Palgrave Studies in Adaptation and Visual Culture

Series Editors
Julie Grossman
Le Moyne College
Syracuse, NY, USA

R. Barton Palmer
Atlanta, GA, USA

This series addresses how adaptation functions as a principal mode of text production in visual culture. What makes the series distinctive is its focus on visual culture as both targets and sources for adaptations, and a vision to include media forms beyond film and television such as videogames, mobile applications, interactive fiction and film, print and nonprint media, and the avant-garde. As such, the series will contribute to an expansive understanding of adaptation as a central, but only one, form of a larger phenomenon within visual culture. Adaptations are texts that are not singular but complexly multiple, connecting them to other pervasive plural forms: sequels, series, genres, trilogies, authorial oeuvres, appropriations, remakes, reboots, cycles and franchises. This series especially welcomes studies that, in some form, treat the connection between adaptation and these other forms of multiplicity. We also welcome proposals that focus on aspects of theory that are relevant to the importance of adaptation as connected to various forms of visual culture.

Thomas Leitch
Editor

The Scandal of Adaptation

Editor
Thomas Leitch
Department of English
University of Delaware
Newark, DE, USA

ISSN 2634-629X   ISSN 2634-6303 (electronic)
Palgrave Studies in Adaptation and Visual Culture
ISBN 978-3-031-14155-3   ISBN 978-3-031-14153-9 (eBook)
https://doi.org/10.1007/978-3-031-14153-9

© The Editor(s) (if applicable) and The Author(s), under exclusive licence to Springer Nature Switzerland AG 2023
This work is subject to copyright. All rights are solely and exclusively licensed by the Publisher, whether the whole or part of the material is concerned, specifically the rights of translation, reprinting, reuse of illustrations, recitation, broadcasting, reproduction on microfilms or in any other physical way, and transmission or information storage and retrieval, electronic adaptation, computer software, or by similar or dissimilar methodology now known or hereafter developed.
The use of general descriptive names, registered names, trademarks, service marks, etc. in this publication does not imply, even in the absence of a specific statement, that such names are exempt from the relevant protective laws and regulations and therefore free for general use.
The publisher, the authors, and the editors are safe to assume that the advice and information in this book are believed to be true and accurate at the date of publication. Neither the publisher nor the authors or the editors give a warranty, expressed or implied, with respect to the material contained herein or for any errors or omissions that may have been made. The publisher remains neutral with regard to jurisdictional claims in published maps and institutional affiliations.

This Palgrave Macmillan imprint is published by the registered company Springer Nature Switzerland AG.
The registered company address is: Gewerbestrasse 11, 6330 Cham, Switzerland

ACKNOWLEDGMENTS

Our heartfelt thanks are due to Julie Grossman and Barton Palmer, whose vigorous support of this project from its beginnings was indispensable in bringing it to birth, and to Lina Aboujieb, Lakshmi Radhakrishnan, Petra Treiber, and the entire production staff at Palgrave Macmillan, who did everything humanly possible to keep it on track. We are also grateful to Lawrence Venuti, whose example in writing *The Scandals of Translation* has been inspiring. Our greatest debt is to the South Atlantic Modern Language Association, who have extended their hospitality to the adaptation studies community for over ten years, and whose topic for their 2020 conference, "Scandal!", was an open invitation to produce this collection.

Contents

Introduction Thomas Leitch	1
Succès de Scandale: From Adultery to Adulteration Irina Makoveeva	19
Fritz Lang's *Scarlet Street* (1945): Designing for Scandal R. Barton Palmer	43
Sweet Smell of Success: Noiradaptation "in This Crudest of All Possible Worlds" Julie Grossman	63
On Incest and Adaptation: The Foundational Scandal of *Cecilia Valdés* Elisabeth L. Austin and Elena Lahr-Vivaz	81
"We Need More Input!": John Hughes's *Weird Science* (1985) and Scandals from the Red Scare to the Twitter Mob Jerod Ra'Del Hollyfield	99
Adaptation and Scandal in *The Goldfinch* Kate Newell	119

vii

Scandalous Dystopias: Hyping *The Last of Us Part II* and
Cyberpunk 2077 During the Pandemic   139
Daniel Singleton

Bowdlerizing for Dollars, or Adaptation as Political
Containment   157
Glenn Jellenik

(Re-)Writing the Pain: War, Exploitation, and the Ethics of
Adapting Nonfiction   177
Geoffrey A. Wright

Adaptation and Censorship   195
Thomas Leitch

Cinematic Contagion: *Bereullin* (*The Berlin File*, 2013)   213
William Mooney

Periphery and Process: Tracing Adaptation Through
Screenplays   229
Jonathan C. Glance

The Narcissistic Scandal of Adapting History   251
Kristopher Mecholsky

Index   271

NOTES ON CONTRIBUTORS

Elisabeth L. Austin is Associate Professor of Spanish in the Department of Modern and Classical Languages and Literatures at Virginia Tech. Her research explores reading practices, gender, and science discourses in nineteenth- and early-twentieth-century Spanish America. She is the author of *Exemplary Ambivalence in Late Nineteenth-Century Spanish America*.

Jonathan C. Glance is Professor of English at Mercer University in Macon, Georgia. His earlier scholarship examined depictions of the supernatural in Gothic drama and literary dreams in nineteenth-century British novels. His more recent work in adaptation studies is based in part on archival research in the John Huston Papers and the Billy Wilder Papers housed in the Margaret Herrick Library at the Fairbanks Center for Motion Picture Study in Beverly Hills. Glance has presented his research at adaptation studies panels at the South Atlantic Modern Language Association conference (2016, 2019, 2020), at the Last Pages, Last Shots conference in Caen, France (2017), and at conferences of the Association of Adaptation Studies (2018, 2021, 2022). He also contributed chapters to *John Huston as Adaptor* (2017) and *Adapting Endings from Book to Screen: Last Pages, Last Shots* (2020).

Julie Grossman is Professor of English and Communication and Film Studies at Le Moyne College. She is the author of *Rethinking the Femme Fatale in Film Noir* (2009), *Literature, Film, and Their Hideous Progeny* (2015), and *The Femme Fatale* (2020); co-author of *Ida Lupino, Director* (with Therese Grisham, 2017) and *Twin Peaks* (with Will Scheibel, 2020);

and co-editor of the essay collections *Adaptation in Visual Culture* (with R. Barton Palmer, 2017) and *Penny Dreadful and Adaptation* (with Will Scheibel, 2022).

Glenn Jellenik is Associate Professor of English at the University of Central Arkansas, where he teaches eighteenth- and nineteenth-century British literature and film. His research approaches adaptation from a historical perspective that acknowledges a thriving history of adaptation before the advent of cinema. He focuses primarily on long-eighteenth-century adaptation and the productive intersections between literature and mass culture. His essay "The Origins of Adaptation, as Such: The Birth of a Simple Abstraction," in *The Oxford Handbook of Adaptation Studies,* traces the rise of our current cultural notions of adaptation to the late eighteenth century, and his book, *Adaptation Before Cinema: Literary and Visual Convergence from Antiquity to the Nineteenth Century* (co-edited with Lissette Lopez Szwydky), is forthcoming from Palgrave.

Elena Lahr-Vivaz is an associate professor in the Department of Spanish and Portuguese Studies at Rutgers University, Newark, where she specializes in Latin American literature and film. She is the author of *Mexican Melodrama: Film and Nation from the Golden Age to the New Wave* and *Writing Islands: Space and Identity in the Transnational Cuban Archipelago.*

Thomas Leitch is Unidel Andrew B. Kirkpatrick, Jr. Chair in Writing at the University of Delaware, where he teaches undergraduate courses on film and graduate courses on literary and cultural theory. His most recent books are *The Oxford Handbook of Adaptation Studies* and *The History of American Literature on Film.*

Irina Makoveeva is Director of CIEE Study Centers in Russia. She started her teaching career as a graduate student at the Faculty of Philology in the Moscow Lomonosov State University and later continued it at Virginia Tech, the University of Pittsburgh, Vanderbilt University, and Saint Petersburg State University, where she has taught courses on Russian cinema, culture, literature, and language. Her research focuses on transmedia adaptations of canonical literary texts and women filmmakers in post-Soviet cinema.

Kristopher Mecholsky is Professor of English at the Savannah College of Art and Design. His work on the history of crime narratives and the relationship between theories of narrative, genre, and personal and cultural identities has been published by McFarland, Palgrave, and Salem Presses, and has appeared in *South Atlantic Review*, the *Baker Street Journal*, the *Faulkner Journal*, and elsewhere.

William Mooney is Professor of Film and chairperson of the Film, Media, and Performing Arts Department at the Fashion Institute of Technology in New York City. His publications include *Dashiell Hammett and the Movies* (2014) and *Adaptation and the New Art Film: Remaking the Classics in the Twilight of Cinema* (2021).

Kate Newell is the Dean of the School of Liberal Arts and Library Services at the Savannah College of Art and Design. Her areas of research include adaptation and intersections of literature and visual culture. She is the author of *Expanding Adaptation Networks: From Illustration to Novelization* (2017) and essays on adaptation, illustration as adaptation, and intermediality.

R. Barton Palmer is Calhoun Lemon Professor of Literature Emeritus at Clemson University, where he is the founding director of the world cinema program. He has written widely in the field of adaptation studies. The most recent of his many books include edited collections on British and American biopics, French fiction on screen, Irish fiction and drama on screen, the Hollywood Renaissance, and autism on screen. With Julie Grossman, he is the author of the forthcoming *Film Noir Performers*.

Jerod Ra'Del Hollyfield is Associate Professor of Film and Communication at Carson-Newman University, whose work primarily examines Hollywood cinema within a settler-colonial context. His book *Framing Empire: Postcolonial Adaptations of Victorian Literature in Hollywood* was released in 2018. Hollyfield has contributed essays to *Settler Colonial Studies, The Journal of Commonwealth and Postcolonial Studies, Graham Greene Studies, Film International, CineAction*, and several edited collections from Routledge, Palgrave, and other publishers. He is also a filmmaker whose work, largely set in the American South, has been screened at international film festivals.

Daniel Singleton is an independent scholar, freelance educator, and political organizer based in Pittsburgh, Pennsylvania. He holds a PhD in English with a specialization in film and media studies at the University of Rochester, and he has taught courses in film, media, and writing at the

University of Iowa, SUNY Brockport, and St. John Fisher College. His scholarly interests include media convergence, fan/audience studies, screen theory, and adaptation. His articles have appeared in the *Quarterly Review of Film and Video*, *Adaptation*, and *South Atlantic Review*.

Geoffrey A. Wright is Professor of English at Samford University, where he has worked since 2007. He teaches courses in American literature, film history, and film adaptation, and sponsors the English department's undergraduate journal, *Wide Angle*. His research interests lie broadly in American literature and film since 1900, focusing on American war narratives and adaptation studies, especially on problems of identity, trauma, gender, storytelling, and the postmodern condition. His articles have appeared in *PMLA*, the *South Atlantic Review*, the *Literature/Film Quarterly*, and *War, Literature, and the Arts*, among other venues.

LIST OF FIGURES

Introduction

Fig. 1   The Gestapo's Col. Ehrhardt (Sig Ruman) reacts with delight to the report that he is called "Concentration Camp Ehrhardt" in *To Be Or Not to Be*   11

***Succès de Scandale*: From Adultery to Adulteration**

Fig. 1   The candle's light in Anna's hand emphasizes Garbo's divinity in an invented scene of the Easter service in Edmund Goulding's *Love* (1927)   23

Fig. 2   In 1937 *Theatrical Decade* made its display of Alla Tarasova as Anna in the novel's stage adaptation into a major event of the season   29

Fig. 3   Even the lovers' costumes play tricks on the spectators' memory of Tolstoi's story in John Neumeier's updated version   31

Fig. 4   The creators of the 2012 version of *Anna Karenina* staged and filmed an impressive episode of races on theater boards, with spectators occupying the theater space   33

Fig. 5   The lovers' *pas de deux* introduced in Joe Wright's 2012 film adaptation aspires to convey a moment of intimate connection between Anna (Keira Knightley) and Vronskii (Aaron Taylor-Johnson) outside their society   35

Fig. 6   In Radda Novikova's 2019 film, Anna restores her dignity by murdering an abhorrent Vronskii   39

Fritz Lang's *Scarlet Street* (1945): Designing for Scandal

Fig. 1 Chris (Edward G. Robinson) in his role as unrewarded love slave to Kitty (Joan Bennett) in *Scarlet Street* 50

Fig. 2 The unintended memorial to the woman (Joan Bennett) whom Chris (Edward G. Robinson) loved and killed in *Scarlet Street* 61

Sweet Smell of Success: Noiradaptation "in This Crudest of All Possible Worlds"

Fig. 1 The fur coat Susie Hunsecker (Susan Harrison) wears throughout *Sweet Smell of Success* is a symbol of the toxic control of her brother J.J. (Burt Lancaster) 74

Fig. 2 The shadow cast by her brother J.J. (Burt Lancaster) helps establish the unblinking Susie (Susan Harrison) as a femme fatale 75

On Incest and Adaptation: The Foundational Scandal of *Cecilia Valdés*

Fig. 1 Cecilia (Daisy Granados) and Leonardo (Imanol Arias), from Humberto Solás's *Cecilia* (1982) 86

Fig. 2 José Dolores (Miguel Benavides) yearns for Cecilia (Daisy Granados) in Solás's film 87

"We Need More Input!": John Hughes's *Weird Science* (1985) and Scandals from the Red Scare to the Twitter Mob

Fig. 1 Gary (Anthony Michael Hall) and Wyatt (Ilan Mitchell-Smith) cull the perfect woman from multiple sources in *Weird Science* 111

Fig. 2 Chet (Bill Paxton) oozes the toxic masculinity typical of the '80s "hard body" in *Weird Science* 115

Adaptation and Scandal in *The Goldfinch*

Fig. 1 *The Goldfinch*, 1654 (oil on panel), Carel Fabritius (1622–54), Mauritshuis, The Hague, the Netherlands 121

Fig. 2 Donna Tartt, *The Goldfinch*, cover, Back Bay Books, 2015 125

(Re-)Writing the Pain: War, Exploitation, and the Ethics of Adapting Nonfiction

Fig. 1	An agrarian vista from the opening minutes of *Heaven and Earth*	185
Fig. 2	Le Ly Hayslip (Hiep Thi Le, right) meets troubled war veteran Steve Butler (Tommy Lee Jones) in *Heaven and Earth*	186

Adaptation and Censorship

Fig. 1	Marvin Davis, Oscar Polk, and Dawn Dodd are among the Black performers who are cast in offensively stereotypical roles in *Gone with the Wind* (1939)	202
Fig. 2	Michael B. Jordan and Michael Shannon's unapologetic approach to censorship in *Fahrenheit 451* (2018)	209

Cinematic Contagion: *Bereullin* (*The Berlin File, 2013*)

Fig. 1	Hempf (Thomas Thieme) assaults Christa-Maria Sieland (Martina Gedeck) in *Das Leben der Anderen*	223
Fig. 2	Siegmund (Thomas Thieme) explains "how things work" in *Bereullin*	223

Periphery and Process: Tracing Adaptation Through Screenplays

Fig. 1	Realizing that their murder of her husband may soon be discovered, Walter Neff (Fred MacMurray) and Phyllis Dietrichson (Barbara Stanwyck) connive what to do next in *Double Indemnity (1:10:01)*	240
Fig. 2	Daniel Dravot (Sean Connery) weds Roxanne (Shakira Caine) moments before his kingdom crumbles in *The Man Who Would Be King (1:56:00)*	243

The Narcissistic Scandal of Adapting History

Fig. 1	The *Atlantic* used this image from Gustav Doré's illustrations for Samuel Taylor Coleridge's "Rime of the Ancient Mariner" to accompany James Parker's reflection on the Ancient Mariner Big Read in order to reflect humanity as a collective navigating the pandemic	256

Introduction

Thomas Leitch

This collection of fourteen new chapters on adaptation is a valentine—or, more precisely, three valentines. The first is to "Scandal!"—the thematic rubric of the 2020 convention of the South Atlantic Modern Language Association (SAMLA), a perfect subject for adaptation scholars. The second is to SAMLA, which for the past ten years has hosted over fifty sessions on adaptation studies, most of them under the nominal aegis of the Association of Adaptation Studies. In 2011 R. Barton Palmer, who had long been active in SAMLA's governance, approached me with the idea of "colonizing" the conference by proposing a series of adaptation panels that would offer participants the experience of a conference within the conference. The SAMLA organizers were exceptionally hospitable to the project, and Barton and I took turns for several years soliciting proposals and organizing them into panels and roundtables, passing this job on to Dennis Perry and then Kate Newell, who organized the 2020 sessions, as all of us rejoiced in the growing sense of community among the adaptation scholars who returned to the conference year after year. So this volume is intended specifically as a belated celebration of ten years of adaptation events at SAMLA.

T. Leitch (✉)
Department of English, University of Delaware, Newark, DE, USA
e-mail: tleitch@udel.edu

© The Author(s), under exclusive license to Springer Nature Switzerland AG 2023
T. Leitch (ed.), *The Scandal of Adaptation*, Palgrave Studies in Adaptation and Visual Culture,
https://doi.org/10.1007/978-3-031-14153-9_1

The project's third valentine is addressed to Lawrence Venuti's 1998 monograph *The Scandals of Translation*, a groundbreaking intervention into translation studies—though not into adaptation studies, which by and large has ignored its sister field as it has pursued a parallel path. With a few welcome exceptions like the essays Laurence Raw collected in *Translation, Adaptation and Transformation* (2012) and Venuti's own 2007 essay "Adaptation, Translation, Critique," which Venuti chose not to reprint in his 2013 collection *Translation Changes Everything*, there have been few truly productive conversations between translation scholars and adaptation scholars. Instead of seeking to remedy this unfortunate lack, this volume draws inspiration from Venuti's work, especially from the aptly titled *The Scandals of Translation*, whose opening paragraph defines its subject in gratifyingly bracing terms:

> The scandals of translation are cultural, economic, and political. They are revealed when one asks why translation today remains in the margins of research, commentary, and debate, especially (though not exclusively) in English. Any description of these margins risks seeming a mere litany of abuse, the premise of an incredible victimology of translation and the victims it leaves in its wake. Translation is stigmatized as a form of writing, discouraged by copyright law, depreciated by the academy, exploited by publishers and corporations, governments and religious organizations. Translation is treated so disadvantageously, I want to suggest, partly because it occasions revelations that question the authority of dominant cultural values and institutions. And like every challenge to established reputations, it provokes their efforts at damage control, their various policing functions, all designed to shore up the questioned values and institutions by mystifying their uses of translation. (Venuti, *Scandals* 1)

Substituting *adaptation* for every instance of *translation* in this paragraph would preserve its essential truth and indicate just how scandalous adaptation is, how closely the scandals it poses academic fields and entertainment and communication establishments resemble the scandals of translation, and how these institutions have protected themselves against these scandals by policing, disavowing, and marginalizing it.

The parallel between the scandals of adaptation and those of translation is not perfect. What Venuti calls "perhaps the greatest scandal of translation"—"asymmetries, inequities, relations of domination and dependence [that] exist in every act of translating, of putting the translated in the service of the translating culture" (Venuti, *Scandals* 4)—is not equally true of adaptation because the borders it most often crosses, medial rather than linguistic, do not question national and cultural identities as centrally or persistently as the border-crossings of translation. Even so, each of the eight "categories and practices" (Venuti, *Scandals* 1) Venuti goes on to examine in detail in *The Scandals of Translation*—heterogeneity, authorship, copyright, the formation of cultural identities, the pedagogy of literature, philosophy, the bestseller, globalization—is challenged by adaptation as well; some of them—the bestseller, authorship, and especially copyright, which may without exaggeration have been instituted on a global scale as a specific response to the scandal of unauthorized adaptations—are perhaps even more urgently challenged by adaptation than translation. For its part, adaptation studies has focused recently on interrogating widely shared assumptions about several related categories—media, aesthetics, and the text—whose monolithic status is called into question by adaptation's very existence.

As Venuti acutely notes, "The only authority that translation can expect depends on its remaining derivative, distinguishable from the original compositions that it tries to communicate, and collective, remaining open to the other agents who influence it, especially domestic readerships. Hence, the only prestige that a translator can gain comes from practicing translation, not as a form of personal expression, but as a collaboration between divergent groups, motivated by an acknowledgement of the linguistic and cultural differences that translation necessarily rewrites and reorders" (Venuti, *Scandals* 4). Adaptation studies has clearly been more interested, and more successful, in following the first of these directives (accepting its subject's derivative status) than the second (acknowledging its status as a collective activity open to a wide range of other gatekeepers, stakeholders, and agents). My own research on the relative neglect of the collaborative model of adaptation illustrated by the films of John Huston, which has been far less influential than the auteurist models associated with Alfred Hitchcock and Andrew Davies, suggests that adaptation continues to be theorized as a process of appropriation, to use Julie Sanders's term, rather than collaboration.

Another crucial difference between adaptation studies and translation studies is thrown into sharp relief by Venuti's emphasis on the prestige available to translators who *practice* translation as a collaboration. For better or worse, very few adaptation scholars, unlike virtually all translation scholars, have any practical experience as adapters themselves. So the goal Venuti announces in introducing the essays reprinted in *Translation*

Changes Everything (2013)—"to worry the questionable distinction between translation theory and practice, whether that practice is research or translating" (Venuti, *Translation* 8)—reveals a distinction between theory and practice even more firmly entrenched in adaptation studies.

Even so, virtually every claim Venuti makes in the closing paragraph of his Introduction to *Translation Changes Everything* could be equally urged on behalf of adaptation:

> [T]ranslation [or adaptation] carries the potential to bring about multiple transformations. Translation [adaptation] changes the form, meaning, and effect of the source text, even when the translator maintains a semantic correspondence that creates a reliable basis for summaries and commentaries. Translation [adaptation] changes the cultural situation where the source text originated through an investment of prestige or a creation of stereotypes. Translation [adaptation] changes the receiving cultural situation by bringing into existence something new and different, a text that is neither the source text nor an original composition in the translating language [or adapting medium], and in the process it changes the values, beliefs, and representations that are housed in institutions. Translation [adaptation] deals in contingencies open to variation. To cling to an instrumental model of translation [translation], to insist on the existence of a source invariant, to suppress the translator's [adapter's] interpretation, and to neglect the cultural situation to which it responds must ultimately rest, then, on a fear of change. (Venuti, *Translation* 10)

The last two sentences in this passage suggest that focusing on the scandals of translation, or of adaptation, raises logically unavoidable (though largely avoided) and uncomfortable questions about current events and the public humanities. Adaptation studies has been marginalized by literary studies, which treats adaptations as mere by-products of the creative process; by cinema studies, which is so intent on establishing its independence from literary studies that it resolutely turns its back on the adaptations that link the fields; by intermedial studies, which confines adaptation to a single room in its capacious mansion of medial and intermedial practices; and even by translation studies, which follows Venuti's "choice of translation theory as a source of concepts for adaptation studies" and criticism that adaptation studies often "betrays an ignorance of translation studies over the past three decades" without acknowledging the possibility that translation scholars may prefer to contest outdated versions of adaptation studies for reasons of their own (Venuti, "Adaptation" 28, 29). But this very marginalization gives adaptation studies, like translation studies, the ability to speak truth to power.

Although adaptation scholars have been slow to acknowledge the scandalous nature of adaptation and turn it to account, they have long recognized the scandalous power of individual adaptations that, as Dudley Andrew reminded his audience during a recent conference presentation, can make taboo subjects reserved to elite literary audiences available to everyone. The obvious case is Stanley Kubrick's 1962 film adaptation of Vladimir Nabokov's 1955 novel *Lolita*, which was marketed with the tagline—"How did they ever make a movie of *Lolita?*"—that was designed precisely to emphasize the film's power to intensify the scandals posed by the novel by indicating that its presumed visual explicitness would make it even more scandalous. More recently, the field's continued emphasis on novel-to-film adaptations has provided still another scandal to practitioners and theorists who rightly claim the neglect of a wide range of adaptations from operas to podcasts whose study would greatly enrich the field.

The leading question the contributions to this volume seek to address is the relation between scandalous individual adaptations and the scandal of adaptation as such. What Simone Murray has called the adaptation industry, which is closely intertwined with the publishing and filmmaking industries (and with other industries Murray does not consider), accepts, encourages, and depends on the production of many individual adaptations. Any number of adaptations are accepted as a necessary part of Murray's adaptation industry: adaptations of contemporary bestsellers seeking to reach a larger audience, adaptations of forgotten or neglected classics yearning to be rediscovered, adaptations of established classics like *Hamlet* and *Little Women* that are proven properties because they have already been repeatedly adapted. So a large number of stakeholders inside and outside the adaptation industry are not scandalized by adaptations unless their subject or approach offers scandal. These stakeholders routinely set the virtue of adaptability, the ability to generate new adaptations, against the virtue of integrity, the ability to remain true to oneself. This last phrase suggests that in moral philosophy, integrity is typically prized above adaptability, as in Plato, Aristotle, and more recent champions of the Western canon and its works like E.D. Hirsch and Harold Bloom. Adaptability, by contrast, is prized above integrity in the world of fashion, which is sustained by implanting the desire for more or less gratuitous wardrobe purchases unmotivated by any practical necessity. Bodybuilders and weight-loss coaches urge their followers to change themselves until they reach their ideal corporal specifications, then urge them to take continued action to maintain their target weight and muscular ability on the assumption that maintenance requires ceaseless activity. More to the point, adaptability is preached by Hollywood agents and dealmakers who live off new movies and by writing teachers working to help their students adapt models like the five-paragraph essay to their own expressive or argumentative uses. One of the foundational debates in contemporary adaptation studies is between champions of integrity, who frown on adaptations generally and prefer them faithful, and champions of adaptability, who want to do whatever they can to encourage a wider array of adaptations.

The different positions in this debate can readily be traced to different stakeholders in the adaptation community. Authors usually appreciate the money, if not the experience, when their novels and plays and stories are adapted to television or film, even when, like J.K. Rowling, they like to retain tight control over them, or, like Daphne du Maurier, they disapprove of particular adaptations. Unlike Charles Dickens and Victor Hugo, whose campaigns against unauthorized adaptations played a pivotal role in the establishment of international copyright, more recent authors like J.D. Salinger, Thomas Pynchon, and Sara Paretsky who do not want their work to be adapted can easily take measures to avoid it—at least until they die, when their heirs, like Audrey Geisel, can authorize the adaptations that Geisel's late husband, who published his children's books under the byline Dr. Seuss, had resisted. Screenwriters and filmmakers of every sort prefer to have the option of adapting established properties instead of being obliged to invent their own. Fans eagerly await the latest iterations of Spider-Man, *Emma*, and *Lord of the Rings*, even if they end up condemning specific features or whole adaptations online. And adaptation scholars, once united in denigrating adaptations as derivative, have softened this stance, like George Bluestone, or reversed it, like Robert Stam, even as debates over fidelity, repeatedly laid to rest as resolved, have kept rising from the grave, typically circling around variously faithful adaptations that hold out the promise of balancing the claims of adaptability and integrity.

The two constituencies most likely to be scandalized by adaptation as such, then, are academics, especially literature teachers, who do not happen to be adaptation scholars, and movie reviewers who do not happen to be academics. The motives in each case are clear. Academics are famous defenders of established canons, and reviewers lose no opportunity to demonstrate that they are superior to the material they review. It does not follow from this revelation that adaptability should be prized over integrity, but only that in taking positions in this age-old debate, adaptation scholars and others should consider more mindfully which positions they represent, how their views compare to their cohorts' interests, and what arguments can plausibly be made against them.

The rise of adaptation studies as a methodology or discipline poses the kinds of threats to fields like literary studies and cinema studies that would automatically provoke defensive measures by established fields determined to marginalize or devalue or ignore this new interloper along with all the others. Apart from these reflexive reactions, adaptation offers a scandal to aesthetics as such. Recent work in performance studies has sought to complement the canonical archives on which traditional aesthetics has based its methods and prestige with the notion that archives are powerless and inert unless they are performed by active interpreters whose different approaches challenge the archive even as they bring it alive. Aesthetics' central emphasis on the stable identity of the work of art as a *Ding an sich* is challenged by adaptation theory's emphasis on becoming rather than being. The notion of all art as a series of works-in-progress offers scandal even to two areas with which it is often aligned: Mikhail Bakhtin's notion of carnival, which is rooted in a specific historical moment in the Middle Ages, and intermedial studies, which focuses on a set of synchronic intermedial relations, not a diachronic series of processes. Although Kamilla Elliott has recently charged that "the top-down rhetoric of 'theorizing adaptation' pervades adaptation studies, while a reciprocal, inverse rhetoric of 'adapting theorization' remains underdeveloped" (239), adaptation scholars have increasingly been more invested in, and more successful in pursuing, what I have called "petit theories" (Leitch, "Against" 704) that mount new challenges to the quasi-canonical Grand Theory on which they rely. And of course adaptations of nonfictional texts offer scandal to historians who continue to hold film adaptations to monolithic truth standards they have long since waived for their own written histories.

The relations between individually scandalous adaptations and the scandal of adaptation as a practice are on full display in the 1942 United Artists film *To Be or Not to Be*. Although the film, directed by Ernst Lubitsch, is based on a screenplay by Edwin Justus Mayer which is based in turn on an original story by Lubitsch and Melchior Lengyel, contemporaneous reviewers unanimously treated its story of a Polish acting troupe's unwilling entanglement with a Gestapo plot against the Polish Underground in World War II as an adaptation of recent history, and their verdicts were uniformly negative. Bosley Crowther's review in the *New York Times* is typical: "[I]n a spirit of levity, confused by frequent doses of shock, Mr. Lubitsch has set his actors to performing a spy-thriller of fantastic design amid the ruins and frightful oppressions of Nazi-invaded Warsaw. To say it is callous and macabre is understating the case" (883). Even audiences who had made Charlie Chaplin's Hitler-baiting satire *The Great Dictator* the top-grossing American film of 1940 were scandalized by Lubitsch's attempt to make light of the traumas the Third Reich had visited on occupied Poland. Political satires have always been rare in American cinema because of the obvious and gratuitous risks they run of antagonizing half their potential audience, and *To Be or Not to Be* is an even rarer creature, an American political satire that does not involve either elections or Americans.

The film's reputation has risen steadily over the years—it currently holds an 8.2 rating on the Internet Movie Database, a 96% Fresh rating on Rotten Tomatoes' Tomatometer, and a Metascore of eighty-six—but even commentators who have reversed the earlier verdict against it have been slower to appreciate the ways the scandal of its very existence and its irreverent approach to the horrors of the Gestapo are rooted in a more specific series of scandals at the heart of its story. Like *Primary Colors* (1998), which views politics in terms of a romance between the candidate and others (especially, though not entirely, voters), *To Be or Not to Be* is a movie about the relations between politics and love. Since no one runs for public office in the Third Reich, the forms political action take here are demagoguery, resistance, and spying. The film revolves around a romantic triangle including the Polish actors Joseph and Maria Tura, husband and wife (Jack Benny and Carole Lombard), and Stanislav Sobinski (Robert Stack), a young lieutenant in love with Maria who discovers that Professor Siletsky (Stanley Ridges), a friend and mentor of a Resistance bombing squad Sobinski and several other exiled Polish fighters have formed in England, is actually a German spy who plans to turn over to the Gestapo the personal information members of the squad have supplied him when they learned of his upcoming visit to Warsaw and asked him to get in touch with their friends and relatives. In an attempt to defeat Siletsky's plans, Sobinski parachutes into Warsaw, and Maria and Joseph, warned by him of Siletsky's intentions, play a series of roles designed to delay his delivery of the information or trick him into delivering it to them instead of the Gestapo. As David Lehmann, who observes that "there are few movies that mix reality and imposture to such superb effect, with artifice trumping actuality as the actors play their parts not on the stage but in the streets and enemy headquarters of their Nazi-occupied city," has recently noted, "Benny plays five roles" in the film, "and in each of them, he is Jack Benny" (Lehman). Pauline Kael, who opined that Lubitsch "starts off on the wrong foot and never gets his balance," complained that Benny is "bizarrely cast" (774) as Tura, a Shakespearean actor affronted to the point of despair when Sobinski, whom he has never met, repeatedly walks out of his performance as Hamlet during the opening line of the famous soliloquy that begins "To be or not to be," not because he knows his wife has given Sobinski this cue for their romantic backstage meetings, but because he thinks that the unknown audience member has chosen this particularly noisy and disruptive way to criticize Tura's performance. But the scandalous casting of Benny as Hamlet, a noted Shakespearean actor, or ultimately a hero of the Polish underground is very much to the film's point.

The film's satire, which at first seems scattershot, is in fact tightly organized around three thematic concerns: the politics of self-serving bluster, resistance, and espionage; romance, the province of both feuding domestic partners and suitors who threaten the partners' stability; and acting, which includes both the troupe's onstage performances of *Hamlet* and their increasingly improvisational offstage acting by stage-trained actors thrust into high-stakes real-life situations over which they have little control—a reminder that a central theme of *Hamlet* itself, the play to whose leading role Joseph Tura is so clearly inadequate, is the relationship between action and acting. The film's politicians are self-aggrandizing, self-absorbed, and histrionic, a tendency Tura inadvertently parodies when, thinking himself mortally shot in his confrontation with Siletsky, he cries, "Long live Poland!" before the rest of the troupe rushes in to rescue him from his nonexistent wound. Its spies are deceptive, secretive, and competitive. Its lovers are deceptive, secretive, histrionic, self-absorbed, and competitive. And its actors, from the Turas to Rawitch (Lionel Atwill), are deceptive, histrionic, self-absorbed, and competitive. So it is perfectly logical that in the course of the film, each of these activities emerges as an increasingly illuminating metaphor for the others.

The film repeatedly treats politics as acting, acting as romance, romance as politics, and romance as acting for the sake of comic confusion throughout the many situations in which they intermingle, overlap, or are mistaken for each other. Its story is framed by two attempts of the supporting actor Bronski (Tom Dugan) to fool audiences outside the theater into believing he is Adolf Hitler, the first of them laughably unsuccessful, the second breathtakingly consequential. The company stages *Hamlet* only when they are forbidden to stage *Gestapo*, the presumably scandalous play they had originally chosen. Maria, who had earlier proposed to the stage manager Dobosh (Charles Halton) a ludicrously glamorous staging of her first appearance in a concentration camp, accepts Sobinski's suit by telling him, "This is the first time I've ever met a man who could drop three tons of dynamite in two minutes," and agreeing to join him aboard his bomber. Later, Siletsky warns Maria, who wants to seduce and assassinate him, how important it is to take the right side in politics as in love, and she responds to his kiss by murmuring dreamily, "Heil, Hitler." Tura, outraged at both Maria's danger and her activism, attempts to reassert himself by announcing, "I'll decide with whom my wife will have dinner, and whom she's going to kill." In the film's best-known sequence, Tura, masquerading as Col. Ehrhardt of the Gestapo, finding himself unable to make convincing small talk with Siletsky, whom the troupe has lured to the theater they have disguised as Gestapo headquarters, can only repeat, "So they call me Concentration Camp Ehrhardt"—a scandalous juxtaposition of comic ineptitude, serious danger, and jaw-droppingly inappropriate reference to the concentration camps where, as the real Col. Ehrhardt (Sig Ruman) says when Tura approaches him in disguise as Siletsky, "We do the concentrating and the Poles do the camping." Ehrhardt, who, when he is asked by the false Siletsky if he is familiar with "that great, great Polish actor Joseph Tura," replies, "Oh, yes. What he did to Shakespeare we are doing now to Poland," gets to top Tura's most famous line with an even more scandalous repetition. When Tura repeats to him Siletsky's remark that he is known as Concentration Camp Ehrhardt, he muses, "So they call me Concentration Camp Ehrhardt" (Fig. 1)——an echo that prompts Tura's self-satisfied remark, "I had a feeling you would say that," and confirms Bronski's response to Dobosh's criticism that his opening performance as Hitler was unsuccessful because he is "only a little man with a mustache": "So is Hitler," the ultimately scandalous takedown of the fearsome dictator's posturing hubris. The story appropriately climaxes with a pair of bravura performances. The actor Greenberg (Felix Bressart), emerging from a women's lounge in a Warsaw theater Hitler is visiting, gives a stirring rendition of Shylock's "Hath not a Jew eyes?" speech from *The Merchant of Venice* in order to provide a distraction while Bronski, masquerading as Hitler, leads Greenberg and Hitler's attendant troops from the theater.

Fig. 1 The Gestapo's Col. Ehrhardt (Sig Ruman) reacts with delight to the report that he is called "Concentration Camp Ehrhardt" in *To Be Or Not to Be*

These conflations of politics, spying, romance, and acting, along with what Scott Eyman has called the film's "daring analogy between the rape of a nation with the aesthetic rape of a playwright" (302), offer scandal to audiences' assumptions about both the idealism and the transactional brutality of politics, the purity, glamour, and transcendence of romantic love, and the apparently necessary social assumption that you can trust other people because they act only when they are onstage. What makes these conflations both comic and scandalous ("how *could* you?") is their constant implication of a third-party audience that the performances of politics, spying, and romance depend on as surely as any performance does. But film's most penetrating scandal is its persistent use of deflating analogies between politics and romance, romance and acting, acting and politics, with the constant implication that no matter which of these deeply human activities is defined in terms of any of the others, the results are scandalously reductive. So too the deepest scandal of adaptation is not that a given adaptation will betray the original text it adapts, but that it will reveal productive fissures, limitations, and invitations in that text, and in the process challenge the very idea of originality.

Although the chapters in this volume are organized into two parts, "Scandalous Adaptations" and "Scandalous Adaptation," that respectively emphasize the scandals many individual adaptations have occasioned and the scandalous nature of adaptation itself, this distinction is largely a matter of degree, for they all share a common concern with the relation between these two kinds of scandal.

Irina Makoveeva begins Part I with an examination of some of the many adaptations of *Anna Karenina*, a novel that manages to be at once canonical and scandalous. The unapologetic adultery at the heart of Tolstoi's novel and the many social transgressions that surround it made it a *succès de scandale* to many of its earliest readers, and the torrent of adaptations of Anna's story, which Makoveeva treats selectively but incisively, are distinguished from each other not only by their choice of presentational medium or their handling of the novel's nineteenth-century setting but by the ways they choose to treat that scandal in times that consider themselves less hidebound, beginning but not ending with the questions of whether they have sought to efface or inflate that scandal and how they have linked, or failed to link, the infidelity of Tolstoi's heroine to their own infidelities.

The production history of *Scarlet Street*, the subject of R. Barton Palmer's chapter, illustrates almost exactly the opposite premise: the ways an adaptation of a story relatively free of scandal could seek commercial success precisely through "the provocation of public outrage" even as it cannily complied with the strictures of the Production Code Administration and the Legion of Decency. The filmmakers' concerted attempts to minimize its ties to the fifteen-year-old novel on which it was based and its "continuation" of several crucial features of Fritz Lang's previous film, *The Woman in the Window*, are faithfully echoed within the film by the plot of the lowlife heroine and her accomplice to pass off the paintings she is given by her starry-eyed accountant lover as her own. The censor-baiting tactics of Universal Studios not only extended the time *Scarlet Street* remained in the public eye and swelled its box-office receipts but helped provide an "antiestablishmentariasm" blueprint for over a decade of films noirs that would follow.

One of the last entries in this first-generation noir cycle, *Sweet Smell of Success*, provides the subject for Julie Grossman's chapter on the seamy side of adaptation. The film, like the novella it adapts, focuses on the circle around a gossip columnist, a professional scandalmonger. Walter Winchell, who supplied the model for the baleful J.J. Hunsecker, was himself a quintessential adapter of other people's words, poses, and ideas whose practice showed just how dirty adaptation can be—a revelation that is intensified by the film's noir sensibility. Nor is this dirty adaptation restricted to the narrative, for accounts of the film's contentious production display many instances of "maladaptation in the workplace." Repeated examples of maladaptation in the narrative, in its real-life model, and in its production history blur the lines between fact and fiction, showing that "[b]ecause they are the products of complex social contexts and multiple wranglings, adaptations can never 'come clean.'" Grossman makes the resonance of these lessons for contemporary American sociopolitical culture disturbingly clear.

Elisabeth L. Austin and Elena Lahr-Vivaz explore the relationship between adaptation and incest in three adaptations of Cirilo Villaverdes's novel *Cecilia Valdés*. Just as *Cecilia Valdés* is widely considered Cuba's national novel, the unwittingly incestuous relationship at its heart reveals "the *foundational scandal* of Spanish American literature" by disclosing "the fabricated nature of paternity and fidelity, of knowable origins and predictable futures" as violations of the taboo against incest and its potentially monstrous offspring affront the social norms designed to contain it. Each of these "hideous progeny," in Julie Grossman's term, treats the scandalous revelation of incest differently than the novel. The first one, like MGM's 1935 *Anna Karenina*, creates a new scandal by effacing the forbidden relationship, displacing it onto a coupling with a dramatically different social valence; the second doubles down on the original scandal in order to mount a sociopolitical critique of 1987 Cuba; and the third broadly hints that not only all adaptations of *Cecilia Valdés* but perhaps all adaptations of anything are inherently and productively incestuous.

Instead of analyzing acknowledged adaptations of an equally canonical text, Jerod Ra'Del Hollyfield plumbs the controversy surrounding the recent video release of *Weird Science*, an iconic '80s teen movie that draws its central concept from Mary Shelley's *Frankenstein*, rendered retrospectively controversial by revelations of writer-director John Hughes's misogyny, which made the film's objectification of women seem even more toxic. He treats dismissive online commentary on the film as a manifestation of what he calls "BuzzFeed Theory: Internet writing aiming for optimal dissemination that acts as full-fledged adaptations of the texts it discusses in order to curtail the web of intertextuality by deposing and replacing source texts via scandal, a strategy that protects it from resistant scholarly interventions." Focusing on the ways the film's scandalous video release provoked social media distillations of nuanced assessments into memes and hot takes that flattened the debates that spawned them with the effect, and perhaps the goal, of supplanting and burying both the film itself and its earlier commentary, Hollyfield makes a compelling case for academic, non-academic, and anti-academic analyses as adaptations.

Taking off from the proposition that Donna Tartt's bestselling novel *The Goldfinch* is an adaptation of Carel Mauritius's 1654 painting, which continues in different ways to inform John Crowley's 2019 film adaptation of the novel, Kate Newell focuses on the question "What is it?" to interrogate the status of Crowley's film—which was widely viewed as too faithful to Tartt's novel either to replicate the experience the novel provided or to establish its own independent cinematic credentials—the novel itself, and Fabritius's trompe l'oeil painting as at once "the thing and yet not the thing" each one seeks to represent. For Newell, the continuing debates over the generic categories that might best describe the painting, the novel, or the film reveal that "[t]he scandal of *The Goldfinch*(es) is the scandal of trompe l'oeil" at the heart of adaptation and adaptation studies, "which likewise remains caught in a dilemma of how to discuss adaptations as adaptations without having categories of 'the thing' and 'yet not the thing' overdetermine that discussion."

Daniel Singleton brings Part I into the very recent past by detailing the ways in which the [COVID] pandemic undermined two of 2020's most highly anticipated video game releases, *The Last of Us Part II* and *Cyberpunk 2077*. The delay of *The Last of Us Part II* provoked impatient hackers to release game footage that included a major spoiler that turned many avid fans against the game; the developers' determination to incorporate material from an ever-expanding pool of media from earlier video games to role-playing games to film franchises to immersive platforms weighed down *Cyberpunk 2077* with a hopeless array of bugs and contradictory expectations that encouraged its target audience to turn from players into outlaw adapters who posted GIFs of its bugs, produced patches to address its shortcomings, or hacked into the production company's servers, downloaded the game's source code, and auctioned it on eBay. Both episodes, as Singleton notes, "reveal how thoroughly the process of adaptation pervades the production as well as consumption of video games, setting the stage for scandals that erupt."

Part II begins with Glenn Jellenik's analysis of a double scandal: the widely acknowledged bowdlerization of so many texts by their adaptations, and the generally overlooked critical under-reading of acts of bowdlerization that scholars eagerly call out but then ignore. Focusing on the stage and screen adaptations that sought to tame two subversive novels, William Godwin's *Things As They Are, or The Adventures of Caleb Williams* and Theodore Dreiser's *An American Tragedy*, he argues that despite George Colman's insistence that he was approaching Godwin's novel without regard to its politics, such a stance is already politically conservative, as David O. Selznick unwittingly indicated when he rejected Sergei M. Eisenstein's screenplay for *An American Tragedy* on the grounds that by giving audiences "a most miserable two hours," it would fail in its primary responsibility to provide mass entertainment. Because Jellenik regards all adaptations, whatever their ideological intentions, as acts of political containment, he enjoins adaptation scholars to resist extending this containment by reading their chosen texts and their own arguments more critically.

Asking "what happens when filmmakers adapt a war memoir into a film," Geoffrey A. Wright emphasizes the scandalously exploitative nature of all adaptation's dependence on "*using* the source text to make money and of changing it to meet ends for which it was not designed." This exploitative quality becomes central in adaptations of war memoirs like *When Heaven and Earth Changed Places* that introduce new complications into those memoirs' original goal—to write the author's pain—by filtering them through the sensibilities of any number of collaborators. Considering both aesthetic and ethical dimensions of nonfictional film adaptation, Wright reasons that its goal can be only subjective, not objective truth. His analysis draws on concepts from quantum physics to demonstrate that whatever its creators' intentions, it is a "*composite nonfiction*" that "exhibits both fictional and nonfictional qualities"—a conclusion that adds new urgency to the question of whether all adaptation, as Deborah Cartmell has suggested, is exploitation.

My own chapter draws on the controversy surrounding HBO Max's decision to temporarily withdraw *Gone with the Wind* from its streaming platform before returning it with new framing material that sought to respond to outcries against the film's racism. Although all parties to the controversy, like most Americans, insisted that they were against censorship, a problematic behavior they ascribed only to other people, the chapter explores the possibility that adaptation is a mode of censorship that audiences and analysts find acceptable because it does not feel like censorship, even though it is "a mode of reframing or recontextualizing that chooses certain textual details to emphasize and systematically suppresses other details," a mode that raises hard questions about what Americans want their history to say and how they want this history, or histories, to be inscribed.

William Mooney analyzes Ryoo Seung-wan's 2013 film *Bereullin* (*The Berlin File*) as a site of contagion that supplements its echoes of Florian Henckel von Donnersmarck's 2006 film *Das Leben der Anderen* (*The Lives of Others*) with narrative elements and memes drawn from spy thrillers like *The Bourne Supremacy*, the political history of North and South Korea, and the city of Berlin as a site of both heightened Cold War conflicts and the possibility of resolving such conflicts. What is scandalous in Ryoo's film is not its infection by all these memes but its narrative foregrounding of its uneasy combination of materials, beginning with the title *The Berlin File*, which indicates "this film's composite nature as a *file*, containing separate documents that relate to a particular subject, but which are yet to be integrated," and the more general implication that "[t]he creator of such works becomes, at most, one who *discovers* rather than one who *invents*, one who observes affinities among elements in a reservoir of cultural consciousness that invite recombination," establishing or revealing adaptation as contagion.

Comparing the ways translation and screenwriting have been scandalously marginalized and stigmatized in academic writing, Jonathan C. Glance builds on Lawrence Venuti's call for a reassessment of translation by inviting a reconsideration of screenplays' formative role in the adaptive process. Glance draws on a rich trove of primary materials to inform his studies of two films by noted writer/directors, Billy Wilder's *Double Indemnity* and John Huston's *The Man Who Would Be King*, that sharpen debates about authorship, fidelity, and medium specificity. He focuses especially on the relations between extrinsic pressures like casting, budgeting, and censorship and intrinsic pressures like the wish to retain specific scenes, characters, and plot devices from the adapted texts, the investment in pivotal images and dialogue tags, and the desire to resolve or extend the adapted texts' moral ambiguities by casting their leading characters as heroes or scoundrels. Glance's detailed studies illuminate the process of endless rethinking and revision in successive screenplay drafts and incidentally debunk some long-standing myths like veteran novelist Raymond Chandler's allegedly limited and amateurish contributions to the first screenplay on which he worked.

Part II concludes with an examination of perhaps the most widespread and unremarked scandal of all: the process of "living in the present as an adaptation of the past" through what Kristopher Mecholsky calls "historical–poetic interpolation," understanding the present by seeking out analogies in the historical past. He uses figures as diverse as Samuel Taylor

Coleridge, John Wilkes Booth, and Vladimir Lenin to ask, "What do we lose and gain when we compare our experiences to past experiences we take as their pattern?" Drawing on the historical theories of Paul Ricoeur and Friedrich Nietzsche, he argues that although the processes of writing and living history are inescapably intertwined, the constant attempt to "wear a mantle of the past and dress in the trappings of other narratives and times of historical import" threatens "to erase our particularity in favor of memorability." His boldly speculative and ambitious chapter makes an appropriately inconclusive conclusion to this volume, right down to its final word—"fuhgeddaboudit"—although it is to be hoped that readers of all these perceptive and provocative contributions, suitably stimulated by their many sharp provocations, will have exactly the opposite reaction.

References

Crowther, Bosley. "*To Be or Not to Be.*" 1942. *The New York Times Guide to the Best 1,000 Movies Ever Made*, edited by Peter M. Nichols, Times Books/Random House, 1999, p. 883.
Elliott, Kamilla. *Theorizing Adaptation*. Oxford University Press, 2020.
Eyman, Scott. *Ernst Lubitsch: Laughter in Paradise*. Johns Hopkins University Press, 1993.
Kael, Pauline. *5001 Nights at the Movies*. Owl Books, 1991.
Lehmann, David. "Hamlet vs. the Nazis: A Look Back at Ernst Lubitsch's 1942 movie, *To Be or Not to Be*." *American Scholar*, 4 Jan. 2021, theamericanscholar.org/hamlet-vs-the-nazis/. Accessed 27 June 2022.
Leitch, Thomas. "Against Conclusions: Petit Theories and Adaptation Studies." *The Oxford Handbook of Adaptation Studies*, edited by Thomas Leitch, Oxford University Press, 2017a, pp. 698–709.
Leitch, Thomas. "Introduction: Adapted by John Huston." *John Huston as Adapter*, edited by Douglas McFarland and Wesley King. SUNY P, 2017b, pp. 1–20.
Lolita Directed by Stanley Kubrick, performed by James Mason and Sue Lyon, MGM, 1962.
Murray, Simone. *The Adaptation Industry: The Cultural Economy of Contemporary Literary Adaptation*, Routledge, 2012.
Primary Colors. Directed by Mike Nichols, performed by John Travolta and Emma Thompson, Universal, 1998.
Raw, Laurence, editor. *Translation, Adaptation and Transformation*, Continuum, 2012.

To Be or Not to Be. Directed by Ernst Lubitsch, performed by Carole Lombard and Jack Benny, United Artists, 1942.

Venuti, Lawrence. "Adaptation, Translation, Critique." *Journal of Visual Culture*, volume 6, 2007, pp. 25–42.

Venuti, Lawrence. *The Scandals of Translation: Towards an Ethics of Difference*, Routledge, 1998.

Venuti, Lawrence. *Translation Changes Everything: Theory and Practice*, Routledge, 2013.

Succès de Scandale: From Adultery to Adulteration

Irina Makoveeva

The eye says 'Here is Anna Karenina.' A voluptuous lady in black velvet wearing pearls comes before us. But the brain says, 'That is no more Anna Karenina than it is Queen Victoria.' For the brain knows Anna almost entirely by the inside of her mind—her charm, her passion, her despair. All the emphasis is laid by the cinema upon her teeth, her pearls, her velvet.—Virginia Woolf (269–70)

What's the point of doing a safe adaptation? If you're going out you might as well go out with a bang.—Keira Knightley (qtd. in Palmer)

TOLSTOI'S ANNA

All adaptations of literary classics have the potential to scandalize the public by disturbing their sources' integrity, but revivals of Lev Tolstoi's *Anna Karenina* (1875–1877) are doubly inflammatory given that the novel itself epitomizes scandal. Like Pandora's box, the narrative offers a wide array of shocking events and ideas from which its adapters can select and

---

I. Makoveeva (✉)
Council on International Educational Exchange, St. Petersburg, Russia

© The Author(s), under exclusive license to Springer Nature Switzerland AG 2023
T. Leitch (ed.), *The Scandal of Adaptation*, Palgrave Studies in Adaptation and Visual Culture,
https://doi.org/10.1007/978-3-031-14153-9_2

appropriate whatever corresponds best with their chosen art form, their production goals, and their own understanding of the novel. And while reintroducing some of its diegetic scandals, they have the option of making scandalous changes to them or avoiding such alterations entirely.

Of course, what generates a scandal in one era may merely impress another era's society, critics, readers, and viewers as an admirably bold treatment. This particular novel's publication aroused scandal through topics then under vehement public discussion, thereby guaranteeing contemporaries' agitated reception; moreover, its initially serialized release over three years helped the scandal stew by maintaining suspense and thus prolonged the effects of a *succès de scandale*. Not yet as radical as later in his life, Tolstoi nevertheless explicitly filled the text with incendiary views on marriage, sexuality, women's emancipation, and religious and state institutions, igniting heated debates at the time of its publication. The readers' assessment of the plot gradually unfolding in the *Russian Messenger* issues was hardly laudatory. In fact, many prominent literary critics and writers in Russia, including Vladimir Stasov, Fedor Dostoevskii, and Ivan Turgenev, expressed their disappointment with the novel's first chapters. Mikhail Saltykov-Shchedrin, for instance, in one of his letters from 1875, condemned *Anna Karenina* as structured entirely on "sexual drives," though later he apparently changed his mind. According to Count Vladimir Golitsyn's diaries, equally scandalous for the public were the "disgustingly" realistic scenes describing Anna's labor and Konstantin Levin's confession, seen by contemporaries as inappropriate in a literary work (qtd. in Gornaia 18–23). Also shocking was (and still is) the inclusion of controversial details from the author's intimate life, with Levin regaling his innocent wife-to-be with an account of his premarital sexual encounters to help initiate her into a happy married life. For this part, Stasov later attested to the lasting shock value of Anna's form of suicide in his description of the Lumières' *Arrival of a Train at La Ciotat Station* (1895): "All of a sudden a whole railway train comes rushing out of the picture towards you; it gets bigger and bigger, and you think it's going to run you over, just like in *Anna Karenina*—it's incredible" (qtd. in Tsivian 3).

What most scandalized Tolstoi's contemporaries, however, was his largely sympathetic portrayal of a Russian woman who not only commits adultery, which she refuses to keep clandestine, but violates the religious and societal prohibitions against the betrayal of her marital vows, abandons her maternal obligations, and sins against the precepts of Russian

Orthodoxy by committing suicide.[1] In the context of the nineteenth century's restrictive norms for married women, Anna's demeanor unambiguously marks her as a deviant adulteress. But her moral fall within the novel's narrative and in the responses of contemporary critics, who found her behavior scandalous, gradually lost its provocative intensity as a disruptive hazard, at least within western cultures. In order to make the infidelity scandal believable for their contemporaries, *Anna Karenina* adapters have to recast it by reassigning faults and shifting emphases on Anna's adultery—most frequently by reimagining her as a victim of high society, her husband, or morphine addiction rather than of her own self-indulgent conduct. Even more audaciously, twenty-first-century artists have resorted to updating the novel through contemporary settings, experimenting with new media or broadening the limits of the old (theater and cinema), and redirecting audiences' attention to less familiar knots in the Tolstoian tapestry.[2]

The novel has an abundance of such knots. While revolving around Anna's adultery, culminating in her suicide, it is also permeated with domestic and societal scandals of various proportions involving other characters as well—the serial marital infidelities of Anna's brother, Stiva Oblonskii; Vronskii's abandonment of his alleged fiancée-to-be, Kitty, who has counted on his proposal at the ball; Betsy Tverskaia's masterful accommodation of both her husband and her lover; Konstantin Levin's adamant rejection of high society and its values; and his brother's common-law marriage to a prostitute—offering additional routes taken by adapters seeking a new *succès de scandale*. At the same time, there are lacunae in the narrative that can be filled in eras that have abandoned restrictive norms for depicting sexual intimacy. Indeed, even though later criticized by his contemporaries for foregrounding "sexual drives" in his work, Tolstoi had

---

[1] The declining trajectory of Anna's affair derives from a real-life scandal involving Anna Pirogova, a housekeeper of the writer's neighboring landowner, who ended her life under a train to punish her paramour for marrying another woman. Tolstoi even went to look at the suicide scene and was powerfully affected by the victim's disfigured body—a reaction echoed in Vronskii's closing complaint that the view of his lover's body at a train station eclipsed all his memories of her glamorous appearance while alive.

[2] One of the most scandalous adaptations of *Anna Karenina* was a graphic novel by Katia Metelitsa (2000), which not only transposed Tolstoi's plot to post-Soviet Russia with its emerging class of New Russians but also employed a medium previously banned from publication in Soviet Russia—a combination that certainly doubled its transgressive effect (Makoveeva 42).

concealed the lovers' first sexual intercourse with two lines of ellipses, mentioning only the shame, disgust, and horror experienced by Anna afterward. However, more explicit lovemaking, no longer considered indecent by the end of the twentieth century, fills this gap, drawing out the repressed in the novel—a natural and inevitable choice across media, especially for cinema in post–Production Code times. By reversing the source text's extreme discretion in describing the affair's consummation, adapters have opened it up to a new scandal, most provocatively visualized by the television rendition by David Blair, with Helen McCrory as Anna (2000). Yet its scenes showing the amorous couple engaged in passionate lovemaking elicit scandalous reactions mainly from viewers familiar with the novel, who perceive such explicitness as a presumptuous clarification of the Tolstoian text. For other viewers, these episodes represent a common, unprovocative element of today's love-storytelling.

The Silver Screen's Anna

With different times, audiences, media, and cultures come different standards for determining whether or not the liberties taken by an adapter are scandalous. Within a single decade, adapters of the same text can end up with versions as radically dissimilar as Edmund Goulding's silent film *Love* (1927) and Clarence Brown's *Anna Karenina* (1935), both starring Greta Garbo as Anna. Paradoxically, the first adaptation's crude deviations from Tolstoi's novel hardly interfered with the public's enthusiastic reaction and the film's transformation into a celluloid archetype at the core of all subsequent renditions. The key to this paradox is Goulding's leading actress, her performance and status, and not least her enigmatic face, capable of infusing Tolstoi's narrative with passion and enthralling her viewers. While the writer foregrounds Anna's earthly traits, such as liveliness, kindness, and vulnerability, Garbo's cameraman, William Daniels, illuminates the star's divinity. Defining *the Divine*—an appellation widely bestowed upon Garbo—Roland Barthes deciphers it as "the essence of her corporeal person, descended from a heaven where all things are formed and perfected in the clearest light" (83) (Fig. 1).

For the sake of the divine image descended onto the Hollywood screen, Goulding's version obliterates the immorality of Anna's adultery and of her abandonment of her son for a lover, thus bypassing the novel's major diegetic scandal. The viewers see a suffering mother unconditionally attached to her son rather than a suffering adulteress destroying her family

Fig. 1 The candle's light in Anna's hand emphasizes Garbo's divinity in an invented scene of the Easter service in Edmund Goulding's *Love* (1927)

and undermining society's foundations. Such intense maternal devotion, reinforced by Garbo's performance, drew attention from various commentators. Barry Paris, one of her biographers, wrote that in her 1927 and 1935 films, "Garbo's main lovemaking is directed toward her child. But in the talkie, it is virtually the *only* lovemaking she does" (317). Matthew Kennedy, describing Goulding's career and life, likewise noted that despite "the combustibility of the Garbo-Gilbert pairing [in 1927], an equally compelling story takes place between Anna and her son Sergei" (66).

Even as it whitewashed Anna's adultery, however, the 1927 rendition itself chose to adulterate the literary plot with potentially scandalous deviations epitomized by scriptwriter Frances Marion's changed ending, in which Anna reunites with Vronskii after her husband's convenient death instead of leaping under a train. The concluding shot depicts Vronskii visiting Anna's son in a military school after a three-year break, when Anna unexpectedly appears through the swinging open doors. But Goulding actually filmed Tolstoi's ending of Anna's affair as well, and then made the two versions available in different locales. While the American distributors on the east and west coasts preferred the tragic closure, the middle portion of the country was introduced to the happy ending (Paris 132). It is unlikely, however, that the distributors' arbitrariness discontented 1920s viewers expecting a love story with Garbo in the title role rather than a screen version of Tolstoi's novel, probably then unknown to most of them. Apparently even Russian audiences were not scandalized by the 1927 double-ending, when the endings were shown as successive parts of the same narrative. According to Russian scholar Lev Anninskii, Goulding's film introduced Anna's suicide only as a dream, optimistically followed by a "happily ever after" ending (174).

If it had been screened two decades later, Marion's tinkering with the already famous classic might well have scandalized audiences, but not then. They anticipated *Love*. The playful marquee for the film, "John Gilbert and Greta Garbo in *Love*," intimated a real-life romance exploiting the spectators' interest in the stars' private lives and predetermined their generic expectations of the onscreen romance. In 1927 *Photoplay* announced to its readers that "it isn't Tolstoy but it is John Gilbert and Greta Garbo, beautifully presented and magnificently acted" (qtd. in Paris 134). Moreover, the audiences who were exposed to the more faithful finale felt perplexed. *New York Times* reviewer Mordaunt Hall wrote that "the spectators were surprised on the opening night of this picture, because they expected Anna to go forth with her child, or that the storyteller of the screen would cause the husband to die and to show Anna and Gilbert happy" (7). And that is exactly how Marion had scripted the other version. Indeed, her triumphant closure corresponds better with Garbo's interpretation of Anna as a transcendental character. In the end, *Love*—toasted on several occasions invented by the filmmakers—triumphs over the unloved and unloving Karenin.

Now less well-known than Brown's *Anna Karenina*, Goulding's version actually served as its proto-text alongside Tolstoi's novel (or more precisely, its abridged version). As a silent film with exaggerated stylistics to compensate for its lack of sound, *Love* appealed less to audiences over the years despite its artistic merit. However, it was critically important in laying a foundation for collective memory of the novel as the narrative of a tragic love affair with a self-sacrificing woman and mother at its center. And all subsequent actresses portraying Anna onscreen have been daunted by the Garbo-as-Anna divinity, trying to recreate her heavenly essence.

But Goulding's downplaying of infidelity was not a viable option for Brown, since the moralistic censorship of the 1930 Production Code forced him to modify the portrayal of Tolstoi's heroine, condemning female adultery and punishing her for her failure to comply with the patriarchal order. Some changes were entirely gratuitous, with Vronskii closer to Karenin than to his suffering paramour in his condemnation of women obsessed with love and who distract men from their manly duties in the military. "I am sick and tired of love," he says in his last conversation with Anna. On the whole, however, the studio was forced into greater fidelity to the novel, inasmuch as Tolstoi's Anna commits suicide. Yet in the struggle to disguise sloppy plot segues caused by endless instructions to alter the script, the film awkwardly motivated her action by her resistance to Vronskii's departure to war and her inability to see him off at the train station. The crowning 1935 shot displays her face entrapped in a shiny picture frame, with Vronskii and his friend contemplating her tragic fate, and betrays a curious transformation of Vronskii the devoted lover, as John Gilbert had portrayed him, into Vronskii the narrator condemning the adultery according to the Production Code's precepts.

Despite its glaring reversal of the 1927 film's happy ending, this closure did not scandalize its viewers either, once again thanks to Garbo, then at the peak of her popularity and no longer silent, her presence seeming to sanction all sorts of deviations. And for her second incarnation of Anna, she won the New York Film Critics' Award for Best Actress. Even in the eyes of Russian cinephiles more familiar with and more protective of their sacrosanct literary works, Garbo's captivating performance nullified "the script's deficiencies," as documented by Russian film critics (Gornaia 91). Likewise invisible to the public were the scandalous peripeteias of the 1935 production, starting with its first director George Cukor's departure from the project because he "couldn't face all the suffering, agony and rat-killing" of the original story (Swenson 331) and ending with its producer David Selznick's considerable compromises on the initial screenplay, supplanted by "the alternative of making a completely vitiated and emasculated adaptation of Tolstoy's famous classic" (Swenson 335).

More generally, another factor was at play in 1920–1930s' tolerance of the liberties taken by adaptations, namely early audiences' expectations of the moviegoing experience. Almost certainly, their expectations were predetermined by their past visits to a movie theater and by the celluloid stories viewed there. Borrowing, developing, and generating a limited number of tales—the seduction and adultery plots were eminently recognizable and popular—the new medium was still learning how and what to narrate. Then its storage of visual associations was still half-empty. The average filmgoer anticipated a simplified love story with familiar obstacles, surmountable or not, rather than a multi-linear narrative of a revered Russian literary classic. To be recognized as a film, with its plot fitting into the extant cinematic memory, was what both filmmakers and spectators expected from a screen adaptation: its adaptability mattered more than its integrity.[3] In many ways, visual texts accumulated before a given period programmed the expectations and the reception of a period's audiences. With cinema's maturation and its film collection's growth came more experienced and better educated cinephiles, and yet the two films with Garbo portraying Anna continue to govern the processes of adapting Tolstoi's novel, watching its celluloid versions, or encountering any of its transmedia renditions. And that remains true despite the two versions' mutually exclusive reimaginings, whose incompatibility just eight years apart could in itself have scandalized audiences. In this context, a *Chicago Sun-Times* review of the Joffrey Ballet's 2019 adaptation contains a particularly revealing slip. In summarizing the Tolstoian plot, the reviewer, Kyle McMillan, unwittingly offered his readers an invented closure of the 1935 film, claiming that "the adulterous wife throws herself under a train, after Vronskii tires of her and goes off to war." No matter how outdated, sexually restricted, narratively abridged and altered, the Hollywood versions by Goulding and Brown represent our collective memory of *Anna Karenina*.

Anna Treading the Boards

Unlike the impact of celluloid reworkings on the collective unconscious, that of theatrical adaptations was (and still is) short-lived and often untraceable given their immateriality and ephemerality. They are, to borrow Renata Miller's words, "ghostly presences of vanished works" (53). Yet it was the stage that took it upon itself to liberate the Tolstoian text

[3] Of course, a body of filmgoers is hardly a homogeneous cohort taking the same approach to adaptations. However, at the risk of simplification, I suggest an all-embracing view of the 1920–1930s spectatorship, since obviously long before adaptation scholars voiced their concerns about the criterion of integrity, the public included people with varied tolerance of adapters' inventiveness. Thomas Leitch, in this volume's introduction, distinguishes three possible positions in the adaptability-integrity debate that adaptation scholars might do well to recognize and choose among (5–7).

from its novelistic shackles and bring its progeny into the multimedia world. *Anna Karenina*'s first stage productions appeared in the 1880s[4] with an aura of scandal, as they could suggest only reductive readings while the novel was still at the epicenter of public discussions—an explosive combination that on the one hand guaranteed full houses and on the other encouraged invidious comparisons with the literary source, at least among theatergoers who had actually read the novel. Only three decades later, the nascent cinema caught up with its then more respected rival with the (lost) Pathé Frères version directed by Maurice-André Maître (1911); the (partially extant) Paul Thiemann and Friedrich Reinhardt Company adaptation by Vladimir Gardin (1914); the (presumably lost) Fox Film rendition by J. Gordon Edwards (1915); and finally the (extant) Hungária Filmgyár interpretation by Márton Garas (1918).

Moreover, *Anna Karenina*'s early renditions on stage, in contrast to their screen counterparts, which primarily zeroed in on a passionate romance, demonstrated more interest in the content of aristocratic gatherings and conversations, a preference that both fanned and dampened the fire of scandal. Unfortunately, the few existing testimonials mainly lament the plays' truncations of the literary source, without describing the productions in enough detail for accurate evaluation of the adapters' choices. Several stage adaptations at the beginning of the twentieth century, by Russian authors Mavrov (1900) and Marina Morskaia (1914) and well-known French stage adapter Edmond Guiraud (1907), included many episodes focusing on the society itself. Although these three interpretations took liberties with the material—especially Guiraud's, which rearranged and merged many of the novel's episodes and reshuffled its characters[5]—all followed Tolstoi's lead in making the beau monde important, almost a separate personage in its own right. By contrast, in more recent versions, Anna's elite world seems only a backdrop, portrayed indirectly through representatives embodying the conventions and decorum

---

[4] As evident from a hand-written copy of a play by S.F. Rassokhin's Company, with a censor's permission to stage it in public theaters across Russia, the first theatrical adaptation of *Anna Karenina* can be dated to 1882. However, the letters to Tolstoi from his novel's enthusiastic admirers either asking for his permission to rework it as a play or describing their endeavors to him show that the very first renditions were undertaken by non-professionals in the 1870s (Gornaia 83).

[5] One of the most shocking innovations in his adaptation, which was not mentioned in any reviews I read, is that one of the officers, Makhotin, declares his love for Anna and even demands sexual favors from her at a train station right before her suicide (Guiraud 154–58).

against which her affair plays out, thus securing undivided attention to the Anna–Vronskii–Karenin scandal.

A rare exception that claimed the stage for an exceptionally long time was the Moscow Art Theater's *Anna Karenina*, based on the 1935 play by Nikolai Volkov and staged by the esteemed Vladimir Nemirovich-Danchenko and Vasilii Sakhnovskii. Premiering in 1937, it was filmed in 1953 and dominated the Russian stage until 1983, when another Moscow theater, the Vakhtangov, broke the spell with a new revival of the novel, "a breakthrough created as a polemic against its precursors" (Poliakova 86). Whereas the Moscow Art Theater's protracted monopoly earned contemporary approval as the definitive interpretation, today it seems scandalously long to theatergoers able to enjoy an overwhelming variety of *Anna Kareninas* on multiple stages throughout Russia. Back then, the adaptation's success depended partly on the fame of the leading actress, Alla Tarasova, but a more important element was its ideologically welcome interpretation of Anna as the victim of an aristocratic society that throws her under the train, with Stalin and Molotov's attendance at its premiere as an official seal of approval. Undoubtedly censored in accord with the historical moment's precepts by the playwright himself, this version secured a long life on the country's foremost dramatic stage, then branched out into provincial theaters. Even if it was not always successful, as local newspaper reviews suggest,[6] these far-and-wide public performances were ideologically safe. Unlike many other post-revolutionary literary texts chastised for any sort of criticism of the Soviet regime, *Anna Karenina* was hardly threatening because of Tolstoi's solidified status as a literary colossus censorious of his contemporaries' lifestyle and values. Praised as the novel's exemplary adaptation despite its misleading emphasis on gender inequality and the complexities of divorce in pre-revolutionary Russia and its omission of the Kitty–Levin line, it haunted the Soviet cultural landscape for several decades, impeding new interpretations. Yet it has since sunk into oblivion, vanquished by a rival medium's power to influence masses for a much longer period (Fig. 2).

Notwithstanding the theatrical productions' transience, it is exactly this medium that demonstrated its urge to scandalize by undermining

---

[6] One such testimonial examines an "irresponsible" adaptation by the Saratov theater that presents "Anna's fate as a banal family drama" and shows her suicide as a result of her lover's breaking up with her rather than a consequence of "the old society moral trampling a human personality," as demonstrated in the Moscow Art Theater interpretation (Sappak).

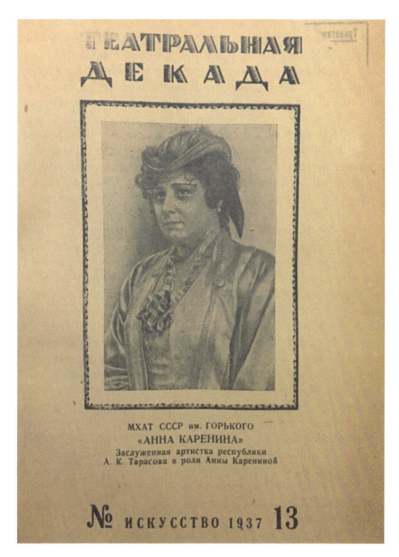

Fig. 2 In 1937 *Theatrical Decade* made its display of Alla Tarasova as Anna in the novel's stage adaptation into a major event of the season

sacrosanct texts, and *Anna Karenina* in particular. The last turn of the century was especially favorable to such experiments, mostly, but not exclusively, on Russian soil. While many twenty-first-century adapters zealously seek to assert themselves by creating a version of *Anna Karenina* that outshines their predecessors', such competition has become a form of rebellion for the Russian stage. Once policed to ensure an ideologically correct interpretation by emphasizing the imperial society's and Karenin's oppressive roles in Anna's demise and simultaneously downplaying her own failings (abuse of morphine, failure to normalize her life with Vronskii after leaving her husband, lack of maternal care for her second child), Tolstoi's text has been subjected to the new era's (mis)management. As if following in the steps of the 1990s crowds who celebrated the Soviet empire's collapse by toppling its monuments, the adapters dared to approach Tolstoi's *Anna Karenina*. Of its many revisions, Oleg Shishkin's play *Anna Karenina–2* (2002) stands out for shaking spectators' memory of the Tolstoian plot and totally besmirching the novel. Resurrected from the dead, Anna as an invalid in a wheelchair and her lover Vronskii as a paralyzed veteran drag out their deplorable existence with Karenin as their caretaker. The critics' explicit hostility in branding the version's authors "grave desecrators" (Tukh 8) and the audience's receptivity to Vladimir Epifantsev's staging of the play at the 2002 New Drama Festival laid bare an essential moment in culture, still predominantly logocentric, yet ready to challenge its nineteenth-century classics and stir up scandal.

Most theaters, however, resorted to a less rebellious stance. Eager to win back their laurels and audiences in the 1990s, theaters adopted cinematic tricks while catering to the spectators' changed tastes and attempting to shake their expectations. Thus directors provocatively challenged the customary limitations of the stage by adding kinetic images in the background to widen stage dimensions and eliminate visible borders (still the most obvious and most easily executed adjustment today). More recently, Aleksei Ratmanskii's ballet production at the Mariinskii Theater and Roman Ignat'ev's musical version at the Moscow Operetta Theater mark the first indications of an attempted media merger. While the inclusion of cinematic elements in stage performances helps accelerate the progression of scenes[7] and reconstruct episodes previously unmanageable for

---

[7] Curiously, in 1914 a reviewer criticized the Korsh Theater's version of *Anna Karenina* because of scenes that flashed at the theatergoers like a kaleidoscope and therefore were reminiscent of the cinematic experience, which that critic seemed to dislike (Pasmurov). Without a doubt, a century of making and watching films radically changed viewers.

theater, the refitting of *Anna Karenina*'s setting and its mise-en-scène to non-verbal (rather traditional) art forms like ballet can readily arouse a furor like the one that greeted John Neumeier's 2018 rendition at the Bolshoi Theater. A famous choreographer, known for his skillful set designs, audacious stage lighting, and passion for literary classics, Neumeier shifted the novel to today's reality by opening his ballet with Anna at a political rally supporting her husband's re-election. His version reimagines Stiva Oblonskii as a restless chaser of Bolshoi dancers, Levin as a cowboy-landowner driving a tractor on stage, Vronskii as an ardent lacrosse player, and Kitty as a tormented patient at a sanatorium after her broken engagement. Even more noticeable is Neumeier's choice of composers: predictably, Piotr Tchaikovskii; less expectedly, Alfred Schnittke; and surprisingly, if not scandalously, Cat Stevens (Yusuf Islam) (Fig. 3).

Although unorthodox, Neumeier's is a striking transposition to the dance stage, thanks to his selective use of Tolstoi's text to provide a coherent and engaging multi-line narrative. What is questionable, however, is which text really governed the choreographer's choices. In an interview before the premiere that stresses the time constraints of a ballet as an

Fig. 3 Even the lovers' costumes play tricks on the spectators' memory of Tolstoi's story in John Neumeier's updated version

obstacle to adapting the complex 800-page novel, he alludes exclusively to the cinematic adaptations starring Keira Knightley, Greta Garbo, and Vivien Leigh (73). And his discussion of the powerful motif of dreams and the subconscious in Tolstoi's narrative, both evident in his choreographic rendition, reveals that not only were *screen* adaptations a starting point for his own production but also that he had not seen the Russian versions including Anna's dreams. While it would be unfair to expect a choreographer to be familiar with the rare footage of the 1914 version, which displays Anna describing her nightmare to Vronskii and the peasant (*muzhik*) striking the train's wheels with a hammer in the frame's upper right, it is surprising to learn that he was unaware of the 1967 Soviet adaptation by Aleksander Zarkhi, especially since his own *Anna Karenina* was scheduled to premiere in post–Soviet Russia. Neumeier's long interview omits any mention of Maia Plisetskaia's breakthrough 1972 ballet *Anna Karenina*, which, performed on the same stage as Neumeier's almost half a century previously, had paved the way for future choreographic interpretations of Tolstoi's novel. Conversely, a choreographer of the Joffrey Ballet's adaptation premiering in Chicago in 2019, Yuri Possokhov, identified Plisetskaia's Anna as his source of "guidance" (McMillan). Whether Neumeier's neglect points to a Harold Bloomian anxiety of influence or a collective unconscious fixated on Anglophone filmings of the canonical Russian novel, these moments add an inflammatory spark to a production that from the very beginning was meant to scandalize through the director's choice of hypotext.

Multimedia's Anna

Another production that reopened the Anna Karenina hypotext was Joe Wright's aforementioned adaptation with Keira Knightley as Anna (2012), the most flamboyant and ballyhooed version of the new millennium. Working with Tom Stoppard's screenplay, Wright injected new blood into the narrative, the potential for scandal residing not so much in its deviations from the novel as in its unprecedented counterpoising of two genres. In this interpretation, an enclosed theatrical building serves as the primary filming set; the filmmakers extravagantly envelop the screen action with a theatrical frame—a metatextual choice that distances audiences from a familiar narrative and juxtaposes the dynamics of stage and screen, all while insisting on the constructed nature of the written narrative as well. Although the director's final decision to use a single theatrical space

Fig. 4 The creators of the 2012 version of *Anna Karenina* staged and filmed an impressive episode of races on theater boards, with spectators occupying the theater space

instead of multiple locations in Russia resulted from the production's budgetary constraints, it was later introduced as an idea borrowed from Orland Figes's academic monograph *Natasha's Dance* (2003). In the end, an impressive execution of Wright's unique conception created a stir, proved its adaptive legitimacy, and led to a *succès de scandale* (Fig. 4).

At the same time, the film's apparently incongruous framing actually relays a crucial thematic dichotomy in Tolstoi's text. The artificial stage arrangement mirrors the *modus operandi* of the novel's high society, contrasting the aristocracy's artificial existence with the dissenters' authenticity. Accordingly, Wright unlocks a narration restricted to a dilapidated theater only for the open-space scenes celebrating the countryside as the opposite to urban life and to the characters who strive to escape the confines of the beau monde—Levin in his search for truth, Anna and Vronskii in pursuit of their forbidden passion, and Karenin on his path of forgiving Anna and reconciling with her and his own fate. In fact, the film's concluding sequence transfers the audience to the pastoral setting of a flowering meadow where both Anna's son by Karenin and her daughter by Vronskii play together happily and Karenin lovingly watches over them.[8]

---

[8] Wright's adaptation offers an overwhelmingly idealized portrayal of the cuckolded husband in the Tolstoian love triangle—a post-millennial trend of shifting the focus from a suffering adulteress to her suffering husband. It should be noted that it was the British screen that established and maintained a tradition of sympathetic treatment of Karenin, starting with Julien Duvivier's *Anna Karenina* (1948), with Ralph Richardson as Karenin.

Equating theater space with falsity (so despised by Tolstoi) and the realm beyond it with truth (the ultimate goal of Tolstoi's writings), the director creates a binary opposition of artifice versus authenticity. This thematic tension derives from the two media's contrasting modes: theater binds characters and narration to the stage, while film takes them into nature and the open.

In many ways the impact of the film does indeed depend on the interplay between these two respected genres. But paradoxically, it is exactly theatricality—and exaggeration as its grounding principle—that makes the 2012 cinematic adaptation stand out as fresh and creative. Whereas harking back to the medium to which the novel was first adapted might seem retrograde, making the staging insistently artificial rather than realistic like early theater presentations actually revitalizes the narrative. Moreover, Wright's most striking visual innovations include Sidi Larbi Cherkaoui's choreography, which is deliberately accentuated and especially palpable in the ball sequence initiating Anna and Vronskii's sensuous love affair. In the midst of the ballroom dancing, the pair's movements resemble a *pas de deux*—an unexpected replacement for the whirlwind waltz prevailing in earlier versions (Fig. 5).[9]

The dancers' intricate balletic steps combined with their arms' "evocatively swan-lake" gestures encouraged Catherine Nepomnyashchy to suggest Tchaikovskii's ballet *Swan Lake* and Darren Aronofsky's film *The Black Swan* (2010) as illuminating contexts for those particular moments (326). Indeed, in an interview with *The New York Times*, Wright said that he had conceived his film "as a ballet with words" (qtd. in Backstein 54). Another striking innovation, most effectively used in the opening sequence, is a swiftly choreographed succession of scenes lacking the transitions customary for cinematic storytelling, with characters moving from one space to another while changing attire on the go. As each episode morphs into the next, their quick passing is reminiscent of watching the world through the window of a moving train. What makes this film device even more

---

[9] Most cinematic adapters gratify viewers with Anna and Vronskii intimately waltzing, oblivious to the other ball attendees. Their choice has required re-interpretation of the novel's mazurka—a regulated dance by contrast with the waltz, once forbidden in the ballroom as a reprehensible "form of erotic temptation" (Sandler 256). Not necessarily aware of the nineteenth-century perception of the waltz as a "passionate, insane and close to nature" dance (Lotman 526), adapters employ a visually effective and suitable metaphor for a whirlwind romance alongside the speeding train and the snowstorm essential to Anna's story.

Fig. 5 The lovers' *pas de deux* introduced in Joe Wright's 2012 film adaptation aspires to convey a moment of intimate connection between Anna (Keira Knightley) and Vronskii (Aaron Taylor-Johnson) outside their society

daring is that Seamus McGarvey's camerawork registers the movements within the theater arena.

Without doubt, however, most moviegoers thought it was the luster of Keira Knightley starring as Anna that earned Wright's rendition laurels as a cultural event and placed its leading actress alongside Greta Garbo and Vivien Leigh. Already a worldwide celebrity thanks to her roles in such popular films as *Pirates of the Caribbean* (2003, 2006, 2007), *Pride and Prejudice* (2005), *Atonement* (2007), *The Duchess* (2008), and her appearances as a new face for Chanel's perfume and jewelry commercials, Knightley was a major force in promoting the new British adaptation of *Anna Karenina*. While mass media were circulating a plethora of her interviews before the film's release, the internet, that most powerful tool for global reach, was (and still is) inundated with her posing, model-like, in glamorous Anna-costumes, occasionally revealing their complex undergarments. Such slippage from Wright's aesthetic interplay of theater, film, and ballet apparently did not strike audiences as a scandalous commercialization of a classic. Rather, it probably made Anna seem all the more contemporary, given social media's aggressive promotion of the film as a blockbuster.

The publicity surrounding the star's imminent appearance on the silver screen presented Wright's film not only as an adaptation of *Anna Karenina* but also as the right vehicle for Keira Knightley's re-embodiment of Anna in the new millennium, her assumption of that heroine's persona (and costumes). While her fame will hardly last as long as Anna's or Greta Garbo's, the 2012 adaptation will retain its position among its precursors as a celluloid version that daringly uses theater, its long-term rival, to transpose Tolstoi's classic to the screen. At the same time, however, the film might well offend the collective memory of the novel, shaped by twentieth-century cinema as the narrative of a passionate affair. By displaying Anna in dazzlingly splendid costumes, Wright seems at times to reduce her to a fashion plate, a glamorous icon far removed from Tolstoi's character. Whereas the novel's Anna at one point joins her maid in altering old dresses for high society engagements, onscreen Anna's splendid wardrobe earned the Oscar for Best Costume Design (by Jacqueline Durran), inspired by the fashion houses of Balenciaga and Dior and accordingly matched by Chanel's jewelry of not less than "$2 million apiece," as publicized before the film's release (Betker).

While the film did turn out to be a financial blockbuster—with a budget of $40.6 million, it earned $68.9 million worldwide—it met with strong critical disapproval, with some reviewers clearly scandalized not by its wholesale deviations from the novel but by its cinematic shortcomings. Christy Lemire, for instance, blamed Wright's artifice for failing to engage the viewers emotionally: "Rather than feeling the suffering of the adulterous Anna, we're more likely to notice how beautiful the suffering looks—the flattering lighting, her wild mane of dark curls spread meticulously across her pillow case." *Cineaste* reviewer Karen Backstein went even further, identifying the leading actress as the production's Achilles heel and its "big black hole, sucking in energy and illuminating nothing" (55). Intriguingly, while denying the 2012 star her literary prototype's "grace" as an intrinsic component of Anna's beauty, Backstein reanimated the praises for the divine Garbo, whose performances as Anna ultimately outweighed the plot deviations so obvious in her 1927 and 1935 films. Thus, in the critic's view, it was Knightley, on whose status the publicity campaign rested, who obstructed the adaptation's success—an opinion shared in Simon Fallaha's posting on *Si's Sights And Sounds*, which expresses his disappointment with "cardboard characters" (except for Jude Law's Karenin), and especially with Anna, "a cipher, a plot device, a nobody." More analytical yet equally disapproving was Richard Brody's review in *The New Yorker*, criticizing the filmmakers for their adaptation's artificiality and their borrowing of Tolstoi's plot and characters simply to enhance their work's status by the literary association. Brody's verdict was categorical: "Wright, with flat and flavorless images of an utterly impersonal banality, takes Tolstoy's plot and translates it into a cinematic language that's the equivalent of, say, Danielle Steel, simultaneously simplistic and overdone." A week later *The New Yorker* published Joshua Rothman's reflections on the novel after his viewing of Wright's film at its New York premiere. Rothman described the interpretation as "fanciful and expressionistic" and its sets as "inventive and metafictional"; even so, he faulted it as "too romantic," with a simplified representation of love discordant with Tolstoi's nuanced treatment of it. While softening Brody's harsh criticism, Rothman used Wright's rendition to talk about the novel, mostly about its representation of multi-faceted family love and happiness. In doing so, he adhered to his colleague's binary opposition, privileging the literary source over its screen version—a dead-end approach for evaluating transmedia adaptations.

As long as they are compared to Tolstoi's narrative, versions like these will scandalize book-oriented audiences with the truncation and alteration inevitable in relocating it to other media, none of which can convey the psychological complexities and subtleties of free indirect speech in the voluminous novel. In estranging the literary text through performances on a stage, moving images on a screen, or comic-strip characters on a page, the renditions "foreignize" the novelistic discourse and make an adapter and her/his artistic genre visible—to echo Lawrence Venuti's notion of foreignization from his influential *The Translator's Invisibility* (1995), which advocates laying bare a translated text as not the original. And it is precisely such "making visible" in adapting *Anna Karenina* that led some to reject Wright and Stoppard's interpretation as deviancy rather than mere deviation. However, the advertising frenzy around this production drowned out the voices of the displeased public, blocking an accurate assessment of the scandal's proportions. To hear more of these voices, I looked at *The New York Times*' thread of posts following A.O. Scott's laudatory review of the 2012 film as "risky and ambitious enough to count as an act of artistic hubris, and confident enough to triumph on its own slightly—wonderfully—crazy terms." Surprisingly or not, the critic's opinion did not significantly affect the public reception: out of twenty-five comments, only eight assessed it as a stellar, five-star adaptation, whereas on the opposite end, ten responders graded it as a one-star production; in between, three commentators gave it four stars while four others ranked it as a mediocre three- or two-star movie. At the risk of overestimating statistical indicators, it is tempting to affirm the *Times* reviewer's definition of the film as "Mr. Wright's brilliant gamble" and conclude that the wager paid off as it managed to stir up a scandal. What is noteworthy in these comments, whose contradictions faithfully reflect the fickleness and subjectivity of public tastes, is the frustrated spectators' irritation with the action unfolding on a theatrical stage, characters climbing a ladder to enter the next scene, the camera playing visual tricks, and other spatial transformations. Unlike the critics, audiences seem to have been more outraged by the director's transgeneric liberties.

At the opposite extreme from Wright's grand 210-minute conception, Radda Novikova's eight-minute *Dark Like the Night. Anna Karenina–2019*, released in Russia, is thus far the most remarkable, if not shocking, onscreen rendition of the novel. In her brutally abbreviated interpretation of Tolstoi's magnum opus, Novikova managed to include all the desiderata for a *succès de scandale*. For one thing, she collaborated on the script with a well-known author of satirical short stories, Aleksandr Tsypkin: together they did away with the original trajectory of Anna's tragic fate and relocated the action to today's Russia. For another, she engaged an extraordinary number of stars, given the brevity of the screenplay. Perhaps most egregiously, she chose to make the short film all the more reminiscent of a music video by having a rock soundtrack accompany its abrupt editing. Not accidentally, at the Prague Independent Film Festival it was recognized as Best Music Clip of 2019. About half of the action is accompanied by the famous song *Dark Like the Night* by Boris Grebenshchikov, a cult figure in rock, who shares something of Tolstoi's celestial status in contemporary Russia. Traditionally reimagined even by modern adapters as a victim, Anna here morphs into a feisty, strong woman-avenger who speaks and acts aggressively. Mistreated by both men in her life, she ends up punishing her husband, a terrifying tycoon, by reporting his illegal affairs to authorities and her narcissistic, unfaithful lover by pushing him under a subway train (Fig. 6).[10]

---

[10] Rejection of the Tolstoian paradigm of a woman committing suicide under a train's wheels creates a niche for further challenging the creator's authority and censoring his vision of the events' inevitability. Indeed, whether reproduced or rejected by adapters, the culmination of Anna's romance does constitute a provocation. One can only speculate how many troubled minds, fictional or real, were served by Anna's tragic finale. The writer's own wife, Sofia Tolstaia, was among the first victims attempting to replay the last stunt of her husband's creation. Her diary entry on July 21, 1891 describes a conjugal quarrel resulting in her decision to take her life "like Anna Karenina" (Basinskii 422). Luckily, on her way to the train station she was met by her brother-in-law, who escorted her back home.

Fig. 6　In Radda Novikova's 2019 film, Anna restores her dignity by murdering an abhorrent Vronskii

The film toys with audiences' expectations of the finale by crosscutting between the main action and the subway driver on his route, until Anna's last encounter with her jilter turns suicide into homicide. As she strides off purposefully, no police in sight, she is emancipated, her new, shorter hair style adding to the feminist outlines of this version. Tolstoi himself would surely have been scandalized. Unlike the happy 1927 ending that will presumably inspire future Disney World interpretations of Anna's story, the 2019 portrayal of Tolstoi's protagonist as a nemesis retaliating against men intimates a dissimilar development for this heroine. With rock, computers, email, and strenuous sex on the boardroom table updating the original story, the film presages the novel's possible future as a wandering text open to unpredictable metamorphoses. The potential for scandal lives on.

The twentieth and twenty-first centuries have seen the public outrage that the novel ignited both doubled and replaced by responses to its seemingly endless adaptations on stage, screen, and page, only a few of them discussed here. While a faithful rendition focusing on the novel's original provocations can certainly scandalize audiences, an unfaithful version intentionally elicits a similar reaction by betraying its literary source or going against the grain of previous adaptations. Whereas scandal once revolved around the immorality of Tolstoi's female protagonist and her suicide, outrage has more recently been stimulated by transgeneric liberties. Like Anna in her adultery, adaptations also betray and prove unfaithful—in short, they adulterate the original narrative. Both cinematic and theatrical adaptations have been lambasted, not for Anna's deviancy, but for their deviation from Tolstoi's conception of his adulteress and for their violation of familiar media boundaries. The time and place of reading and adapting *Anna Karenina* inevitably affect its comprehension and its new reappearances across media. The more removed audiences are temporally and spatially from the novel's publication, the less they recognize and engage with Tolstoi's encyclopedic portrait of 1870s Russian society. It is up to adapters delivering the nineteenth-century narrative to their contemporaries to choose how best to reanimate their interest. And a *succès de scandale* unquestionably makes their work more visible.

References

Anninskii, Lev. *Lev Tolstoi i kinematograf,* Iskusstvo, 1980.
Backstein, Karen. *Cinéaste* 38, no. 2, 2013, pp. 54–55. http://www.jstor.org/stable/43500827.
Barthes, Roland. "The Garbo Face." *A Barthes Reader,* Hill and Wang, 1982.
Basinskii, Pavel. *Lev Tolstoi: begstvo iz raia,* AST, 2016.
Betker, Ally. "In New *Anna Karenina* Film, Dior Couture for the 1870s." *The Cut,* 26 October 2012, https://www.thecut.com/2012/10/anna-karenina-dior-couture-for-the-1870s.html. Accessed 27 June 2022.
Brody, Richard. "An Anna Karenina That Forgets Tolstoy." *New Yorker,* 16 Nov. 2012, https://www.newyorker.com/culture/richard-brody/an-anna-karenina-that-forgets-tolstoy. Accessed 27 June 2022.
Fallaha, Simon. "The pointless adaptation of Tolstoy's masterpiece is a missed opportunity." *Si's Sights And Sounds,* 11 Sept. 2012, https://sights403.rssing.com/chan-6669412/all_p1.html. Accessed 27 June 2022.
Gornaia, Viktoriia. *Mir chitaet "Annu Kareninu,"* Kniga, 1979.
Guiraud, Edmond. *Anna Karenina.* Translated by Frank J. Morlock, 2009.
Hall, Mordaunt. "Anna Karenina." *New York Times,* 30 Nov. 1927, p. 22.
Kennedy, Matthew. *Edmund Goulding's Dark Victory,* U Wisconsin P, 2004.
Leitch, Thomas. "Introduction." *The Scandal of Adaptation,* ed. Thomas Leitch. London: Palgrave Macmillan, 2022, 1–18.
Lotman, Yurii. *Pushkin,* Iskusstvo-Spb, 1999.
Makoveeva, Irina. "Revisualizing *Anna Karenina.*" *Tolstoy Studies Journal,* vol. 16, 2004, pp. 42–54.
McMillan, Kyle. "With 'Anna Karenina,' Joffrey Ballet continues its journey into story ballets." *Chicago Sun-Times,* 6 Feb. 2019, https://chicago.suntimes.com/2019/2/6/18391065/with-anna-karenina-joffrey-ballet-continues-its-journey-into-story-ballets. Accessed 27 June 2022.
Metelitsa, Katia. *Anna Karenina by Leo Tolstoy,* Mir Novykh Russkikh, 2000.

Miller, Renata Kobetts. "Nineteenth-Century Theatrical Adaptations of Novels: The Paradox of Ephemerality." *The Oxford Handbook of Adaptation Studies*, edited by Thomas Leitch, Oxford University Press, 2017, pp. 53–70.
Nepomnyashchy, Catherine. n.d. "A Tale of Two *Annas*." *Tolstoy on Screen*, edited by Lorna Fitzsimmons and Michael A. Denner, Northwestern University Press, pp. 317–27.
Neumeier, John. "Po motivam L'va Tolstogo." *Anna Karenina. Ballet by John Neumeier*, Teatralis, 2019, pp. 73–82.
Palmer, Martyn. "Keira Knightley's theatre of dreams: The stage is set for a stunning new take on Anna Karenina," https://www.dailymail.co.uk/home/moslive/article-2182673/Keira-Knightley-Anna-Karenina-An-exclusive-look-lavish-production-directed-Joe-Wright.html. Accessed 27 June 2022.
Paris, Barry. *Garbo: A Biography*, Knopf, 1995.
Pasmurov, N. "Anna Karenina." *Teatr*, no. 1609, 1914.
Poliakova, E. "Svechi, otrazhennye v zerkalakh." *Teatr*, no. 5, 1984, pp. 86–92.
Rothman, Joshua. "Is 'Anna Karenina' a Love Story?" *New Yorker*, 23 Nov. 2012, https://www.newyorker.com/books/page-turner/is-anna-karenina-a-love-story. Accessed 27 June 2022.
Sandler, Stephanie. "Pleasure, Danger, and the Dance: Nineteenth-Century Russian Variations." *Russia-Women-Culture*, edited by Helena Goscilo and Beth Holmgren, Indiana University Press, 1996, pp. 247–72.
Sappak, Vl. "Legkomyslennye uprazhneniia nad klassicheskim romanom." *Soviet Art*, 15 Sept. 1951.
Scott, A.O. "Infidelity, Grandly Staged." *New York Times*, 15 Nov. 2012, https://www.nytimes.com/2012/11/16/movies/anna-karenina-from-by-joe-wright-with-keira-knightley.html. Accessed 27 June 2022.
Swenson, Karen. *Greta Garbo: A Life Apart*, New York: Scribner, 1997.
Tsivian, Yuri. *Early Cinema in Russia and Its Cultural Perception*, U of Chicago P, 1994.
Tukh, Boris. "Oskverrniteli grobnits, ili stolichnye shtuchki v provintsii." *Teatral'naia Zhizn'*, no. 2, 2002, pp. 8–9.
Woolf, Virginia. "Cinema." *Collected Essays*, vol. 2, Hogarth P, 1966, pp. 268–72.

Fritz Lang's *Scarlet Street* (1945): Designing for Scandal

R. Barton Palmer

Translation, Lawrence Venuti proclaims, is scandalous because it exists on the margins of other cultural practices, including literary production as authored expression, which is why translation is "discouraged by copyright law" (1). Not just troublesome in its vexing marginality, translation, as he argues, is also disruptive because it "occasions revelations that question the authority of dominant cultural values and institutions" (1). In fact, translation often "provokes their efforts at damage control" (1). Scandal in the ordinary sense of that term is a predictable, if not inevitable, result of such challenges in the sense that the revelation of the violation of cultural norms or laws can and often does provoke public outrage. Not only, then, are translations bad objects in themselves, deserving to be stigmatized or scorned. Venuti also offers an extensive catalog of ways in which they threaten the cultural order; among these is their rejection of the neoromantic notion of literary expressions as linked uniquely and inviolably to their ostensible authors.

R. B. Palmer (✉)
Clemson University, Clemson, SC, USA
e-mail: ppalmer@clemson.edu

© The Author(s), under exclusive license to Springer Nature Switzerland AG 2023
T. Leitch (ed.), *The Scandal of Adaptation*, Palgrave Studies in Adaptation and Visual Culture,
https://doi.org/10.1007/978-3-031-14153-9_3

In so doing, translations call attention to the central, and perhaps most subversive, aspect of textuality: the fact that no text is ever closed or finalized, but remains open and thus subject to continuation, to gestures of furthering or remaking whose direction and result can be predicted only in a very rough sense, if at all. The once and future authors of any text might be, and often are, many, and no definitive list of them can ever be compiled. Completion and finality are forever deferred. This is true because, as I have observed elsewhere, "all texts are fragments in the sense that they await gestures of continuation that challenge the mirage of self-containment in which they are mistakenly thought to naturally endure" ("Continuation" 76).

As one of many forms of continuation, translation reduces to an unstable liminality the identity of the text, the sense that it belongs to and is expressive of one someone. The translation is, even as it is not, the original; its translator is, and is not, an author of that original; translators speak but do not own the words of the text they produce. I can affirm from my own experience as a literary translator that, as a form of substitution ungoverned by any rules, translation is haunted at every stage by an infinity of equally plausible choices and, since alternatives are excluded once choices are made, by the subsequent certainty that any re-languaged version will fail to re-speak the full meaning of the original (see the case history in Palmer, "Translation"). The notion of an "accurate" translation is nothing more than a convenient fiction, necessary in the sense that social actions and cultural knowledge depend on thinking that precise equivalencies between texts in different languages are an achievable goal.

The re-authoring essential to literary/film adaptation fosters similar complications. Adaptation is also a form of continuation focused on labile objects that are thereby provided with, among other qualities, an intentionality that is foreign to them. Moreover, adaptation too problematizes the sense in which a text might be understood as "owned" by its original author. Like translation, adaptation promotes the paradoxical notion of subsequent-order creation, in which the source is reconfigured for some purpose that its original creator likely would never have imagined, much less approved. Yet this re-versioning never forecloses the possibility of even greater alterations, of the emergence of further redactors with different purposes in mind. In their engineering of similar forms of re(dis)placement, adaptations and translations dispose of much the same destabilizing, recreative power, which is, of course, their raison d'être. It is hardly surprising that the public outrage of scandal in some form always looms as a possibility when texts are cut loose from their expressive moorings in order to serve some other purpose. This can in fact be deliberately to foster provocation, even scandal, as we shall see. It follows that the key to understanding the cultural value of any particular adaptation is the discovery and evaluation, insofar as this is possible, of the purpose it was meant to serve. Expressive theories of literary creation can dispense with intentionality, conceived by some as a fallacy. Perhaps, as Archibald MacLeish famously maintained, a poem can simply "be" rather than "mean." However, such an understanding of a film adaptation—a form of secondary creation dependent on deliberate co-optation and the formulation of a complex plan involving many others—is simply not tenable.

The subject of this chapter is the production history of Fritz Lang's *Scarlet Street* (1945), produced by Lang, with Walter Wanger functioning as executive producer, from a script by Dudley Nichols based on Georges de la Fouchardière's novel *La Chienne*; the film was distributed by Universal Pictures, with Joan Bennett, Dan Duryea, and Edward G. Robinson in the featured roles. This project demonstrates how through adaptation a fictional work can in fact be deliberately turned toward the provocation of public outrage even while conforming closely enough to merit approval according to operative censorship standards. In this case, these were set officially by the industry through the Production Code Administration (PCA), which had been instituted to enforce the regulations of the Production Code (PC), but also, and unofficially, by the Legion of Decency, a lay organization, under the purview of the Council of Bishops, that was formed in order to regulate the filmgoing habits of the nation's millions of Catholics (see Leff/Simmons; Black). By 1945, wielding the power of potential boycotting, the Legion possessed significant influence over Hollywood production, reflecting the view of the cinema as a moral danger that had been posited by Pope Pius XI in his bull *Vigilanti Cura* (1936), an admonition that was taken very seriously by the American church.

In the project that became *Scarlet Street*, Lang, Wanger, and Nichols managed to confect a multivalent text that would be acceptable to both the PCA and the Legion and yet also provocative in bending, arguably even breaking, the moral strictures of the PC in order to appeal to and, to a limited degree, satisfy a public taste for the salacious. Interestingly, the Legion's head, Monsignor McClafferty, responding to pressure from Universal, opined that the film offered a "moral lesson," justifying its rating as suited for adults and only "objectionable in part" (qtd. in Bernstein

160). The exhibition marketplace did not punish but rewarded this borderline malfeasance. To be sure, the exhibition of *Scarlet Street* did become a scandal, prompting its official condemnation followed by its banning by state and local officials in three states, threatening the film's earnings and prompting a promise from the PCA to oversee future submissions more carefully (Bernstein 160). The film's immediate legal problems in all three markets were not resolved for more than a year, and the resulting brouhaha kept the story alive for weeks, generating considerable national notoriety. The controversy did the filmmakers a favor by providing *Scarlet Street* with an enormous amount of free publicity; it became the studio's most successful release that year, earning almost $3 million on a production budget of a little more than $1 million.

The scandalous adaptation of de la Fouchardière's novel paid handsomely even as it persuaded the filmmakers involved to pursue similar projects, furthering the reach of what would become known as the film noir, the production series that would become an enduringly significant if in important respects contrarian element of the American cinema (see Bernstein for a perceptive and full account of the controversy and its aftermath; on the early history of noir, see Esquenazi; Lesuisse). Billy Wilder's *Double Indemnity* (1944), as Richard Schickel suggests, was the first Hollywood film to showcase appropriately the raw, socially disruptive energies of the period's crime fiction written in a popular, naturalistic style, even if the most disturbing aspects of the story were soft-pedaled in the film's final release version, including a new conclusion that can only be termed sentimental (53–69). The following year, *Scarlet Street* showed how far this representational revolution could be pushed, setting the tone for an antiestablishmentarian vein of taste that endures in American filmmaking and in many other national traditions to this day.

This film's case history, in other words, not only illustrates both a more general property of screen adaptation and the enduring appeal of the salacious to US filmgoers, as later developments in the industry would confirm (see Lewis). More important, perhaps, it brings to light details otherwise difficult to trace of the institutional developments within Hollywood that led to the emergence and flourishing of the film noir. *La Chienne*, published in 1930, with a film version by Jean Renoir released in France the next year, more likely attracted interest in 1944 because a significant shift was already occurring in the American film industry, one to which Lang and Nunnally Johnson (who produced and wrote the screenplay) had contributed with the very similar *The Woman in the Window* just the year before. *Window* was a semi-indie production by International Pictures, which RKO distributed. Interestingly, International would soon merge after the war with Universal, which would handle the release of what eventually became, with a significant shift in titling, *Scarlet Street*, in which the three featured players of *Window* would star. Screenwriter Dudley Nichols had worked with Lang on *Man Hunt* (1941), a wartime thriller that was a considerable box office success, with Joan Bennett's turn as a supporting player drawing considerable praise from the critics and those in the industry. In a letter to the director/producer, Nichols showered praise on *Window* and expressed a desire to work with Lang again on yet another Joan Bennett picture.

On the heels of his success with *Window*, this was the moment, as Wanger must have recognized, to resurrect this long-ignored French property from the studio files. He was, as Matthew Bernstein notes, a producer who "always excelled at finding properties if directors did not bring them to him" (Bernstein, private communication). But even if Wanger initiated discussions of adapting *La Chienne*, the decision to go ahead would not have been made without Lang's strong endorsement. Both men were aware that the two stories shared much in common, as the production plans demonstrated. As Bernstein suggests, "*Woman* was definitely the inspiration for making *Scarlet Street*. They hired Milton Krasner, who shot *Woman*, for *Scarlet Street*. Dudley Nichols's involvement stemmed from his admiring letter to Lang about *Woman*. He commented, 'it's been too long since *Man Hunt*.' He wanted to collaborate with Lang again and they brought him in as Ludwig Bemelmans didn't work out. Also, Wanger acknowledged that Joan's best films of all time had been made with Lang (*Man Hunt*, *Woman*), so let's continue this" (private communication).

Wanger and Lang were correct in predicting that the PCA would in 1945 not approve for screen adaptation a property that did not readily conform to the strictures of the PCA, established with tough-minded Joseph Breen in charge not long after Ernst Lubitsch obtained the rights to the novel for the studio (McGilligan 317). In the 1930s, Lubitsch likely thought that the artful mixture of sex and violence in *La Chienne* would make for a profitable project in a cinema marketplace that had seen *The Story of Temple Drake*, an adaptation directed by Stephen Roberts, of William Faulkner's salacious and fabulously profitable novel *Sanctuary*, become one of the highest grossing films of 1933. That film's exhibition had turned into a quite troublesome public scandal for the industry because it spawned widespread protests over its depictions of rape and other forms of sexual misconduct, forcing Hollywood to institute the PCA in order to enforce compliance with the Code (see Doherty). Lubitsch, it seems likely, hoped to repeat *Temple*'s success with a film version of *La Chienne*, but several attempts to get preliminary approval from the PCA failed (*Scarlet Street* case file). However, this sudden change in the operation of industry censorship meant that *La Chienne*'s failure to deliver its immoral and criminally minded characters to official justice, as well as its dwelling on adulterous sexual relationships and the discontents of marriage, would likely have barred a screen version at the time from receiving a certificate. And so the property sat for over a decade on a metaphorical shelf from which it might never have been plucked.

By 1945, the industry, reflecting developments in the culture that had already shown up in the popular fiction market, was moving toward the making and exhibition of films that took as their collective subject the dark underside of contemporary America, thus undermining and in some cases reversing the long-standing Hollywood practice of providing what were, if often in complex senses, positive screen versions of the national experience. Hollywood was not giving up on forms of cinematic entertainment that were lighter in tone and more supportive of conventional values, but these darker films provided a strong contrast to them, their popularity dependent on an increasing taste for such representations, suitable material for which was found in the fiction of Dashiell Hammett, Raymond Chandler, Vera Caspary, and James M. Cain (see Rabinowitz).

Although this emerging series of films was dependent on Anglophone crime fiction, there was no reason, as Wanger and Lang must have realized, that this kind of material could not be found elsewhere, especially (in a huge cost savings measure) by bringing to the screen an older property, already purchased but as yet unproduced, that experienced screenwriter Dudley Nichols could easily turn into a bitterly pessimistic portrayal of human weakness and criminal depravity. *Scarlet Street* charts a landscape roiled by unexpectedly treacherous and often violent encounters between two feckless members of the underclass and a dissatisfied, henpecked older man whom they easily exploit. With no little humor and grim irony, the film anatomizes the frustrated desires of this trio of misfits for prosperity and sexual indulgence.

As a *tranche de vie*, the film does not lack a political critique of sorts. *Scarlet Street*'s first sequence implies something of a Nietzschean explanation for what follows: a patronizing executive, J.J. Hogarth (Russell

Hicks), confident of his wealth and position, bestows at a company dinner a gold watch and an expensive cigar on a faithful employee, accountant Chris Cross (Edward G. Robinson), for his decades of service. Abandoning the honoree and his fellows to further indulgence in free alcohol, Hogarth then departs the scene in a flashy limousine, accompanied by an attentive and beautiful young woman who is clearly not his wife. Blinded by the glamor of his own accomplishments, he seems unaware of the *ressentiment* that such unself-conscious display of privilege might have aroused in those not similarly blessed.

In the afterglow of this celebratory dinner, Chris mentions to one of his fellows the wish that, like Hogarth, he too could bask in the affection of a lovely young girl. He also dreams that he might be recognized for his artistic talent. For years, he has been painting, pursuing this hobby on the margins of a dull marriage to a shrew who makes him set up his easel in the bathroom. Making his way home that night, Chris has a chance encounter that sets him on a path to make both these wishes come true. Spotting a woman in distress, he intervenes, wielding his umbrella like a sword, and rescues Kitty (Joan Bennett) from a man who seems bent on causing her harm, knocking him out. It is made clear to the viewer, but not to Chris, that Kitty's attacker, Johnny (Dan Duryea) is actually her pimp; he recovers and escapes before Chris can fetch a policeman. This sudden turn of fortune promises at first to grant him the affection of this beautiful young woman, with whom he ardently pursues a connection she encourages, thinking he is a well-off artist (a misimpression he does not correct). She describes herself as an actress even though it should be plain enough what profession she follows. The two begin a tentative relationship, and Kitty persuades Chris to set her up in an artist's garret, where he can visit to paint. Working furiously, he perfects a kind of late-Impressionist style, prioritizing, as he says, an inner sense of how people and objects should be rendered. Interestingly, this refusal to see things as they are has everything to do with the tragedy that follows (Fig. 1).

Meanwhile, Johnny and Kitty develop a scheme to rob Chris blind, exploiting the very talent that his new situation in the garret helps him develop: without Chris knowing, Johnny takes the canvases he turns out at a prodigious rate to sell them at a prestigious gallery, with Kitty providing signatures and posing as the artist. This betrayal of Chris seems to be counterbalanced by a stroke of apparent good luck. His wife's first husband, presumed dead, suddenly appears and tries to blackmail Chris, not realizing that he would be happy to be rid of the woman. In a manner that

Fig. 1 Chris (Edward G. Robinson) in his role as unrewarded love slave to Kitty (Joan Bennett) in *Scarlet Street*

the conniving Johnny might admire, Chris schemes to effect the couple's reunion, making him a bachelor once again. Because he now expects Kitty to marry him, disaster for all concerned is soon in the offing once the love-smitten man realizes that Johnny is more than Kitty's "friend."

In this stealth adaptation—or perhaps better, appropriation, since Lang's film marginalizes any connection to its ostensible source—the slipperiness of expressive ownership (in this fictional case, of paintings as objects of sale) becomes a major theme, as easily faked affirmations and illicit seizure become central elements in the plot, driving an ultimately murderous love triangle. This unauthorized co-optation and re-purposing of another's creative work in order to "earn" huge sums asks to be read as a *mise-en-abyme* of sorts for the film itself, which treats this theme with more nuance and complexity than either the original novel or Renoir's version. Lang's film, in fact, seems especially conscious of the disruption threatened by this second-order "creation," which would be one way to describe this fraud. It is perhaps not too great a stretch to see the film as illustrating cinema's inherent disposition toward the incorporative predation of other forms of culture so that they might be monetized. Such a facility to re-present what might be found elsewhere is of course the most important capacity of the medium that Lang and Wanger would be putting to their own quite scandalous advantage.

The popular success in France of both novel and film explains why a translation, under the title *Poor Sap*, was published in the United States, where it attained only a limited popularity, its English title making clear the novelist's sardonic, Zolaesque attitude toward these stereotypes from the lower orders. *La Chienne* presents the immorality and self-destructiveness of its characters with wry, *weltschmerzig* detachment. In the end, the ironically named LeGrand, despite the degradation to which he has been subjected, has attained a self-satisfied peace of mind even as he is reduced to penury and homelessness. Renoir's faithful adaptation of this vision of human resilience in the face of moral weakness and bad luck was exhibited in France without attracting the condemnation or either the Catholic church or local censors.

In contrast, the retitled US screen version, now staged in a fictionalized version of New York's Bohemian Greenwich Village, reframes the tale as a small-scale apocalypse in which all involved are destroyed by their vanity, indifference, and criminality in ways that absolutely defy the capacity of social institutions to come to know, much less regulate or judge, them. Absent from Lang's film is any vestige of the genial tolerance for human fallibility evident in both the original novel and the Renoir version, which lightheartedly opens with a Punch and Judy puppet show in a humorous anti-realist gesture. *Scarlet Street*'s deadly serious portrayal of wrongdoers as evading official justice for their crimes ran contrary to the spirit and letter of the PC, but the film seems to have received a grudging pass from the censors and thus a certificate because its finale emphasizes a poetic justice administered through the vagaries of circumstance and the workings of individual conscience. This was a judgment with which the Legion also concurred, recognizing that the film could not reasonably be understood as straightforward exploitation even though it was suitable fare only for adults. One might even say that the US filmmakers encourage a moral reading by emphasizing a kind of Dantean *contrapasso*, in which sinfulness entails its own retribution, rendering judges and juries superfluous.

Nothing could be further from the half-seriousness of the original fiction. The novel's "poor sap," desperate for deliverance from domestic dullness and eager for some sexual diversion, is in his American reversioning ennobled by a consciousness of responsibility that leads him to embrace a never-ending self-flagellation. Now supplied with a name that suggests his victimization, Chris Cross becomes something of a Raskolnikov denied the release of death and condemned to wander instead the landscape of his degradation and malfeasance. Viewers of *Scarlet Street* at the time might have been surprised to learn that the novel and Renoir's film both feature something of a happy ending in which the murderer, LeGrand (Michel Simon), embraces life as a self-satisfied vagrant, living off handouts. First he engineers an exit from a marriage he finds suffocating, and then in a rage ends an exploitative love affair, which had pressured him into embezzling from his firm, by murdering his conniving paramour, Lulu (Janie Marèse). For these crimes he feels no guilt. LeGrand is not troubled in the least by the role he plays in sending the woman's pimp, DéDé (Georges Flamant), to the guillotine in his stead.

Lang's version is instead imbued with what his biographer Patrick McGilligan appropriately calls a "somber fatalism" even as all involved did their best to play up the more salacious aspects of the story as visualized, with the several scenes between Johnny and a scantily attired Kitty played for as much flirtatiousness and flesh as the PCA would permit (321). This kind of radical re-orientation is typical of the appropriation, which, as Julie Sanders writes, offers "a more decisive journey away from the informing source into a wholly new cultural product and domain" (28).

Why was that journey undertaken, and what were its shaping pressures? In *Scarlet Street*, the intentions of the characters as well as the bewildering ways in which they connect, often in ignorance but always self-serving, never become fully visible to the authorities, who are present only as off-screen shadows. Much the same might be said about the intentions of the filmmakers, which, though easily read out from their actions, were certainly kept on the downlow. One of those intentions was turning out a film that could be profitably viewed as scandalous even as they and their attorneys vehemently denied the charge, insisting instead that *Scarlet Street* "reflects a serious dramatic theme and presents its thesis with a dignity and propriety commensurate with the importance of the subject matter" (City of Atlanta vs. Universal Pictures). This view of the film, which may seem cynical and self-serving, reflects long-standing justifications for the shocking representations of literary naturalism (as in the case of *Sanctuary/Temple Drake*). *Scarlet Street* engages with those broad issues of justice and accountability that seem to weigh so heavily on Cross. Lang would explore these further in his later noir films, particular *Beyond a Reasonable Doubt* (1956) (see Gunning). In a larger sense, of course, his wrongdoing does not go unpunished, nor does that of either Kitty or

Johnny. One could say, as the studio's lawyers did, that *Scarlet Street* takes on a "serious dramatic theme" that it develops with "dignity and propriety." However, *Scarlet Street* could be, and was, read otherwise. Christina Smith, Atlanta's official censor, was unimpressed by its evident literary pretensions. She spoke for conservative forces in American culture when she dismissed what Lang and Wanger were peddling to baser instincts with a story that was "licentious, profane, obscure, and contrary to the good order of the community" (qtd. in Bernstein 157). And it is certainly true that the film depicts unconventional sexual pairings whose details are never publicly condemned. It is easy enough, in fact, to point to evidence that the film was intended to be exploitative and, because it was not adapted from a well-known literary source, had to advertise itself as such. The title chosen by Wanger had no connection to either version of the novel. "Scarlet Street" was easily decoded as "red light district," a fictional setting, trading on a cultural stereotype, whose essential qualities were indicated clearly by the film's advertising materials. Prospective viewers were to be enticed by the notion that the film would somehow manage to deal with prostitution, an officially banned subject, but one allowed sometimes to creep into Hollywood films, and they were not disappointed. Lang and company created a studio-bound version of New York's lower Manhattan, famed for its saloons and night life. In such environs, the sight of a man like Johnny giving the provocatively dressed woman a beating does not seem out of place. After all, as it is soon revealed, she only earned fifteen dollars that night—a detail that the film delivers without so much as a wink.

There were no alternative explanations for "their" situation as a couple, as the filmmakers knew very well. Chris is soon cast in the role of the couple's john. Kitty's refusal to marry him quickly leads to his discovery that Johnny and Kitty are intimately connected, precipitating the murderous rage in which he fatally stabs her. Johnny's unfortunate arrival on the scene just after Chris slinks away leads to his arrest. Because the actual killer remains unsuspected and silent, Johnny is speedily convicted and dispatched in a gruesomely evoked electrocution. Even though there is some moral fairness in the death Johnny endures, an aura of a miscarriage of justice lingers as the whole truth of what happened never comes to light.

Lang's film has been much discussed as not only a literary adaptation of the de la Fouchardière novel but also as a remake of the Renoir original. However, these two ways of understanding *Scarlet Street*'s trans-textuality prove irrelevant in explaining why the property was adapted in this way at this particular moment and in the way it was brought to the screen. Instead, this film reflects a contrasting form of "continuation," one that does not easily fit into the usual critical categories because it is not based on an exchange or replication of textual features as such, but on a symbiotic relationship forged between two distinct productions that results in deep and unusual connections between the two texts. Here, in other words, the process of appropriation reflects the cinema's nature as a performance art making use of resources that are for the text (and most importantly for its performers) but not of it. For example, the repeat casting of the three major performers, properly speaking, is a resource, not a feature.

In their mounting of *La Chienne*, Lang and his colleagues appropriated the story materials of *La Chienne* to devise a profitable reshaping of the director's previous project, *The Woman in the Window*. In *Scarlet Street*, the three principals of *Window* play much the same roles in an eerily similar narrative that also borrows several of the earlier film's incidental elements: the lower Manhattan location of the apartment where the killing takes place and, most startlingly, framed portraits of Joan Bennett's character on exhibit in two Fifth Avenue galleries, the object of the gaze, in each case, of Edward G. Robinson's characters. The two films are linked as productions, not as narratives. In no sense, however, was *Scarlet Street* marketed or even publicly acknowledged by those involved as a repetition of sorts of *Window*, even though advertising did mention that film as one of the stars' previous appearances. So effective was the attempt on the part of all concerned to obscure the connection between the two films that this crucial fact is overlooked in most critical discussions not only of Lang but also of film noir (see Palmer, "Fritz Lang").

Repetition, of course, does not precisely describe the links between these two films; these are not elements as such of either one, as would be the case in sequels, where the trans-textual link would position each film to be understood through the terms "initial" and "subsequent" in terms of both narrative and production time. This pairing evidences no "seriality." These resemblances are, instead, better understood as evidence that the object of those involved in the *Scarlet Street* project was to turn out a steamier, more sensational version of *Window*, reusing what had proved successful in that earlier project. From that point of view, *Scarlet Street* improves on its "source." With its focus on the middle-aged Wanley, *Window* had largely wasted the considerable glamour and what would have been marketed at the time as sex appeal of Joan Bennett. The second version of the casting plan takes more titillating advantage of Joan Bennett's glamor and of her evident chemistry with Dan Duryea, discovered during their brief—and very late—scenes in *Window*. *Scarlet Street* makes them lovers rather than antagonists, providing a number of scenes where the two, living in the apartment Chris rents, enjoy an intimacy away from prying eyes. Such scenes have a stronger erotic charge than any in *Window*, and they provide the film with the opportunity to showcase a lithe and scantily dressed Bennett prancing around their home.

More important, in refusing the all-too obvious moralism of *Window*'s finale, *Scarlet* pushes harder against institutional restraints, reflecting how the circumstances of production and release had altered considerably in the course of 1944–45, which was an annus mirabilis of sorts for the film noir series. The industry that year witnessed the profitable release not only of *Window* but of three similar films, all adapted from risqué literary properties: *Murder, My Sweet*, adapted by Edward Dmytryk from Raymond Chandler's *Farewell, My Lovely*; *Laura*, adapted by Otto Preminger from Vera Caspary's novel; and, most important, Billy Wilder's *Double Indemnity*, adapted from James M. Cain's novella. This production trend was a signal that, as Bernstein observes, Hollywood was growing "more adept at creating naturalistic, gritty, noiresque dramas" that would pass muster for the most part with the emerging values of communities around the country, which in many cases were still then at that time supervised by local censors (176). This adeptness had much to do with the particular circumstances that brought Cain's *Double Indemnity*, previously banned, to the screen. Wanger and Lang had enough experience to discern the meaning of an ongoing production trend behind these rule-bending adaptations of novels that offered compelling, layered narratives of the intersection between sexual desire and criminal intent (McGilligan 317). They evidently thought that *La Chienne* would make a perfect follow-up project to the success that Lang, working with Dudley Nichols, had just recently achieved with *Window*. It would also provide another choice role for Joan Bennett, who had married Wanger in 1940.

This film also chronicles the fall into adultery, murder, and criminality of a middle-aged man experiencing a midlife crisis. Professor Wanley (Edward G. Robinson), left on his own while his wife and son go on vacation, wanders New York City streets after a dinner with friends and is there accosted by a beautiful young woman of dubious morals, Alice (Joan Bennett), as Wanley stares at a portrait of her in a gallery window. Enchanted by this somewhat mystical experience, he accepts her tempting invitation for a late-night drink, and perhaps more, in her upscale nearby apartment. Their encounter has just turned personal and romantic when it is suddenly interrupted by the violent intrusion of an enraged man, who it turns out is entrepreneur Claude Mazard (Arthur Loft), who has been supporting Alice in this fine style. Mad with jealousy, Mazard attempts to throttle Wanley, who is forced to kill him, stabbing him with a pair of scissors Alice puts in his hand.

Wanley obviously acts in self-defense, but reporting the incident to the police, he and Alice fear, would bring ruinous scandal on them both, so they attempt to get rid of the body, dumping it miles away, where it is quickly found. Wanley's bad luck continues when he becomes accidentally involved in the investigation of the crime, which is being conducted by a good friend. As the investigation continues, he seems unable to resist implicating himself in the crime. Meanwhile, Alice is threatened by yet another visitor when a private detective, Heidt (Dan Duryea), barges his way into the apartment. Heidt, hired as Mazard's bodyguard, had been following him, and now that Mazard has disappeared, he suspects that Alice and Wanley killed him. Alice resists the detective's attempts at blackmail, while, partly because of his own continued bungling, the professor becomes the prime suspect. He is just about to be arrested for the crime when Heidt is misidentified as the culprit and shot dead by police.

Ironically, this exculpation comes too late for the hapless academic, who is informed of the fact only after having taken poison in an attempt to avoid a public shaming. However, *Window* backs away from this grim finale when all that has occurred is revealed as what the professor dreamed after falling asleep at his club. Awakening with a start, he hastens into the street, passing by an uncannily familiar gallery of figures in the dream, which he realizes are all versions of people he met during an evening spent at the club. At that same window, looking at the portrait, he is accosted by a beautiful streetwalker, from whom his recoils in terror, lesson obviously learned. *Window* bakes a cake that in the end it is too hesitant to eat; a similar judgment could be passed on the other noirs from 1944, all of which feature endings more restorative of conventional values. In their re-versioning of *Window* that next year, however, Lang and Wanger refused to retreat from their bleak vision of contemporary American life.

That a significant shift in Hollywood production was happening passed more or less noticed in the United States with few exceptions (see, e.g., Kracauer). However, in France, where American films were taken seriously, this shift occasioned much discussion among the intelligentsia, especially on the left. Some, like Pierre Kast, saw nothing threatening in the fact that many recent Hollywood films were making a "deliberate use of despair, failure, and fear," moving away from the pseudo-optimism of the happy ending (45). Others, including Georges Sadoul, deplored what they saw as a slide into a decadence and scandal that threatened the future of the cinema. Henri-François Rey felt compelled to ask: "What is the meaning of these shocking representations of American life?" Only one conclusion was possible: Hollywood had abjured its customary role as a booster of the national culture and was now conjuring up a "disturbed America in chaos" (Rey 28, 29).

As Jean-Pierre Chartier observed at the time, these American releases bore a resemblance to the 1930s films of Marcel Carné, Jean Renoir, and others, but while in these French noirs "love offers the mirage of a better world," the American films provide no such possibility of redeeming emotion and hope for social change (27). A bitter, ironic view of the human condition prevails in *Scarlet Street*, which is in effect an anti-romance that trades more in sexual obsession and exploitation than in any meaningful human connection. The film lacks any vision, however self-deluding, of a world beyond evil, weakness, and social decline comparable to what French dark films such as Carné's *Le Jour se lève* (1939) poignantly offer in their tragic finales, which fully deserve to be called, as they customarily are, poetic. There is no sense, as there is in both the de la Fouchardière novel or the Renoir film, that life goes on. It says much about American culture at the time, however, that one of the nation's most influential film critics, Bosley Crowther, pronounced it nothing more than "a painfully moral picture and, in the light of modern candor, rather tame" ("*Scarlet Street*"). But then Crowther seems to have been strangely unreceptive to the startling thematic innovations of *Double Indemnity*, which he rates as merely "a variably intriguing crime game" ("*Double Indemnity*").

Such reactions to the advent of film noir in America bespeak a remarkable form of cultural blindness, one that contrasts starkly with the shock French cinephiles felt when Hollywood's wartime films, not available during the war, were suddenly exhibited en masse in 1946 following the conclusion of a trade agreement between the two countries that weakened restrictive quotas. *Scarlet Street* and the American noirs more generally focus instead on the distressing failure of self-fashioning, of violent death endured or barely escaped, of the flimsy contingency of relationships, communal values, and ostensible identities, and of the grim realization that evil and perfidy entail their own punishment, requiring little from the seemingly weak official institutions of the law by way of regulation, restoration, or retribution. When Henri-François Rey suggested that these films reflect a "disturbed America in chaos," he meant not only that these films offered in microcosm images of social breakdown, but also that the PCA was suddenly, if somewhat mysteriously, receptive to approving the release of such projects.

It was a remarkable sign of a significant change in Hollywood when in 1944 Breen ended his long-standing reluctance to approve screen versions of James M. Cain's fiction. Cain had achieved considerable success with *The Postman Always Rings Twice* (1934), but RKO, interested in purchasing the screen rights, was warned that same year by the PCA that the property was "unsuitable." Although Warners was also discouraged from proceeding at the time, MGM took a gamble and purchased the rights but postponed the project after it became obvious that the PCA was serious about enforcing the PC. And so the property sat on the shelf unproduced, suffering much the same fate as *La Chienne*. In 1944, Cain, still hoping for a big sale, sent around to studio production departments copies of *Double Indemnity*, a lurid tale of adultery and murder originally serialized in *Liberty* magazine in 1936, now reprinted with two of Cain's other novellas in *Three of a Kind* (1943). The negotiations between Paramount Pictures and the Production Code Administration ended with a development that stunned many in the industry. Without any explanation for this change in course, the PCA reversed its earlier decision that the studio's projected film version, though incorporating considerable changes from the novella, would bring to the screen intact much of Cain's bitter view of depravity, greed, and ruthlessness—the very ingredients, it seems likely, that then led to the film's considerable success.

Back-channel negotiations with studio executives had undoubtedly influenced Breen's decision, as many in the industry must have been aware. In any case, that *Double Indemnity* was approved with relatively few changes demanded in the treatment Paramount originally submitted, making it clear that the institutional way was once again clear to submit for approval properties that had previously been refused a green light. The most notable of these apart from *La Chienne* was Cain's own *The Postman Always Rings Twice*, finally released in 1946, more than a decade after the initial the acquisition of the rights, and reversing the order in which the two narratives had originally been composed. In its novella form, *Double Indemnity* had been clearly modeled on *Postman*, much of whose material (including a plot involving a wife and lover murdering an inconvenient husband for the insurance money) it simply recycled. The similarities between the two narratives, needless to say, proved useful in a Hollywood where reuse and imitation were of paramount importance in shaping the market for each new release.

Similarly, strictly for commercial motives, including the effective reuse of already purchased or contracted resources, Lang and Wanger had every reason to make another film about the misadventures of a would-be middle-aged and decidedly unhandsome Lothario, who this time would be permitted to do more than dream of sexual hijinks and the troubles that such indulgence might bring down upon him (qtd. in Lally 126). *Scarlet Street* met with even more fervent moral disapprobation than Wilder's film, proving to be more scandalous after being banned, if only temporarily, from exhibition in three US film markets. This sporadic official disapproval, however, did not harm but enhanced its popularity with the filmgoing public. Its scandalousness was a carefully designed effect achieved through the co-optation and revisioning of its literary source. What it reveals about the poisoning of human relationships is not softened as it is in *Double Indemnity*, whose finale offers a poignant image of the restored brotherhood that the confession of wrongdoing and the persistence of empathy can effect.

Few Hollywood films end as despairingly as *Scarlet Street*. Chris is set free only to be destroyed by his sense of guilt, and he is reduced to anonymous and beggarly wandering through the upscale precincts of a New York from which he is even more estranged than when he was simply a "poor sap" and still lacking in street smarts. His ignorance, in fact, strangely redounds to his moral credit. Discovering that Kitty proved able to sell his work as her own to a famous dealer, he feels no sense of violation, but rejoices to see his talent recognized. Kitty's "crime" in co-opting his paintings is never exposed, because after her death, Chris successfully conceals his involvement in the whole affair. In the film's last scene, he shuffles by a gallery window, dressed in rags, and there spies the portrait he had painted of Kitty on display. Her face catches his eye, which fixes with grim recognition on her signature. This glimpse afforded him by circumstance is a reminder that his two wishes have in a sense come true, but only in a way that has denied him their possession. Pretending to be rich and accomplished, he managed to persuade a beautiful young woman to be his companion, and his affection seems undimmed even though she refused his clumsy attempts at lovemaking while robbing him of his money and respectability. He has achieved success as an artist; at least, what he has painted has become widely admired. His paintings have established a reputation that a treacherous pretender has not lived to enjoy. But their creator cannot reclaim this as his own even though "his" paintings survive. Any connection to what he has created is now as irrecoverable as the position in society he forfeited. His vision, once intensely personal, has now been assigned, through a fraud that cannot be corrected, to someone else. Unloved, unconfessed, unknown, he is now truly nothing. Or, put another way, Chris's identity as established by his self-expression is forever put under erasure. In discussing the several films noirs, like this one, in which male characters deploy "fetishized images of women to bolster their own identities or fashion new ones," Mark Osteen observes that "in blurring the lines between originality and forgery, subjectivity and objectivity, real and representation, these films [...] advance the idea that identity is not an entity but a never-ending process [...] implying that self-reinvention may occur not as a result of individual choice but as an inevitable by-product of the gap between humans and our representations" (106) (Fig. 2).

Chris's final view of the woman he loves is not of her, but of an image of what he felt, and wished, her to be. He looks now at what he saw when first gazing with an artist's eye at Kitty. The portrait is of a creature of his own fashioning. Most importantly, it is a record of the idealizing feelings that motivated and shaped the creative act. As Pierre Duvillars, writing in 1951, commented on the closed circuit of male desire so central to these innovative films:

> In these films, the crime seems a fatal destiny born of a look, which issues from between two open lips, and the thriller, born, not from the consequences of a crime that we know is inevitable from the film's first images, but from obsession, and from the fatal destiny of the crime that cannot help but be committed. From this follows the man's lack of responsibility. [...] The sense of tragedy is lost, and thus the sense of humanity as well. (11)

Lang's masterpiece, much-imitated but never equaled, is the first of the many Hollywood noirs to configure the full dimensions of the erotic as a form of self-generating male *fatalité*.

Fig. 2 The unintended memorial to the woman (Joan Bennett) whom Chris (Edward G. Robinson) loved and killed in *Scarlet Street*

REFERENCES

Bernstein, Matthew. "A Tale of Three Cities: The Banning of *Scarlet Street*." *Controlling Hollywood: Censorship and Regulation in the Studio Era*, edited by Matthew Bernstein, Rutgers University Press, 1999, pp. 157–85.

Black, Gregory D. *Hollywood Censored: Morality Codes, Catholics, and the Movies*, Cambridge University Press, 1996.

Chartier, Jean-Pierre. "Les Américains font aussi des films noirs." *Revue du cinema*, vol. 2, Nov. 1946, pp. 67–70. English translation in Palmer, *Perspectives*, pp. 25–27.

"City of Atlanta vs. Universal Pictures," https://casetext.com/case/city-of-atlanta-v-universal-film-exchanges. Accessed 27 June 2022.

Crowther, Bosley. Review of *Double Indemnity*. *New York Times*, 7 Sept. 1944. https://www.nytimes.com/1944/09/07/archives/the-screen-double-indemnity-a-tough-melodrama-with-stanwyck-and.html. Accessed 27 June 2022.

Crowther, Bosley. Review of *Scarlet Street*. *New York Times*, 15 Feb. 1946, https://www.nytimes.com/1946/02/15/archives/the-screen-dan-duryea-edward-robinson-joan-bennett-at-criterion-in.html. Accessed 27 June 2022.

Doherty, Thomas. *Pre-Code Hollywood: Sex, Immorality, and Insurrection in American Cinema: 1930–34.* 2nd ed., Columbia University Press, 1999.
Duvillars, Pierre. *L'Érotisme au cinema,* Éditions du xxme siècle, 1951, pp. 69–73. English translation in Palmer, *Perspectives,* pp. 10–12.
Esquenazi, Jean-Pierre. *Le Film noir,* CNRS, 2015.
Gunning, Tom. *The Films of Fritz Lang: Allegories of Vision and Modernity,* BFI, 2000.
Kast, Pierre. "Court traitié d'optimisme." *Positif,* vol. 6, 1953, pp. 3–9. English translation in Palmer, *Perspectives,* pp. 44–49.
Kracauer, Siegfried. "Hollywood's Terror Films: Do They Reflect a State of Mind?" *Commentary,* Aug. 1946, pp. 132–36.
De la Fouchardière, Georges. *Poor Sap.* Translated by Robert Forest Wilson, Knopf, 1930.
Lally, Kevin. *Wilder Times: The Life of Billy Wilder,* Holt, 1996.
Leff, Leonard L., and Jerold L. Simmons. *The Dame in the Kimono: Hollywood, Censorship, and the Production Code,* University Press of Kentucky, 2001.
Lesuisse, Anne-Françoise. *Du Film noir au noir: traces figurales dans le cinéma classique hollywoodien,* De Boeck univérsité, 2002.
MacLeish, Archibald. "A Poem Should Not Mean, But Be." https://fourteenlines.blog/2019/04/25/a-poem-should-not-mean-but-be/. Accessed 27 June 2022.
Osteen, Mark. *Nightmare Alley: Film Noir and the American Dream,* Johns Hopkins University Press, 2013.
Palmer, R. Barton. *Perspectives on Film Noir,* G.K. Hall, 1995.
Palmer, R. Barton. "Translation and Failure: The Example of Guillaume de Machaut." *Anglistik,* vol. 21, no. 1, 2010, pp. 75–86.
Palmer, R. Barton. "Fritz Lang Remakes Jean Renoir for Hollywood: Film Noir in Three National Voices." *Transnational Film Remakes,* edited by Iain Robert Smith and Constantine Verevis, Edinburgh University Press, 2017a, pp. 36–53.
Palmer, R. Barton. "Continuation, Adaptation, and the Never-Finished Text." *Adaptation in Visual Culture: Images, Texts, and their Multiple Worlds,* edited by Julie Grossman and R. Barton Palmer. Palgrave Macmillan, 2017b, pp. 73–99.
Quigley, Martin. *Decency in Motion Pictures,* Macmillan, 1937.
Rabinowitz, Paula. *Black and White and Noir,* Columbia University Press, 2002.
Sadoul, Georges. "Mettre le accent sur le sujet," *La Nouvelle Critique,* vol. 5, 1949, pp. 92–100.
Scarlet Street case file (n.d.). Production Code Administrations Archive. Margaret Herrick Library.
Venuti, Lawrence. *The Scandals of Translation: Toward an Ethics of Difference,* Routledge, 1998.

Sweet Smell of Success: Noiradaptation "in This Crudest of All Possible Worlds"

Julie Grossman

This chapter explores the peculiarly noir elements of adaptation as a textual practice, using the classic New York film *Sweet Smell of Success* (Alexander Mackendrick, 1957) to establish the links between dirty towns and (adaptations as) dirty texts. Echoing the fatalism in film noir, adaptations inevitably taint their sources, and looking at the ways in which this process occurs can help us to see the contingency of all texts, as we question their stability and their purity. Even "nice" texts, like the "nice guys" and the "good girls" we see at the beginning of many noir films—think Betty Elms (Naomi Watts) in David Lynch's *Mulholland Drive* (2001)— break bad under the pressures of adaptation, change, desire, ambition, and institutionalized social forces. *Sweet Smell of Success* provides instances of "noiradaptation" in the story's diegesis, its production history, and its origins in scandal magazines like *Confidential* (1952–78), as well as the ambitions, successes, and failures of famed gossip columnist and media icon Walter Winchell. The power dynamics that characterize all these

J. Grossman (✉)
Le Moyne College, Syracuse, NY, USA
e-mail: grossmjj@lemoyne.edu

© The Author(s), under exclusive license to Springer Nature Switzerland AG 2023
T. Leitch (ed.), *The Scandal of Adaptation*, Palgrave Studies in Adaptation and Visual Culture,
https://doi.org/10.1007/978-3-031-14153-9_4

63

layers remind us of the inherent instabilities and proneness to scandal present generally in media and society, but also in adapting and adapted texts. Film noir, with its emphasis on human vulnerabilities and the omnipresence of criminality, as well as its thematic and narrative concerns of surveillance, exposure, and publicity, as Curtis Hanson displays in *L.A. Confidential* (1997), has always been a scandalous means of truth-telling whose creative use of language, stylized performances, and mise-en-scène force a confrontation with the potentials for dark turns in multiple forms of expression and change. Thinking about noir as a sensibility that informs textual adaptation opens a window onto analogous processes of transformation that productively unsettle sacrosanct notions of discrete individual human, social, national, and textual identities. Textuality is often a dynamic process with no clear teleology, and every adaptation stems from multiple causes and contexts and, as R. Barton Palmer has argued, a "never finalizing [...] source" (97).

Sweet Smell of Success presents a Darwinian social world in which press agent Sidney Falco (Tony Curtis) races around New York City desperate to impress J.J. Hunsecker (Burt Lancaster) so that the latter will feature Falco's clients in his censorious newspaper gossip column. Attempting at the same time to adapt to a vicious environment of competition, exploitation, and ego and submitting to utter desperation and loss of self, Sidney tells his secretary, "Watch me run a fifty-yard dash with my legs cut off." Sidney thinks Hunsecker is "[t]he golden ladder to the place where I want to get." The operative words in Sidney's articulation of an illusory American Dream are his last four, "I want to get." His willingness to harm others to achieve success highlights the film's moral insistence on the costs of putting ambition above community and kindness and tapping the basest desires of a citizenry—that is, exploiting the base.

Sweet Smell of Success charts the naturalistic slide of Sidney Falco (who has the less predatory name of Sidney Wallace in the novella) and J.J. Hunsecker (whom Lehman gives the less aloof name of Harvey Hunsecker). At the beginning of Ernest Lehman's original novella, Sidney is described as feeling as if he is on the precipice of success: "all I had been scratching and crawling for was finally drawing within reach" (9). With the possible exception of *A Face in the Crowd*'s "Lonesome" Rhodes, Hunsecker is the Trumpiest film character of the 1950s. His surname, with its honey and sucking references, evokes seductive media vampires who lay bare the weaknesses or failures of social institutions and practices, especially in the realms of family, journalism, politics, and entertainment.

Viewer fascination with the awfulness of the character links Winchell to Donald Trump, another bombastic and fickle egomaniac whose actions and words drew delight from some viewers, readers, and audiences, and horrified shock from others. Winchell and Trump exploited people's public and private lives for entertainment, and watching or listening to such stories can be likened to the bottlenecking human impulse to watch a car crash. Indeed, as *The Portland Oregonian* said about Winchell's radio show *The Lucky Strike Dance Hour* in the early 1930s, "You listen not because you admire [Winchell], but because you expect each night his egotism will overreach itself, plunging [him] up to his neck in trouble" (qtd. in Gabler 127). One of the perspectival shifts resulting from an examination of all of the sources and scripts that inform *Sweet Smell* is that Winchell inhabits the character of Sidney just as fully as Hunsecker. While Winchell emerges in Neal Gabler's biography as an obvious source for Hunsecker, the cold media honcho known for making and breaking the careers and lives of Americans, the real Broadway columnist and media kingpin similarly informs Falco, the young Hunsecker wannabe whose fall and failure is the focus of the story and film. Sidney's manic energy, ambition, and fear of failure capture Winchell's persona, which has been described as "go-getter," "driven," and "ambitious" (Gabler 50); he was "an inveterate table-hopper," his wife Rita said, and "he never sat through his meals without getting up a half dozen times" (qtd. in Gabler 56). In his own role as adaptor, Clifford Odets, who revised Lehman's original script for the film, reportedly advised Tony Curtis on his performance of Falco, emphasizing that Curtis should always be moving: "Don't ever let Sidney sit down comfortably. I want Sidney constantly moving, like an animal, never quite sure who's behind him or where he is" (Kashner). The following description of Winchell by Gabler matches Sidney's affect more precisely than Hunsecker's steely mien:

> A friend said that being with [Winchell] was like being with "human electricity." He smoked furiously, gabbed incessantly, scribbled quickly (usually with a stubby pencil on the back of envelopes or on a folded square of newsprint) and drummed the table with his fingers on the rare occasions when he wasn't talking. (Gabler 109)

The point raises an interesting question about adaptational reading strategies, how our sense of what in an adaptation comes from where shifts when we examine a variety of contexts and sources beyond the film's ostensible source, Ernest Lehman's novella. In this connection, Thomas Leitch's lobbying for the term "scripts" to identify the multifarious and often surprising sources that influence a text is particularly helpful:

> I prefer "scripts" to "sources" or "genres" or "hypotexts" because in the plural form, it already implies both a forward impetus lacking in "sources" and a hybridity that has to be smuggled into each of the other terms through inadequately theorized appeals to multiple sources or contexts. It is no accident that "scripts" is closely related to screenplays, or more precisely to screenplay drafts, because everyone knows that the screenplays that serve as more proximate sources for movies than their avowed novels or plays or stories commonly go through many drafts, none of which has absolute authority. (*History* 23)

Such an understanding of the "hybridity" of sources and contexts is especially useful in a case such as *Sweet Smell of Success*, whose textual, production, and reception histories are a palimpsest of mutually informing layers of authorship.

Early in his career, Ernest Lehman—later famous for his scripts for *Sabrina*, *North by Northwest*, *West Side Story*, *The Sound of Music*, and *Who's Afraid of Virginia Woolf?*—was himself a New York City publicist, working with Irving Hoffman, another agent feeding stories to Walter Winchell. Hoffman, who became an inspiration for Sidney Falco, was reportedly scandalized by Lehman's transparent portrayal of his dealings with Winchell and other press agents. Lehman's adaptation of his own experience—sublimating his guilt about having run in these vulgar crowds, "some form of expiation" (Kemp 140)—illustrates one of the ways adaptors can reframe the past, as Leitch explores in his chapter in the present volume. Lehman's expiative story and original script showed "what adaptation does with real-world problems, and indeed with texts and canons[:] not solve them but reconsider, reframe, reformulate, police, and otherwise manage them" (Leitch, "Adaptation and Censorship" 207). Gabler, who quotes Lehman repeatedly in his biography of Winchell, observes that "[m]ost of [the press agents] deeply resented the power Walter held over them. [...] But just beneath the surface of the image, one found an unsavory and largely forlorn group of men. [...] They lived with a sense of their own corruptibility" (Gabler 247–48). The "forlornness" Gabler adumbrates in his delineation of New York City's cadre of midcentury gossip reporters and publicists is represented in *Sweet Smell* by columnist

Otis Elwell (David White), who describes his own kind of somnambulist cynicism. Looking for brute stimulation, a night with Sidney's sometime girlfriend Rita (Barbara Nichols) in exchange for printing dirt on Steve Dallas, the jaded Elwell drones, "Like most of the human race, I'm bored. I'd go a mile for a chuckle."

Lehman's story seeded the film's obsession not only with world-weariness but also with dirt and dirtiness. The novella begins with Sidney's exchanges with his mother and brother Mike, both ashamed by Sidney's chaotic work in show business. His mother tells him that Sidney's dollars are contaminated by "dirt." Mike, who won't accept money from Sidney, writes a letter to his brother about his job "in a steam laundry" as he works his way through college. Lehman makes it clear to readers that Sidney's office walls are "dirty," and the novel opens with a description of a hot summer day—"one of those dirty, sweltering August afternoons" (9).

Adapting Winchell

A study of adaptational elements in *Sweet Smell of Success* includes three casts of characters—those surrounding the source and production of the film; its fictional men; and its touchpoints in historical and contemporary media/political landscapes, especially Walter Winchell. In 1998, the *New York Times* recalled that by the early 1950s, Americans had been treated to decades of media mogul Walter Winchell's invective: his newspaper column and radio show had him reaching into politics, entertainment, and sports. A McCarthyist media demagogue and gossip columnist, Winchell saw himself as America's savior (Weinraub). But Winchell's commentary could change with the prevailing winds. According to Lehman, who took aim at Winchell's hypocrisies, the columnist and his insincere peers "never believed in their own politics; but this was part of their product, to be patriots" (qtd. in Kemp 150). Winchell's fickleness reflected a personal need to be admired and a fear of losing the public's attention. He had had virtuous moments in calling out Nazis and Anti-Semites in the 1930s. According to Neal Gabler, "Walter took on Hitler in 1933, far earlier and with far more prescience than all but a few political pundits" (195). Penelope Pelizzon and Nancy West observe, however, that the cruelty present in *Sweet Smell of Success* owes more to its source in scandalous gossip magazines such as *Confidential* and *Hush-Hush* (181–84). The scandal sheets of the 1950s were malicious about star culture in a way that Winchell's columns weren't necessarily, the latter gossip-mongering built on what Gabler calls a "common frame of reference [...], a national 'backyard fence' over which all Americans could chat" (Gabler 81; qtd. in Pelizzon and West 182).

According to Gabler, a contemporary of the columnist noted "the amazing adaptability of the Winchellesque style" (297). Winchell held few sustained beliefs; his views were a product of how much interest he was paid in a given moment, predicting Trump's audience-driven populist rhetoric. Brandishing a wit not apparent in Trump's speeches or tweets, Winchell's columns displayed neologisms and clever wordplay: his "slanguage" included calling corrupt press people "presstitutes"; referencing celebrities in romantic trysts as "Adam and Eve-ing it"; referring to Broadway as "the main stem" and liquor as "giggle-water." Winchell's entertaining portmanteaus aptly metaphorize the journalist's willingness to play with existing realities. In this way, they are akin to the "composographs" Gabler describes as part of the tabloid revolution in the 1920s, where journalists could invent images (and thus the news) by layering photographs (heads onto others' bodies, for example). Such composite images presaged the ways Winchell's journalism would adapt the news industry (see Gabler 73). Pelizzon and West similarly discuss the "narrative recycling" that tabloid journals and magazines engaged with, borrowing Mary Desjardin's phrase "composite-fact stories" (184).

Winchell's improvisation—with language, in dispensing his judgments—is artfully evoked in *Sweet Smell*'s use of language appropriation. In the scene at the club, for example, Sidney hears columnist Bartha (Lawrence Dobkin) say that Hunsecker has the "the scruples of a guinea pig and the morals of a gangster." Seizing an opportunity minutes later, Sidney uses the same phrase about Hunsecker to manipulate columnist Otis Elwell; Sidney wants Elwell to plant a story that Susie's boyfriend, Steve Dallas (Martin Milner), is a pot-smoking Communist. Sidney's stealth appropriation of Bartha's words suggests the dangers of imitation when the players are so ruthlessly self-serving. From the virtues of adapting texts and selves to register changes in perspectives or cultural contexts, *Sweet Smell* shows a fallen world of adaptation where we see the exploitative potential of survivalist adaptors turning on a dime, desperately borrowing and stealing other people's words—and entertaining viewers and audiences in so doing. The dynamic suggests the responsibility of viewers and audiences to see past their own immediate pleasures to understand the manipulative processes of media and to read the symptoms of their dysfunction well.

Winchell's desperate and illicit practices reached an apogee when he joined forces with McCarthy during the HUAC years. Regarding *Sweet Smell*'s adaptation of the tabloid magazines, Pelizzon and West comment on the perfect storm of 1950s tabloids and McCarthyism: "Fomenting, extorting, and circulating rumor and innuendo all thrived in cold-war America because conventional 'morality,' despite the uncertainties gripping the country, was being asserted more vigorously than ever" (183). At the same time, *Sweet Smell* spoke to an abiding element of modern tabloid culture that the film's director, Alexander Mackendrick, saw as a hinge to the story: the complicity of readers and audiences in making gossip columns and the likes of Walter Winchell viable and often successful. Mackendrick wrote extensive notes on the script Lehman based on his own novella, making it clear that Hunsecker and Sidney are not the real villains of the film but symptoms of a damaging media culture. His prescient commentary helps explain why the exploitations on display in *Sweet Smell of Success* are uncannily adapted across time, Sidney and Hunsecker appearing merely as "the product of a very questionable feature of our civilization" (Lehman papers). If noir is a transhistorical tone, as Christopher Breu and Elizabeth A. Hatmaker argue, that is "characterized by negative affect" (3), its sensibility sheds a gloomy light on the persistently dangerous convergence of cultural power dynamics and individual susceptibilities to narcissism and megalomania. While the portrait of J.J. Hunsecker is stylized and melodramatic—in Kemp's words, "an expressionistic study in irresponsible power" (150)—Trump's towering self-absorption and malice compel us to rethink Hunsecker less as a symbolic distillation of historical figures than a realistic portrayal of the extreme dangers of corrupt media demagoguery.

Still, *Sweet Smell of Success* didn't do well when it was released. As Gary Giddins observes, "Audiences in 1957 did not go to see Burt Lancaster and Tony Curtis movies to find the characters they played steeped in a disdain that also defiled venerable commonplaces of American life, from brotherly love to dogged ambition, not to mention newspaper columnists, cigarette girls, senators, the police, and all that glittered along the Great White Way." Audiences found *Sweet Smell of Success* too cynical to make it commercially successful—it opened against *Tammy and the Bachelor* (Buford 183)—but its acute anatomizing of the American public's craving for excess and invective in its media hype, gossip, and presentation of politics as entertainment constitutes a searing adaptation of real-life social and political traumas and demagogues, dirty players and earnest writers and artists. As time passed, the poetry of its noir performances, visual qualities, and script have led to fuller appreciation of the film's art—and its visual rendering of not only Lehman's novella but an aspect of America's history and culture that remains bewildering to many who might still be surprised that Donald Trump, an offspring of Winchell's America, became a successful political candidate. In 2020, Paula Rabinowitz designated Trump's America a melodramatically adapted "new United States of Noir Affect (USNA)," linking the fictional worlds of film noir to the current "slimy world run by powerful and corrupt men" (262).

Although Winchell turned his attention from Broadway to politics in the 1930s, he never lost his desire to entertain, thus contributing to a cultural shift commentator Cleveland Amory called "publi-ciety," a society that values publicity and entertainment above all else (Gabler 184). Winchell played with the facts to get the news, as Walter Neff from *Double Indemnity* might say, up on its feet. However, what made Winchell and the servile press agents who fed him items for his columns such good material for a work of fiction—and for a film noir—were the writer's larger-than-life personality and his rise and fall from fame that mostly resulted from his energy, cleverness, outsized ego, deep insecurity, and bullying habits. Winchell's gymnastic use of language also made his story ripe for noir, whose scripts are often characterized by cynical wit, metaphor, and clever urban patter. Lehman's original story described the fast-talking, often corrupt and corrupting city denizens; Clifford Odets added much of the film's noir poetry and dialogue. James Naremore discusses the film's "baroque verbiage," saying that "few films have employed such deliberately 'stagy' language, in this case a mixture of gutter poetry and Winchell-ese of a sort that was never actually spoken in New York" (40). Odets also adapted the stars' bodies and personae into the script, poetically riffing on actor Tony Curtis's looks and contrasting his prettiness—Rita calls Sidney "Eyelashes" and the cop Harry Kello refers to Sidney's "ice-cream face"—with the film's menacing environment.

Lehman, Lancaster, and Mackendrick as Adaptors

Lehman first published "Hunsecker Fights the World" in *Collier's* in 1948. In 1950, this thinly veiled story about Walter Winchell appeared in expanded form in *Cosmopolitan* under the title "Tell Me About It Tomorrow!"—a phrase that appears repeatedly in the novella, capturing the self-serving tone of denial in the press agents' amoral activities. Lehman had wanted to call the novella "Sweet Smell of Success," but the editor didn't want the word "Smell" in the title (Kemp 140). The piece caught the interest of a new production company actor Burt Lancaster had formed with literary agent Harold Hecht and screenwriter James Hill. Lehman saw the three as crass and pushy men who were constantly in conflict, and he wasn't alone in that assessment. Actors Elizabeth Taylor and Montgomery Clift urged Alexander Mackendrick to avoid working with Lancaster, Hecht, and Hill, calling the men "monsters" (Kemp 140).

An early plan was to cast Orson Welles as J.J. Hunsecker, though Lancaster saw himself playing the role. The earlier casting choice would have made explicit an additional source for the film's story, *Citizen Kane*, another adaptation of a real-life media mogul, William Randolph Hearst, Winchell's boss for much of his career. Welles's description of *Kane* as "a failure story" (Mulvey 81) applies equally to Winchell's career trajectory and to the crash of fortunes in *Sweet Smell of Success*. Lancaster feuded with Mackendrick during what Lehman described as "long and exhausting story conferences" (Lehman papers); the Scottish-American Mackendrick, known for directing dark Ealing–Studios British comedies like *The Ladykillers* (1955), had strong ideas for the story and characters. Though he thought Mackendrick "brilliant," Lehman hand-wrote in his annotation of Mackendrick's notes in the film's pre-production that "it is very difficult for a writer to have a director who wants to 'express' himself" (Lehman papers), illustrating the competitive side of collaboration in adaptation. Lehman's frustration with Mackendrick's auteurist bent was due in part to the writer's disappointment that another early plan, for Lehman himself to direct the film, had been rejected by the producers.

Mackendrick clashed continually with Lancaster on shooting decisions (see Kemp, Naremore, and Rashner). Lancaster, another "rival director" to Mackendrick, called him a "mad professor" (Buford 181). Naremore reports an incident in which Sidney is supposed to sidle in beside Hunsecker at "21" (adapting Winchell's home away from home of The Stork Club). Because Lancaster didn't believe Hunsecker would allow himself to be blocked in by Sidney, he demanded the scene be restaged, eventually pushing the table over in a violent act of frustration. Mackendrick usually prevailed in such commotions, but even after Lehman had left the production, the hostile working environment persisted. Naremore describes the result: "a group of talented artists working under high tension in an atmosphere sometimes as malodorous as the world depicted on screen" (8). An egregious form of maladaptation in the workplace, such bullying demonstrated a hyper-masculine drive in the production that mirrored Hunsecker's attitude and approach and Winchell's quickness to anger. Burt Lancaster's forcefulness was repeatedly observed. Naremore comments that "an aura of violence had always surrounded the star" (Naremore 26) and quotes composer Elmer Bernstein: "Burt was really scary. He was a dangerous guy. He had a short fuse" (Naremore 29). The comment brings to mind Dixon Steele, from the noir classic *In a Lonely Place* (1950); in the film, Sylvia worries that Dix is "dangerous," and Brub prefers to romanticize his deviance as stemming from an artistic sensibility, calling him "an exciting guy." Neal Gabler reports Lehman's assessment of the men producing the film as "a rapacious and amoral bunch" (501); Lehman recalled, "there was a whiff of violence about the place" (Kashner). Lancaster's vulgar displays of machismo took center stage: "His sheer physical presence was overwhelming; his shadow fell over you before he even entered the room" (Kashner). Lehman later reported that the men were always "scratching around for women. They were the most corrupt group. I really sank into the depths when I decided to work with them" (Kashner).

Adding to other stresses during production, the script kept changing from day to day. As Sam Kashner points out, "Mackendrick would note years later, 'There never was a final shooting script for the movie. [...] It was all still being revised, even on the last day of principal photography. It was a shambles of a document'" (Kashner). Battles over the representation of all of the characters, as well as the tone of the film's ending, so exacerbated a stomach ailment of Lehman's that the writer left the project on doctor's orders. Lehman high-tailed it all the way to French Polynesia, about which he remarked in the hand-written notes on the film, "I loved Tahiti" (Lehman papers). This is when Clifford Odets, famed for '30s social-problem plays like *Waiting for Lefty*, came in to revise the script. In adapting Lehman's work, Odets added much of the film's wickedly witty dialogue (Kemp 143), cauterizing the film's noir tone and illustrating the "centrality [of the history of the adapted screenplay] to the collaborative authorship that is at the heart of film adaptation" (Boozer 1). For example, the dialogue reveals Hunsecker's casual yet brutal wit in the line, "You're dead, Sidney. Get yourself buried." The line is an interesting echo of the language of death that characterized Winchell's treatment of others. His well-known "Drop Dead List" announced the columnist's exile of press agents or performers from his reportage. Gabler notes that Winchell's ally McCarthy learned something of character assassination from the columnist, another instance of bullying and power-mongering tactics whose high stakes are reflected in a language of violence and death.

THE NOIR ADAPTATION OF *SWEET SMELL* AND ADAPTATION AS NOIR

Despite Lehman's frustration at sharing authorship with Mackendrick and Lancaster, the cinematography of the film and its famed jazzy score by Elmer Bernstein would contribute significantly to the art of the film, as would its directing labor, its fictional source, the revised script, and the charismatic performances of the actors. With his glistening black-and-white exterior shots of New York City, cinematographer James Wong Howe added his signature to the film—for example, putting Vaseline on Burt Lancaster's glasses to help define Hunsecker's villainy as opacity (Giddins); using unnerving low-angle shots throughout the film; and manipulating lighting to accentuate character and theme. Howe recalled, "Even in restaurants and other interiors with a lot of fill light, Hunsecker was lit so that his chiseled features stood out and his steel-rimmed eyeglasses gave him a sort of owlish look, like a predator." His cinematography worked at "replicating and heightening reality" (Giddens), achieving that paradoxical combination of realism and expressiveness characteristic of classic film noir.

Bernstein's viscerally jazzy score is linked to another aspect of the story. Lehman had transposed Winchell's overprotective relationship with his daughter Walda into Hunsecker's more blatantly incestuous desire to keep Susie for himself. Susie's lover in the film is a musician, unlike real-life itinerant scammer Billy Cahn, whose relationship with Walda Winchell it became Walter Winchell's mission to destroy. Walda's birth name, in its closeness to Walter's own, reflects the cloying attention Walter paid to his daughter. According to Gabler, Winchell also gave Walda a fur coat, which *Sweet Smell of Success* adapts into a visual metaphor. Susan Harrison, playing Susie Hunsecker, is accoutered with a fur coat throughout the film, yet as *Sweet Smell* progresses, she changes from wearing it full on to draping it across her shoulders, as if she is sublimating a resistance to J.J. and his withering power over her (Fig. 1); at the end of the film, she throws off the fur, leaving J.J. and walking into the city's dawn.

Fig. 1 The fur coat Susie Hunsecker (Susan Harrison) wears throughout *Sweet Smell of Success* is a symbol of the toxic control of her brother J.J. (Burt Lancaster)

As dark as the film is, this more hopeful conclusion was another change wrought by Mackendrick after continued arguments with Lancaster about the ending. Lancaster wanted the final scene to focus on the two men (Falco and Hunsecker) and planned to recut Mackendrick's ending. The director noted, "I became devious, as a director has to be […] I shot the whole thing with a moving camera, which makes it much harder to cut. I wanted to be sure they couldn't massacre the scene" (Buford 182). It is worth noting that the novella *Sweet Smell* ends with a fierce, fateful, one-word exclamation by Sidney, as J.J. lurches toward him after finding him with Susan: "Don't!"

Given the hyper-masculine atmosphere of the production set, it is no surprise that Harrison reportedly struggled with the work environment (see Kashner), perhaps contributing to a performance Naremore rightly characterizes as "insecure and melancholy" (55). The fact that the actor shares her given name with her character further symbolizes the blurred lines between fact and fiction in these layers of noiradaptation. Lehman, who didn't like the addition of Susie's attempted suicide in the script, wanted the character to reflect a kind of strength that her intermittent hopelessness belied. However, there is a significant shot of Susie in the film as it dawns on Sidney that she has set him up to be caught by J.J. in a compromising situation with the sister in whom he is perversely overinvested. As Harrison's face is partially in shadow, the film casts her now as a femme fatale of sorts, having wreaked vengeance on Sidney for setting up her lover Steve Dallas (originally called Vic Dallas in Lehman's 1956 script). Though Susie has lost her innocence, the lighting and Harrison's steely stare at Sidney reveal her agency here, the noir features of the film honoring Lehman's earlier intent to show Susan as a formidable character (Fig. 2).

Steve Dallas's status as a beleaguered musician aligns the film with several noir portraits of aggrieved men with artistic values (expressive, yet unyielding, putting in place the possibility of violence): the romantic yet violent screenwriter Dix In a Lonely Place; the defeated-idealist actor Charlie Castle (Jack Palance) in The Big Knife; Lancaster's own starry-eyed boxer Swede in The Killers; Bogart's hyper-principled Sam ("when a man's partner is killed, he has to do something about it") Spade in The Maltese Falcon; Sunset Blvd.'s writer Joe Gillis, who came to Hollywood as an energetic kid hoping to make it as a writer in the movie business—not to mention Norma Desmond herself, described by Cecil B. DeMille as "a

Fig. 2 The shadow cast by her brother J.J. (Burt Lancaster) helps establish the unblinking Susie (Susan Harrison) as a femme fatale

lovely kid of seventeen with more courage and wit and heart that ever came together in one youngster." All of these characters are innocents, or idealists, who came to lose their perspective, while Steve Dallas, a secondary character who is central to the plot, represents a stalwart romantic whose art represents his virtue. Surrounded by fakers and scammers, Steve speaks in a way that echoes his value as a talented musician when he tells Susie, "don't leave me in a minor key." He is a genuine article, a "real man," in Susie's words: an artist in a grubby, competitive world.

In fact, going back to the wrangling negotiations during pre-production, it was director Mackendrick who took a strong stand in making Steve Dallas, the artist figure, a moral center in the film. Mackendrick's notes, annotated by Ernest Lehman and archived at the Harry Ransom Library, include impassioned commentary on why the earlier plan to make Susie's lover a "bobby-sox singer" was problematic. Mackendrick felt strongly that Dallas should be singular and authentic. For Mackendrick, Dallas's goodness was a crucial foil to Hunsecker's narcissistic megalomania: "Vic [later, Steve] has talent and ignores Hunsecker's power. Nothing would be more certain to excite the columnist's fury. He would regard Vic much as Senator McCarthy regards Communists, as Hitler regarded Jews, as a General regards a pacifist. […] The boy is unnatural, un-American and all things most foul" (Lehman papers). Mackendrick's notes not only reveal his auteurist interventions (and help to explain Lehman's anxiety and Lancaster's anger and frustration) but also indicate the film's efforts to promote an idealism in proximity to corruption, a fundamentally noir double vision that is a direct result of the complex extra-diegetic story of adaptation undergirding the film.

If *Sweet Smell*'s transposition of hapless scammer Billy Cahn into an artist figure adds to the film's noiradaptation, so too does the presence of the Chico Hamilton Quintet performing on-screen. Indeed, part of the film's thematic noirness lies in its allusion to the social justice issues surrounding an authentic artist in a society deeply stratified according to race, class, and gender. The role of a hunted and haunted jazz musician in the '50s evokes a racialized postwar America like that in James Baldwin's "Sonny's Blues." The whiteness of Martin Milner's Steve Dallas inversely reflects a history of Black jazz artists trying to thrive in a racist country.

Describing the mutations and transformations of texts in their adaptations can be likened to a scandal sheet—storytelling that goes into difficult negotiations, wranglings among players and collaborators, and various versions of what the adaptation might be. In this way, Hunsecker's famous command to Sidney to light the columnist's cigarette—"Match me"— occasions some thinking about why "matches" often fail. Sidney wants to be like Hunsecker, to match him (see Kemp 153), and he's bound to fail. In Lehman's novella, Susan tells Sidney, "Stop trying to be a pale imitation of my brother. You weren't born to it. You haven't got the makings. [...] I came here [...] to warn you to stop trying to be another J.J. Hunsecker" (24). Like Sidney's slavish attention to Hunsecker, texts that try to match sources without thinking through their own aims and objectives and establishing their independence and creativity can be overbound to and imprisoned by previous scripts and texts that can never "match" the adaptation. For example, *Sweet Smell of Success* was adapted in 2002 to musical theater, with a book by Nicholas Hytner and a score by Marvin Hamlisch. Instead of taking the tone and emotional timbre of the musical theater players fully into account, the show attempts to "match" the film's meanness without an equally scandalous venue or structure. Because the show isn't self-conscious about its adaptation of the personae of its actors, John Lithgow's vulnerability ends up forcing a match with Hunsecker's trademark coldness. If Hunsecker called Tony Curtis's Sidney a "cookie full of arsenic" in the film, the charming performer Brian D'Arcy James plays Sidney instead as "starry-eyed" (Jefferson). Stopping to soliloquize in snappy song doesn't work for a story whose characters were riveting in the film because of their fraught and antsy movement within the cityscape, as when Tony Curtis's Sidney says, "the cat's in the bag, and the bag's in the river." Not surprisingly, theater critic Ben Brantley observed that "dialogue that seemed cool and mordant on screen registers as phony and bombastic onstage."

Hunsecker's comment to Steve Dallas that it's "difficult to be an artist in this crudest of all possible worlds" reveals the abiding messiness of adaptations and their composite status as blends of multiple scripts. Because they are the products of complex social contexts and multiple wranglings, adaptations can never "come clean." Rather than rendering simple judgments on the muddle of adaptation, it is much more productive and rewarding to anatomize its contents, contexts, and contradictions. *Sweet Smell* and its Janus-faced look at real and fictional American media moguls confront a truth about how social worlds, like texts, change and also repeat, revealing the noir griminess of adaptive processes and the importance of taking an unstintingly full look at them. Noir revelation as an adaptive process of examining social worlds seems at the heart of Breu and Hatmaker's study of "noir affect" when they suggest that "only by tarrying with these negative affects as they appear in the story of two-time losers, violent criminals, and death-haunted subjects can a truly transformational politics become possible" (7). To Breu and Hatmaker's twinning of cynicism and idealism in film noir, I would add the related values of empathy, perceptiveness, and understanding, even if "transformational politics" is not readily on hand.

Gabler describes the work of publicists in Lehman, Hoffman, and Winchell's era: "Most of the press agents themselves were so absorbed in the details they were myopic to the rest; they never saw the system whole this way or gave a moment's thought to its effect" (248). The myopia adapted across the texts and historical contexts discussed in this chapter serves, I hope, as a useful provocation to readers, viewers, and audiences to "see" "the system" of texts and social symptoms holistically, in all of their endlessly adaptive and detailed forms, complications, and seeming obscurities.

References

Boozer, Jack, editor. *Authorship in Film Adaptation*, U of Texas P, 2008.
Brantley, Ben. "A Faustian Pact in a City of Demons," review of *Sweet Smell of Success*. *New York Times*, 15 Mar. 2002, https://www.nytimes.com/2002/03/15/movies/theater-review-a-faustian-pact-in-a-city-of-demons.html. Accessed 27 June 2022.
Breu, Christopher, and Elizabeth A. Hatmaker. "Introduction: Dark Passages." *Noir Affect*, edited by Christopher Breu and Elizabeth A. Hatmaker, Fordham University Press, 2020, pp. 1–27.
Buford, Kate. *Burt Lancaster: An American Life*, Da Capo, 2000.
Gabler, Neal. *Walter Winchell: Gossip, Power and the Culture of Celebrity*, Knopf, 1994.
Giddens, Gary. *"Sweet Smell of Success:* The Fantastic Falco," Criterion 2011 DVD, 2 Feb. 2011, https://www.criterion.com/current/posts/1761-sweet-smell-of-success-the-fantastic-falco. Accessed 27 June 2022.
"James Wong Howe (1899–1976)," interview by Alain Silver. *Film Noir Reader 3: Interviews with Filmmakers of the Classic Noir Period*, edited by Robert Porfirio et al., Limelight, 2002, pp. 137–47.
Jefferson, Margo. "Why 'Sweet Smell of Success' Went Sour on Stage," *New York Times*, 24 March 2002, https://www.nytimes.com/2002/03/24/theater/theater-why-sweet-smell-of-success-went-sour-on-stage.html. Accessed 27 June 2022.

Kashner, Sam. "A Movie Marked Danger," *Vanity Fair*, April 2000, https://archive.vanityfair.com/article/2000/4/a-movie-marked-danger. Accessed 27 June 2022.
Kemp, Philip. *Lethal Innocence: The Cinema of Alexander Mackendrick*, Heinemann, 1991.
Lehman, Ernest. *Sweet Smell of Success (and other stories)*, Overlook, 2000. Ernest Lehman papers at the Harry Ransom Archive, University of Texas, Austin.
Leitch, Thomas. *The History of American Literature on Film*, Bloomsbury, 2019.
Leitch, Thomas. "Adaptation and Censorship." *The Scandal of Adaptation*, edited by Thomas Leitch, Palgrave Macmillan, 2022, 195–212.
Mulvey, Laura. *Citizen Kane*. BFI Film Classics, BFI, 1992.
Naremore, James. *Sweet Smell of Success*. BFI Film Classics, Palgrave Macmillan, 2010.
Palmer, R. Barton. "Continuation, Adaptation Studies, and the Never-Finished Text," *Adaptation and Visual Culture: Images, Texts, and Their Multiple Worlds*, edited by Julie Grossman and R. Barton Palmer, Palgrave Macmillan, 2017, pp. 73–99.
Pelizzon, V. Penelope, and Nancy West. *Tabloid, Inc.: Crimes, Newspapers, Narratives*, Ohio State University Press, 2010.
Rabinowitz, Paula. "Melodrama, Noir's Kid Sister, or Crying in Trump's America." *Noir Affect*, edited by Christopher Breu and Elizabeth A. Hatmaker, Fordham University Press, 2020, pp. 261–73.
Weinraub, Bernard. "He Turned Gossip into Tawdry Power; Walter Winchell, Who Climbed High and Fell Far, Still Scintillates." *New York Times*, 18 Nov. 1998, https://www.nytimes.com/1998/11/18/arts/he-turned-gossip-into-tawdry-power-walter-winchell-who-climbed-high-fell-far.html. Accessed 27 June 2022.

On Incest and Adaptation: The Foundational Scandal of *Cecilia Valdés*

Elisabeth L. Austin and Elena Lahr-Vivaz

This chapter explores the twinned scandals of adaptation and incest, focusing on three key adaptations of Cuban author Cirilo Villaverde's novel *Cecilia Valdés*, published in its definitive version in 1882. Villaverde had published two earlier versions of *Cecilia Valdés*, both in 1832: a short story, published in two parts in the magazine *La siempreviva*; and a novella titled *Cecilia Valdés, o la Loma del Ángel*. Neither of the 1832 versions brings incest into the relationship at the center of the 1882 novel (Genova), in which Cecilia, the eponymous young *mulata* (mixed-race) protagonist, has a tumultuous affair with a young Creole named Leonardo. Their relationship, already scandalous because of their relative social positions, proves even more so when it is revealed at the 1882 novel's end that the two are in fact half-siblings who share the same father. Compounding this

---

E. L. Austin
Virginia Tech, Blacksburg, VA, USA
e-mail: elaustin@vt.edu

E. Lahr-Vivaz (✉)
Rutgers University, Newark, NJ, USA
e-mail: el431@newark.rutgers.edu

© The Author(s), under exclusive license to Springer Nature
Switzerland AG 2023
T. Leitch (ed.), *The Scandal of Adaptation*, Palgrave Studies in
Adaptation and Visual Culture,
https://doi.org/10.1007/978-3-031-14153-9_5

tragic denouement, Leonardo is killed by the jealous José Dolores, a free black who is in love with Cecilia, and Cecilia, who has given birth to a baby girl, is imprisoned in a mental institution.

Often referred to as Cuba's national novel, *Cecilia Valdés* offers ripe material for the musicians, novelists, and filmmakers who have adapted it since its publication (see, among others, Bravo Rojas and Mejías Alonso). This story of cross-caste lovers who are unknowing kin has been adapted frequently to the stage, page, and screen, including a zarzuela (light opera) (Gonzalo Roig, 1932); the novels *Sofía* (Martín Morúa Delgado,1891), *Cecilia después, o por qué la tierra?* (F. Mond, 1987), and *La isla de los amores infinitos* (Daína Chaviano, 2006); the play *Parece blanca* (Abelardo Estorino, 1994); and the films *Cecilia Valdés* (James Sant-Andrews, 1949) and *Un paraíso bajo las estrellas* (Gerardo Chijona, 2000). The present chapter focuses on three adaptations of *Cecilia Valdés*: director Humberto Solás's 1982 film *Cecilia* (released in three different cuts), writer Reinaldo Arenas's 1987 novel *La loma del Ángel (The Graveyard of the Angels)*, and playwright Norge Espinosa Mendoza's 2004 puppet play *La Virgencita de Bronce (The Little Bronze Virgin)*.[1] These adaptations suggest that the scandal of Cecilia—replayed and adapted over many decades, both in Cuba and abroad—reflects not only questions of colonial power and racial control, but also questions of creativity and cultural patrimony. The incestuous character of Cecilia's multiple adaptations brings the lines that delineate race, sex, gender, and genre to the surface of this mixed group of texts, showcasing the fecundity of adaptation within a (not-so-) insular system of cultural and intellectual kinship in Cuba, as well as Spanish America more broadly. These adaptations of an incestuous story suggest a resonance between the self-reflexive, endogamous, and scandalous practices of both adaptation and incest in these texts, a not-uncommon coupling in Spanish American literature and film.

SCANDALOUS ROMANCE

Among the myriad social and political themes that Spanish American literature explores from the nineteenth century to the present, the narrative trope of unintentional incest—an illicit love between family members who do not know they are bound together by blood—is an unsettlingly

---

[1] Unless otherwise noted, translations of *The Graveyard of the Angels* are by Alfred J. MacAdam; translations of *The Little Bronze Virgin* are our own.

frequent theme. In addition to *Cecilia Valdés*, such incest is featured in canonical nineteenth-century novels like Juan León Mera's *Cumandá* (1877, Ecuador) and Clorinda Matto de Turner's *Aves sin nido* (*Birds without a Nest*, 1889, Peru); in twentieth-century epics like Gabriel García Márquez's *Cien años de soledad* (*One Hundred Years of Solitude*, 1968, Colombia); and even in contemporary Latinx novels like Silvia Moreno-García's bestselling *Mexican Gothic* (2020, U.S.).

Michel Foucault's provocative observation that "sexuality is 'incestuous' from the start [...], an object of obsession and attraction" (108–9) and Gilles Deleuze and Félix Guattari's proposition that "Instead of assuming [...] from the legal prohibition of incest that there is a natural aversion to incest, we ought rather to assume that there is a natural instinct in favor of it" (114) suggest why incest continues to be a scandalous companion to many Spanish American narratives. Legal and social prohibitions against incest—considered in almost all societies to constitute a clear-cut line between civilization and barbarism—have sought to regulate desire and sexuality as a means of preserving wealth and creating bonds outside of the family through marriage (Foucault 111, 120). Among such measures, the incest taboo, which proved to be the "keystone of alliances" (Foucault 111), ended competition inside families and allowed for the creation of inter-family alliances (Maryanski and Turner 4–5).

In the specific case of nineteenth-century novels like *Cecilia Valdés*, the relationship between unknowing siblings signals a generalized preoccupation with race and identity. As an example, Adriana Méndez Rodenas's Lacanian reading of incest in *Cecilia Valdés* blames slavery for a disturbance of the Symbolic realm (85) and concludes that *Cecilia Valdés* "confirms incest as a component of the Cuban psyche" (101). In Spanish America, the need for such alliances and the regulation of desire came into sharp focus for Creoles (Latin Americans of European descent) as they sought to maintain their power and prestige, in part through the fiction of racial superiority. With economic and social clout on the line, the ability to see race—and protect self-beneficial alliances—was paramount.

While Doris Sommer proposes the well-known concept of "foundational fictions" to describe nineteenth-century narratives from Spanish America that depict idealized political futures through allegorical romances (5–7), incest may be considered the *foundational scandal* of Spanish American literature, following on the heels of the "foundational frustrations" of the earlier versions of *Cecilia Valdés* published in 1832 (Genova). In the context of the violent colonial and post-independence history of

Spanish America, in which caste societies were divided according to an invented racial hierarchy, incest reveals the dark underbelly of a (supposedly) post-colonial modernity. Scandalously upending the potentially happy endings of foundational fictions and their same-caste alliances, incest lays bare the fabricated nature of paternity and fidelity, of knowable origins and predictable futures. Incest here is the child of power and abuse, marked by a secrecy that sometimes characterizes the mixed ancestry denoted by Spanish American *mestizaje* (racial mixing). At the same time, violating the incest taboo serves to contest the rules and regulations of society, even when, as in John Sayles's border film *Lone Star* (1996, U.S.), an incestuous romance does not end with potentially monstrous progeny (Lahr-Vivaz, "Passing" 209–10).

The myriad and ever-multiplying adaptations of *Cecilia Valdés* point in turn to what Anibal Quijano terms the "coloniality of power," the persistence of colonial power structures beyond independence in Spanish America. Cuba outlawed slavery only in 1886 and did not gain full independence until 1902. For Quijano, globalism represents the end of the colonial process, from which Euro-centered capitalism emerges as the newest global power, one that depends on social hierarchies based on race as a tool of oppression (533). As we show here, the multiple adaptations of Villaverde's novel across time and space signal the ongoing valence of this coloniality of power and the continued preoccupation with race as its instrument. Following Quijano, race continues to serve as both a marker of identity and a gatekeeper of privilege: "The racial axis has a colonial origin and character, but it has proven to be more durable and stable than the colonialism in whose matrix it was established" (533). The interlocked narratives of incest and miscegenation that remain the cornerstones of Cecilia's foundational scandal underscore the ways in which coloniality of power might be contested, as directors, writers, and playwrights employ incest as a metonym of the often hidden yet nonetheless pervasive social, cultural, and intellectual practices of Spanish America's past that linger into an occasionally monstrous present.

As Cecilia is written into song, adapted to the screen, and recast on the page, adaptations of Villaverde's novel form a growing, self-referential corpus of texts: a "hideous progeny" (Grossman 1–2) that contains a potential for monstrosity and invites deeper questions. In some adaptations, this potential is amplified and satirized; in others, it is sidelined. In all instances, the incestuous interrelations of Cecilia Valdés and her progeny signal the fertile ground of scandalous adaptations of all stripes, not only within the context of Cuba, but within all cultures that struggle with the persistence of the genetic, cultural, and colonial heritage of the past (Quijano 533–34) within a continuously adaptive present.

CECILIA (1982): THE REVOLUTIONARY ECONOMICS OF LOVE AND RACE IN CUBA

Conceived in the womb of the Cuban state, and produced with funding from Spain as well as Cuba, director Humberto Solás's "free" adaptation *Cecilia* (1982) is imbued with revolutionary rhetoric.[2] Solás (1941–2008), a contributor to the New Latin American Cinema that arose in the late 1950s, focused throughout his storied career on creating a local and national social cinema that opposes capitalist representation and foreign, market-controlled film production (Martin and Paddington 2). Solás's cinematic retelling of the Cecilia story therefore highlights national concerns of race and economics in Cuba. His Cecilia (the "no longer young" Daisy Granados, playing a part originally intended for an ingenue [Chanan 391]), first appears on the screen as a beautiful *mulata* who hopes either to marry well or to live as a courtesan. When *criollo* Leonardo Gamboa (Imanol Arias) flirts with her, she is attracted not only by his youth and beauty, but also by his potential as an economic benefactor. After professions of love and an afternoon of passion, he vows to marry her. Despite the couple's infatuation, however, the vast differences in their social positions make such an ending first unlikely and then impossible once Cecilia becomes more deeply involved in revolutionary activities (Fig. 1).

The director suggests from the start that Cuba's colonial history determines the transactional nature of relations between *mulatas* and *criollos*, as well as between *criollos* themselves. In the first frames, a written script, white against a black screen, details Spanish imperial control and the abuse of slaves who were forced to labor for wealthy Creole landowners. The title sequence is followed by images of black bodies, first ancient, then dressed in nineteenth-century garb, Afro-Cuban bodies dancing in the street to chants to the Yoruba deity Oshún and brown bodies in a Catholic

---

[2] *Cecilia* was released in three cuts, per its co-production agreement: a six-hour version for Spanish television, a four-hour version for the Cuban cinema, and an almost-three-hour film version for the international screen (Chanan 392). Michael Chanan notes the difficulty of producing a film, in three different versions, that would satisfy such diverse conditions and audiences (392–93). The version we analyze here is the three-hour international cut.

Fig. 1 Cecilia (Daisy Granados) and Leonardo (Imanol Arias), from Humberto Solás's *Cecilia* (1982)

street procession singing *Kyrie eleison* and carrying images of the Virgin and the crucified Christ. Liturgical music is juxtaposed with African music and rhythms, overlapping and softly discordant, as the camera lingers with a medium shot on several figures dragging crosses and self-flagellating as the procession fades from view. The script describes the syncretic cultural elements produced throughout Cuban history, suggesting that they lay the groundwork for independence and eventually for the 1959 Revolution.

From its first frames, the film roots Cuban culture in its rejection of coloniality and celebrates the fusion of African and Hispanic cultures as the heritage of the modern nation. This idea is reinforced with a sequence just after the opening that tells the story of Oshún, a river *orisha* (goddess) of the Yoruba religion. Desired by all but captured by white men, Oshún was eventually freed by the *orisha* Changó. A jump cut from Oshún bathing in honey to Cecilia bathing in honey and water confirms the parallel between these two females. Rather than concocting a romance from Cecilia and Leonardo's dalliance, *Cecilia* offers instead a loose metaphorical comparison, voiced by several characters, between the situation of black Cubans, enslaved and freed, and women—especially women of color—who were marginalized by both race and sex, and thereby doubly limited economically and socially within colonial and pre-Revolutionary Cuba.

Underscoring that Cecilia initially pursues economic security rather than love, an evocative scene with José Dolores Pimienta (Miguel Benavides), a black musician and fellow revolutionary, clarifies the economic nature of Cecilia's interest. Although Pimienta complains that Cecilia does not like black men, an erotic exchange between the two, complete with heavy breathing and licked lips, shows that this is not the case. Pimienta laments that if he were white, he would have her as a slave at his feet, recognizing both her economic interest in the power associated with whiteness and the metaphorical equivalence between slavery and women in a pre-Revolutionary society. Cecilia does not deny his accusation, and she permits his caresses, implicitly admitting that her interest in the *piel blanca* (white skin) of Leonardo—a character wearing, like all the film's *criollos*, white makeup that gives him a vampiric glow—is purely economic (Fig. 2).

Revealing sex, skin, and breathy promises alongside whispers of Revolution, the true scandal of Solás's *Cecilia* is that, while there is plenty of melodrama (Lahr-Vivaz, "Qué cosa" 155), there is no incest: Solás's film ends with the death of Leonardo and the possible death of Cecilia, but no suggestion of blood ties between them. The film hints instead at an incestuous desire between Leonardo and his mother, amplifying, as do some other adaptations, the echoes of this forbidden desire in Villaverde's

Fig. 2 José Dolores (Miguel Benavides) yearns for Cecilia (Daisy Granados) in Solás's film

novel. This change to Villaverde's plot became a scandal itself (Chanan 393), suggesting an emotional investment in the symbolic importance of the incest between Cecilia and Leonardo on the part of the Cuban filmgoing public (Alberto 10).

The film provoked a public outcry that critics attributed to a frustration with its blockbuster budget, its poor performance at Cannes, and the director's casting, narrative, and aesthetic choices (Alberto 10, Chanan 388-94). Solás himself interpreted the public's reaction as "masked racism," a rejection of the film's celebration of racial syncretism in Cuba (Martin and Paddington 11). The scandal surrounding Solás's *Cecilia*, which prompted the firing of the director of the Cuban Institute for Cinema (ICAIC) (Chanan 393–94), ultimately presents a predictable reading of the colonial past from a Revolutionary perspective. In Villaverde's novel, the lovers' unwittingly shared paternity marks a foundational scandal that signals the impossibility of overcoming the abuses of Cuba's founding fathers and their exploitation of slavery, a rotten cornerstone to the national foundation. Solás shifts the incest to Leonardo and his mother, marking *criollo* heritage as the tainted element in Cuba's foundation and leaving open the path to a *mulato* revolutionary narrative of future racial equality.

Chaotic sequences end the film: an incipient revolution, Leonardo's murder at the hands of José Dolores, and Cecilia dressed in carnival garb as Ochún throwing herself off a tower in a scene reminiscent of Hitchcock's *Vertigo* (Fisher xx, n. 25). Thus the film separates the future Revolutionary Cuba from the colony's foundational scandal and the resultant coloniality of power that established the imbalance between whites and blacks, and men and women, before 1959. Solás's elision of the incest between Cecilia and Leonardo highlights the racial and economic differences that impede their union, laying the blame for their (and Cuba's) tragic demise on the incestuous nature of *criollo* society, as Leonardo metonymically portrays the decadence of that caste.

In this adaptation of Cecilia's story, it is through revolution that Cuba achieves a future free of the chains of the colonial past. Although adaptation and incest are both endogamous operations, Solás's adaptation of Cecilia's story reworks Villaverde's narrative to make room for a future *mulato* revolutionary state unfettered by the ghosts of Cuba's imperial sins. When Solás places incest within the *criollo* household instead of between inter-caste lovers, he points to Cuba's *criollo* history as the true foundational scandal. In contrast to the *criollos* who undermine the nation's future potential, brave *mulato* revolutionaries, including Cecilia, Pimienta, and many others, work to free themselves and their nation from the colonial powers that still grip them. Their revolutionary zeal continues uncorrupted, suggesting a connection with the Revolutionary Cuban government which Solás steadfastly supported, and which he sought to advance and interrogate through film (Martin and Paddington 13). The backlash against the film and its revision of the incest narrative, however, suggests a continued desire on the part of Cuban spectators to acknowledge, and live with, the colonial past and its persistent ghosts. This "haunting," to borrow Linda Hutcheon's apt metaphor, signals the ongoing impact of the coloniality of power, even for a Revolutionary state dedicated to its eradication.

THE GRAVEYARD OF THE ANGELS (1987): THE SCANDAL OF EXCESS

In *Cecilia*, Solás elides incest to retell the history of the Revolutionary present. In *The Graveyard of the Angels* (1987), by contrast, exiled Cuban author Reinaldo Arenas centers his gaze on the incestuous desires that riddle Villaverde's novel, multiplying and magnifying the scandalous sexual proclivities of Villaverde's text in a scathing critique of the Cuban nation.

Arenas (1943–1990) was an openly gay writer who left Havana for New York in the 1980 Mariel Boat Lift. Although Arenas initially supported the Revolution, he later became one of its fiercest critics, calling attention to the abhorrent treatment of gays during the 1960s and 1970s and to the censorship that limited the publication of his work in Cuba. In the preface to *The Graveyard of the Angels*, Arenas characterizes his literary adaptation as both a recreation and a betrayal (*Loma* 9–10). In a sharp critique of Cuba's Revolutionary regime, which continues to teach *Cecilia Valdés* in schools as a tale of abolition and national beginnings, Arenas amplifies this "betrayal" by asserting that Villaverde's novel and his own both tell of redemption (*Loma* 10), implying a recuperation of Cuba's past. Criticizing the literary underpinnings of the Cuban nation, which, as Solás's cinematic adaptation shows, would just as soon sweep under the rug the incest that problematizes Cecilia's relationship with Leonardo, Arenas instead proffers a parodic tale of lurid, incestuous power and class struggles (*Loma* 9).

To some extent, Arenas remains faithful to Villaverde's novel in *The Graveyard of the Angels*, retaining the rough contours of the 1882 novel's plot, including the fatal end to the relationship between Leonardo and Cecilia. At the same time, however, Arenas sends up the nineteenth-century novel by foregrounding and amplifying what he terms its "incessant, skillfully suggested incestuous patterns" (*Graveyard* 1). He announces that Cecilia and Leonardo's love is tainted from the start, rather than waiting until the end to announce the shocking news of their shared bloodlines: Cecilia loved Leonardo, he writes, "not exactly in a brotherly way" (11). Arenas suggests, furthermore, that it is not only Cecilia and Leonardo who lust after kinfolk, but all the members of the esteemed Gamboa family. As in Villaverde's novel, Leonardo's sister Adela is characterized as Cecilia's double (7, 70). Yet while the transgressive desire between Leonardo and Adela is merely hinted at in Villaverde's novel (and absent from Solás's *Cecilia*), *The Graveyard of the Angels* makes the illicit lust between siblings explicit: "The mere sight of this [courtship of Adela] threw her brother Leonardo into a rage because he could not conceive of Adela's loving any man—except, of course, himself" (80). Similarly, whereas in Villaverde's novel Leonardo's mother, Doña Rosa, is characterized as having an unhealthy attachment to her son, in *The Graveyard of the Angels* her incestuous, intergenerational desire is foregrounded even more than in Solás's adaptation, at the same time that Leonardo's father don Cándido is shown to harbor possible desire for his future daughter-in-law. During a heated family debate in *The Graveyard of the Angels*, Doña Rosa reacts vehemently with an expression of incongruous interest in her own son: "'Hold it right there, don Cándido de Gamboa!' bellowed Doña Rosa. 'Leonardo has not chosen a wife, nor will he ever as long as I'm alive, because there's no woman—except me—who could love him, spoil him, put up with him, and understand him as he so richly deserves!'" (88).

In addition to drawing attention to the incestuous desires that problematize even the most nominally upstanding of Creole families, Arenas intimates that incest is largely unavoidable, regardless of intent, by showcasing the scandalous, illicit relationships that result in a populace of bastardized progeny. In a satirical reference to slave owners' siring of children with slaves, Doña Rosa insists that the slave Dionysus give her a black baby to restore her honor when she discovers that her husband has betrayed her with Cecilia's mother: "Right now you are going to possess me and make me pregnant with a black baby boy. A black boy, understand? If you don't, you'll go straight to the cane grinder out on the plantation and end up as brown sugar" (14). In Arenas's retelling, Doña Rosa's *mulato* son is later revealed to be José Dolores Pimienta. Arenas's narrative choice in this instance in fact serves to place incestuous desire in check: while Nemesia Pimienta desires her "supposed brother" (32), their shared surname obscures their lack of shared blood. Doña Rosa's insistence on her slave's compliance to her whims, however, also points to the unknown bloodlines of Cubans past and present.

In another instance of scandalous offspring, the esteemed bishop of Havana admits that he has fathered an untold number of children when he dresses up as an angel to offer solace to women of the upper class, suggesting the procreative perils of unclaimed progeny. "Wearing my splendid robes, I would venture out into the city almost every night and appear on the balconies of the most devout, most beautiful, and richest ladies. I don't suppose I have to tell you about the obedience and devotion with which a beautiful woman attends an angel who enters her boudoir at midnight. Yes, brother, I have angelically possessed practically every woman in this city" (16–17). The bishop offers a neat solution to the unwanted pregnancies that result from his angelic perambulations: "I solved the problems of the married women by absolving them and then baptizing one more supposedly legitimate child. The unmarried women had to enter the convent which I had built out back for just that purpose. Thanks to those ladies, the church is now filled with nuns, altar boys, sacristans, gravediggers, coachmen, and gardeners" (17). Jorge Olivares has noted the importance of this chapter in the novel, arguing that it can be considered "an interior duplication, a *mise en abyme* of *The Graveyard of Angels*" (171; our translation). In Villaverde's novel, love that crossed the color line was fraught by the uncertainty of paternity associated with slavery and the systemic abuse that yielded *mulato* children, presenting the specter of incest as a back-door argument for abolition. In Arenas's retelling, even those who opt to partner solely with those of their class and race may find themselves in bed with their family members—for, with the bishop revealed as the secret biological father to many in his flock, even those who wish to avoid an incestuous liaison might find it impossible to do so. Considered in this regard, the sly reference to "brother" in the bishop's deathbed confession signals the insidious possibility that the term, in colonial-era Cuba, is more than mere metaphor.

In drawing a line between past and present, and in characterizing both his text and Villaverde's as tracts in favor of redemption, Arenas signals the need for a decolonizing narrative that reveals the coloniality of power that lies at the heart of the Cuban nation, revolutionary or not. In this Arenas criticizes the same colonial abuses as Solás and others, but with very different implications, in effect "mak[ing] their denunciations of all desires that do not fit the heterosexual norm seem rather prudish" (Fischer xxv). Even (or especially) in Revolutionary Cuba, Arenas suggests, the stain of past sins continues to affect the present. With incest omnipresent and unavoidable, there is a clear need for a truthful approach to history, untainted by colonial power structures, in order to address the concerns of the nation past and present. Arenas's solution is not an attempt to avoid incest—as the reception of Solás's film showed, incest would continue to haunt any Cecilia adaptation—but to recognize the bones of the past buried in the national graveyard.

These bones are both black and white, and Arenas suggests that the true scandal of Cuban nationality, past and present, is the ongoing obsession with separating the two. In one of the most memorable scenes of *The Graveyard of the Angels*, Cecilia paints her great-grandmother white in an attempt to hide her black past from Leonardo: "Cecilia, dipping her brush in a pot of white paint, was changing Doña Amalia's black skin into ivory" (63). Whitewashing her past, Cecilia attempts to secure her future with Leonardo by passing as white in a parody of the discourse of *blanqueamiento*, or "whitening" as a means of accessing social privilege (Rosell). Yet Arenas shows that such endeavors are foiled from the start: no Cuban family is left untouched by the intersecting web of bloodlines that result from illicit, often incestuous, liaisons. Arenas foregrounds the remnants of black flesh amidst the white paint, here rendered as what a horrified Leonardo glimpses as "the black breast Cecilia hadn't as yet painted" (64), showcasing the twinned scandals of adaptation and incest in the name of national critique.

THE LITTLE BRONZE VIRGIN (2004): HIDEOUS PROGENY HIDDEN NO MORE

Appearing decades after the release of Solás's revolutionary *Cecilia* and the publication of Arenas's scandalously excessive *The Graveyard of the Angels*, Norge Espinosa Mendoza's *The Little Bronze Virgin* (2004) adapts Villaverde's novel to the stage in a transgressive rendition that intimates that all adaptations—at least in the case of *Cecilia Valdés*—are themselves inherently incestuous, and productively so.

Espinosa (1971–) is a Cuban playwright, poet, critic, and LGBTQ activist whose work has been produced in Cuba, Puerto Rico, and the U.S. He wrote *The Little Bronze Virgin*, an adult puppet play, for the Teatro de las Estaciones in Matanzas, Cuba, at the request of its director, Rubén Darío Salazar (ix). His title is a reference to José Dolores Pimienta's characterization of Cecilia as "my little bronze virgin" in Villaverde's *Cecilia Valdés*. Taking advantage of the potential presented by the uncommon genre of puppet representation, Espinosa's drama offers a theatrical reading of adaptation and incest that is both strange and compellingly human, embracing both incest and previous adaptations of Cecilia's story, portraying them as open secrets, and using them to create and maintain a dramatic tension between the characters of the play that extends to include the audience.

The Little Bronze Virgin opens by revealing the secret that lurks at the end of Villaverde's novel: Cándido Gamboa acknowledges to the audience that he has fathered the infant Cecilia and places her in an orphanage in order to conceal his relationship with her. He asks the child's grandmother, Chepilla, for her silence as he takes the baby, ignoring the cries of her mother (23–24). In the next scene, the puppets of the village, acting as a Greek chorus, sing about incest: "and if they knew the truth/ they would have avoided disgrace/ the disgrace that will come/ brother and sister in love/ bastard love, how horrible!" (31). Here the incest is openly discussed among most of the characters, and, in a continuous play of dramatic irony, the lovers are the only characters unaware that they are siblings. In the opening scene, Cecilia cries, "I love you, Leonardo, I love you! [...] But wait, slow down. Something tells me our love is prohibited" (30). To which a servant responds in an aside, "Oh, shoot, someone already told her the end of the book!" (30). In this case, Cecilia and Leonardo remain ignorant of their shared paternity: while Cecilia may suspect something is awry, the audience, along with the entire puppet village that surrounds the lovers, know all about their parentage and the prohibited nature of their amorous liaison. Incest remains a topic of open discussion between Leonardo and his mother (35), as well as Cándido and Chepilla (39), throughout the play.

From the description of the characters at the beginning of *Virgencita* that describes Cecilia as "seems white" (21), the title of Abelardo Estorino's play adapting *Cecilia Valdés (Parece blanca)*, to the strains of Gonzalo Roig's *zarzuela*, or light opera, that open the play's prologue (23), mark its conclusion (67), and accompany many scenes, adaptations of the Cecilia story constitute a fundamental part of Espinosa's work. The rich intertextuality that characterizes this play recognizes a cultural reality regarding Cecilia: that for most Cubans, Roig's 1932 *zarzuela* is inseparable from the novel (Espinosa 72), if not better known than the original. The zarzuela's prominence in the Cuban cultural imaginary recalls Hutcheon's suggestion that adaptations are "second without being secondary" (9), indicating that chronology does not determine cultural authority or stature. Illustrating Grossman's metaphor of adaptations as "monstrous progeny," Cecilia's story evokes the image of Frankenstein's monster to signal a close, and often contentious, relationship between adaptations and the parent texts they "destroy" (1–2). In Grossman's formulation, the intertexts that inform, shape, precede, and follow any adaptation represent "elastextity" (2), the web of dynamic interrelations between texts that persist and expand, a corrective to Hutcheon's idea that we experience adaptations as palimpsests (8). By acknowledging elastextity, the connections between texts, whether parent or progeny, are never quite forgotten or erased, but rather coexist within and through every new adaptation, a multiplying inheritance comparable to a genetic relationship, through which the past coexists within every (potentially monstrous) offspring. These relationships between parent and progeny, whether textual or diegetic, are marked from the first scene as incestuous, interrelated too closely for the comfort of everyone but the whole puppet village that habitually remarks on the presence of incestuous relations and desires.

The elastextity of the Cecilia story in *The Little Bronze Virgin* is further conveyed narratively, referenced through the layers of related texts that contribute to the creation of the puppet play. Such layers include sound, as songs from the zarzuela precede almost every scene, as well as through the written descriptions and spoken dialogue that play on the page and stage such as the character descriptions, above, and references to Villaverde. The use of puppets allows Espinosa another visual way to signal such elastextity, nodding to the embedded relationships between his adaptation and the many others that have preceded it, as well as those that will almost certainly follow. Espinosa uses what John Bell calls the inherently uncanny nature of puppet theater (48–50) not only to evoke the intertextual connections between this presentation and previous Cecilia adaptations but also to encourage a material and emotional separation between the audience and events on the stage. As Cecilia sobs in front of a broken mirror when she believes that Leonardo has left her, images of her "twins" appear, "disfigured by her desperation" (53): Crazy Cecilia, Sick Cecilia, Old

Cecilia. In a nod to Charles Dickens's *A Christmas Carol,* these Cecilias tell the protagonist that they represent what she is and what she will become. When Cecilia requests that she be left alone, or *sola,* Crazy Cecilia riffs on her request, quoting Villaverde: "I am alone, I was born alone ...." (53). The other Cecilias soon join in, each adding one of the well-known lines from the novel:

Old Cecilia: *(Imitating her.)* "My mother had me alone"
Sick Cecilia: *(The same.)* "I must make my way alone." (53, trans. Helen Lane)

The reiteration of the word "alone," however, highlights the paradoxical futility of any attempt to find solitude (see Lahr-Vivaz, "Passing for Solitude"). In Espinosa's play, as in any other adaptation of *Cecilia Valdés,* the existence of a multiplicity of Cecilias—not only the Old and the Sick, but also the Revolutionary icon created by Solás in his film and the defiant, whitewashing girl in Arenas's novel—mean that each iteration of Cecilia necessarily finds herself as one of many in an incestuous *elastextity.*

Including a chorus of Cecilias in *The Little Bronze Virgin,* Espinosa intimates that the potentially incestuous, always scandalous, progeny of *Cecilia Valdés* should remain hidden no more, hideous though they may be. In an epilogue, the playwright underscores this point: "One Cecilia Valdés exists. Many Cecilia Valdéses exist" (69). Espinosa goes on to explain that he has drawn on multiple "pages and adaptations [...] trying to find in them that one uniquely multiple face of a character, which will continue invoking herself at other opportunities to come, from whatever other form of artistic expression" (69). In this regard, Espinosa would seem to posit an idea similar to elastextity, as he acknowledges the inherent singularity and plurality of the Cecilia story and its many voices and incarnations, past and present. Espinosa's description of Cecilia refers not only to the multiplicity of adaptations but to the scandalous omnipresence of incest. In both processes, there is a conflation, and an uncomfortably uncontrolled proliferation, of genes as well as of genres, that is considered scandalous (and/or sinful), a creative liberty that Espinosa here celebrates: a "game of searches, reading and memories" (69), an uncanny history of Cuba.

Adapting the Future from the Bones of the Past

As *Cecilia Valdés* and its adaptive progeny suggest, incest shocks, transgresses, and scandalizes even as it marks limits, crosses borders, and questions fundamental assumptions of family origins and futures. In so doing, it reminds us of the scandal of adaptation(s), the theme of this volume. In concluding this analysis of three of the many adaptations of *Cecilia Valdés*, we note that adaptation—both verb and noun, practice and product of that practice—is remarkably similar to the metaphor of incest. Not only do both provoke intense emotional reactions in their audiences, but as they create new pairings outside of the allowed schemes for reproduction, they are both irreducibly self-referential and culturally cannibalistic, and they both carry a potential for monstrosity. Both incest and adaptation are instruments of creative endogamy, one oriented toward the past (incest), the other offering the potential for future change (adaptation). As we see with Cecilia, both processes reveal a past not as well known as we assumed and a future that is continually adaptive.

To Lawrence Venuti's insight regarding the potential for translations to "question the authority of dominant cultural values and institutions" (1), we might add another from Argentine author Jorge Luis Borges, who once quipped that "the original is unfaithful to the translation" (146). Villaverde's Cecilia appears anemic in comparison with the adaptations that have transformed Cecilia into a cultural touchstone that becomes enriched through every incestuous incarnation.

References

Alberto, Eliseo. "Cecilia: entre la pluma y la pantalla," *Caimán barbudo*, vol. 16, no. 176, 1982, pp. 10–11.
Arenas, Reinaldo. *La loma del ángel*. 2nd edition, Ediciones Universal, 2001.
Arenas, Reinaldo. *The Graveyard of the Angels*. Translated by Alfred J. MacAdam. Avon, n.d.
Bell, John. "Playing with the Eternal Uncanny: The Persistent Life of Lifeless Objects." *The Routledge Companion to Puppetry and Material Performance*, edited by Dassia N. Posner et al., Routledge, 2014, pp. 43–52.
Borges, Jorge Luis. *Other Inquisitions*. Translated by Ruth L.C. Simms, Washington Square Press, 1966.
Cecilia. Dir. Humberto Solás 1982. *Films On Demand*, Films Media Group, 1981, digital.films.com/PortalPlaylists.aspx?wID=256779&xtid=160506.

Chanan, Michael. *Cuban Cinema*. U of Minnesota P, 2003. *ProQuest Ebook Central*, ebookcentral.proquest.com/lib/vt/detail.action?docID=310656.
Deleuze, Gilles and Félix Guattari. *Anti-Oedipus: Capitalism and Schizophrenia*. Translated by Robert Hurley et al., Penguin, 2009.
Fischer, Sibylle. "Introduction" and "Bibliography." *Cecilia Valdés or El Angel Hill*. By Cirilo Villaverde. Edited by Sibylle Fischer, translated by Helen Lane, Oxford University Press, 2005, pp. xi–xxx and 499–501.
Foucault, Michel. *The History of Sexuality. Volume I: An Introduction*. Translated by Robert Hurley, Vintage, 1990.
Genova, Thomas. "Foundational Frustrations: Incest and Incompletion in Cirilo Villaverde's *Cecilia Valdés*." *Decimonónica: revista de producción cultural hispánica decimonónica*, vol. 13, no. 1, Winter 2016, pp. 66–86.
Grossman, Julie. *Literature, Film, and Their Hideous Progeny: Adaptation and ElasTEXTity*. Palgrave, 2015.
Hutcheon, Linda. *A Theory of Adaptation*. Routledge, 2006.
Lahr-Vizav, Elena. "Passing for Solitude: Incest and Ideology in the 'Lone Star' State." *Journal of American Studies*, vol. 46, no. 1, 2012, pp. 203–17.
Lahr-Vizav, Elena. "Qué cosa eres?": Reading Refractive Melodrama in Humberto Solás's *Cecilia*." *Chasqui*, vol. 46, no. 1, 2017, pp. 153–66.
Martin, Michael T., and Bruce Paddington. "Restoration or Innovation? An Interview with Humberto Solás: Post-Revolutionary Cuban Cinema." *Film Quarterly*, vol. 54, no. 3, 2001, pp. 2–13. *JSTOR*, www-jstor-org.ezproxy.lib.vt.edu/stable/10.1525/fq.2001.54.3.2.
Maryansky, Alexandra, and Jonathan Turner. "Incest, Theoretical Perspectives on." *The International Encyclopedia of Anthropology*. Edited by Hilary Callan, John Wiley, 2008, pp. 1–14. *Wiley Online Library*, onlinelibrary.wiley.com/doi/https://doi.org/10.1002/9781118924396.wbiea2041.
Olivares, Jorge. "Otra vez Cecilia Valdés: Arenas con(tra) Villaverde." *Hispanic Review*, vol. 62, no. 2, 1994, pp. 169–84.
Quijano, Aníbal. "Coloniality of Power, Eurocentrism, and Latin America." *Nepantla: Views from the South*, vol. 1, no. 3, 2000, pp. 533–80.
Méndez Rodenas, Adriana. "Identity and Incest in 'Cecilia Valdés': Villaverde and the Origin(s) of the Text." *Cuban Studies*, vol. 24, 1994, pp. 83–104. *JSTOR*, www-jstor-org.ezproxy.lib.vt.edu/stable/24485771.
Rosell, Sara. "*Cecilia Valdés* de Villaverde a Arenas: la (re)creación del mito de la mulata." *Afro-Hispanic Review*, vol. 18, no. 2, 1999, pp. 15–21.
Bravo Rozas, Cristina, and Almudena Mejías Alonso, editors. *El mito de Cecilia Valdés: de la literatura a la realidad*. Verbum, 2014.
Sommer, Doris. *Foundational Fictions: The National Romances of Latin America*. U of California P, 1991.

Venuti, Lawrence. *The Scandals of Translation: Towards an Ethics of Difference.* Routledge, 1998. *ProQuest Ebook Central,* ebookcentral.proquest.com/lib/vt/reader.action?docID=169424.

Villaverde, Cirilo. *Cecilia Valdés or El Angel Hill.* Edited by Sibylle Fischer, translated by Helen Lane, Oxford University Press, 2005.

"We Need More Input!": John Hughes's *Weird Science* (1985) and Scandals from the Red Scare to the Twitter Mob

Jerod Ra'Del Hollyfield

When Molly Ringwald reassessed her collaborations with John Hughes post—#MeToo in a 2018 article for the *New Yorker*, she created an Internet firestorm that branded the director's seminal teen films canceled. As Twitter and publications from *The Guardian* to *Jezebel* began riffing on Ringwald's comments over the next year, one film took the brunt of criticism and became the poster child for Hughes's alleged rampant misogyny and other cultural transgressions: 1985's *Weird Science*. The backlash against the movie was so prominent that when Arrow Video released a collector's edition of *Weird Science* on Blu-Ray in 2019, the accompanying critical essays by Alexandra Heller-Nicholas and Amanda Reyes both sought to justify why the film merited analysis at all. *Weird Science* details the accidental creation by teen outcasts Wyatt (Ilan Mitchell-Smith) and Gary (Anthony Michael Hall) of perfect woman Lisa (Kelly LeBrock) to

---

J. Ra'Del Hollyfield (✉)
Carson-Newman University, Jefferson City, TN, USA
e-mail: JHollyfield@cn.edu

© The Author(s), under exclusive license to Springer Nature Switzerland AG 2023
T. Leitch (ed.), *The Scandal of Adaptation*, Palgrave Studies in Adaptation and Visual Culture,
https://doi.org/10.1007/978-3-031-14153-9_6

fulfill their sexual fantasies and climb the high-school hierarchy. Regardless of its surface violations of current cultural standards, the film's nuances and complicated politics make it a much more valuable text than its recent reception would admit.

Deviating from the norms of both film criticism and academic conventions, the genre of Internet-based commentary eschews analysis of texts in favor of a haphazard application of diluted cultural studies terminology it relies on to manufacture scandal. Lacking the rigor of academic criticism and actively resisting context, this type of social-media discourse opts to depose and supplant source texts while seizing their place within popular culture, a trait that has serious implications for *Weird Science* and adaptation studies generally that the discipline has yet to address. In response, this chapter inverts the customary trajectory from close analysis to general conclusions. Instead, it begins *in medias res* by considering the barrage of recent viral articles and tweets that so quickly shifted the film's legacy as themselves essentialist adaptations that willfully evade the typical relationships adaptation studies has developed to understand connections between texts before using the ways the film comments on the lingering effects of the Cold War by adapting numerous texts from *Frankenstein* to the E.C. Comics series of the same name in order to challenge the more recently emerging norms of what I call BuzzFeed Theory.

SCANDAL AS ADAPTATION AND THE MAKING OF BUZZFEED THEORY

If not for a serendipitous collision of classroom instruction and academic research that occurred in the spring of 2018, I likely would have never considered online pop-culture writing within the framework of adaptation studies. After suspending our department's undergraduate critical theory course for half a decade due to lack of interest from both faculty and students, my department head suggested that I teach it as a way to increase upper-division offerings. Though the course barely made with its seven enrolled students, it easily became one of the most rewarding teaching experiences of my career. The students proved curious and dedicated to the material despite its demands as we moved from Aristotelian aesthetics through disability studies in fifteen weeks. I naturally expected the class to struggle with the material, but I perceived a greater sense of confusion than I was initially prepared for. One April day after forty-five minutes of reluctant discussion of Homi Bhabha and hybridity, I could feel the concepts finally clicking with the students. As we concluded, an art major taking the course as an elective before she began graduate school remarked, "This would have been so much easier if I didn't have to unlearn everything I read online." When I asked her to elaborate, she rattled off a host of listicles and tweets written in the wake of sundry cultural appropriation controversies from Miley Cyrus to Kylie Jenner before concluding, "It seemed that once it had a label, there couldn't be any more to it."

That same semester, I was also teaching a class on the history of the teen movie, a course that dovetailed with an essay I had begun that focused on the curious cycle of five teen-science movies released over the course of one month from July to August of 1985: *Back to the Future, Explorers, Real Genius, My Science Project,* and *Weird Science.* I found this cycle of films intriguing both because it was produced in the wake of the Reagan Administration's seminal 1983 education report *A Nation at Risk,* which, as Holly G. McIntush writes, "stripped the nation of the myth that our schools were the best in the world, legitimized state and local efforts to reform education systems [...] and inspired a new discourse and a new round of reform," and because, except for *Back to the Future* and the research niche the franchise has spawned in recent years, the films are neglected in studies of the teen movie (423). Apart from *Back to the Future,* which became the year's highest-grossing title, and *Weird Science,* these films were also box-office failures (boxofficemojo.com). Though the latter's $23 million box-office take cemented John Hughes's brand of teen movies, it earned half of what *The Breakfast Club* had the previous February and a third of what *Pretty in Pink* and *Ferris Bueller's Day Off* would the following year.

As I began the project, I noticed a curious antipathy in recent reviews and popular criticism of the films I had never encountered in my academic career that ballooned when Ringwald released her essay a few weeks into my research. In "What About *The Breakfast Club?*" Ringwald reassesses Hughes's earlier work as a writer for *National Lampoon* and her collaborations with the filmmaker that made her such an '80s icon that she appeared on the cover of *Time*—a descent into her past for which *Sixteen Candles* and *The Breakfast Club*'s inductions into the Criterion Collection served as the impetus. Alternating between effusive praise and out-of-context cheap shots at the auteur who reinvented the teen film in the '80s, Ringwald highlights Hughes's complicated legacy:

John's movies convey the anger and fear of isolation that adolescents feel, and seeing that others might feel the same way is a balm for the trauma that teen-agers experience. Whether that's enough to make up for the impropriety of the films is hard to say—even criticizing them makes me feel like I'm divesting a generation of some of its fondest memories, or being ungrateful since they helped to establish my career. And yet embracing them entirely feels hypocritical. And yet, and yet ....

Despite her retrospective misgivings about some of the content of Hughes's films and her roles in them, Ringwald's essay is a largely thoughtful and personal piece about her own cinematic legacy and how motherhood changed her perceptions of the past, albeit one that fails to acknowledge alternative readings or previous academic work on Hughes's oeuvre and the teen film as a genre. As much as the article feels like a stab at relevancy and promotion of her guest-star stint as Archie's mother on the comic-based CW teen soap *Riverdale* (2017–), it conveys a productive ambivalence that merits real conversation. But that's not what happened. Minutes after its publication, Internet news outlets from *Vulture* to *IndieWire* to *Mashable* distilled the essay into hot takes filled with pull quotes that were variably invested in preserving the tensions with which Ringwald's essay grapples. Others further sensationalized the piece, a trend epitomized by a *Showbiz Cheatsheat* article that bears the headline, "Molly Ringwald Found John Hughes to Be 'Racist, Misogynistic, and, at Times, Homophobic' after Rewatching His Films That Made Her Famous" (Williams). As expected, Ringwald trended on Twitter, where users linked directly to the story accompanied by their own commentary or, in many cases, to articles about the essay from other outlets. Then online publications began covering the Twitter commentary, deepening the controversy Ringwald kindled while barely acknowledging her initial work, a response most thoroughly on display in the *Daily Edge*'s "Molly Ringwald Divides Twitter by Highlighting Problematic Elements of *The Breakfast Club*," a piece that collects embedded tweets about the scandal supplemented with an assessment of Ringwald as simply "troubled by her character's treatment" (McClelland). One could watch in real time as Ringwald's piece became aggregated, remixed, and retweeted until it barely resembled itself beyond vague and superficial summaries of its thesis that wouldn't pass muster on an annotated bibliography for English 101.

While it is important to reiterate that this cancel campaign was not Ringwald's intent, the fallout continues to influence Hughes's place in pop culture, especially for the films he wrote or directed that do not feature the actress, such as *Weird Science*, which Internet-based pieces have increasingly demonized since the *New Yorker* essay appeared. A week after the publication of Ringwald's essay, the *Guardian*'s Hadley Freeman published a listicle titled "Times Move Pretty Fast! Rewatching 80s Favorites in the Age of #MeToo" that extended Ringwald's critique to a host of '80s movies, including *Die Hard* and *Ghostbusters*. Yet for Freeman, *Weird Science* clocked in as the greatest offender, Hughes's "one teen film that is pure fratboy, and thus has aged the worst." In the *Jezebel* article "The Only Gender-Swapped Remake I Want to See Is *Weird Science*," Hazel Cills writes, "*Weird Science* is dated in nearly every way but mostly for its gender politics. It's a movie built for bros who think the world owes them hot girlfriends and its gaze is strictly that of a 15-year-old boy." Blogger Dan Hall gave the movie a backhanded positive review as an entry in his series (and now self-published book) *Problematic Movies of the 1980s*: "In 1985, there was a horny, stupid ideal of the perfect woman and the movie *Weird Science* exemplified it." This discourse was given further energy by the unavailability of the film on home video until Arrow released the collector's edition Blu-Ray in late 2019 at a premium price of $39.99 and its inaccessibility on any streaming platform; it became sporadically available on HBO Max when the service launched in summer 2020. As a result, such thinkpieces on *Weird Science* became a fleeting pop-culture phenomenon that saw a largely unavailable movie popularly evaluated without substantial textual analysis, triggering a lasting impact on the film's reception.

The viral sensation Ringwald's essay initiated and its influence on public perceptions of Hughes's filmography typify the type of exposure to critical terms that my literary theory student claimed she had to unlearn to grasp our course's leading concepts. Though posing as critical analysis and keen insights into oppressive social structures, this genre of popular online commentary has no intention of furthering debate, privileging instead affirmation and the type of imitation Freedman's *Guardian* piece illustrates. As my student remarked, it exists to formulate a label and put an end to any productive conversation, a goal antithetical to academic writing in the humanities. These commentaries are not produced in a spirit of inquiry rooted in textual evidence. Yet they clearly have a greater reach than peer-reviewed journal articles despite their dearth of inquiry, a trait that endows the genre with a clear anti-expertise streak. Indeed, part of the reason the critical theory course I taught was on hiatus for so long may well be that students felt sufficiently exposed to such concepts through their use of social media.

In her discussion of the adaptation industry, Simone Murray positions scholars and their writing about particular films as firmly entrenched within the adaptation process, serving to give legitimacy to certain texts as they evolve into future iterations, rescuing neglected works from the historical dustbin, and calling for reexaminations of existing adaptation situations as they embody the "mechanisms of evaluation" that drive how texts circulate (12). In her interrogations of the intertextual relationships among source texts, adaptations, and industry contexts, however, Murray does not deem scholarly writing a type of adaptation, but merely the related output of the academic branch of the adaptation industry that serves as a stakeholder in the process. In contrast, the online criticism for which Ringwald's essay and its responses serve as examples is best understood as what I call BuzzFeed Theory: Internet writing aiming for optimal dissemination that acts as full-fledged adaptations of the texts it discusses in order to curtail the web of intertextuality by deposing and replacing source texts via scandal, a strategy that protects it from resistant scholarly interventions.

The moniker BuzzFeed Theory has less to do with the online news outlet's coverage of Ringwald's *New Yorker* essay than with the pioneering form of journalism the site developed in 2006 and has since exploited to grow into a hub that rivals the web traffic of the *New York Times* (Berman 4113). Sharing many similarities with the yellow journalism of the nineteenth century like William Randolph Hearst's *New York Journal*, BuzzFeed has, as David Elliot Berman observes, undertaken its sensationalist media forms—clickbait headlines, listicles, and personality quizzes—as "institutional adaptations to spaces in which information and sensation were heavily *concentrated*": the Facebook news feeds on which his article focuses as well as tweets, Instagram stories, and TikTok videos (4109). Though *BuzzFeed* did not cover the initial fallout from Ringwald's essay, it did more than perhaps any other publication to fan the flames of scandal for years to come. The news site invited Ringwald to rehash the controversy in 2019 on its Twitter news show *AM to DM* and published a subsequent article about the appearance entitled "Molly Ringwald Said Fans Thanked Her for Her #MeToo Essay on *Sixteen Candles* and *The Breakfast Club*" (Yandoli). It also ran several quizzes in the vein of "Everyone Has a Molly Ringwald Character Who Matches Their Personality—Here's Yours" days before Ringwald's editorial came out and "Which *Pretty in*

Pink Character Are You Most Like?" during the July following Ringwald's article (Leggett; juliaaurane). Such pieces were a far cry from the warmed-over nostalgia of Susan Cheng's *BuzzFeed* article "Molly Ringwald and Ally Sheedy Explain Why *The Breakfast Club* Is Still Relevant Today," which recounts a 2015 interview with the two actors at South by Southwest.

As Berman implies, the online genres that result from *BuzzFeed*'s adaptation of news to the social-media landscape have led to other digital-native publications adopting formats like the listicle and secondhand coverage of stories published in legacy media. Similarly, traditional media outlets produce work that resembles the structure of *BuzzFeed* pieces more and more closely than articles appearing in their archives as recently as a decade ago in the hope that content adapting to the clickbait style indicative of *BuzzFeed* will catch users' attention on social media and redirect them to the websites of formerly illustrious publications (Lewis and Molyneux 11). Within this online news ecosystem, an adaptation cycle emerges that is apparent in the Ringwald essay's effect on Hughes's reputation. Though Ringwald's piece appeared in a publication as storied as the *New Yorker*, editors designed it for online viral dissemination. Its release coincided with the canonization of Hughes's films in the Criterion Collection; its author made up for her lack of journalistic and literary bona fides fundamental to the *New Yorker*'s ethos with her celebrity status; and its central argument avoided any close reading of Hughes's work in favor of generalizations anchored in personal anecdotes. In addition, its title directly referenced aspects of scandal related to online discussions of critical theory both through the inclusion of the hashtag #MeToo and in its allusion to the rhetorical fallacy of whataboutism through its title, "What About *The Breakfast Club*?" Through a tactic of dismissal and distancing buoyed by its gestures to online appeal, the essay attempted to replace Hughes's films, not facilitating debate but claiming the status of a definitive statement that has assumed the role of source text.

Establishing itself as dominant, the essay encourages the propagation of further adaptations it hopes will link to the *New Yorker*. Some resemble Freeman's listicle for the *Guardian* that apply Ringwald's claim to Hughes's other work and 1980s Hollywood in general through a mode of writing that would have been anathema to the newspaper until recently. Others simply rehash and summarize the *New Yorker* piece or inspire amateur authors to write their own thinkpieces on sites like *Medium*. Further adaptations appear when the article or its aggregate summaries are shared, tweeted, and retweeted—conforming to various social-media conventions by privileging scandal over close analysis. In the early years of Twitter, scholars like Chuck Tryon called the site's ability to effect box-office grosses for new films through the accumulation of positive or negative reviews "The Twitter Effect" (119). However, as the site gained relevance, The Twitter Effect has also adapted, now appraising the value and upsetting the financial stability and reputations of existing texts and their creators. As the Ringwald essay's trajectory indicates, Twitter can transform an innocuous positive piece or a cautiously critical one into a scandal through its toxic essentialism. Adaptation for use on Twitter and other social-media sites allows for what Emily Snydor defines as "partisan selective exposure"—consumers' ability to filter out media that is not likeminded, leading to increased polarization and a lack of productive dialogue that seeks to close off the adaptation process and deny the existence of further intertextual relationships (76). Such adaptations must render texts like *The Breakfast Club*, *Weird Science*, and the rest of Hughes's filmography effectively extinct beyond allusions to it online.

This process of annihilation through adaptation would be fruitless if its only source texts were the cultural artifacts it made scandalous. As its name suggests, BuzzFeed Theory must also adapt critical theory, severing it from research methodologies and the productive conversations that ensue in academic environments. In *Culture and Imperialism*, Edward Said advocates for the contextualization of Empire's cultural products through the process of "contrapuntal reading," a strategy that "must take account of both processes, that of imperialism and that of resistance to it, which can be done by extending our reading of the texts to include what was forcibly excluded" (66–67). Although Said's critical approach is not apologetic, it also resists dismantling the canon, a view most clearly expressed in his chapter on Rudyard Kipling's *Kim* (1901) that probes the novel for its contradictions but does not dismiss its more anti-imperial stances. In contrast, the iterations of postcolonial, feminist, queer, and other critical lenses central to BuzzFeed Theory avoid such nuance, replacing the contrapuntal with the "problematic" or an endless stream of uninterrogated -isms and -ists—rhetoric that calls attention to the exclusions so important to Said but seems more interested in a text's fall from grace and installation of itself as omnipotent than any further investigation.

Adaptations may strive to replace their predecessors and annex their cultural clout, but, as Thomas Leitch argues in Chap. 10 of this collection, in general, adaptation theory "encourages us to ask another series of meta-questions about adaptation, cancelation, and censorship" (207). In Leitch's view, a film like *Gone with the Wind* (1939) can dislodge Margaret Mitchell's novel as the dominant iteration of the narrative, but it does not discourage comparison to the text. Rather, it acts as most adaptations do, in the words of Kamilla Elliott, to ensure "the survival of works into future generations" (48). Yet adaptations taking the form of BuzzFeed Theory actively repel such questions, accusing the adaptation theorist of complicity with the systems it dismantles for questioning the authority of its word and the dominion it has appropriated. They embody what Helen Pluckrose and James Lindsay call a "reified postmodernism" in which "[a] moral person aware of The Truth According to Social Justice must serve its metanarrative by actively asserting a Theoretical view of how the world works and how it ought to work instead" (183). Although many of the claims Pluckrose and Lindsay make about humanities departments in their controversial book *Cynical Theories* neglect the utility of critical theory such as Said's work in their cataloguing of extremes, this reified form of postmodernism is alive and well on the Internet in the form of BuzzFeed Theory as it exerts a greater influence on popular culture than the esoteric debates scholars have trained for all their lives, a force that threatens to cancel not only texts but also the type of critical inquiry Leitch sees as fundamental to adaptation studies (Pluckrose and Lindsay 183).

In recent years, critics have associated adaptation with infection—especially the concept of "going viral," as William Mooney discusses in Chap. 11 of this volume (213). Yet while the adaptations within the realm of BuzzFeed Theory aim to go viral to sustain their cultural impact, their dissemination mechanisms more closely resemble the bacterial. As viruses evolve, they become less lethal. Their primary goal, maximum reproduction and transmission, requires their host to stay alive. In his discussion of settler colonialism operating under a bacterial logic, Lorenzo Veracini differentiates it from the viral qualities of extraction colonialism: "Unlike viruses, bacteria *attach* to surfaces and form aggregations called biofilms or bacterial mats. Bacteria do not need living cells to reproduce. […] Likewise settler collectives attach to the land but generally do not need indigenous 'Others' for their reproduction and operation" (22). While most adaptation contexts aspire to a viral mutualism—an aspiration Elliott considers one of the likely reasons adaptation has served such a consistent role in various colonial projects—BuzzFeed Theory does not need to keep its host alive, but greatly benefits from the death of the source text, which permits it to grow exponentially without the threat of expert intervention

(80). Such terminology also highlights BuzzFeed Theory's blindness to its own reliance on settler colonial formations and class privilege. However, this bacterial relationship exists only between BuzzFeed Theory and its source text, not among the other adaptations in its online cycle. As Vivian Roese writes, "News media are economically dependent on social media and its users. Social media are economically dependent on the users and, to some extent, on news media. The users appear to be dependent on social media as part of their everyday lives and sources of information" (328). In the end, BuzzFeed Theory adapts with the hope that we too are the virus built on the foundation of its initial and deadly bacterial infection.

Within the context of this metaphor, Elliott's recent attempts to encompass adaptation's history and theorize it productively prove integral to developing strategies that better deal with the hybrid adaptations of BuzzFeed Theory that defend themselves by adopting the fluidity of postmodern relativism and replacing textual analysis with scandal. As Elliott writes: "Adaptation is not for aesthetic purists, political ideologues, or systemic cataloguers: it violates and exceeds their principles; it takes both sides of their theoretical debates and no side at all; it crosses boundaries, resists containment, resides outside borders, occupies middle grounds and no-man's land" (124). In situating BuzzFeed Theory within adaptation studies, scholars must conceive a textual situation that leaves no room for academic conversation, analysis, or interrogation—just obliteration. While the presence of Silicon Valley in developing the sites and apps where such discourse takes root seems to conform to Murray's industrial model of adaptation, BuzzFeed Theory flourishes outside the rights agreements and studio deals that govern the transitions of films into properties such as board games, soundtrack albums, and theme park rides. Like Meta, Twitter, and the other social-media sites so vital to its existence, outlets like *BuzzFeed* are disrupters, while competitors like *Vulture* under the umbrella of *New York* magazine are grasps at relevancy from legacy publications outmoded for the synergy-obsessed conglomerates in Hollywood.

In attempting to bring BuzzFeed Theory into the fold, adaptation studies has much to learn from anarchism. For Jesse Cohn, singular representations such as those central to BuzzFeed Theory serve as a dominating force that actively denies alternatives:

> Meanings (i) and (ii) are related but not coterminous; both are to some extent indeterminate and meanings in the second register will fluctuate depending on who is asking (and in what situation), but neither is indepen-

dent of the material actuality of the thing being investigated. In short, we hold that an *actual* text conditions its multiple *conditional* meanings for different readers in different times and places. This anarchist account of meaning has the distinct advantage of avoiding the pitfalls of antirepresentationalist theories. In ethically balancing the claims of self and other, it avoids the extremes of instrumentalism for which the other only exists as a use-value and a passive stance of letting-be. (88)

In their advocacy for a multiplicity of meanings and lack of boundaries within textual interpretations, both Elliott and Cohn signal a framework that acknowledges and absorbs the salient points BuzzFeed Theory raises while directly challenging its rigid ideology, disguised as do-gooderism, as well as its denial of its own ethical compromise. Cohn's discussion of conditional meanings is especially important to adaptation studies and notions of intertextuality that seek to situate a text in relation to material conditions and its sources. Approaching a film like *Weird Science* through the lens of broad and open inquiry underscores both the flaws in BuzzFeed Theory and its threat to the future of productive discourse on adaptation.

Weird Science and Resistant Adaptation

Before examining how *Weird Science*'s rich use of adaptation and rewriting make a case that BuzzFeed Theory's scandalmongering has resulted in its own problematics for our field, it is important to note that, like the seven other films Hughes both wrote and directed—*Sixteen Candles* (1984), *The Breakfast Club* (1985), *Ferris Bueller's Day Off* (1986), *Planes, Trains, and Automobiles* (1987), *She's Having a Baby* (1988), *Uncle Buck* (1989), and *Curly Sue* (1991)—it is based on an original screenplay. After writing *Home Alone* (1990), adapting *Uncle Buck* into a CBS sitcom that ran for one season during 1990–1991, and directing his final film, Hughes spent the last act of his career largely writing remakes and adaptations, including *Dennis the Menace* (1993), *Miracle on 34th Street* (1994), the live-action *101 Dalmatians* (1996), and *Flubber* (1997). *Weird Science* spawned a USA Network television series that ran for five seasons and reused the film's eponymous theme song by the New Wave band Oingo Boingo, led by Danny Elfman, which charted in 1985 and serves as an adaptation of the film in its own right. Though *Deadline* reported that the original film's producer, action-movie legend Joel Silver, was developing an R-rated remake in the style of *The Hangover* (2009) and *21 Jump Street* (2012), no news of the project has appeared since 2013 (Fleming). Accordingly, the primary space for *Weird Science*'s intertextual life has for the past two decades been the Internet, where its reputation has most recently remained in thrall to BuzzFeed Theory.

Despite its status as an original film, *Weird Science* voraciously adapts a host of source texts, incorporating them into its narrative to undercut the frat-boy misogyny of which so many of its detractors accuse it. My intent is not to discredit or trivialize critiques of the film's gender politics, many of which are legitimate. Instead, I take up Julie Sanders's call to "restore to the subgenres or practices of adaptation and appropriation a genuinely celebratory comprehension of their capacity for creativity, and for comment and critique"—goals clearly at odds with BuzzFeed Theory's reductiveness (160). *Weird Science* is a clear adaptation of Mary Shelley's *Frankenstein* (1818) that also reworks James Whale's *Frankenstein* (1931) and *Bride of Frankenstein* (1935), going so far as to edit colorized and black-and-white clips from Whale's sequel into the scenes leading to the montage of Gary and Wyatt creating Lisa. It also, according to Amanda Reyes, takes its title and much of its plot from the short-lived E.C. Comics series *Weird Science* (1950–53), especially the story "Made of the Future!" (1951), in which a man travels to 2150 and orders a wife he can grow in a bathtub (25). Reyes has made a compelling argument for the film as an adaptation of "Made of the Future!" But although Silver owned the film rights to E.C.'s entire library and was responsible for developing its horror comic *Tales from the Crypt* into an HBO series (1989–1996) and movie franchise (1995, 1996), he has fervently denied that the film is based on "Made of the Future!"—claiming that the adaptive impulse was limited to Hughes seeing a cover of the comic and coming up with the concept on the fly before writing the script over a weekend (Reyes 32). Since he held the rights and would likely have tried to cash in on the brand, given how lucrative *Tales from the Crypt* became, Silver had no financial incentive to deny the film was an adaptation (Fig. 1).

While *Weird Science* is often a frivolous film, its melding of Whale's *Frankenstein* adaptations, E.C.'s '50s aesthetic, and Hughes's now iconic take on the teen movie allows for direct commentary about adolescence and Cold War ideology, a topic the film explicitly broaches in its final act in an over-the-top sequence in which Gary and Wyatt accidentally conjure a nuclear missile instead of a second woman when they try to impress popular bullies Ian (Robert Downey, Jr.) and Max (Robert Rusler). As I have argued elsewhere, the five films in 1985's teen-science cycle situate

Fig. 1 Gary (Anthony Michael Hall) and Wyatt (Ilan Mitchell-Smith) cull the perfect woman from multiple sources in *Weird Science*

their presentation of classroom and extracurricular science within the context of *A Nation at Risk* at a time when the last days of the Cold War required a science-proficient generation that was also technologically savvy as the country began to experience the first threats to its superpower status from Asia's economic ascendancy. What resulted was the adoption of a new iteration of "yellow peril" in politics and pop culture present both in Hollywood cinema and in documents like *A Nation at Risk* (Hollyfield 74–75). Consequently, American teenagers in the 1980s found themselves in an impossible situation, dangerously undereducated by the school system, according to *A Nation at Risk*, and transitioning into an economy that exposed America's limitations in the world of global capital Reagan facilitated in which the specters of Marx were replaced by the ghosts of Orientalism's past.

Such economic concerns permeated the spaces teenagers inhabited to such an extent that they were inescapable. In their work on sites of teen socialization in American film, Steve Bailey and James Hay identify the home, the classroom, and the shopping mall as locations in which "[t]he articulation of the teenager as a 'mobile' subject becomes linked to a sense of the teen as a kind of well-rounded individual, occupying the place of a family member, a citizen-in-training and a consumer, and developing the ability to shift between all three subject positions as circumstances demand" (219). Bailey and Hay's work surveys teen films through the early 2000s, but their claims have especially direct relevance to a 1980s cinema preoccupied with teenagers who constructed their identities in a society that interrogated the efficacy of citizen training in the classroom and contemplated the teenager's place as consumer in homes and shopping malls overrun with imported goods widely perceived as threatening Reagan's American exceptionalism.

In addition, 1985 was the first full summer in which the PG-13 rating was widely adapted by studios after its introduction the previous July, an attempt at public service for parents that led Hollywood to target teen audiences with even more precision. Noting the rise of teen protagonists like Marty McFly (Michael J. Fox) in Robert Zemeckis's *Back to the Future*, Leitch views the trend as departing from previous relationships between Hollywood and teenage audiences, especially in the "[John] Hughes teen-bonding film" and "the psycho-slasher cycle" that "reflect and foster a specifically teenage sensibility quite without precedent in earlier American films" ("The World" 43–44). Leitch sees these new takes on teen movies, which feature adults primarily as either buffoonish (loser parents and bumbling cops) or threatening figures (draconian vice-principals, Jason Voorhees and Freddy Krueger), as "reassuring the audience that [growing up] will never happen to them at the same time they valorize adolescent values—directness, outspokenness, independence, self-idealization, the will to success—by arranging their triumph over the discredited adult values they oppose" (45).

Considering that the teen film first developed in the wake of the Hollywood studio system's collapse in the mid–twentieth century, its resurgence in the '80s appears a logical shift for the industry (Smith 11). Leitch's analysis is an apt assessment of this second wave of the genre. Yet the 1985 cluster of teen-science films is an outlier, deviating sharply from the adolescent-values mode. The toxic masculinity of weekend chaperone Chet Donnelly (Bill Paxton) serves as a central obstacle for his younger brother Wyatt and his best friend Gary amid *Weird Science*'s teenage-Frankenstein shenanigans. Rather than expressing a fear of adulthood, the adolescent characters in *Weird Science*—and those in the other four entries in the cycle—embrace an adulthood that preserves their teen values as a result of their pursuit of scientific endeavors under the guidance of adult mentors like *Back to the Future*'s Doc Brown (Christopher Lloyd) and Gary and Wyatt's dream girl Lisa, who model for their charges that true maturity hinges upon a personal ethics built on a critical inquiry rooted in science.

As a result, *Weird Science* is both aware of and playful in its use of the male gaze, a strategy Hughes largely achieves through his references to *Frankenstein* under the cloud of *A Nation at Risk*. In its devastating assessment of education in America, *A Nation at Risk* extends the Cold War's rhetoric to the classroom: "We have even squandered the gains in student achievement made in the wake of the Sputnik challenge. Moreover, we have dismantled essential support systems which helped make those gains possible. We have, in effect, been committing an act of unthinking, unilateral educational disarmament" (National 1). The comical level of scientific aptitude Gary and Wyatt exhibit, however, contradicts the report's stark portrayal of youth lacking education and technological skill. Tired of bullies and Friday nights alone, the boys become inspired by a late-night airing of Whale's *Bride of Frankenstein*, seamlessly transitioning to creating Lisa without any hesitation or research into the process. While Frankenstein collected body parts from cemeteries, Gary and Wyatt engage in postmodern cultural leveling to make their ideal woman. In a New Wave-scored montage, they easily hack into the Pentagon's Internet system and feed it a host of input items: pages ripped from their stash of *Playboys*, articles from *Sports Illustrated*, *Vogue*, and *Cosmopolitan*, sheet music, and photos of Einstein, Beethoven, and Houdini. As the program crafts a genius-level IQ for their creation, Gary exclaims, "It's working by itself!" before the duo attaches a scantily clad Barbie to wires in a parody of *Frankenstein*'s most famous scene that also includes a sudden and inexplicable lightning storm outside Wyatt's suburban home. As Timothy Shary writes of the sequence, "they want a voluptuous and smart woman who can fulfill their carnal *and* intellectual demands" (193).

While one could dismiss the film's allusions to Whale's *Frankenstein* films as merely clever, Hughes's choice to ground the movie in this intertextual relationship provides *Weird Science* with its ethical sensibilities. For David J. Skal, the mad scientist *Frankenstein* made famous serves as a figure who, "[i]nstead of pressing us to confront the serious questions of ethics, power, and the social impact of technological advances [...] too often allows us to laugh off notions that science might occasionally be the handmaiden of megalomania, greed, and sadism" (18). Gary and Wyatt may have created Lisa because of their egos and a desire for female companionship that is a by-product of their upper-middle-class entitlement. As Lisa assumes the role of mentor for the boys, however, she not only calls attention to their objectification of women and their inclination to flout wealth, but also molds them into more honest versions of themselves. As deeper feminist analyses of the film such as Alexandra Heller-Nicholas's essay for the Arrow Blu-Ray indicates, *Weird Science*'s entire point is centered on the boys' creation of a female who is too much woman for them: "In the face of her confidence, her attractiveness, her intelligence, and her kindness, which are products of their *exact* making, the result of their *exact* desires, they *still* can't handle her," a subtext most apparent in the scene where Gary and Wyatt shower with Lisa as Hughes tilts down to reveal that both boys are still wearing pants (15).

Although the film may endow Gary and Wyatt with mad-scientist tendencies, it also implies that without the aid of the military technology they hack into, Lisa would remain a two-dimensional AI barely able to pass a Turing Test. Whether or not Hughes directly adapted *Weird Science*'s "Made of the Future!" or just alluded to the series in the film's title, he bridges the military-industrial complex of the '50s and the Reaganite politics of the '80s. Throughout the early Cold War, science fiction increasingly adopted what J. Hoberman refers to as the "subversion scenario" that channeled nuclear anxieties and commented on the era's commie paranoia (306). Coupled with the manufactured juvenile delinquency scandal so well lampooned in films like Nicholas Ray's *Rebel Without a Cause* (1955), the nation was under a web of suspicion that linked the Reds to wayward youth. Such hysteria led to a Senate subcommittee hearing on the ties between the type of violent and grotesque comics E.C. printed and teenage deviance, which marked the beginning of the end for the publisher (Geissman 8). To combat this phantom threat, schools and other local authorities began implementing dress and behavior codes that, in light of the 1958 National Defense Production Act's increased funding for math and science instruction, aimed to cultivate a technologically adept generation equipped for the demands of the Cold War (Palladino 162, 171).

Working within *Weird Science*'s goofy sci-fi style and against *A Nation at Risk*'s warmed-over Sputnik rhetoric in his teen-bonding film mode, Hughes creates a parallel between the disciplined Cold War teen and what Susan Jeffords calls the "hard body" politics of Reagan's America—an ideology that valued "enveloped strength, labor, determination, loyalty, and courage" in contrast to the softness of computer nerds and couch potatoes as well as the disease-ridden bodies of the AIDS epidemic that clouded Reagan's presidency (24). While Lisa tries to mold Gary and Wyatt beyond their entitled softness, Hughes satirizes the hard-body concept through his portrayal of Wyatt's older brother Chet, a military cadet.

Throughout the film, Hughes pits Lisa against Chet as they vie for authority over Gary and Wyatt. Chet is abusive to the boys, blackmailing them for cash and electronics (largely made in Japan) while droning on and on about his military school training as his state of dress dwindles from underwear to a towel to full nudity by film's end. Chet is the rampant misogynist Twitter accused Hughes of being, objectifying Lisa instead of acknowledging her emotional maturity and intelligence, which the boys learn to value. In teaching Gary and Wyatt not only to be themselves but also to stand up to Chet, Lisa serves as a rebuke to the era's hard-bodied culture, a critique Hughes directly employs when Lisa turns Chet into a soft-bodied slime monster in the film's final act to force him to atone for his behavior (Fig. 2).

Weird Science's inventive use of adaptation to draw distinct links between historical periods in its meditations on masculinity and scientific ethics seriously challenges BuzzFeed Theory's dismissive assessment of it. One could adopt Pluckrose and Lindsay's critique of social justice warriors in the academy and online for the fallacy of operating under postmodern theory while exempting sanctioned ideologies from poststructuralist play and its march toward oblivion. While this view is suggestive, it reduces critical theory to the same type of oversimplified interpretations scandalmongers on social-media use to evaluate popular culture. A more helpful framework originates in Cohn's update of Bakunin's anarchist vision of art

Fig. 2 Chet (Bill Paxton) oozes the toxic masculinity typical of the '80s "hard body" in *Weird Science*

"that represents living beings in evolution and releases them from the ideas which they contain," which Cohn refers to as a "social anarchist aesthetic' ("Anarchism, Representation, and Culture"). However the field decides to address BuzzFeed Theory's online cycle of adaptation that this chapter discusses, *Weird Science*'s recent reception is but one example of how viral-ready Internet content that disguises its bacterial roots calls adaptation studies from the battle to dislodge fidelity into a world of evolution versus extinction.

References

Back to the Future. Directed by Robert Zemeckis, performed by Michael J. Fox and Christopher Lloyd, Universal, 1985.

Bailey, Steve, and James Hay. "Cinema and the Premises of Youth: 'Teen Films' and Their Sites in the 1980s and 1990s." *Genre and Contemporary Hollywood*, edited by Steve Neale, BFI, 2002, pp. 218–35.

Berman, David Elliot. "The Spaces of Sensationalism: A Comparative Case Study of the *New York Journal* and *BuzzFeed*." *International Journal of Communication*, vol. 15, 2021, pp. 4109–28.

Cheng, Susan. "Molly Ringwald and Ally Sheedy Explain Why *The Breakfast Club* Is Still Relevant Today." *BuzzFeed*, 24 Mar. 2015, https://www.buzzfeed.com/susancheng/why-there-hasnt-been-another-film-like-the-break. Accessed 1 Feb. 2022.

Cills, Hazel. "The Only Gender-Swapped Remake I Want to See Is *Weird Science*." *Jezebel*, 5 Apr. 2018, https://jezebel.com/the-only-gender-swapped-remake-i-want-to-see-is-weird-s-1825020058. Accessed 1 Feb. 2022.

Cohn, Jesse. "Anarchism, Representation, and Culture." *Culture and the State*, vol. 4, 2003, pp. 54–63.

Cohn, Jesse. *Anarchism and the Crisis of Representation*. Susquehanna University Press, 2006.

Elliott, Kamilla. *Theorizing Adaptation*. Oxford University Press, 2020.

Fleming, Michael Jr. "Universal, Joel Silver to Remake John Hughes Comedy *Weird Science*." *Deadline*, 18 Apr. 2013, https://deadline.com/2013/04/weird-science-remake-joel-silver-universal-477704/. Accessed 1 Feb. 2022.

Freeman, Hadley. "Times Move Pretty Fast! Rewatching 80s Favourites in the Age of #MeToo." *Guardian*, 13 Apr. 2018, https://www.theguardian.com/film/2018/apr/13/80s-films-molly-ringwald-john-hughes-metoo. Accessed 1 Feb. 2022.

Gaines, William M., and Al Feldstein. "Made of the Future!" 1951. *The E.C. Archives: Weird Science Volume 1*. Dark Horse, 2015, pp. 149–56.

Geissman, Grant. "Introduction." *The E.C. Archives: Weird Science Volume 1*. Dark Horse, 2015, pp. 7–8.

Hall, Dan. "Problematic Movies of the 1980s: *Weird Science*." *Literate Ape*, 1 Dec. 2018, https://www.literateape.com/blog/2018/12/1/problematic-movies-of-the-80s-weird-science-1985. Accessed 1 Feb. 2022.

Heller-Nicholas, Alexandra. (n.d.) "Electric Venus; or How I Learned to Stop Caring and Love *Weird Science*." *Weird Science* Blu-Ray liner notes, Arrow Video, pp. 7–20.

Hollyfield, Jerod Ra'Del. "Why is Everything so Heavy in the Future?": Science and *A Nation at Risk* in the American Teen Movies of 1985." *The Scientist in Popular Culture*, edited by Rebecca Janicker, Lexington, 2022, pp. 71–92.

Jeffords, Susan. *Hard Bodies: Hollywood Masculinity in the Reagan Era*. Rutgers University Press, 1993.

Julialaurane. "Which *Pretty in Pink* Character Are You Most Like?" *BuzzFeed*, 30 June 2018, https://www.buzzfeed.com/julialaurane/which-pretty-in-pink-character-are-you-25qi7. Accessed 1 Feb. 2022.

Leggett, Tabatha. "Everyone Has a Molly Ringwald Character Who Matches Their Personality—Here's Yours." *BuzzFeed*, 4 Apr. 2018, https://www.buzzfeed.com/tabathaleggett/which-molly-ringwald-character-are-you. Accessed 1 Feb. 2022.

Leitch, Thomas. "The World According to Teenpix." *Literature Film Quarterly*, vol. 20, no. 1, 1992, pp. 43–47.

Leitch, Thomas. "Adaptation and Censorship." *The Scandal of Adaptation*, edited by Thomas Leitch, Palgrave Macmillan, 2023, pp. 195–212.

Lewis, Seth C., and Logan Molyneux. "A Decade of Research on Social Media and Journalism: Assumptions, Blind Spots, and a Way Forward." *Media and Communication*, vol. 6, no. 4, 2018, pp. 11–23.

McClelland, Niamh. "Molly Ringwald Divides Twitter by Highlighting Problematic Elements of *The Breakfast Club*." *Daily Edge*, 7 Apr. 2018, https://www.dailyedge.ie/the-breakfast-club-3945916-Apr2018/. Accessed 1 Feb. 2022.

McIntush, Holly G. "Defining Education: The Rhetorical Enactment of Ideology in *A Nation at Risk*." *Rhetoric and Public Affairs*, vol. 3, no. 3, 2000, pp. 419–43.

Mooney, William. "Cinematic Contagion: *Bereullin* (*The Berlin File*, 2013)." *The Scandal of Adaptation*, edited by Thomas Leitch, Palgrave Macmillan, 2023, pp. 213–28.

Murray, Simone. *The Adaptation Industry: The Cultural Economy of Contemporary Literary Adaptation*, Routledge, 2012.

National Commission on Excellence in Education. *A Nation at Risk: The Imperative for Educational Reform*, U.S. Department of Education, 1983.

Palladino, Grace. *Teenagers: An American History*, Basic, 1996.

Pluckrose, Helen, and James Lindsay. *Cynical Theories: How Activist Scholarship Made Everything about Race, Gender, and Identity*, Pitchstone, 2020.

Reyes, Amanda. "Pictures from a Magazine: Reflecting on E. C. Comics' Influence on *Weird Science*." *Weird Science* Blu-Ray liner notes, Arrow Video, 2019, pp. 21–42.

Ringwald, Molly. "What About *The Breakfast Club*? Revisiting the Movies of My Youth in the Age of #MeToo." *New Yorker*, 6 Apr. 2018, https://www.newyorker.com/culture/personal-history/what-about-the-breakfast-club-molly-ringwald-metoo-john-hughes-pretty-in-pink. Accessed 1 Feb. 2022.

Roese, Vivian. "You Won't Believe How Co-Dependent They Are or: Media Hype and the Interaction of News Media, Social Media, and the User." *From Media Hype to Twitter Storm: News Explosions and Their Impact on Issues, Crises and Public Opinion*, edited by Peter Vasterman, Amsterdam University Press, 2018, pp. 313–32.

Said, Edward. *Culture and Imperialism*, Vintage, 1993.

Sanders, Julie. *Adaptation and Appropriation*, Routledge, 2006.

Shary, Timothy. *Generation Multiplex: The Image of Youth in Contemporary American Cinema*, U of Texas P, 2002.

Skal, David J. *Screams of Reason: Mad Science and Modern Culture*, Norton, 1998.

Smith, Frances. *Rethinking the Hollywood Teen Movie: Gender Genre, and Identity*, Edinburgh University Press, 2017.

Snydor, Emily. *Disrespectful Democracy: The Psychology of Political Incivility*, Columbia University Press, 2019.

Tryon, Chuck. *On-Demand Culture: Digital Delivery and the Future of Movies*, Rutgers University Press, 2013.

Veracini, Lorenzo. *The Settler Colonial Present*, Palgrave Macmillan, 2015.

Weird Science. Directed by John Hughes, performed by Anthony Michael Hall and Ilan Mitchell-Smith, Universal, 1985.

Williams, Bre. "Molly Ringwald Found John Hughes to Be 'Racist, Misogynistic, and, at Times, Homophobic' after Rewatching His Films That Made Her Famous." *Showbiz Cheatsheat*, 16 Jan. 2021, https://www.cheatsheet.com/entertainment/molly-ringwald-found-john-hughes-to-be-racist-misogynistic-and-at-times-homophobic-after-rewatching-the-directors-films-that-made-her-famous.html/. Accessed 1 Feb. 2022.

Yandoli, Krystie Lee. "Molly Ringwald Said Fans Thanked Her for Her #MeToo Essay On *Sixteen Candles* and *The Breakfast Club*." *BuzzFeed*, 15 Jan. 2019, https://www.buzzfeednews.com/article/krystieyandoli/molly-ringwald-metoo-breakfast-club-sixteen-candles. Accessed 1 Feb. 2022.

Adaptation and Scandal in *The Goldfinch*

Kate Newell

Carel Fabritius's *The Goldfinch* (1654), which measures a scant 33.5 cm × 22.8 cm, depicts a small goldfinch perched on a feeding box mounted to a wall. *The Goldfinch* went missing in the Delft Thunderclap of 1654, when a store of gunpowder housed in the cellar of a former convent exploded, destroying much of the city and contributing to the untimely death of thirty-two-year-old Fabritius. While much of Fabritius's work was believed to have been permanently lost, *The Goldfinch* resurfaced some 200 years later in Brussels, where it came to the attention of Théophile Thoré-Bürger, the French art critic also responsible for rediscovering Johannes Vermeer. The Mauritshuis in The Hague purchased *The Goldfinch* at a Paris auction in 1896 and it has remained in the public eye ever since.

The history of *The Goldfinch* is essential to understanding its position as a source text and its role within a broader adaptation network that includes Donna Tartt's 2013 Pulitzer Prize–winning novel and the 2019 film written by Peter Straughan and directed by John Crowley. The Delft explosion and consequent loss and reemergence of *The Goldfinch* opened a debate over what exactly audiences experience as *The Goldfinch* as they consider

K. Newell (✉)
Savannah College of Art and Design, Savannah, GA, USA
e-mail: knewell@scad.edu

© The Author(s), under exclusive license to Springer Nature Switzerland AG 2023
T. Leitch (ed.), *The Scandal of Adaptation*, Palgrave Studies in Adaptation and Visual Culture,
https://doi.org/10.1007/978-3-031-14153-9_7

its materiality, subject matter, and genre. This chapter examines the discursive scandals that shape iterations of and critical responses to *The Goldfinch*(es). "Scandal," as used here, signifies a rift between the expectations and experiences of a particular *Goldfinch*—a rift that prompts audiences to ask "What is it?" and come up with differing and even contradictory answers. As answers to this question, Tartt's novel and the 2019 film adapt the painting's subject matter, materiality, and history.

TROMPE L'OEIL OR STILL-LIFE: FABRITIUS'S *THE GOLDFINCH* (1654)

Fabritius's *The Goldfinch* is itself a type of adaptation, of course, capturing an impression of an already captured goldfinch. In the sixteenth and seventeenth centuries, goldfinches were common household pets that appear regularly in paintings. In many such cases, the bird plays a role in a larger scene, as in Hieronymus Bosch's *The Garden of Earthly Delights* (1495–1505), in which the goldfinch evokes fertility, and in Raphael's *Madonna del cardellino* (1505–1506), in which the goldfinch foreshadows Christ's crucifixion. Goldfinches could be trained to use a thimble to fetch water from a small pail fastened to their perch, as in Abraham Mignon's *Fruit Still-Life with Squirrel and Goldfinch* (second half of the seventeenth century) and Gerrit Dou's *A Girl in a Window with a Bunch of Grapes* (1662). Fabritius's painting depicts a small goldfinch perched on a feeding box mounted to a wall, painted ochre to resemble wall plaster. The box is slightly rectangular in shape, and two semi-circular perches—upper and lower—enclose the box in arcs of slightly different sizes; two support braces emerge from the base. The bird perches on the top band to the right of the box, its body turned to the right and its head facing the viewer; a metal ring encircles the bird's ankle and a slim chain tethers the bird to the perch. The realism with which Fabritius painted the bird and the perch, coupled with the verisimilitude of the background and the close cropping, suggests that *The Goldfinch* was intended as a trompe l'oeil designed to trick viewers into momentarily believing that they were seeing a real goldfinch. These qualities likewise place the painting in the broader generic categories of still life and portraiture (Fig. 1).[1]

---

[1] My goal here is not to suggest that trompe l'oeil and still life are exclusive genres, but rather to explore how the characteristics of trompe l'oeil or still life are emphasized in discussions of *The Goldfinch*.

Fig. 1 *The Goldfinch*, 1654 (oil on panel), Carel Fabritius (1622–54), Mauritshuis, The Hague, the Netherlands

Fabritius's early death and the unknown whereabouts of *The Goldfinch* in the period between the Delft explosion and the latter half of the nineteenth century have left many questions about the painting unanswered. Nonetheless, patterns emerge in how historians have "read" the painting by assigning it to a particular genre. For example, the National Galleries of Scotland label *The Goldfinch* a "portrait" and note that while the painting is consistent with Dutch tradition in choice of subject, Fabritius's "isolated depiction of the bird falls outside such traditions," rendering the bird's "meaning" as "more elusive." Emilie Gordenker, director of the Mauritshuis, likewise affirms that "what's unusual about Fabritius's painting [...] is that it is, as it were, a portrait. Before Fabritius, you find birds in genre paintings and landscapes, as well as dead birds in still lives. But to see one isolated in this way is revelatory" (qtd. in Sooke). Linda Stone-Ferrier highlights the ways in which *The Goldfinch* works within and outside of generic conventions, explaining that "Fabritius's *Goldfinch* offers a trompe l'oeil variation on seventeenth-century Dutch genre and still-life paintings, which consistently depicted goldfinches within prominent window-settings." Stone-Ferrier adds that, Fabritius "omitted characteristic details of the conventional site, which results in a tight focus and intimate scale." This variation "increase[s] the viewer's proximity to, and engagement with, the little bird" (2, par. 6). For art historian Walter Liedtke, Fabritius "raise[s] the stakes" of trompe l'oeil, "going beyond the imitation of solid forms and textures [...] to suggest the behavior of light and an actual movement—a twitching response—of the bird" (262). Discussions of Fabritius's *The Goldfinch* tend to follow this pattern, noting the ways in which the painting exceeds established expectations for trompe l'oeil in achieving intimacy and exceeds expectations for still life or portraiture by achieving this "trick of the eye."

In part, the attempt to understand *The Goldfinch* in terms of genre involves a debate over the painting's original method of display.[2] Fabritius made changes and additions to the painting after its initial creation that complicate efforts to settle on an original use or intention and suggest "the experimental or exploratory nature of the painter's artistic endeavor" (Stone-Ferrier 2, par. 6). Scans of *The Goldfinch* show that it was completed in two phases and suggest that Fabritius may have been uncertain about how he wanted the painting to communicate with viewers. *The Goldfinch* is painted on a very thick piece of panel that lacks beveling or other amendments that would point to its having been designed for display within a frame. While at one point Fabritius "hammered a gilded frame onto the panel," he later removed the frame "and extended the white paint of the plaster background to the panel's right edge." He also

---

[2] Stone-Ferrier provides a comprehensive overview of critical positions on the question of display. See in particular paragraphs 7–11, pages 2–3, and notes 7 and 9, which I summarize here.

"retouched his signature, and added the goldfinch's lower perch" (Stone-Ferrier 3, par. 7–8). Historians point to these additions as evidence that the painting was intended for display without a frame (Stone-Ferrier 3, par. 7–8). Furthermore, markings on the back and side and the remnants of a dowel on the right edge suggest that the painting was initially mounted as a sign for a shop or cabinet door. M.L. Wurbain proposes that *The Goldfinch* might have been commissioned by Cornelis de Putter, "a shoemaker, wine- and bookseller in The Hague," as the bird "may have alluded to the proprietor's name and also referenced his wares since *putten* in Dutch means 'pitching water or wine'" (Stone-Ferrier, note 7). Stone-Ferrier explains, though, that some historians dismiss this theory, arguing that such signs would have "typically exhibited the shop owner's name rather than the artist's signature." Mariët Westermann speculates that "Fabritius may well have embedded the small panel in a fake window, cabinet opening or wall to create a trompe-l'oeil effect." Similarly, Liedtke ventures that *The Goldfinch* may have appeared in the construction of a perspective box, and Ariane van Suchtelen and A.B. de Vries agree that "*The Goldfinch* probably functioned as a little door of a 'painting case'" (Stone-Ferrier, note 7).

This overview suggests that asking "What is it?" of *The Goldfinch* leads to different answers. Some material qualities signal *The Goldfinch* as not a conventional still life and others as not a conventional trompe l'oeil. Clearly, the painting can be both. Far from being "scandalous," *The Goldfinch*'s failure to conform to conventional generic standards is invoked in arguments that attest to "originality," a characteristic of masterpieces and source texts alike. The painting's status as "original," as source text, is confirmed both by its being displayed in a frame on a Mauritshuis gallery wall and by its reproduction on notebooks, glasses cases, shawls, tote bags, and other merchandise available for sale in the gift shop. Such acts of reproduction retain Fabritius's subject matter while experimenting with new materialities and genres. If *The Goldfinch* were to follow the path of most adaptation histories, its status as an "original" would designate the painting as the starting point of future iterations. In the next sections I explore the ways in which Tartt's novel and the 2019 film adapt Fabritius's painting, as well as the deprioritization of this "source" in critical discussions of those adaptation as adaptations.

Nature Morte and Donna Tartt's *The Goldfinch* (2013)

Tartt's novel adapts *The Goldfinch* eponymously as well as through meditations on the painting's broader themes and nods to the art historical discourse it inspires. The cover design, for example, alludes to the painting's simultaneous categorization as trompe l'oeil and still life. The front cover creates the illusion of Fabritius's *The Goldfinch* wrapped in white paper as if protected for storage or shipping, the bird detail visible only through a small tear. Here Fabritius's trompe l'oeil of a bird perched on a wall takes a back seat to that of a painting of a bird hidden behind paper—a more believable illusion in this new context and medium. For the 2015 trade paperback edition, the book's back cover features a thumbnail of Fabritius's painting presented, this time, as a wall-mounted still life. In this way, the design of the book participates in the discourse attending Fabritius's painting and foreshadows art critical observations voiced by the novel's characters (Fig. 2).

The painting's place in a tradition of art historical analysis is echoed in the title of the novel's fictional exhibition where it is first seen by the narrator Theo, "Portraiture and Nature Morte: Northern Masterworks of the Golden Age," and in the commentary on the painting provided by various characters.[3] For example, at the novel's close, Theo, considering the cultural significance of *The Goldfinch*, comments that Fabritius's focus on a live goldfinch "was in no way characteristic of his age and time, where animals featured mainly dead, in sumptuous trophy pieces, limp hares and fish and fowl, heaped high and bound for table" (765). Similarly, Horst, an underground art dealer Theo meets through his childhood friend Boris, reflects debates on *The Goldfinch*'s generic affiliation in his doubt as to whether Fabritius's painting is truly trompe l'oeil:

> [P]eople call it trompe l'oeil and indeed it can strike the eye that way from afar. But I don't care what the art historians say. True: there are passages worked like a trompe l'oeil. [...] But Fabritius ... he's making a pun on the genre ... a masterly riposte to the whole idea of trompe l'oeil ... because in other passages of the work—the head? the wing?—not creaturely or literal in the slightest, he takes the image apart very deliberately to show us how he

---

[3] While still life and nature morte are used interchangeably, the French phrase, as Michael Petry points out, is more "suggestive of the layered symbolism of the genre and its poignant reminders of the transience of life and the ever-present threat of death" (6).

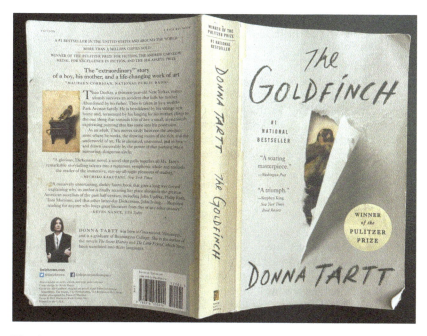

Fig. 2 Donna Tartt, *The Goldfinch*, cover, Back Bay Books, 2015

painted it. [...] There's a doubleness. You see the mark, you see the paint for the paint, and also the living bird. [...] The thing and yet not the thing. (578–79)

Such observations, drawn directly from scholarship on Fabritius's painting, educate Tartt's readers on how to understand *The Goldfinch* within a particular theoretical framework of illusion and play. Significantly, Tartt does not group *The Goldfinch* in a trompe l'oeil exhibition, but opts instead to place the painting within the critical context of still life and portrait, of paintings that communicate the "doubleness," the scandal, of representation more subtly.

Tartt adapts these generic considerations in other ways, most notably through Theo, whose perspective becomes determined by the last moments he spends with his mother in the exhibition before a terrorist bombing in the museum and who comes to understand his physical world through analogies to nature morte and forms of static visual representation. When Theo returns to the apartment he shared with his mother, for example, he describes the scene before him as though describing a still life painting:

> When I walked into the living room, I was confronted by a sweater of my mother's lying across the chair where she'd left it, a sky-blue ghost of her. Shells we'd picked up on the beach at Wellfleet. Hyacinths, which she'd bought at the Korean market a few days before she died, with the stems draped dead-black and rotten over the side of the pot. In the wastebasket: catalogues from Dover Books, Belgian Shoes; a wrapper from a pack of Necco Wafers. (193)

Theo's description of his home parallels his description of the "Portraiture and Nature Morte" exhibition upon first entering:

> Ruined banquet tables littered with peeled apples and walnut shells; draped tapestries and silver; trompe l'oeils with crawling insects and striped flowers. And the deeper we wandered, the stranger and more beautiful the picture became. Peeled lemons, with the rind slightly hardened at the knife's edge, the greenish shadow of a patch of mold. Light striking the rim of a half-empty wine glass. (23)

Within the tradition of still life, objects reflect the class and taste of the owner and imbue the scene with layered symbolism: Audrey's discarded sweater and collection of shells, of course, speak to her absence and the vacancy of home, and hyacinths signal a message of "forgive me" according to the Victorian "cult of florography" (Petry 22, 12–16).

Throughout the novel, when Theo is faced with the "What is it?" of an unfamiliar environment or situation, he turns to genres of artistic representation for answers. He describes the Barbours's home, where he goes to live temporarily after his mother's death, as "like those dioramas," "like those scenes with the taxidermy animals at the Natural History Museum" (167); the sun in Amsterdam as "hazed and gloomy, casting a low, weak, purgatorial light like a stage effect in some German opera" (700); and the clerk at the train station as "pillowy at the bosom and impersonally genial like a procuress in a second rate genre painting" (709). In adapting *The Goldfinch*, Tartt retains Fabritius's subject matter in the character of Theo, who like Fabritius's avian subject, chained to its perch and denied flight, remains immobilized by the memory of his dead mother. More broadly, however, Tartt adapts from the art historical discussion those questions of generic blur, the exploration of the space between reality and representation and the scandal of representation as "the thing and yet not the thing" (579).

"The Record of an Enthusiasm": Adapting *The Goldfinch* to Film

The 2019 film adapts Fabritius's painting through its color palette and more generalized evocations of still life, and Tartt's novel through its characters and story. The film participates, though this is less openly announced than in Tartt's novel, in the art historical discourse generated in response to Fabritius's painting as well as in the literary critical discourse attending Tartt's novel, and anticipates the form of its own critical analysis. In an interview with Trevor Hogg, Crowley explains that, though Fabritius's painting "is central to the plot," differences between painting and film create "a tricky balance because it's almost as if they talk different languages." He clarifies, "When you experience a painting in a gallery, you stand in front of it and your experience is immediate. The camera," by contrast, "does something to the surface of a painting, which mean[s] that you [can't] rely on the power of the original painting." The film attempts to generate an aesthetic emotional experience and to evoke painterly qualities through visual analogies and references to still life, and to reinforce the impact of specific artworks on individuals through images of Fabritius's *The Goldfinch*.

The film's evocation of Fabritius's painting and nature morte is evident from the opening shot, which may recall for viewers familiar with Tartt's novel Theo's description upon first entering the "Portraiture and Nature Morte" exhibition: "The walls glowed with a warm, dull haze of opulence, a generic mellowness of antiquity" (23). In the opening sequence, the camera tracks down a hotel corridor designed and lit in colors analogous to those of Fabritius's painting: glowing tones of gold, brown, and ochre. The sequence includes a series of dissolves and panning shots of discarded newspapers and hotel dishware with remnants of coffee and half-consumed meals that recall Tartt's catalogs of objects and other references to the genre of still life. Further, the sequence includes images of Theo (Ansel Elgort) at a desk writing goodbye letters in preparation for his suicide superimposed over a nature morte of a skull and feather hung on the hotel room wall. This type of painting, called a vanitas still life, offers, Michael

Petry explains, "a commentary that pair[s] symbols of the joys of a life well lived with symbols of death" (9). The superimposition joins the cinematic and painted image into a vanitas composite that reinforces the transience of Theo's life of excess and materiality and the futility of his earthly obsessions.

Still life invites contemplative reflection on the commonplace and subtle atmospheric changes, and the film evokes analogies to the genre at various moments, as in the scene depicting the journey of young Theo (Oakes Fegley) to and arrival in Las Vegas, where he has been moved by his father (Luke Wilson) in the wake of his mother's death. Xandra (Sarah Paulson), Theo's father's girlfriend, gives Theo a Vicodin to steady his nerves for the flight. Visibly disoriented under the influence of the drug, Theo stares at the space between himself and the seat in front of him, mesmerized by the dust particles circling seemingly suspended. The camera lingers in this moment, inviting viewers to contemplate the space as Theo does. Similarly, an aerial shot of the Las Vegas subdivision to which Theo moves offers what might be described as an architectural nature morte, with roads that end abruptly in the desert, sand moving in rhythmic waves through abandoned properties and housing structures, and the general omnipresence of death and decay. The scene in which Theo encounters Welty Blackwell (Robert Joy) in the wake of the explosion also invites atmospheric contemplation as the camera settles on the gray expanse of dust and dark, framing a composition reminiscent of studies by Turner and Monet.

Compared to Tartt's novel, in which Fabritius's painting plays a visible and central role, the painting seems largely absent from the film adaptation. The *Washington Post*'s Stephanie Merry observes, "In the book, when Theo isn't looking at the painting [...] he's thinking about it. It's a constant source of anxiety and fascination but also solace." In the film, by contrast, the painting "barely makes an appearance." Fabritius's painting does appear physically in a handful of scenes, but mostly only the verso is visible. For example, when Theo encounters Welty in the gallery of the museum immediately following the explosion, Welty tells Theo to "take it," pointing to an object lying in the rubble. The camera shows only the verso as Theo puts the painting hastily in his bag. When packing to leave New York for Las Vegas, Theo wraps the painting in newspaper, but the camera again shows only the verso. And when Boris and Theo reunite in New York as adults, Boris proves that he has the painting by showing Theo a photograph of the verso. Commonly, the film signifies the painting through a bundled package, as when, in a drug-inspired flashback, the adult Theo recalls writing a letter to young Pippa (Aimée Laurence) telling her how unhappy he is in Las Vegas, and, in an imbedded flashback-within-the-flashback, Pippa asking, "Do you remember your mother?" The film depicts Theo curled in a fetal position on the floor of his bedroom clutching the bundled painting as he describes his mother to Pippa in voiceover. In each instance, the painting functions as a deeply personal object, a fetish for a greater loss or absence. Rather than attempt to create the immediate experience of standing in front of *The Goldfinch*, the film attempts to create corollary moments of emotional impact.

If the scenes focused on the verso underscore personal connections to *The Goldfinch*, those focused on the recto underscore the painting as a public cultural artifact that unites individuals in a common experience. The film's opening sequence features an image of *The Goldfinch* on the floor of the museum covered in dust from the explosion. Theo, in voiceover, relates: "It doesn't matter that I'm going to die. But for all time, for as long as history is written, that painting will be remembered and mourned." The film returns to this image toward its close as Theo's voiceover tells the story of Fabritius, the explosion at Delft, and the painting's survival. In this sequence, the camera alternates between shots of the young Theo and his mother at the museum and the explosion and shots of the older Theo preparing to overdose in his hotel room in Amsterdam. Other than the obvious link between the painting and Theo's grief, these alternations establish a link between the appreciation of art and the appreciation of life—a link further reinforced in the last ten minutes of the film, which emphasize visually the human connection built through shared experiences of art. This closing sequence, including a flashback to a moment when Theo's mother (Hailey Wist) shares with him details about techniques of the Dutch masters as they walk through the galleries, concludes with Theo and his mother standing before *The Goldfinch* next to Welty and Pippa, the four visually united in their common appreciation of the painting. In such moments, the film distinguishes between the deep personal connection individuals form with certain art objects, the object's "cult value," in Walter Benjamin's terms, and the role of the object as a cultural artifact, the object's "exhibition value" (224–26). The "cult" moments use the verso to signify the physical object as a repository of Theo's memories of his mother, whereas the "exhibition" moments use the recto to signify the masterwork that is *The Goldfinch* to audiences within and outside of the film's diegesis.

The film's non-linear structure and prioritization of character and psychological reconciliation inflect the story's meditation on questions of art and representation. The film adapts the painting and the related art historical discourse in a manner that remains yoked to character development and revelation. Unlike the novel, which includes passages of exposition voiced by the characters, the film's meditation occurs largely through Theo's voiceover as the camera displays specific reference points and art objects in full view and in close-up. This slideshow presentation focuses attention on select details from specific works that haunt or interest Theo and provides fewer moments of generalized aesthetic contemplation. In an interview with Rebecca Pahle, Crowley says that, with *The Goldfinch*, he and writer Peter Straughan were interested in making a "piece of *cinema* [...] as opposed to just an adaptation." With this distinction, Crowley indicates that he wanted to make a film that would stand alone as an example of its medium, independent of its association with Tartt's novel. The repeated pairing of voiceover and visual positions the cinematic apparatus as the epitome of art historical lecturer and film as the generalized visual masterpiece into which all others, including Fabritius's *The Goldfinch*, are imbedded. Despite this bold assertion of medial authority, the film, in retaining the painting's and novel's titles and subject matter, foregrounds its own position within an adaptation network and anchors its own creative course.

What Is It? Critical Responses to *The Goldfinch*(es)

Like the painted bird in a window that passersby mistakenly take for a real one, unique characteristics of each adaptation challenge audiences' expectations about medium and genre and force the question, "What is it?" However, whereas Fabritius's work was praised as "revelatory" (Gordenker) and stake-raising (Liedtke) for exceeding and expanding expectations, both Tartt's novel and the 2019 film faced criticism for generic disunity and disappointing audiences' expectations about Pulitzer Prize–winning novels and film adaptations. In their attempts to make sense of *The Goldfinch*(es), many critics propose situating these works in related or unrelated genres and media, and sidestep any close consideration of the announced relationship to Fabritius's painting. This practice removes the work from its adaptive legacy, downplays the intentionality of any genre play, and in so doing heightens the sense of scandal.

Audiences of Tartt's *The Goldfinch* turn to genre categorization to describe the novel's pacing and, in some cases, to resolve the rift between their expectations and experience of this work. Evgenia Peretz labels *The Goldfinch* "a sprawling bildungsroman." *Kirkus Reviews* calls the novel a "lovely addition to what might be called the literature of disaster and redemption." Christopher Tayler of the *London Review of Books* describes *The Goldfinch* as "a consciously neo-Victorian romp," "a kind of displaced 9/11 novel," and a "picaresque story." For the *New Yorker*'s James Wood, *The Goldfinch*'s "tone, language, and story belong to children's literature"—a view seconded by Tayler. Anthony Domestico comments on the challenge of classifying Tartt's novel: "*The Goldfinch* is not a work of literary realism. It uses many of the tools of that genre, but in pursuit of different ends" (29). Reading Tartt's novel in light of mixed genres could generate new methods of responding to adaptation, as Domestico and other reviewers suggest; instead, though, that Tartt's novel does not fitly neatly into a single undisputed generic category magnifies its scandalous nature.

Rather than unpack how Tartt's "pursuit" expands generic expectations in the fashion of Fabritius, reviewers more commonly underscore the novel's stylistic similarities to recognizable literary works and authors, such as Charles Dickens, an evident influence on this and her two previous books, *The Secret History* (1992) and *The Little Friend* (2002). Michiko Kakutani calls Fabritius's painting "the MacGuffin at the center of [Tartt's] glorious, Dickensian novel." She adds that "Ms. Tartt is adept at harnessing all the conventions of the Dickensian novel—including startling coincidences and sudden swerves of fortune." Stephen King writes, "Like the best of Dickens [...] the novel turns on mere happenstance," and points to the manner in which specific characters find corollaries in Dickens. Similarly, *USA Today*'s Kevin Nance writes that the novel is "full of moral confusion, hairpin plot turns and, best of all, a vivid, rather raucous cast of characters drawn with the fond yet gimlet-eyed insight of Charles Dickens, whose spirit hovers over this book like a guardian angel" (see also Jacklosky). Reviewers mention Fabritius's painting as a plot point or recurring symbol of Theo's grief, but rarely as a source text.

Responses to the 2019 film, by contrast, are so deeply rooted in comparisons to Tartt's novel as the nominal source text that despite Crowley's best intentions, few focus on the film as an example of cinema. Some noted exceptions include *VultureHound*'s Tom Beasley, who praises the film for "real moments of visual splendour," and Linda Marric, who lauds its "moments of unfathomable beauty." Wenlei Ma particularly praises cinematographer Roger Deakins: "The way he lit the Las Vegas sequences is truly stunning, the ochres of the bone-dry desert blended in with the striking blues of the night sky." Ricky Church is one of the few critics to note "how many of the colour hues resemble the Goldfinch painting." Commonly, reviewers approach the 2019 film as an adaptation, yet that classification does not fully resolve the question "What is it?" The critical consensus is that *The Goldfinch* is both too faithful to Tartt's novel and not at all like it. Marric calls the film "an ambitious yet decidedly muddled adaptation" that is "primarily let down by its inability to break away from the original source material." *Hyperallergic*'s Dan Schindel describes *The Goldfinch* as "more a transplantation of the book's plot than an invested adaptation," and *Variety*'s Owen Gleiberman labels it a "faithful-in-a-literal-way yet somehow skittery cinematic transcription of" the novel. Most critics attribute the film's failures to the very structural features Crowley employed to make a "piece of *cinema* [...] as opposed to just an adaptation" (Pahle). *The Guardian*'s Simran Hans reads Crowley's and Straughan's inventions as a sign that, "intimidated by their source material," they "rearrang[ed] the novel's linear chronology into a fractured, jumbled timeline." Similarly, for Church, the film "feels more like a collection of mini-episodes throughout Theo's life." Richard Brody, writing for *The New Yorker*, describes the film as taking Tartt's "teeming plot" and "trim[ing] [it] to index-card snippets detached from a sense of place."

Like Tartt's novel, the film frustrates those who expect generic conformity. Gleiberman calls the film a "a kind of glazed picaresque," and describes it as "a thematically organized but disjointed drama that sometimes feels like three separate movies jammed together." Similarly, Allen Almachar, reviewing the film for *The MacGuffin*, writes that "the tonal shifts of this story—or stories—varies [sic] so wildly that you'll be watching one type of movie and then ten minutes later will be watching something completely different." Unable to quite make sense of *The Goldfinch* as a film, some reviewers turn to analogies to visual works in other media. A.O. Scott likens the film to "a Pinterest page or piece of fan art, the record of an enthusiasm that is, to the outside observer, indistinguishable from confusion." Gleiberman describes the film as a "labored live-action illustration" and Joseph Walsh as "a series of elegant tableaux" whose "overall effect" is "akin to the porcelain mannequins in a store window at Christmas." Although remarks on the film's aesthetic stillness are made in support of arguments on the film's failure as an adaptation, these same comments point to key features of the film as an adaptation and features of *The Goldfinch*'s adaptation history overall.

The tendency to respond *The Goldfinch*(es) in terms of media or genres outside the work—a children's book, a Pinterest page, an illustration—can limit audiences' understanding of this work, or indeed any work, and its role as a cultural artifact. Rather than read Tartt's novel in terms of Fabritius's *The Goldfinch*, for example, evoking Dickens directs the path of response toward influences and intertexts. As Matthew Sherrill challenges, foregrounding "*Dickensian* [...] denies, then, as it must, a certain amount of *Tarttness*. And isn't it in part the critic's job to suss out what that *Tarttness* might be?" At the same time, however, considering works in light of unannounced signposts also point to a common strategy by which adaptation networks expand. Approaching Tartt's novel as an adaptation of *Oliver Twist* or *David Copperfield* expands our understanding of adaptation and adaptive influence in directions not possible if we limit the sphere of adaptation to Fabritius's painting. Similarly, reading Tartt's novel through the lens of disaster fiction likewise results in a different understanding of the novel than reading it through the lens of children's literature. Likewise, reading the 2019 film through the lens of Pinterest invites reflection on medial and generic similarities between cinema and web-based social media—a line of inquiry quite different from that of the similarities between cinema and illustration.

"The Thing and Yet Not the Thing": (Not-So-) Scandalous Adaptation

The scandal of *The Goldfinch*(es) is the scandal of trompe l'oeil: "the thing and yet not the thing." The initial play between trompe l'oeil and still life, between expectation and experience, evident in Fabritius's painting and developed in the critical discourse, shapes the adaptation strategies of *The Goldfinch*(es) as well as their critical response. The 2019 film's moments of stillness, for example, temporarily "trick the eye" and invite viewers to see through the technology of the moving image to see the still image. Tartt's use of signifiers of disaster fiction may "trick" readers into believing that they are reading one type of book, only to "trick" them again by folding in signifiers of children's literature. *The Goldfinch*(es)' mediation on trompe l'oeil unfolds as well at the story level through Theo's work as an antiques restorer who tricks unknowing clients into believing that a composite cobbled together in the shop's workroom is "the thing"—for example, an authentic Chippendale highboy. The meditation on trompe l'oeil shows up also in the critical response. Scott quips that the 2019 film "looks and sounds like a movie without quite being one." Domestico, considering Tartt's use of fairy tale tropes, concludes: "Tartt hasn't written a pure fairy tale. Instead, she has written a novel that, on its surface, looks an awful lot like a work of conventional literary realism" (29).

That such "tricks" are perceived as such reinforce the challenges of adaptation—how to represent a creative work in a manner that is believable and authentic to the broadest range of audiences. For many audiences, the pleasure of adaptation lies in the "doubleness," the play between bird and paint, between the original and the reproduction, between the source and the adaptation (Tartt 579). To many audiences this play may not be evident, and therein lies yet another scandal: some passersby may see only the bird; some viewers may take the film as the book. The fear that an "original" may go unnoted or uncelebrated as superior, expressed most commonly in critical and popular responses to adaptations, can interfere with the ability to appreciate "the experimental or exploratory nature of the [...] artistic endeavor" (Stone-Ferrier 2, par. 6). Each iteration of *The Goldfinch* generates an interpretive disconnect as audiences attempt to answer the question "What is it?" The answer commonly highlights a range of genres and styles evident in the work or to which the work can be compared. As a critical approach, comparison ensures that we never arrive at "the thing," but, rather, base our understanding of a work on varied layers of "yet not the thing." The elements of 2019 film that stand out to Scott as more in keeping with a Pinterest page or fan experience, for example, need not negate the work's role as a film nor be assumed to be unintentional; rather, the play between film and seemingly external intermedial and intermodal signifiers can be explored as meaningful features of the adaptation process. The challenges evident in *The Goldfinch*(es)' adaptation network are those of adaptation studies in general, which likewise remains caught in a dilemma of how to discuss adaptations as adaptations without having categories of "the thing" and "yet not the thing" overdetermine that discussion. In an enterprise as multiform as adaptation, the lines between such categories are always shifting. Rather than continue perpetuate divisions between "the thing" and "yet not the thing," *The Goldfinch*(es), through the tandem lenses of still life and trompe l'oeil, invite us to conceptualize seeming divisions as essential to the comprehensive whole.

Acknowledgments I am grateful to David A. Stivers, who offered invaluable feedback on early drafts of this chapter.

References

Almachar, Allan. "Film Review—*The Goldfinch*." Review of *The Goldfinch*, directed by John Crowley. *The Macguffin*, 12 Sept. 2019, https://macguff.in/film-reviews/the-goldfinch/. Accessed 13 June 2021.

Beasley, Tom. "'It Was My Fault, Just Like Everything That's Happened Since'– The Goldfinch (Film Review)." Review of *The Goldfinch*, directed by John Crowley. *VultureHound*, 29 Sept. 2019, https://www.vulturehound.co.uk/2019/09/it-was-my-fault-just-like-everything-thats-happened-since-the-goldfinch-film-review/. Accessed 13 June 2021.

Benjamin, Walter. "The Work of Art in the Age of Mechanical Reproduction." *Illuminations* edited by Hannah Arendt, translated by Harry Zohn, Schocken, 1968, pp. 217–42.

Brody, Richard. "The Goldfinch." Review of *The Goldfinch*, by Donna Tartt. *New Yorker*, vol. 95, no. 28, 23 Sept. 2019, http://www.newyorker.com/goings-on-about-town/movies/the-Goldfinch. Accessed 20 Sept. 2020.

Church, Ricky. "Blue-ray Review–The Goldfinch (2019)." Review of *The Goldfinch*, directed by John Crowley. *FlickeringMyth.com*, 7 Dec. 2019, http://www.flickeringmyth.com/2019/12/blu-ray-review-the-goldfinch-2019/. Accessed 20 Sept. 2020.

Domestico, Anthony. "Bookmarks | Fairy Tales Are More Than True." *Commonweal*, 4 Dec. 2014, https://www.commonwealmagazine.org/bookmarks-fairy-tales-are-more-true. Accessed 13 Aug. 2020.

Fabritius, Carel. *The Goldfinch*. 1654, Mauritshuis, The Hague, Netherlands.

Gleiberman, Owen. "Toronto Film Review: 'The Goldfinch.'" Review of *The Goldfinch*, directed by John Crowley. *Variety*, 8 Sept. 2019, http://www.variety.com/2019/film/reviews/the-goldfinch-review-ansel-elgort-1203325606/?sub_action=logged_in. Accessed 20 Sept. 2020.

Hans, Simran. "*The Goldfinch* Review—The Plot Thickens to Sludge." Review of *The Goldfinch*, directed by John Crowley. *Guardian*, 28 Sept. 2019, https://www.theguardian.com/film/2019/sep/28/the-goldfinch-film-review-donna-tartt-ansel-elgort-sarah-paulson. Accessed 2 Apr. 2021.

Hogg, Trevor. "Uncaging a Narrative: How 'The Goldfinch' Director John Crowley Brought an Epic Tale from the Page to the Screen." Review of *The Goldfinch*, directed by John Crowley. *Sound and Picture*, 30 Sept. 2019, http://www.soundandpicture.com/2019/09/the-goldfinch-director-john-crowley/. Accessed 2 Apr. 2021.

Jacklosky, Rob. "'The Thing and Not the Thing': The Contemporary Dickensian Novel and Donna Tartt's *The Goldfinch* (2013)." *Dickens After Dickens.* Edited by Emily Bell. White Rose UP, 2020. DOI: 10.22599/DickensAfterDickens.

Kakutani, Michiko. "A Painting as Talisman, as Enduring as Loved Ones Are Not." Review of *The Goldfinch*, by Donna Tartt. *New York Times*, 7 Oct. 2013, http://www.nytimes.com/2013/10/08/books/the-goldfinch-a-dickensian-novel-by-donna-tartt.html. Accessed 5 May 2021.

King, Stephen. "Flights of Fancy." Review of *The Goldfinch*, by Donna Tartt. *New York Times*, 10 Oct. 2013, http://www.nytimes.com/2013/10/13/books/review/donna-tartts-goldfinch.html. Accessed 24 Oct. 2020.

Kirkus Reviews. "The Goldfinch." Review of *The Goldfinch*, by Donna Tartt. 22 Oct. 2013, http://www.kirkusreviews.com/book-reviews/donna-tartt/the-goldfinch/. Accessed 24 Oct. 2020.

Liedtke, Walter, et al. Vermeer and the Delft School, exh. cat., Metropolitan Museum of Art/Yale UP, 2001, pp. 260–63.

Ma, Wenlei. "The Goldfinch isn't a disaster, but it's not great either." Review of *The Goldfinch*, directed by John Crowley. *Courier Mail*, 26 Sept. 2019, http://www.couriermail.com.au/entertainment/movies/the-goldfinch-isnt-a-disaster-but-its-not-great-either/news-story/d045df7b-f9ec6f4aaf191c5233137470. Accessed 5 May 2020.

Marric, Linda. "The Goldfinch review: It is a beautifully shot mess of a film." Review of *The Goldfinch*, directed by John Crowley. *HeyUGuys*, 28 Sept. 2019, http://www.heyuguys.com/the-goldfinch-review/. Accessed 24 Oct. 2020.

Merry, Stephanie. "'The Goldfinch' movie left a lot of the book out—but not what you'd expect." Review of *The Goldfinch*, directed by John Crowley. *Washington Post*, 13 Sept. 2020, http://www.washingtonpost.com/entertainment/books/the-goldfinch-movie-left-a-lot-of-the-book-out%2D%2Dbut-not-what-youd-expect/2019/09/13/65dfd6f2-d62f-11e9-9610-fb56c5522e1c_story.html. Accessed 5 May 2021.

Moore, Fernanda. "Oliver Twit: A review of Donna Tartt's *The Goldfinch.*" *Commentary*, Dec. 2013, http://www.commentary.org/articles/moore-fernanda/oliver-twit/. Accessed 5 May 2021.

Nance, Kevin. "With 'The Goldfinch,' Donna Tartt proves her greatness." Review of *The Goldfinch*, by Donna Tartt. *USA Today*, 20 Oct. 2013, http://www.usatoday.com/story/life/books/2013/10/20/the-goldfinch-donna-tartt-review/3004303. Accessed 5 May 2021.

National Galleries Scotland. "The Goldfinch." Exhibition, 4 Nov. 2016–18 Dec. 2016. http://www.nationalgalleries.org/exhibition/goldfinch.

Norton Simon Museum. "Significant Objects: The Spell of Still Life." Exhibition, 20 July 2012–21 Jan. 2013, http://www.nortonsimon.org/exhibitions/2010-2019/significant-objects-the-spell-of-still-life.

Pahle, Rebecca. "Cinema Gold: John Crowley Takes on a Literary Behemoth with *The Goldfinch*." *Boxofficepro.com*, 11 Sept. 2019, https://www.boxofficepro.com/john-crowley-the-goldfinch-interview/. Accessed 05 May 2020.
Peretz, Evgenia. "It's Tartt—But Is It Art?" *Vanity Fair*, 11 June 2012, https://www.vanityfair.com/culture/2014/07/goldfinch-donna-tartt-literary-criticism. Accessed 19 Dec. 2020.
Petry, Michael. *Nature Morte: Contemporary Artists Reinvigorate the Still-Life Tradition*, Thames and Hudson, 2013.
Schindel, Dan. "Short on Substance, *The Goldfinch* Falters on Screen." Review of *The Goldfinch*, directed by John Crowley. *Hyperallergic*. 10 Sept. 2019, https://hyperallergic.com/516828/goldfinch-movie-review/. Accessed 20 Sept. 2020.
Scott, A.O. "'The Goldfinch' Review: Strictly for the Birds." Review of *The Goldfinch*, directed by John Crowley. *New York Times*, 11 Sept. 2019, http://www.nytimes.com/2019/09/11/movies/the-goldfinch-review.html. Accessed 20 Sept. 2020.
Sherrill, Matthew. "Ditching *Dickensian*." *Paris Review*, 30 Apr. 2014, http://www.theparisreview.org/blog/2014/04/30/ditching-dickensian/. Accessed 20 Sept. 2020.
Sooke, Alastair. "The Intriguing Mystery of *The Goldfinch*." *BBC*, 12 Dec. 2016, http://www.bbc.com/culture/article/20161207-the-intriguing-mystery-of-the-goldfinch. Accessed 2 Feb. 2020.
Stone-Ferrier, Linda. "The Engagement of Carel Fabritius' Goldfinch of 1654 with the Dutch Window, a Significant Site of Neighborhood Social Exchange." *Journal of Historians of Netherlandish Art*, vol. 8, no. 1 Winter 2016, DOI: https://doi.org/10.5092/jhna.2016.8.1.5.
Tartt, Donna. *The Goldfinch*, Little, Brown, 2013.
Tartt, Donna. *The Goldfinch*, Back Bay, 2015.
Tayler, Christopher. "Death among the Barbours." Review of *The Goldfinch*, by Donna Tartt. *London Review of Books*, 19 Dec. 2013, http://www.lrb.co.uk/the-paper/v35/n24/christopher-tayler/death-among-the-barbours. Accessed 19 Dec. 2020.
The Goldfinch. Directed by John Crowley, written by Peter Straughan. Amazon, 2019.
Walsh, Joseph. "The Goldfinch Review—a Pale Reproduction: Adaptation of Donna Tartt's novel is less than the sum of its parts." Review of *The Goldfinch*, directed by John Crowley. *Theartsdesk.com*, 27 Sept. 2019, http://www.theartsdesk.com/film/goldfinch-review-pale-reproduction. Accessed 19 Sept. 2020.
Wark, Kirsty. "Donna Tartt Shares *The Goldfinch*'s Secret History." *BBC Culture*, 28 Oct. 2013, http://www.bbc.com/culture/article/20131028-donna-tartt-on-the-goldfinch. Accessed 1 March 2020.
Wood, James. "The New Curiosity Shop." Review of *The Goldfinch*, by Donna Tartt. *New Yorker*, 14 Oct. 2013, http://www.newyorker.com/magazine/2013/10/21/the-new-curiosity-shop. Accessed 19 Dec. 2020.

Scandalous Dystopias: Hyping *The Last of Us Part II* and *Cyberpunk 2077* During the Pandemic

Daniel Singleton

Few events disrupted established media playbooks like the COVID-19 pandemic. As movie theaters closed, high-profile movies were delayed or dumped onto streaming platforms. But the Great Hibernation seemed like a godsend for video games. Console manufacturers Sony and Microsoft had already been planning to replace the PlayStation 4 and Xbox One with next-generation upgrades, the PlayStation 5 and Xbox Series S/X, by the 2020 holidays, and developers had been preparing a slew of games for machines new and old. The highest-profile games were adaptations: sequels like *Animal Crossing: New Horizons* and *Doom Eternal*, prequels like *Half-Life: Alyx*, and remakes like *Resident Evil 3* and *Final Fantasy VII Remake* of popular game series; licensed games like *Marvel's Avengers*, an action-adventure game based on Disney's eponymous franchise; and officially sanctioned homages like *Ghosts of Tsushima*, a samurai action

D. Singleton (✉)
Pittsburgh, PA, USA

© The Author(s), under exclusive license to Springer Nature Switzerland AG 2023
T. Leitch (ed.), *The Scandal of Adaptation*, Palgrave Studies in Adaptation and Visual Culture,
https://doi.org/10.1007/978-3-031-14153-9_8

game approved by the estate of Akira Kurosawa. Pandemic lockdowns increased the hype for these games. Millions of people could not attend movies, concerts, or sports, but they could sit on the couch playing video games for weeks or months. But soon lockdowns began to upend publishers' best-laid plans (Schreier).

This chapter explores the ways in which the pandemic scandalized two of 2020's most highly anticipated releases: *The Last of Us Part II* and *Cyberpunk 2077*. These case studies will reveal how thoroughly the process of adaptation pervades the production as well as consumption of video games, setting the stage for scandals that erupt under the wrong conditions. Both games built enough hype to justify their ballooning budgets and nearly decade-long development cycles by adapting a range of other media in complex ways. *The Last of Us Part II* is a sequel to an older game, *The Last of Us* (2013), which itself adapts zombie movies like *28 Days Later* (2003) and TV shows like *The Walking Dead* (2010–2022). The games would also be adapted into HBO miniseries in late 2022 or early 2023. *Cyberpunk 2077* is nominally based on the cult tabletop roleplaying game *Cyberpunk 2020*, which itself adapted gameplay from the fantasy-themed *Dungeons & Dragons* to the cyberpunk dystopia of William Gibson's novel *Neuromancer*. But it would also outfit a familiar game genre—the open-world sandbox game—with cyberpunk iconography from *Blade Runner* (1982) and *The Matrix* (1999). Adaptation has been imbricated in every stage of game production from design to marketing. On the design front, producers use existing media properties or even entire genres as well as time-honored gameplay mechanics to reassure risk-averse investors of games' broad marketability. Adaptation also plays a crucial role in hyping games. Marketing departments use the promise of adaptation—the alluring potential to play around with familiar worlds—to capture players' attention in an increasingly oversaturated market.

The COVID-19 pandemic exposes the risks of this approach. Hyping games in relation to other media texts can increase their visibility, but these associations risk creating expectations that can quickly exceed producers' control. It was difficult for Naughty Dog and Sony to balance *The Last of Us Part II*'s competing impulses to be a sequel to the first game, an homage to prestige TV shows like *The Walking Dead*, and an extended teaser for an HBO miniseries. It was even harder for CD Projekt Red (CDPR) to fulfill *Cyberpunk 2077*'s promise of playing with retro-futuristic sci-fi gizmos and gadgets in time for Christmas. These gaps between expectations and reality might have gone unnoticed if the games had been released under more favorable conditions, but scandals exploded as the pandemic disrupted the games' carefully planned releases, leading to delays, leaks, and disappointments.

PRESTIGE TV, PLOT SPOILERS, AND PANDEMICS IN *THE LAST OF US PART II*

The first major casualty of the pandemic was *The Last of Us Part II*. The hype machine framed the game as both a long-awaited sequel to *The Last of Us* and a prelude to an upcoming HBO miniseries. When the developers at Naughty Dog Studios and the publishers at Sony delayed the game in the early days of the pandemic, a few irate hackers released game footage spoiling the unexpected death of a major character from the first game. The ensuing scandal revived debates about how sequels should extend their precursors as well as broader culture-war narratives about everything from the pandemic to cancel culture to social justice campaigns.

The Last of Us games show how completely even avowedly original games are packaged in relation to other media. The first game was sold as an original horror game from the creators of *Uncharted* (2007–2017). Those games had adapted the platforming action from *Tomb Raider* (1996–2022) and Naughty Dog's *Crash Bandicoot* (1996–2020), which itself can be seen as Sony's answer to Nintendo's *Super Mario Brothers* games (1985–2017), to tell the story of Indiana Jones wannabe Nathan Drake. *The Last of Us* would mix and match mechanics from *Uncharted* with mechanics from survival-horror games like *Resident Evil* (1996–2021) to cast players as the stars of a post-apocalyptic story modeled on films like *28 Days Later* (2003) and *Children of Men* (2006) and TV shows like *The Walking Dead*. It takes place in 2033, twenty years into a viral pandemic that has turned billions of people into insane flesh-eating zombies. Players control Joel (Troy Baker), a hardened loner whose daughter was killed during the first outbreak, as he guides Ellie (Ashley Johnson), an orphaned teenager who is miraculously immune to the virus, on a cross-country journey from a military quarantine zone in Boston to a resistance outpost outside Salt Lake City. In addition to adapting character archetypes and dramatic scenarios from other zombie media, the game also adapts the visual style of a mid-2000s prestige television show. Most plot points are conveyed through non-interactive cutscenes. Even the interactive sections are so carefully choreographed that some players felt as if they were not so much characters in the fiction as actors hitting their marks.

The Last of Us marries the survival-horror gameplay of Resident Evil and Silent Hill (1999–2012) to storylines that recalled TV shows like The Walking Dead in a belated rejoinder to Roger Ebert's infamous declaration that games can never be art (Ebert). These acts of adaptation enable The Last of Us to reset the media hierarchy that positioned video games as subordinate to movies and television. (Ironically, the medium's poor reputation was partly sustained by the preponderance of licensed video game adaptations that were commissioned and rushed into production to promote popular blockbusters.) The Last of Us changes these perceptions by changing its approach to adaptation. Rather than directly adapting existing texts or tacking onto existing franchises, the game integrates the conventions of zombie media with familiar gameplay mechanics to tell its own distinct if generic apocalypse story. The effect is to create a sense of cinema-plus, in which the traditional pleasures of watching interesting characters in dire situations are enhanced by players' participation.

When it was announced in 2016, The Last of Us Part II was framed in two ways. First, it was the paradigmatic video game sequel. Although sequels in every medium are expected to send familiar characters on new variations on old adventures, sequels to popular games must also satisfy medium-specific expectations to push technology to new heights of graphical photorealism. Prerelease marketing promised that The Last of Us Part II would upgrade its predecessor's graphics, refine its gameplay, and expand its story. Many fans were particularly eager to see how Naughty Dog would expand upon the first game's shocking ending, in which Joel, who has already lost his biological daughter to the pandemic, murders the innocent surgeons who are trying to synthesize a vaccine from Ellie's brain at the cost of killing her. Second, the sequel would also double down on its precursor's debt to prestige television. To help write the second game, lead designer Neil Druckmann recruited Halley Gross, a writer on HBO's Westworld (2016–). As the second game neared completion, he announced plans to collaborate with Craig Mazin, the showrunner of Chernobyl (2019), on an HBO TV series based on both Last of Us games to be released in late 2022 or early 2023 (Shanley). These announcements further hyped The Last of Us Part II not just as the paradigmatic video game sequel or an interactive HBO TV show but as the first game to warrant its own Masterpiece Theatre–style adaptation.

Naughty Dog and Sony's carefully laid plans for the game's launch crashed when the World Health Organization declared COVID-19 to be a pandemic, sending millions of people into lockdown and forcing entire industries to transition to remote work overnight. Many observers expected that games that had been tentatively scheduled for release in late 2020 or early 2021 would be delayed. Naughty Dog delayed the game because "we couldn't launch *The Last of Us Part II* to our satisfaction" (@NaughtyDog, "A Message from Us"). Instead of being released the following month, the game would presumably debut after the pandemic ended. This indefinite delay outraged gamers, some of whom had been waiting for seven years to see what happened to Joel and Ellie next. Three weeks later, on 27 April 2020, outraged fans hacked into Naughty Dog's servers and released more than an hour of unreleased game footage onto YouTube. The leaks were initially rumored to come from disgruntled employees rebelling against the controversial practice of "crunching" for twelve or more hours a day, seven days a week, for months or years, to meet ambitious deadlines (Franzese, "Devastating"), but it was later learned that outside hackers had exploited security vulnerabilities on Naughty Dog's servers (@jasonschreier).

These leaks hint at how the sequel will further cast itself as an HBO show-in-waiting by adopting one of prestige television's most familiar conventions: the surprising, incredibly violent deaths of major characters. In these clips, Joel is brutally beaten to death with a golf club by a muscular woman named Abby. The footage was accompanied by a list of levels revealing the game's unusual narrative structure: early levels would follow Ellie on a revenge quest in Seattle, but later levels would repeat the same sequence of events from Abby's perspective. The broad outlines of the story were clear. Abby is the daughter of a doctor killed by Joel at the end of the first game. She would kill Joel to avenge her father's death. Then Ellie would travel to Seattle to avenge Joel by killing Abby (Hernandez). As in prestige television shows like *The Sopranos* or *Breaking Bad*, these plot twists would complicate players' identification with characters by challenging their active decisions to perpetuate circular cycles of violence.

Naughty Dog immediately scrubbed the leaked material from the internet and announced a new release date of 19 June 2020. But the damage had been done. For the next three months, countless videos, memes, and descriptions of the leaks were posted onto social media platforms like Reddit and YouTube. When Naughty Dog recognized that social media were even more viral than the deadly infections depicted in their games, the studio would helplessly default to a counterintuitive strategy of using social media to discourage people from using social media: "We know the last few days have been incredibly difficult for you. We feel the same. […] Do your best to avoid spoilers and we ask you don't spoil it for others. [The game] will be in your hands soon. No matter what you see and hear, the final experience will be worth it" (@NaughtyDog, "A Message from the Studio"). But resisting the temptation to avoid googling the phrase "Last of Us spoilers" for another two months turned out to be a hard sell for homebound gamers who had hoped to escape from the horrors of 2020, which had come to encompass racial unrest and a growing partisan divide about COVID's severity, by playing a dystopian zombie game for 40 h.

The viral spoilers became anti-trailers that damaged many fans' perceptions of the game, and the outrage only intensified as more gamers played the game and experienced these twists themselves. Three days after its release, the game had received nearly 16,000 more negative reviews than positive ones. The reviews drove the game's user score down to 4/10, dramatically lower than the 95/100 score awarded to the game by professional reviewers. Fans' debates about how the story developed characters, plot points, and thematic questions from the first game are informed by adaptation. Some gamers defended the plot twists on the grounds of structural similarity to the first game, which had already shifted the players' perspective from Joel to Ellie to distance them from the former's cruelty and selfishness. Haters attacked Naughty Dog for "destroy[ing] characters we loved" and then glamorizing their sworn enemy (@krnmxd). Many fans hoped for a nostalgic retread of the first game, and they read Joel's death as a slap-in-the-face repudiation of these desires. Few seemed to appreciate how the game had adapted conventions of prestige TV shows, notably their tendency to kill off beloved characters.

Adaptation enters the debate in other ways. Many fans were incensed at the supposedly duplicitous marketing tactics used to hype the game. The prerelease trailers had shown Joel following Ellie to Seattle, but the leaked footage included alternative versions of these scenes that replaced Joel with Ellie's friend Jesse. Gamers complained that Naughty Dog had doctored footage to maximize the shock of Joel's death in the opening levels (Person et al.). The ugliest comments on social media adapted the leaks into culture-war narratives about the ideology of mainstream media. A small but very loud contingent of irate players inserted the game into culture-war battles about identity. When they discovered how Abby would befriend the transgender teen Lev, they accused the developers of being social justice warriors pushing an agenda (Glennon et al.). Misogynists harassed and threatened Laura Bailey, the actress who played Abby. Conspiracy theorists sent the Israel-born Druckmann "death threats, anti-Semitic remarks, and just craziness I never could have anticipated. I knew people would get upset at a character they love dying. I never thought it would reach this kind of hate" (Kinda Funny Games).

Every stage of this scandal was informed by adaptation. *The Last of Us Part II* courted scandal by adapting prestige TV series that delight in disrupting expectations and dividing fans but then subordinating its identity as an extended teaser for an HBO miniseries to its status as a long-awaited sequel to a popular game. Its developers sparked controversy by indefinitely delaying the game during the pandemic, prompting disgruntled hackers to post out-of-context spoilers onto YouTube. The spoilers disrupted the official narrative, punctured the game's aura, and reframed players' experience. Players spent the next three months debating whether the developers were justified in killing their favorite characters. The links to the beloved first game and prestige television shows generated great expectations for the game, but these expectations spiraled out of control due to the centrifugal force of adaptation. Because there were so many sources informing how people read the games, individual users had plenty of room to scramble the hierarchy of sources.

The conditions were ripe for misunderstandings in 2020. Even though very few people mentioned the eerie, if not uncanny, parallels between the game's fictional pandemic and the real-life pandemic raging outside their apartments, the scandal would have been unimaginable without COVID. The outrage over what happened during the game's fictional pandemic suggests how millions of homebound people were adapting to the real-life pandemic. The bipartisan solidarity about COVID had waned by April 2020, replaced with partisan bickering about masks and lockdowns. Even though some players had lost interest in playing "a downer game about a pandemic" (OverHaze), most players seemed to be counting on escaping from the real-world dystopia into a fictional one. "The last of us 2 is now real life," wrote one player, "but the game is cancelled" (Series). At the halfway point of 2020, the bleak outlook for fighting COVID-19 made it more important for the sequel to be a power fantasy than a meditation on violence. On some level, the game's violent fights for survival would be an emotionally cathartic outlet for working out frustration about real-world events. Players could express their anger at people who were imposing or flouting mask mandates by stabbing digital zombies in the throat. When delays threatened to make it impossible for players to ride out the pandemic playing this game, fans adapted by turning anger on the developers. These conditions would fuel the next video game scandal less than six months later.

Corporate Capitalists and Movie Stars in the Digital Dystopias of *Cyberpunk 2077*

The troubled production and scandalous release of *Cyberpunk 2077* show how adaptation can increase the potential for controversy. Although the game was pitched as an adaptation of the cult tabletop roleplaying game (RPG) *Cyberpunk 2020* when it was first announced in 2012, it increased its public profile by gradually accumulating more story elements from cyberpunk media and mechanics from popular games. Each new trailer promised that cutting-edge graphics and gameplay would immerse players in dystopian cities drawn from novels like *Neuromancer* and films like *Blade Runner* (1982) and *Strange Days* (1995); it would even team them up with Keanu Reeves, the star of *Johnny Mnemonic* (1995) and *The Matrix* (1999). But the developers struggled to synthesize so many books, movies, and games that when the game was released on 10 December 2020, its graphical glitches, broken mechanics, and unimaginative take on cyberpunk made it all but unplayable, and players vented their outrage on social media. When the game's futuristic dystopia proved incapable of distracting players from the real-world turbulence of 2020, players adapted by immersing themselves in scandal.

The developer of *Cyberpunk 2077*, CD Projekt Red (CDPR), has a long history making video game adaptations. This Polish software company was founded in 1994 to localize English-language games into Polish and port games across hardware systems. In 2008 it launched an online storefront, GOG.com, to sell ports of "abandonware," or games with lapsed copyrights or bankrupt publishers. When a PC port of the fantasy-action console game *Baldur's Gate: Dark Alliance* (2001) was canceled, CDPR repurposed its assets for another series of games based on *The Witcher* books. This series of Polish fantasy novels, published between 1986 and 1999 by Andrzej Sapkowski, follows the escapades of Geralt the Witcher, a mercenary who kills monsters with magic. The books have been popular in their native country, inspiring a Polish television adaptation in 2001.

CDPR employees credit the books with turning them into fantasy fans. Perhaps this explains why all three games—*The Witcher* (2007), *The Witcher 2: Assassins of Kings* (2011), and *The Witcher 3: Wild Hunt* (2015)—play like unauthorized fan fiction (O'Dwyer). The game rewrites the climax of Sapkowski's last novel, *The Lady of the Lake* (1999). In that novel, Geralt dies in a bloody riot. In the game, however, he is rescued by his fellow Witchers and awakens without any memories of his past exploits (Super Bunnyhop).

Sapkowski, who dismissed the games as cheap fanfiction, would even try to reclaim the franchise symbolically by publishing another book in 2013 (Purchese). But most Polish fans enjoyed resurrecting Geralt for non-canonical adventures, and American newcomers to the franchise— English translations of the books were not published until 2007—appreciated how the trope of amnesia excused them from reading several supplementary novels. For many American players, the games offered Eastern-European variations on Tolkienesque fantasy tropes with gameplay mechanics like a quest structure, combat mechanics, and dungeon design adapted from popular RPGs like *Neverwinter Nights* (2002) and *Elder Scrolls IV: Oblivion* (2006) (Super Bunnyhop). The first two *Witcher* games were cult hits, but the third was a bona fide blockbuster that won more than 250 Game-of-the-Year awards from media outlets and trade organizations and sold more than 30 million copies, compared to the 1 million copies the game had sold during the year after its release (Lee). It would even inspire an original Netflix series starring Henry Cavill. The former Superman star was an avid gamer who had played *The Witcher 3* twice, always assumed that Sapkowski's books were spinoffs of the games, and even based his version of Geralt on Doug Cockle's performance of the character in the games (Wasserman; White). Fans and series newcomers immersed themselves in CDPR's digital facsimile of Geralt's world. In short, *The Witcher* games take more circuitous paths to the center of their transmedia franchise than *The Last of Us*. Even though these officially licensed game adaptations of cult fantasy books act like fanfiction on a narrative level, they quickly supplant their sources and become the model for subsequent entries in the franchise.

The *Witcher* games also created design templates and framed expectations for their next project, *Cyberpunk 2077*. The game was billed as a spiritual successor to *The Witcher* when it was announced in 2012. It would also adapt another piece of cult fiction, the tabletop RPG *Cyberpunk 2020* (1988), which itself adapts the format of *Dungeons & Dragons* for the cyberpunk cycle of science-fiction of the early 1980s. *Cyberpunk 2077* would let players participate in near-future dystopian decay that they had only read about in books or seen in movies and play with advanced technologies like artificial intelligence and cybernetics. CDPR proactively authenticated *Cyberpunk 2077* as an officially licensed sequel to the tabletop game by hiring creator Mike Pondsmith to "extrapolate what has happened since the 4th Corporate War in 2024 all the way up to the 2077 timeline" (Grayson, "Mike Pondsmith"). CDPR also commissioned Pondsmith to produce *Cyberpunk Red* (2020), a module set in 2045 that would bridge the gaps between the tabletop and video games (Hall). Early reports promised a "realistic, violent, and mature game just like *The Witcher*" with "a non-linear story where your decisions affect the outcome" that would "cite cyberpunk touchstones like William Gibson's fiction and *Blade Runner*" and "adhere to the archetypal cyberpunk style" (Onyett). The success of *The Witcher 3* raised expectations that *Cyberpunk 2077* would also boast beautifully lifelike graphics, large open-world maps, and deep roleplaying systems. But soon the expectations would start spiraling out of CDPR's control.

By the time *Cyberpunk 2077* entered production in 2016, its scope and budget had expanded to include even more cyberpunk media as well as other games. Prerelease trailers depict a late twenty-first-century cyberpunk city named Night City after the setting of *Neuromancer*, which has been widely credited with kickstarting the cyberpunk genre. Its neon-noir aesthetic, dominated by dangerous streets that are doused with blinding lights and drenched in heavy rain, is modeled after cult blockbusters like *Blade Runner*, *Strange Days* (1995), and *Akira* (1988). Like Sapkowski, Gibson was unimpressed by the project: "The trailer [...] strikes me as [*Grand Theft Auto*] skinned-over with a generic 80s retro-future, but hey, that's just me" (@GreatDismal). But most people were excited about the game's potential. It promised to insert the complex cyberpunk roleplaying of the *Deus Ex* games (2000–2016) into a hyperrealistic, seemingly infinitely interactive open world à la *Red Dead Redemption II* (2018), Rockstar's epic Western video game. The game seemed poised to fulfill the promises of both the science-fiction genre and the video games medium to immerse players in other worlds. Books and movies could depict imaginary worlds through words or images, but only games could let them interact with cyberpunk gadgets like bodily augmentations, virtual realities, and artificial intelligence. By adapting cyberpunk content into game form, *Cyberpunk* would become the Ultimate Video Game, the platonic ideal of modern big-budget gaming as well as the harbinger of its glorious next-gen 4K future.

This strategy of hyping the unfinished game in relation to other texts culminated in a press event at the 2019 Electronic Entertainment Expo. The event began with another trailer focused on the story in which two hackers, V and Jackie Wells, steal a microchip from the Arasaka Corporation. The job goes south; Jackie is killed; and when V sells the microchip to gangster Dexter DeShawn, he is unceremoniously shot. But somehow V survives, and the last shots of the trailer show his perspective as he wakes up in a garbage dump. "Wake up, samurai," a gruff voice shouts as the camera tilts up to reveal Keanu Reeves. Reeves points a robotic hand at the camera as he speaks the last line: "We've got a city to burn." As the trailer fades to black, Reeves walks onto the stage to pitch the game:

> They go on and on about how they'd create this vast open world with a branching storyline, how you'd be able to customize your character through in-game choices. [...] *Cyberpunk* is set in a metropolis of the future where body modification has become an obsession. You play as an outlaw, an enhanced mercenary working in the sleazy underbelly of this city. [...] Let me tell you. The feeling of being there, of walking the streets of the future, is really going to be breathtaking. ("Cyberpunk 2077")

Nobody had known that Reeves would be participating in the game, let alone appearing at E3. Hundreds of conference attendees and hundreds of thousands of social media users exploded with excitement at the prospect of conquering a dystopian cyberpunk city alongside a digital Keanu. But players' responses suggest that their expectations varied depending upon which sources they knew. Players of *Cyberpunk 2020* recognized Reeves's character as Johnny Silverhand, a rockstar-terrorist with a metal arm who had been killed while raiding Arasaka's headquarters in 2013. For others, the actor's strong association with the sci-fi films *Johnny Mnemonic, The Matrix, A Scanner Darkly* (2006), and the three *John Wick* movies (2014–2019) authenticated the game as a Next-Gen Cyberpunk Experience. The bullet-time sequences in *The Matrix* had inspired games from *Max Payne* (2001) to *F.E.A.R.* (2005). It seemed as if the industry had finally managed to catch the eye of its star (Rogers).

The cyberpunk connection increased the hype for the game, but it also concealed the troubled state of its production. Even though the game was scheduled for release on 16 April 2020, less than ten months away, it was nowhere close to being finished. Developers became bogged down by "feature creep" as they struggled to integrate mechanics from across the history of tabletop and video games with story elements from seemingly every important cyberpunk text. They also struggled to adapt the game for nine consoles and potentially infinite PC configurations. And like Naughty Dog, they struggled to adapt their business practices to COVID. But even though frequent delays leading up to the game's eventual release on 10 December 2020 should have been warning signs of the game's unfinished state, nobody questioned the official publicity, their credulity testifying to the ways the promise of adaptation can entice audiences to personalize hype. Since the game was more concept than code, CDPR sold it through hyperbolic comparisons to other media and trusted players to fill the gaps. The references in publicity material to books, movies, tabletop games, and video games transformed *Cyberpunk 2077* into the ultimate cyberpunk experience. Players could imagine *Cyberpunk 2077* to be virtually anything they wanted, depending on which sources they had encountered.

But the gambit of hyping the unfinished game by hiding it behind a veil of other texts was bound to backfire because too many references created too many conflicting expectations for players or developers to manage. The hype was punctured a few hours after the game's release on 10 December 2020. Much outrage centered on technical problems; social media users posted JPGs and GIFs of hilarious bugs and infuriating glitches as well as downgraded graphics and sluggish performance on current-generation consoles (Cryer). These technical problems led Sony to make the unprecedented decision to delist the game indefinitely from its online storefront (Serrels). Other criticism focused on the game's broken, seemingly unfinished approximations of outdated mechanics from other games. The team behind *The Witcher 3* had promised to reinvent the RPG genre for cyberpunk sci-fi, but players were disappointed to find a mishmash of familiar mechanics like the leveling system of *Skyrim*, the skill trees of *Far Cry*, the carjacking of *Grand Theft Auto*, and the dialogue wheels of *Mass Effect*.

Other criticism focused on the game's static, superficial, and anachronistic adaptation of cyberpunk sci-fi. As Noah Caldwell-Gervais points out, when *Blade Runner*, *Neuromancer*, and *Cyberpunk 2020* imagined the early twenty-first century from their vantage point in the 1980s, they imagined how unregulated tech corporations would produce mind-blowing but dehumanizing technologies like desktop computers,

Bluetooth earpieces, text messages, web browsing, and VR headsets. But littering the Night City of *Cyberpunk 2077* with these technologies ironically makes the game feel more retro-nostalgic than futuristic. Its stark divisions between rich and poor—the luxurious downtown district is dominated by impressive skyscrapers and plastered in neon ads for body modifications, but the dilapidated outskirts are littered with junked cars and other scraps from an industrial past—are virtually identical to those in modern American cities from Chicago to San Francisco, suggesting that very little will have changed fifty years into the future. As Caldwell-Gervais said, the once futuristic cyberpunk worlds of *Neuromancer* "no longer feel much like the future, and that nostalgic fidelity muffles the punk part of it."

As with *The Last of Us Part II*, these criticisms of technical and design problems are suffused with outrage about unethical marketing of games. Fans engage in heated debates about whether developers should make "fake" trailers from curated footage produced on industrial-grade PCs that few players could afford even before the pandemic exacerbated microchip shortages and supply chain delays. Even though it has long been common for games marketing to boast only the most impressive looking sections that players might encounter, fans objected to the ways the duplicitous marketing aligned CDPR with the soulless media corporations in cyberpunk sci-fi instead of heroic rebels like Neo or Johnny Silverhand. Caldwell-Gervais calls it "a high-profile reminder that corporate capitalism doesn't care if you hate it. In fact, it can take that hate, package it in neon and chrome, and sell it right back to you for $60."

The game's pro-corporate take on cyberpunk became even more scandalous in the context of the scandals of 2020, which drove institutional distrust to an all-time high. As with the zombie pandemic in *The Last of Us Part II*, *Cyberpunk*'s dystopian setting enhanced its utopian potential as the ultimate distraction. Its endlessly immersive, infinitely interactive open-world gameplay seemed like the perfect way to fill the time opened by the cancelations of sports, concerts, and family gatherings. And even though Night City was, if anything, even more divided by climate change, economic inequality, and political polarization than the real world, its bright, colorful art direction and engaging mechanics seemed far more appealing than doom-scrolling through clickbait about the end of the world (Statt, "Cyberpunk 2077"). When the game proved to be an unfinished jumble of popular mechanics and cyberpunk clichés, fans took cues from Johnny Silverhand and refused to pay CDPR for the privilege of being beta testers. Picking up threads of adaptation laid by the developers, some fans posted GIFs of bugs on Twitter or made video critiques for YouTube even as others created mods and patches to fix the worst issues. Hackers even breached CDPR's servers, downloaded the game's source code, and auctioned it on eBay with a starting bid of $1 million dollars (Statt, "Cyberpunk and Witcher Hackers"). The game's reputation would slowly improve as disagreements between management and development came to light and as developers released patches throughout 2021. By then, however, players were already having more fun adapting the game into real-life variations of the archetypal cyberpunk scenario in which solitary hackers use their wits and computers to outwit evil corporations.

Conclusion

Both of these games released in 2020, *The Last of Us Part II* and *Cyberpunk 2077*, are so conceptually complex and technically complicated that they would have been hard for developers to make or publishers to sell under ideal circumstances. But the pandemic unleashed the seeds of scandal that had been planted by adaptation. Leading up to the games' release, adaptation—the promise of guiding familiar characters or playing around generic worlds—generates expectations, hype, and interest. But when *The Last of Us Part II* was delayed and *Cyberpunk 2077* was released too soon, the specter of other texts started contributing to their perceived weaknesses. These gaps between expectations and reality inspired players to adapt the games yet again. Outraged players posted critical GIFs, memes, and videos to media platforms like Reddit, Twitter, and YouTube, trashing these games in relation to other titles and prerelease marketing. Other fans hacked into the companies' servers and released game footage or code online. The games were inserted into broader cultural narratives. *The Last of Us Part II* seemed to cancel the beloved original game to satisfy a "social justice warrior" agenda. *Cyberpunk 2077* seemed like a soulless corporate cash grab, a paint-by-numbers collage of story elements from cyberpunk media and gameplay mechanics from every popular game of the last 5 years.

In short, players adapted to the pandemic more readily than developers and publishers did. The scandalous releases of these complex game adaptations upended the industry's carefully laid plans, but they gave players an excuse to participate in one of the closest substitutes for human contact during the pandemic: arguing about video games on the internet with strangers. It might seem as if the video games industry has revealed how media adaptations unexpectedly follow a Darwinist position: the survival of the fittest. Video game production is too time-consuming, laborious, and expensive for developers and publishers to adapt to pandemic isolation, remote working conditions, supply chain disruptions, and microchip shortages. But gamers adapted to these real-world problems by making video game consumption more disposable, by subordinating the experience of playing games to the work of making memes, tweets, and videos about them.

REFERENCES

@GreatDismal "The trailer for Cyberpunk 2077 strikes me as GTA skinned-over with a generic 80s retro-future, but hey, that's just me." *Twitter*, 10 June 2018, https://twitter.com/greatdismal/status/1005958197654351872?lang=en. Accessed 2 Feb. 2022.

@Naughty_Dog. "A message from the studio." *Twitter*, 27 Apr. 2020a, https://twitter.com/Naughty_Dog/status/1254840504182665219?s=19. Accessed 1 Feb. 2022.

@Naughty_Dog. "A message from us about the delay of The Last of Us Part II." *Twitter*, 2 Apr. 2020b, https://twitter.com/naughty_dog/status/1245773177944281089?lang=en. Accessed 2 Feb. 2022.

Super Bunnyhop. "Replaying The Witchers." *YouTube*, 26 June 2015, https://www.youtube.com/watch?v=ZohodiFCOTU. Accessed 2 Feb. 2022.

Byrd, Christopher. Review of *The Last of Us Part II*. *Washington Post*, 12 June 2020, https://www.washingtonpost.com/video-games/reviews/last-us-part-ii-one-best-video-games-ever-made/. Accessed 1 Feb. 2022.

Caldwell-Gervais, Noah. "What Kind Of Game Did Cyberpunk 2077 Turn Out To Be, Anyway? [SPOILERS]." *YouTube*, 6 Mar. 2021, https://www.youtube.com/watch?v=lWEkeqJ2djM&t=4724s. Accessed 3 Feb. 2022.

Cryer, Hirun. "Cyberpunk 2077 Bugs: All the Weird and Wonderful Glitches We've Seen So Far." *GamesRadar+*, 14 Dec. 2020, https://www.gamesradar.com/cyberpunk-2077-bugs/. Accessed 3 Feb. 2022.

"Cyberpunk 2077 Full Presentation with Keanu Reeves | Microsoft Xbox E3 2019." *YouTube*, "Gamespot," 9 June 2019, https://www.youtube.com/watch?v=pwgrsjHlqas. Accessed 2 Feb. 2022.

Cyberpunk 2020a. R. Talsorian Games, 1988.

Cyberpunk 2077. CD Projekt Red, 2020b.

D'Angelo, William. "The Last of Us Has Sold Over 20 Million Units." *VGChartz.com*, 4 Apr. 2020, https://www.vgchartz.com/article/440912/the-last-of-us-has-sold-over-20-million-units/. Accessed 3 Feb. 2022.

Davis, Chris. "Cyberpunk 2077's Problems Go Much Deeper Than Bugs." *YouTube*, 16 Dec. 2020, https://www.youtube.com/watch?v=bexA1Oolp0k. Accessed 3 Feb. 2022.

Digital Foundry. "Cyberpunk 2077 Xbox One/X vs PS4/Pro Tested—Can Any Last-Gen Console Cut It?" *YouTube*, 14 Dec. 2020, https://www.youtube.com/watch?v=mVWJPYKCMco&t=963s. Accessed 2 Feb. 2022.

Ebert, Roger. "Video Games Can Never Be Art." *RogerEbert.com*, 16 Apr. 2010, https://www.rogerebert.com/roger-ebert/video-games-can-never-be-art. Accessed 3 Feb. 2022.

Faierman, Leo. "The Last of Us Part II Review: You've Never Played Anything Like This." *ScreenRant*, 12 June 2020, https://screenrant.com/the-last-of-us-2-game-review/. Accessed 1 Feb. 2022.

Franzese, Tomas. "Devastating *The Last of Us 2* Leaks Spoil Several Major Ellie Twists." *Inverse*, 27 Apr. 2020a, https://www.inverse.com/gaming/last-of-us-2-spoilers-reddit-abby-ellie-leaks. Accessed 3 Feb. 2022.

Franzese, Tomas. "Everything You Need to Know about Abby in *The Last of Us Part 2*." *Inverse*, 28 Apr. 2020b, https://www.inverse.com/gaming/last-of-us-2-leaks-spoilers-abby. Accessed 1 Feb. 2022.

Gingerich, Megan Elisabeth. "The Last of Us 2 Had An Eventful First Year." *GameRant*, 19 June 2021, https://gamerant.com/the-last-of-us-2-release-success-controversy-anniversary/. Accessed 3 June 2020.

Glennon, Jen, et al. "The Rest of Us: *The Last of Us Part II* Trans Controversy, Explained." *Inverse*, 14 May 2020, https://www.inverse.com/gaming/last-of-us-2-trans-controversy-explained-abby-tlou. Accessed 1 Feb. 2022.

Grayson, Nathan. "Mike Pondsmith Talks Reinventing Cyberpunk." *Rock, Paper, Shotgun*, 5 Feb. 2013, https://www.rockpapershotgun.com/mike-pondsmith-talks-reinventing-cyberpunk. Accessed 2 Feb. 2022.

Grayson, Nathan. "*Cyberpunk 2077*'s Genital Customization Options Leave A Lot To Be Desired." *Kotaku*, 11 Dec. 2020, https://kotaku.com/cyberpunk-2077s-genital-customization-options-leave-a-l-1845863407. Accessed 3 Feb. 2022.

Griever114. "[SPOILERS] The Last of Us 2 has been leaked onto YouTube from a dev build of the game." *Reddit*, 26 Apr. 2020, https://www.reddit.com/r/Games/comments/g8rpb7/spoilers_the_last_of_us_2_has_been_leaked_onto/. Accessed 1 Feb. 2022.

Hall, Charlie. "Cyberpunk Red, tabletop RPG and prequel to Cyberpunk 2077, out in November." *Polygon*, 9 Oct. 2020, https://www.polygon.com/2020/10/9/21509131/cyberpunk-red-tabletop-rpg-launch-date-price-cyberpunk-2077. Accessed 2 Feb. 2022.

Hernandez, Patricia. "The Last of Us Part 2 Leak Seems to Show Massive Spoilers." *Polygon*, 27 Apr. 2020, https://www.polygon.

com/2020/4/27/21238104/the-last-of-us-part-2-leak-gameplay-spoilers-ellie-joel-naughty-dog-sony-ps4-story-ending. Accessed 3 Feb. 2022.
"Is Joel Really Dead in The Last of Us: Part 2?" *GameRant*, 22 Dec. 2016, https://gamerant.com/last-of-us-part-2-joel-dead-105/. Accessed 1 Feb. 2022. @jasonschreier. *Twitter*, 3 May 2020, https://twitter.com/jasonschreier/status/1256893466564603906?lang=en. Accessed 3 Feb. 2022.
Jones, Camden. "The Last of Us 2 Controversy Explained: What Reviewers Couldn't Talk About." *ScreenRant*, 8 July 2020, https://screenrant.com/last-us-2-review-embargo-restrictions-abby-joel/. Accessed 1 Feb. 2022.
Kain, Erik. "'Cyberpunk 2077' Receives Unprecedented Consumer Warning from OpenCritic." *Forbes*, 15 Dec. 2020, https://www.forbes.com/sites/erikkain/2020/12/15/cyberpunk-2077-cd-projekt-red-reviews-ps4-xbox-one-opencritic-metacritic-betray-gamer-trust/?sh=197747a1231c. Accessed 3 Feb. 2022.
Kinda Funny Games. "Last of Us 2 Spoilercast w/ Neil Druckmann, Ashley Johnson, Troy Baker — Gamescast Ep. 26." *YouTube*, 25 June 2020, https://www.youtube.com/watch?v=g6rRfK-V2jY&t=2s. Accessed 1 Feb. 2022. @krnmxd. "It's not worth it. You destroyed characters we loved." *Twitter*, 27 Apr 2020, https://twitter.com/krnmxd/status/1254840907003826176. Accessed 1 Feb. 2022.
Lee, James. "The Witcher Hits 1 Million Sales." *GamesIndustry.biz*, 31 Oct. 2008, https://www.gamesindustry.biz/articles/witcher-hits-1-million-sales. Accessed 2 Feb. 2022.
O'Dwyer, Danny. "The Witcher Series." *YouTube*, "Noclip—Video Game Documentaries," 19 Oct. 2017, https://www.youtube.com/playlist?list=PL-THgg8QnvU6WuPJmh19U8cAFjzXHCgvk. Accessed 2 Feb. 2022.
Onyett, Charles. "CD Projekt RED Announces Cyberpunk." *IGN*, 12 May 2012, https://www.ign.com/articles/2012/05/30/cd-projekt-red-announces-cyberpunk. Accessed 2 Feb. 2022.
OverHaze. "[SPOILERS] The Last of Us 2 has been leaked onto YouTube from a dev build of the game." *Reddit*, 27 Apr. 2020, www.reddit.com/r/Games/comments/g8rpb7/comment/foq1z7y/?utm_source=share&utm_medium=web2x&context=3. Accessed 1 Feb. 2022.
Person, Chris, et al. "Naughty Dog Showed A Fake *Last of Us 2* Scene to Preserve One of the Game's Surprises." *Kotaku*, 19 June 2020, https://kotaku.com/naughty-dog-showed-a-fake-last-of-us-2-scene-to-preserv-1844099589. Accessed 1 Feb. 2022.
Purchese, Robert. "Meeting Andrzej Sapkowski, the Writer Who Created The Witcher. Does He Really Hate Games?" *Eurogamer*, 25 Mar. 2017, https://www.eurogamer.net/articles/2017-03-24-meeting-andrzej-sapkowski-the-writer-who-created-the-witcher. Accessed 2 Feb. 2022.

Rogers, Tim. "Story #1 ACTION BUTTON REVIEWS Cyberpunk 2077." *YouTube*, 26 Oct. 2021, https://www.youtube.com/watch?v=o1G_qhFHw4Q&list=PLJ30Ch0mLmzJH9qX4VsWZUC73YoQqHNkS&index=2&t=3862s. Accessed 2 Feb. 2022.

Sapkowski, Andrzej. *The Lady of the Lake*. SuperNOWA, 1999.

Schreier, Jason. "Gaming Sales Are Up, but Production Is Down." *New York Times*, 21 Apr. 2020, https://www.nytimes.com/2020/04/21/technology/personaltech/coronavirus-video-game-production.html. Accessed 31 Jan. 2022.

Series. Comment on "The Last of Us Part II Delayed Indefinitely Due to Novel Coronavirus." *The Verge*, 2 Apr 2020, https://www.theverge.com/2020/4/2/21205819/sony-the-last-of-us-part-ii-delayed-indefinitely-coronavirus-iron-man-vr. Accessed 1 Feb. 2022.

Serrels, Mark. "Sony removes Cyberpunk 2077 from the PlayStation Store." *CNet*, 18 Dec. 2020, https://www.cnet.com/news/sony-is-removing-cyberpunk-2077-from-the-playstation-store/. Accessed 3 Feb. 2022.

Shanley, Patrick. "'The Last of Us' Series in the Works at HBO from 'Chernobyl' Creator Craig Mazin, Neil Druckmann." *Hollywood Reporter*, 5 Mar. 2020, https://www.hollywoodreporter.com/movies/movie-news/last-us-series-works-at-hbo-chernobyl-creator-1282707/. Accessed 1 Feb. 2022.

Statt, Nick. "Cyberpunk 2077 Hands-On: Night City Overflows with Choices." *The Verge*, 25 June 2020, https://www.theverge.com/21302888/cyberpunk-2077-preview-demo-hands-on-ps4-xbox-stadia-cd-projekt-red-impressions. Accessed 3 Feb. 2022.

Statt, Nick. "Cyberpunk and Witcher Hackers Auction Off Stolen Source Code for Millions of Dollars." *The Verge*, 10 Febcyberpunk-witcher-hackers-auction-source-code-ransomware-attack. Accessed 3 Feb 2022.

Tassi, Paul. "It's Time For A Fourth 'Cyberpunk 2077' Roadmap." *Forbes*, 20 Jan. 2022, https://www.forbes.com/sites/paultassi/2022/01/20/its-time-for-a-fourth-cyberpunk-2077-roadmap/?sh=4fca2e3133a3. Accessed 3 Feb. 2022.

The Last of Us. Naughty Dog Studios, 2013.

"The Last of Us Part II — PlayStation Experience 2016: Reveal Trailer | PS4." *YouTube*, 3 Dec. 2016, https://www.youtube.com/watch?v=W2Wnvvj33Wo. Accessed 1 Feb. 2022.

The Last of Us Part II. Naughty Dog Studios, 2020.

Wasserman, Ben. "The Witcher's Henry Cavill Praises Doug Cockle — and the Feeling Is Mutual." *CBR.com*, 12 Dec. 2021, https://www.cbr.com/the-witcher-henry-cavill-doug-cockle-approval/. Accessed 2 Feb. 2022.

White, Sam. "Henry Cavill: Gaming on My Own Is Much More Fun than Going Out." *GQ*, 19 Dec. 2019, https://www.gq-magazine.co.uk/culture/article/henry-cavill-interview-2019. Accessed 2 Feb. 2022.

Bowdlerizing for Dollars, or Adaptation as Political Containment

Glenn Jellenik

"It's not even my story at all—it's a freak mutation, like if someone who hadn't read the book told someone else about it at a cocktail party and then that person went out and wrote a script from memory." (Kleeman, *Something New Under the Sun*, 77)

This essay traces and examines a double scandal in adaptation studies. The first, represented by my title's first clause, is an offense perpetrated by adapters: the bowdlerization of a source by its adaptation. The second scandal, represented by the title's second clause, is an omission perpetrated by scholars: the critical under-reading of those bowdlerizations. With this dual focus, I engage with one scandal we know all too well and one that issues from a critical blind spot. Adaptation critics, both popular and scholarly, never tire of pointing out examples that illustrate bowdlerization but spend very little critical energy exploring their implications. As a result of both scandals and their attendant critical treatment or lack of

G. Jellenik (✉)
University of Central Arkansas, Conway, AR, USA
e-mail: gjellenik@uca.edu

treatment, the field has limited its understanding of what adaptations do and how they function in the society that produces and consumes them. Indeed, I argue that any adaptation—specifically an adaptation that bowdlerizes an activist target text—functions as a political containment. Beyond simply removing the radical politics, the adaptation subverts subversion; it performs an act of appropriation, repositioning the text to help maintain the status quo.

This essay uses adaptations of two activist novels: William Godwin's *Things As They Are, or The Adventures of Caleb Williams* (1793) and Theodore Dreiser's *An American Tragedy* (1925) in order to explore the ways that merely dismissing such adaptations as bad art ignores their function in a capitalist society. Further, such criticism normalizes the political valences of bowdlerized versions that mainstream subversive literature.

We all know the story: writers like Godwin and Dreiser pen subversive novels, works that shake the foundations of the systems that they explore. But as those texts are adapted into regulated socio-cultural systems like theater and cinema, their subversions are ... subverted, undermined, systematically contained. And of course, critics raise their voices en masse against this aesthetic affront.

Julie Sanders constructs a spectrum for adaptations: "Adaptation is frequently involved in offering commentary on a sourcetext. [...] Yet adaptation can also constitute a simpler attempt to make texts 'relevant' or comprehensible to new audiences" (19). Here Sanders distinguishes between two different types of adaptation—one in dialogue with its source, interpreting and commenting, and one simplifying its source for mass appeal. The first merits exploration and explication; the second is scorned and quickly dismissed. But Sanders warns against that impulse: "Adaptation studies [...] are not about making polarized value judgments, but about analyzing process, ideology, and methodology" (20). Viewed as mere bowdlerizations, as simply bad art, these texts will be seen to have removed their sources' philosophy and politics. They bowdlerize for dollars and are simply misreadings.

They are misreadings, but not *simply* misreadings. They function more as Bloomian clinamen—purposeful and productive misreadings that enable reinterpretations of the text. No text exists outside of philosophy or politics, though adaptations may well swap out the philosophy and politics of their sources. Here the secondary scandal becomes primary, because to under-read these adaptations is to obscure their work: they prop up and reinforce the status quo, baiting-and-switching progressive and conservative valences to slip texts into the mainstream.

To proceed as if mainstreaming surgically removes the politics from the text, leaving an apolitical adaptation, is to ignore the sociopolitical functioning of adaptations. Each of the texts explored in this chapter guts its source's philosophical activism. However, the question remains where such characterizations belong in the process of analysis. Often critics make them endpoints whose softening disqualifies such prototypical adaptations from serious analysis. I argue, however, that this observation belongs at the beginning of the process of analysis. It serves not as a conclusion, but as a launching point. Yes, an adaptation can gut its source's philosophical and political engagements. But other engagements inevitably fill the void. To ignore that fact and focus critical energy on what an adaptation fails to do, as opposed to exploring what the adaptation's choices produce, is to abdicate our critical responsibility.

THE SCANDAL OF BOWDLERIZATION: SUBSISTING ON THE BODY OF AN UNFORTUNATE VICTIM

Myriad examples can illustrate adaptive bowdlerization. Both George Colman's stage adaptation *The Iron Chest* and Josef von Sternberg's screen adaptation *An American Tragedy* can be read as gutting their sources, presumably to suit the tastes of broader audiences. Viewed from that angle, they are anodyne, bastardizing, and bowdlerizing. Virginia Woolf viewed any such adaptation as simultaneously predatory and parasitic, falling "on its prey with immense rapacity, and [...] largely subsist[ing] upon the body of its unfortunate victim" (268).

Such adaptations have so long served as a go-to straw man for essentialists like Seymour Chatman who would contain and marginalize adaptation that adaptation-as-watering-down has become a critical truism, repeated again and again to illustrate the things that movies shouldn't do. David Cowart's *Literary Symbiosis* (1990) presents the clearest critical expression of adaptation as bowdlerization: "Hollywood is notorious for the happy ending and other methods of pithing the many respectable and even great fictions it adapts. When Miss Lonelyhearts marries Betty in the Hollywood version of Nathanael West's dark novel, a vulgar myth of fulfillment ruins a grimly comic—and brilliant—morality play. The same monstrous alteration figures in Hollywood's adaptation of *The Sound and the Fury*, in which Jason marries Quentin [...] such [adaptations] prove short on aesthetic means and thematic ends" (8). For Cowart, film adaptation is parasitic and so associated with adulteration that the term becomes too degraded to salvage. Thus he coins "literary symbiosis," which describes "reconfiguration," not adaptation, though the two acts perform identical functions. Significantly, Cowart employs the language of scandal—parasitic adaptations are notorious, vulgar, and monstrous; they pith, corrupt, and ruin their esteemed hosts.

Fredric Jameson repackages many of Cowart's ideas two decades later in "Adaptation as a Philosophical Problem." Jameson reconfigures "symbiosis" through a different metaphor, insisting that a successful adaptation must "breathe an utterly different spirit [than its source] altogether" (218). Most adaptations fail and function only as "toxic twins" (216). Parasite or toxic twin, for these critics, the adaptation functions as derivative and lesser-than, a scandalous sullying of its source, and both work through a dizzying series of fallacies underpinned by subjective evaluation.

Still, even critics staunchly averse to evaluative criteria would be hard-pressed to look at Colman's *The Iron Chest* and Sternberg's *An American Tragedy* and not see them as bastardizing bowdlerizations. E.J. Clery zooms in on *The Iron Chest* as illustrative of a widespread phenomenon: "*Caleb Williams* represents the terrorist genre at the peak of its potential as a means of conscious intervention in the political events of the day. Yet, just like any Minerva Press bestseller, the work was duly adapted as an anodyne stage play" (172). Robert Stam recognizes a pattern in such critical rhetoric: "The language of [adaptation] criticism [...] has often been [...] awash in terms such as *infidelity, betrayal, defamation, violation, vulgarization,* and, *desecration*" (54). While he works to unwind unproductive critical moralizing, Stam himself asks, "are we not entirely wrong to regret" what he calls "misreadings" of a source? (75). Many adaptations cheapen and water down, soften and bowdlerize their sources, presumably for profit. Viewed through this lens, adaptation is scandalous—it destroys art through "vulgar myth fulfillment and monstrous alteration" (Cowart 8).

The Iron Chest adapts William Godwin's philosophical gothic *Things as They Are, or The Adventures of Caleb Williams* into a musical melodrama. On its surface, the play seems a paradigmatic example of adaptation as butchery, bowdlerization, and botched translation of a literary text. Colman's Preface acknowledges his adaptive alterations: "Much of Mr. GODWIN's story I have omitted; much, which I have adopted, I have compressed; much I have added; and much I have taken the liberty to alter. All this I did that I might fit it, in the best of my judgment, to the stage" (1).

As the Licensing Act of 1737 demanded, the dramatization conspicuously avoids all overt political engagements. In his Advertisement to the publication of *The Iron Chest*, Colman strikes a pose of utter political ignorance with regard to Godwin's novel: "I have cautiously avoided all tendency to that which, vulgarly (and wrongly, in many instances), is termed Politicks; with which, many have told me, *Caleb Williams* teems. The stage has, now, no business with Politicks; and, should a Dramatick Author endeavour to dabble in them, it is the Lord Chamberlain's office to check his attempts, before they meet the eye of the Publick" (xxi). The playwright removes "Politicks" so completely from consideration that Godwin's obvious political engagements become hearsay: in his reading of the novel, Colman encounters no politics, though he has been told by others that some politics may possibly reside there.

Following that ethos, Colman's play refuses to engage with the Jacobin aspects of Godwin's novel and the tragic consequences that spin out of those elements. In their place, the playwright inserts healthy doses of melodrama, romance, and even comic elements that have little in common with his source's tone, themes, and concerns. Colman's instincts proved correct; the play met with great popular success in its first season at Drury Lane (where it received twenty-four performances) and later as a regular part of the Haymarket's repertory.

Colman represents a potentially productive and illuminating cultural-historical character. Throughout his career, he occupied four different socio-cultural public positions: playwright, adapter, theater manager, and examiner of plays. As such, he created, adapted, marketed, and censored content. Each position engages a different set of socio-cultural and economic concerns, and the last two are particularly interesting for their gatekeeping functions and the ways in which they mesh and clash with the first two. According to Colman's Preface, the bowdlerization of his source's politics is connected directly to the "business" of the London stage, adapting Godwin's novel specifically in order to yield a more economically productive text.

Interestingly, Colman's formula for *The Iron Chest* parallels David O. Selznick's theory of filmmaking as it appears in his letter on Sergei Eisenstein's screenplay for an unproduced adaptation of *An American Tragedy*. The film that Paramount produced, directed by Josef von Sternberg, is perhaps the most crystalized example of scandalous bowdlerization. Dreiser sued Paramount to block the release of the film, claiming that it would damage the reputation of the author and the novel on which it was based. Colman and Selznick both simultaneously negotiate systems of censorship (the Licensing Act and the Production Code) and center audience expectations when it comes to producing an adaptation.

In his letter, Selznick argues against producing Eisenstein's treatment of Dreiser's novel. Eisenstein's screenplay, which Dreiser eagerly endorsed to Paramount, maintains the novel's withering critique of American capitalism. Selznick takes no issue with the quality of Eisenstein's work, which he calls "the most moving script I have ever read" (Eisenstein). The problem, it seems, is that Eisenstein's adaptation maintains its source's tone and themes. This leads Selznick to the conclusion that, if filmed, "it cannot possibly offer anything but a most miserable two hours to millions of happy-minded young Americans" (Eisenstein). Selznick positions filmmaking in industrial terms, arguing that it is not "the business of this organization to experiment for the advancement of the art. [...] Let's try new things, by all means. But let's keep these gambles within the bounds of those that would be indulged by rational businessmen" (Eisenstein). For both Colman and Selznick, what matters most in the business of producing commercial successes is not the translation of philosophical concepts, but rather the ability to work within the parameters of a medium's strictures and encourage a broad audience to connect with the text.

In the name of business, both Colman and Selznick advocate for bowdlerizing adaptations, for conscious shifts away from the philosophical stances of source material. Still, I must confess that I haven't engaged with the scandal of bowdlerization in good faith. Rather, I've used it in a bait-and-switch capacity to approach my second scandal: under-reading in adaptation studies. Adaptation critics don't need rehashings of the scandal of bowdlerization. We know that they happen; we have a pretty good idea why, and we understand that film is simultaneously an art form and an industry. Moreover, criticism suffers no shortage of voices raised in complaint about various dumbed-down adaptations.

In fact, it is with those voices that I take issue, not because adaptations like Colman's *Iron Chest* and Selznick and Sternberg's *American Tragedy* haven't drastically pruned back their sources' political and philosophical engagements, but because too often our critique stops with pointing out what an adaptation has failed to do. On the contrary, what an adaptation does to, with, and through its audience doesn't stop just because it has softened, simplified, or gutted the philosophical concepts of its source. If nature abhors a vacuum, then such texts aren't merely emptied; they're also refilled. While adaptation critics have done a thorough job of tracing the emptying process, we've done less work covering the refilling.

From the perspective of adaptation theory, this focus on bowdlerization might be literary criticism's way of marginalizing adaptation. As Cowart and company position them, such texts are disposable and not worth consideration precisely because of their derivative status. Even if the novel does exactly the same thing, when it does it, that's not parasitic bowdlerization: it's literary symbiosis.

The Scandal of Under-Reading: You Can't Stay Neutral on a Moving Train

The simplicity of this discourse has become a critical truism. Adaptations simplify. Colman's *Iron Chest* transforms a novel about systemic corruption and social rupture into a melodrama centering on romance and harmony. Sternberg transforms a novel about systemic corruption and social rupture into a cautionary tale about personal responsibility. Extra-textual documents name "business" as the catalyst for these changes, returning us to bowdlerizing for dollars.

Recently however, Simone Murray has picked up a line of inquiry begun by Lester Asheim in the 1950s that works to broaden our consideration of the adaptation industry and account for adaptation as a practice and not simply as a product. Asheim begins with the assumption that many film adaptations simplify their sources (Bazin's "digesting"). From there, he points out that criticism has "too frequently been based upon highly impressionistic criteria and broad generalizations [...] erected on the basis of [critical] predispositions" (289). Asheim seems to channel Selznick and Colman when he writes: "The [adapter's] major question is not, 'Is it art?' but 'Will it sell?'" (292). Indeed, Asheim points out that producers like Selznick "stand between the audience and the product" (292), attempting to shape an adaptation that accords with a sizeable audience's preferences. Colman describes a similar process when he admits to omitting, compressing, altering, and adding to Godwin's story in order to "fit it, in the best of my judgment, to the stage" (1). To fit a property to the stage can be seen as submitting to the government's censorship of the theater or as adapting material from one medium to the different proclivities of another medium, but it can also be seen as altering the text in order to appeal to an expanded audience.

Both Colman and Selznick position this move as one that avoids politics, each insisting that the genres into which they adapt have "no business with politics." Murray engages more directly with these concepts when she charges that adaptation critics have remained too much on the surface of the texts they treat: "The goal of this chapter in approaching adaptation socioeconomically is to engender self-reflexivity in readers as consumers and analysts of adaptation by encouraging them to look beneath the surface of certain adapted works" (123). Murray moves away from evaluative criticism in order to consider the complex systems that produce and consume adaptations and to do this because the system of adaptation has potentially "tremendous influence in shaping the contours of contemporary culture" (123). This influence stems directly from the adaptation's ability to deliver an ideological argument. In the case of the texts explored in this chapter, those arguments move away from radical explorations of the corruption of status quo socioeconomic systems toward conservative endorsements of "things as they are."

It is understandable that producers like Colman and Selznick rhetorically positioned themselves as outside or above the political fray. Reaching the largest audience often requires a pose of political neutrality. It is far less understandable, however, that adaptation critics have left such claims largely unchallenged and unexplored.

This secondary scandal, the serial under-reading of adaptations, underscores the crisis of oversimplification in adaptation scholarship. Adaptations are commonly viewed as critically wanting, debauched, and dumbed-down texts. The concept stretches back to the biases and assumptions of the Romantic mind/body split, leveraging the difference between concept and percept. Woolf zooms in on this dynamic in her dismissal of adaptation: "Eye and brain are torn ruthlessly asunder as they vainly try to work in couples" (168). George Bluestone's seminal work on adaptation maintains this distinction by essentializing the genres: novels deal in concepts that reach the audience through mental images, films in percepts that reach us through visual images. Bluestone's concept echoes Sir Walter Scott's positioning of the novel in contradistinction to theater, which Scott posits in terms of the eye and the "mind's eye." Each case depends on a categorical distinction between the verbal and the visual: verbal concepts are complex and nuanced; visual percepts are simplified and flat. These mindsets construct a foundation of critical assumption: there's little to see in a film beyond what you see. Because philosophy exists at a level deeper than spectacle, there is little of it in the percept-driven text. Film and adaptation theory have taken issue with these essentialist assumptions, but the under-reading problem persists.

Fidelity criticism occasionally dismisses such adaptations as butchery. But *Variety*'s early review of the adaptation of *An American Tragedy* hints at something else at work: "[I]t would have taken a director who liked the novel to [successfully] mold it into film form" ("Review," p. 19). The reviewer suggests that the adapter has adopted an adversarial stance toward his source. Robert Stam includes this model in his "constellation of tropes": "[J]ust as any text can generate an infinity of readings, so any novel can generate any number of adaptations. [...] An adaptation, in this sense, is less an attempted resuscitation of an originary word than a turn in an ongoing dialogical process" (62, 64). Hutcheon echoes this analysis, referring to adaptation as "an interpretive act" (8), one "just as likely to [...] contest the aesthetic or political values of the adapted text as to pay homage" (20). Both these concepts may owe something to Harold Bloom's clinamen, from *The Anxiety of Influence*. Clinamen, or misprision, involves a deliberate misreading of a precursor that enables the adapter to swerve in a new direction (14).

Clearly these bowdlerizations function along the lines of Stamian readings, Hutcheonesque interpretations, or Bloomian clinamen. Both adaptations were subject to fundamental alterations necessitated by censorship: the Licensing Act of 1737 for Colman's play and the Motion Picture Production Code of 1930 for Selznick's film. It is no accident that such methods of censorship would yield adaptations that propped up the status quo, since that is precisely what the Licensing Act and the Production Code were designed to do. Under these systems, and perhaps under capitalism in general, adaptation can be seen to act according to conservative rather than progressive drives.

The scandal here is not bowdlerization but rather the critical under-reading of it, the ignoring of a bowdlerization's political valences. Far from having "no business with politics," these adaptations subvert the subversive potential of their sources. It is sadly ironic that in looking at adaptations as hopelessly oversimplified, critics oversimplify the political valences of adaptations.

Although Colman positioned himself as apolitical, *The Iron Chest* presents a rich, specific, and telling negotiation of many emerging, late-century social, political, and economic issues. Indeed, a close look at it demands that we think differently about the play, that we read it as a conservative containment of Godwin's radical philosophy. In place of Godwin's radical questioning of things as they are, Colman performs a bait-and-switch typical of the period's dramatic adaptation. In the end, the adaptation functions not merely as an emptying out of Godwin's politics but as an installation of an intervening system of Foucauldian governmentality by way of a love story.

Colman steadfastly refuses to engage with both the Jacobin aspects of Godwin's novel and the tragic consequences that spin out of those elements. In their place, he inserts healthy doses of melodrama, romance, musical duets, and comic elements that have little in common with the tone and concerns of the source text. From a literary perspective, the play guts the novel and is difficult to take seriously. From a social perspective, however it shifts the textual focus in a direction that should not be ignored, stabilizing the shifting ground of the social landscape by focusing on harmony rather than rupture. While it might seem to function as a simple example of the sorts of adaptations for which Cowart damns Hollywood, a forward-gazing look engenders a far more productive cultural engagement. A focus on what the adaptation says to and about its audience reveals *The Iron Chest* as yet another example of a written intervention, of what Kevin Gilmartin calls writing against revolution, or "interventional conservatism" (9).

In *Writing Against Revolution* (2007), Gilmartin argues: "[R]adical discontent was put down not by extreme methods of state repression ('Pitt's reign of terror'), but rather by relatively ordinary mechanisms of public deliberation and civic enterprise" (20). The radical discontent evoked by Gilmartin found symbolic expression in the Jacobin novel. Clearly, the government-sanctioned legitimate theater functioned as a moderately conservative force, one that worked in direct opposition to Jacobinism; it positioned its audience to process modernity as meshing harmoniously with a shifting socioeconomic landscape. Colman's adaptation of Godwin's work obscures the Jacobin lens through which the Gothic is so often filtered. In the end, the play confronts Godwin's revolutionary text on what can be seen as its own territory, unwriting radical elements through its investment in the systems of governmentality.

How does Colman adapt Godwin's conflict-novel into a continuity-play? Simple: marriage.

The play stabilizes a shifting social landscape by developing harmony rather than rupture. Godwin's novel launches Caleb Williams on a journey of democratization, but rather than achieve equality, Caleb's quest for truth and justice reveals a deeply and hopelessly corrupt social structure. Colman's dramatization of that novel writes directly against Godwin's revolutionary urges. *The Iron Chest* uses marriage, or at least the domestic romantic drive that leads to marriage, to forge its specific adaptation. The main work of the adaptation transforms the novel for mass theater consumption by grafting a series of romance plots onto Godwin's narrative. Thus, the play begins and ends with the seemingly "minor" plot of Wilford's (Caleb's) romance with Barbara, and the overarching story of Wilford's uncovering of Mortimer's (Faulkland's) crime takes place against the backdrop of an added romance between Mortimer and Helen. The romances simultaneously code the characters and the consequences of their actions. Wilford's fitness as a suitor is matched by his virtuous behavior. Thus his story ends in productive union. Further, the specific dynamic of the central courtship (Wilford's marriage to Barbara will lift her out of rustic poverty and into the emerging middle class) speaks to a functional social system and the utility of the changes brought on by encroaching modernity.

Mortimer's tragic existence is shown to the audience not through his loss of honor and a subsequent questioning of Britain's corrupt aristocratic and judicial systems but through the interruption of his marriage plot. As the drama unfolds, Mortimer's crime and his corruption threaten not Wilford's body and security, as in the novel, but his romance plot. Thus, the central tension of the adaptation is transferred from a systematic threat to Wilford's liberty and rights to a threat to his love and marriage. The play strategically positions the audience to feel threats not in terms of political justice, but rather as interruptions to love. The victory (and the injury) belongs not to the emerging individual but to the romantic couple. Political/collective concerns worth fighting for have been transferred to the domestic.

Once again, the amputation of radical politics from the text might make it seem apolitical. But the adaptation has an internally informing ideology. In both *Caleb Williams* and *The Iron Chest*, the corrupted noble is written out of the emerging society. However, the implications of this removal vary tellingly. Godwin's Falkland-removal occasions an inspection and questioning of a political system formed by him. Colman's Mortimer-removal leads to a celebration of love, marriage, and happy endings.

Cowart dismisses such a move as a distasteful "myth of fulfillment" that ruins the aesthetics of a morality play. Clery offers a similar reaction to Colman's text when she dismisses it as "anodyne." But such adaptations function as political acts of containment of the same order as the other forms of writing against revolution that Gilmartin explores, such as the tracts of Hannah More and the anti-Jacobin novel. While not as overtly hostile to radical ideas as these other forms of anti-revolutionary writing, the theater's acts of containment are just as complete. They represent a flanking rather than a direct frontal assault. It's not that, as Colman says, "the stage has [...] no business with Politicks" (xxi), but rather, the politics of the stage and of adaptation is business. Colman's adaptation serves an ideology that directly contrasts with that of its source. *The Iron Chest*, as a mainstream Romantic-period drama, brings Godwin's Jacobin novel into harmony with encroaching modernity in the form of emerging industrial capitalism and the burgeoning bourgeoisie that drove British theater. Godwin's work is informed by his view of encroaching modernity as conflict, Colman's by his view of encroaching modernity as continuity. In the end, the focus is on love, because when love conquers all, things as they are work as they should.

The film adaptation of *An American Tragedy* covers similar ideological ground. Dreiser's lawsuit suggests that he understood this, claiming that the adaptation amounted to libelous distortion, a charge that implies the adaptation's agency. Yet critics have been satisfied to read it as a simple bowdlerization, read it at only half capacity, exploring what Robert Ray calls "the same unproductive layman's question (How does the film compare with the book?), getting the same unproductive answer (The book is better)" (44). Such studies tend to focus on questions of how the adaptation fails to measure up to its source and what it fails to do, questions that construct a closed loop between source and adaptation and produce little of critical value.

Even the most casual (layman) reader/viewer can recognize Sternberg's adaptation of *An American Tragedy* as a sharp turn away from its source. Dreiser's 1925 novel clearly delineates and sharply critiques the systems of American society that combine to pervert the American dream. Following Clyde Griffiths's bildungsroman-journey from naïve Kansas City Evangelist to social-climbing murderer, the reader traces the myriad ways in which American socioeconomic systems seduce and absolutely corrupt those who strive within them. By the time Clyde murders his poor and pregnant girlfriend Roberta Alden in order to pursue a relationship with a wealthy debutante, the systems' vital role in his moral degradation is clear.

Eisenstein's script maintains that critique, using montage to repeatedly conflate religion, sex, and capitalism. He pointed out that his treatment drove Dreiser's themes by centering "the leit-motif of destroying the psychology and ruining step by step the character of [Clyde] by the surrounding social conditions" (quoted in Haberski 68). However, as mentioned earlier, Selznick and Paramount rejected Eisenstein's script. The film that Sternberg shot abandons Dreiser's (and Eisenstein's) socioeconomic critique in ways I have explored in detail in "The Task of the Adaptation Critic." Where Dreiser's literary naturalism and Eisenstein's cinematic montage place the audience inside Clyde and Clyde inside a brutal system, Sternberg's treatment maintains an odd distance. The camera remains far from Clyde for the entire film, as if content to stay on the outside and not allow the audience to consider the deeper swift currents that Dreiser and Eisenstein depicted as carrying him throughout the story. The result is an inability of the viewer to relate to Clyde, which allows the adaptation to transform him from a complex victim/monster into a psychotic heel. His fall is not fated or directed by the corrupt systems he tried to navigate but follows as the result of his individual choices throughout the story.

Critics immediately recognized this departure and remarked on it. Dreiser's claim that the film libeled his novel not only attempts to retroactively negotiate an absurd fidelity contract for adaptations but demands that the audience receive the adaptation without considering its capacity for agency. The Paramount film certainly turns its back on Dreiser's philosophical arguments, but that does not empty the text of philosophy as much as clear a space for a new set of arguments, despite the author's (and many critics') refusal to grant the adaptation philosophical agency.

Ironically, the judge in Dreiser's suit, New York State Supreme Court Justice Graham Witschief, understood this in ways the plaintiff did not. In finding against Dreiser, Witschief recognizes the inherently political nature of adaptation: "The plaintiff claims that instead of an indictment of society the picture is a justification of society and an indictment of Clyde Griffiths. The difficulty in picturing that viewpoint of the book is apparent. That view depends upon the frame of mind of the individual, upon his outlook upon life, and whether a fatalist or a believer in the power of the individual to overcome the weaknesses of character and rise above his environment, to subdue his desires, and to be master of his body, rather than be mastered by it" ("Decision"). Witschief's ruling against Dreiser hinges on the interpretive nature of adaptation. The judge exhibits a keen cultural sensibility, implicitly acknowledging that the two texts deliver different arguments about the cause of the tragedy. The adapters did not misread Dreiser; they rejected and replaced his conclusions.

Witschief recognized that Dreiser had written a novel about the corrosive potential of capitalism, materialism, and the American dream. He also recognized that the adaptation effectively contains and stifles that withering critique. Far from seeing such a move as libelous, however, he declares a preference for the film's interpretation. His ruling implies that the case was not a potato/potahto argument, but rather a potato/tomato argument. The argument isn't about the proper way to express something; it's about two completely different things. And Witschief prefers tomatoes. He reads the adaptation not as a bowdlerization, but rather as a cultural correction.

In their 1947 *Dialectic of Enlightenment*, Max Horkheimer and Theodor Adorno address the same dynamic from the opposite end of the ideological spectrum, positing the culture industry as mass deception. Mainstream culture constructs a system that inherently validates "monopoly capitalism": "The result is a circle of manipulation and retroactive need in which the unity of the system grows even stronger [...] movies keep the whole thing together until their leveling element shows its strength in the very wrong which it furthered [...] The need which might resist central control has already been suppressed" (121). Horkheimer and Adorno would not be surprised by Paramount's ethos-bending in *An American Tragedy*. For them, it represented a constituent part of the process of such adaptation: "[T]here is the agreement—or at least the determination—of all executive authorities not to produce or sanction anything that in any way differs from their own rules, their own ideas about consumers, or above all themselves" (122). Still, they might be surprised that anyone could view texts such as *The Iron Chest* and the film adaptation of *An American Tragedy* as apolitical. And they might be surprised that the shaping of consumers by "executive authorities" was not original to movies or twentieth-century capitalism but stretched back (at least) to eighteenth-century British theater.

Averting Scandal: Bowdlerization and the Business of Politics

Godwin so clearly expected direct government censure for the publication of both *Enquiry Concerning Political Justice* (1793) and *Caleb Williams*, which adapted *Enquiry*'s radical ideas, that his initial publication of the novel removed a Preface that linked the two texts ideologically. The government never acted—though Gilmartin positions Colman as a subtle proxy—by producing an adaptation that decouples Godwin's story from *Enquiry*'s ideology, Colman subverted subversion.

In the end, the clinamens or swerves evident in the adaptations of *Caleb Williams* and *An American Tragedy* both constitute market-related decisions and business decisions. As Selznick's letter and Colman's Preface make clear, "business" governs these adapters' choices. Indeed, both documents place the term "business" at the head of their argument that the industries and markets in which these texts participate must avoid overt engagements with politics. They make no attempt to hide their intention to veer away from their sources' politics. The most cursory glance at the final adaptive products makes their position even more clear: as executive authorities in the culture industry, they will produce nothing that departs from their own rules.

The academic industry has remained satisfied to pretend that those rules are nothing more than misreadings: bowdlerizations that dumb down in search of the greatest common denominator. Yet in that insistence, critics have oversimplified the oversimplifications. When Horkheimer and Adorno insist that the culture industry will not "produce or sanction anything that in any way differs from their own rules, their own ideas about consumers, or above all themselves" (122), they continue to focus on the negative space of the text. They speak of what will not be produced, as opposed to what has been produced. That is, just as with fidelity critics that position adaptations as gutted, they point out what does not appear in the text. Their critique positions texts that support the status quo as unfilled and empty. Again, this (un)critical position neglects to acknowledge, let alone analyze, what actually appears in the text. This act of ignoring has the (surely unintended) consequence of rendering the status quo organic, inevitable, and completely normalized.

Just as Godwin and Dreiser actively and productively use their novels to point out problems with things as they are, these stage and film adaptations actively and productively construct status quo systems. Within these texts, the structures of things as they are exist as solid and safe, and the status quo acts as a dependable and effective bulwark against chaos, destruction, and desperation. Far from a negative space, lack, or philosophical vacuum, these texts are full of philosophy. To be sure, the philosophy is a simple one. There's no need to look too closely. Pay no attention to the man behind the curtain. Things are good as they are. Clyde's American tragedy and Caleb's British nightmare are nothing more than individual crises; there is no socioeconomic fatalism at work, merely a set of individual situations that could be negotiated differently through a series of different individual choices.

Whether or not this philosophy is oversimplified is not the point. Again, ignoring the agency of these texts' ideological moves and investments does not erase that philosophy, it normalizes it. To ignore the specifics of what gets produced by the dialectic between activist source and conservative adaptation for the short-term pleasure of righteous indignation against the culture industry actually works to counter the impetus of these activist source texts. Conversations on aesthetics and bowdlerization actually obscure the larger philosophical processing that might emerge from granting these adaptations philosophical agency and approaching them from a dialectical perspective.

This approach to reading adaptations joins with others that consider the industrial concerns of adaptation. The history of misunderstanding the dynamics of adaptation is long. In his 1797 review of *The Iron Chest*, Tobias Smollett questioned the viability of the act of adaptation: "[I]t is impossible to produce a lively interest where the denouement is already known" (102). This simply proves that Smollett was a far better novelist than he would have been a Hollywood producer. Like Smollett, most adaptation critics are not businessmen and women; we tend to be less attuned to economic concerns than to aesthetics.

As Thomas Leitch points out in "The Ethics of Infidelity," "Adaptations scholars have uncritically adopted [an] ethical rhetoric" (65) on the issue of fidelity wherein "adapters are allowed to change features of their source texts only if they improve them" (65). That ethical rhetoric is tied to critiques that center aesthetics and evaluation, as opposed to a whole set of potential industrial concerns (62). For Leitch, the rhetoric of infidelity links adaptation to marriage, as husbands and wives are "the main things that have been enjoined historically [...] to be faithful" (65). In that sense, a lack of fidelity is adultery, and indeed the rhetoric of bowdlerization certainly presents these texts as adulterations. They cut, dilute, and water down their sources. But we should strive for approaches that explore the alterations as more than adulterations and that examine what gets produced, as opposed to what gets diluted.

In "Mind the Gaps," Leitch works through the ways in which adaptation scholars can account for, engage with, and interactively play with the details omitted, or added, by an adaptation. I join him in calling readers to mind the gaps as a warning against critical under-reading or oversimplification. To the gaps he examines that are produced by the constitutive potentials of the genres of film and literature, rewriting and rethinking the delineations of Seymour Chatman's "What Novels Can Do That Films Can't," I would add the gaps produced by our perception of texts as philosophically emptied, rather than as philosophically shifted and altered.

It is difficult to argue with Clery's characterization of *The Iron Chest* as an anodyne adaptation of *Caleb Williams* or to dispute Dreiser's assessment of Sternberg's adaptation as gutting his novel's central argument. But such assertions do not end the conversation. They merely open out into to a set of critical questions: What specific shapes and directions does such softening take? What does it enable? How does it work on/with its audience? Will such softening be widely recognized as softening? How are future generations likely to read it? What sorts of sociopolitical changes would have to come about to produce new readings? And so on.

Often we position adaptations as complementary texts, as reiterations of their sources, but they can work at cross purposes as well. Despite beginning from the same general point and following the same general story, texts can diverge quickly and completely. Such divergence is not coincidental, nor can it be described as a simple emptying. Central to our inspection of divergent adaptations, we must recognize that each direction represents a facet of the spirit of the age. Reviewers and other nonspecialists routinely consider the source definitive and determinative and point out all that the adaptation fails to do. But this stance ignores the potential work of adaptation. As shown here, adaptations can function as moderately conservative commodifications. That theater managers or movie producers would seek to expand audiences by rhetorically positioning their texts as apolitical is expected and thus no real scandal at all. But when critics ignore ideological shifts or uncritically accept them as apolitical, we fail to read the text fully and critically. And that is scandalous.

REFERENCES

An American Tragedy. Directed by Joseph von Sternberg, performed by Phillip Holmes and Sylvia Sidney, Paramount, 1931.
Asheim, Lester. "From Book to Film: Simplification," *Hollywood Quarterly*, vol. 5, no. 3, 1951, 289–304.
Bazin, André. "Adaptation, or the Cinema as Digest." *Film Adaptation.* Edited by James Naremore, Rutgers UP, 2000, pp. 19–27.
Bloom, Harold. *The Anxiety of Influence.* Oxford UP, 1997.
Bluestone, George. *Novels into Film.* Johns Hopkins UP, 1957.
Chatman, Seymour. "What Novels Can Do That Film Can't (and Vice Versa)." *Film Theory and Criticism*, 6th edition. Edited by Leo Braudy and Marshall Cohen, Oxford UP, 2004, pp. 445–60.
Clery, E.J. *The Rise of Supernatural Fiction.* Cambridge: Cambridge UP, 1999.
Colman, George the Younger. *The Iron Chest. The Plays of George Colman the Younger*, vol. 1. Edited by Peter Tasch, Garland, 1981.
Cowart, David. *Literary Symbiosis.* U of Georgia P, 1993.
"Decision on 'An American Tragedy'." *Lewiston Daily Sun*, 9 Sept. 1931, p. 4, https://news.google.com/newspapers?nid=IT5EXw6i2GUC&dat=19310909&printsec=frontpage&hl=en. Accessed 18 Apr. 2022.
Dreiser, Theodore. *An American Tragedy.* Vintage, 2021.
Eisenstein, Sergei M., et al. *An American Tragedy* screenplay, 1931, https://sfy.ru/?script=american_tragedy. Accessed 18 Apr. 2022.
Gilmartin, Kevin. *Writing Against Revolution: Literary Conservatism in Britain, 1790–1832.* Cambridge UP, 2007.
Godwin, William. *Things As They Are, or The Adventures of Caleb Williams.* Edited by Maurice Hindle. Penguin, 2005.
Haberski, Raymond. *It's Only a Movie: Films and Critics in American Culture.* UP of Kentucky, 2001.
Horkheimer, Max, and Theodor W. Adorno. *Dialectic of Enlightenment: Philosophical Fragments.* Edited by Gunzelin Schmid Noerr, translated by Edmund Jephcott, Stanford UP, 2007.
Hutcheon, Linda, with Siobhan O'Flynn. *A Theory of Adaptation.* Revised ed. Routledge, 2012.
Jameson, Frederic. "Adaptation as a Philosophical Problem." *True to the Spirit.* Edited by Colin MacCabe et al., Oxford UP, 2011, pp. 215–33.
Jellenik, Glenn. "The Task of the Adaptation Critic." *Adaptation in Visual Culture: Images, Texts, and Their Multiple Worlds.* Edited by Julie Grossman and R. Barton Palmer, Palgrave, 2017, pp. 37–52.
Keen, Paul. *Revolutions in Romantic Literature: An Anthology of Print Culture, 1780–1832.* Broadview, 2004.
Kleeman, Alexandra. *Something New Under the Sun.* Penguin, 2021.

Leitch, Thomas. "The Ethics of Infidelity." *Adaptation Studies: New Approaches*. Edited by Christina Albrecht Crane and Dennis Cutchins, Farleigh Dickinson UP, 2010, pp. 61–77.

Leitch, Thomas. "Mind the Gaps." *Adaptation in Visual Culture: Images, Texts, and Their Multiple Worlds*. Edited by Julie Grossman and R. Barton Palmer, Palgrave, 2017, pp. 53–71.

Murray, Simone. "The Business of Adaptation: Reading the Market." *A Companion to Literature, Film, and Adaptation*. Edited by Deborah Cartmell, Blackwell, 2012, 122–39.

Ray, Robert. "The Field of 'Literature and Film.'" *Film Adaptation*. Edited by James Naremore, Rutgers UP, 2000, pp. 38–53.

"Review: *An American Tragedy*," *Variety*, 11 Aug. 1931, p. 19, https://archive.org/details/variety103-1931-08/page/n73/mode/2up?view=theater. Accessed 18 Apr. 2022.

Sanders, Julie. *Adaptation and Appropriation*. Routledge, 2007.

Scott, Walter. "The Death of the Laird's Jock." *The Keepsake for 1829*. Edited by Paula Feldman. Broadview, 2006.

Smollett, Tobias. "Review of *The Iron Chest*." *The Critical Review, or, Annals of Literature*. Hamilton, 1797.

Stam, Robert. "Beyond Fidelity: the Dialogics of Film Adaptation." *Film Adaptation*. Edited by James Naremore, Rutgers UP, 2000, pp. 54–76.

Woolf, Virginia. "The Cinema." *Collected Essays*, vol. 2, Hogarth, 1966, pp. 268–72.

(Re-)Writing the Pain: War, Exploitation, and the Ethics of Adapting Nonfiction

Geoffrey A. Wright

INTRODUCTION: SCANDAL, WAR, AND ADAPTATION

While attending the War, Literature, and the Arts conference at the US Air Force Academy in 2018, I found myself chatting with a veteran of the Iraq War. I was delighted because I had read his memoir and also, it turned out, that of another veteran who was a friend of his. Unexpectedly, he shared with me his chagrin about publishing his memoir, explaining that publishers pressure veterans to "write the pain" (his words) in order to attract readers and boost sales. I was flummoxed, as I had spent years studying and teaching war literature and film and now wondered whether my work was suddenly cast in a negative light by association. Had I been profiting professionally from the pain of people like this veteran?

The ethical challenge this moment presented me demonstrates one way that nonfictional stories about war can scandalize readers as well as the authors themselves. What is scandalous about the genre of the war

---

G. A. Wright (✉)
Samford University, Birmingham, AL, USA
e-mail: gawright@samford.edu

© The Author(s), under exclusive license to Springer Nature 177
Switzerland AG 2023
T. Leitch (ed.), *The Scandal of Adaptation*, Palgrave Studies in Adaptation and Visual Culture,
https://doi.org/10.1007/978-3-031-14153-9_10

memoir is its exploitative quality: publishers exploit veterans to some degree, pressuring them to reveal deeply private traumas because pain, like sex, sells. Authors consent, however, willingly and for whatever artistic and financial reasons. Readers play their part in purchasing and consuming the material, and critics and scholars publish their reviews and articles. Put this way, the arrangement seems parasitic. This might sound like a condemnation of the entire genre, but I do not believe it is. Even though there is an exploitative aspect to creative nonfiction, it is not solely exploitative. Reading war memoirs can enable civilians to engage in the empathic act of seeing beyond the boundaries of our own experience and into the lives of veterans. This is an act of ethical and political import in the age of the all-volunteer forces, when roughly 99% of the US population does not serve in the military.

Asking what happens when filmmakers adapt a war memoir into a film raises a host of interrelated ethical and aesthetic questions. This chapter focuses on nonfictional war literature and cinematic adaptations thereof; questions might well be raised about the relationships among nonfictional storytelling, film adaptation, and other forms of adaptation that lie outside its scope. On the aesthetic front is the question of genre. If a film is an adaptation of a memoir, and a memoir is a work of nonfiction, then is that film also nonfiction? If the genre of the memoir rests on a claim to truth-telling, then can an adaptation of a memoir reasonably make a similar claim? How does the use of actors, sets, scripts, music, and editing inform the status of such a film adaptation? On the ethical front is the question of exploitation. As filmmakers negotiate the complex process of changing a nonfictional literary text into an audiovisual one, are they engaging in exploitative behavior? Is it exploitative to depict in film an author's true accounts of personal matters such as sexual intercourse, mental health, or violence? More generally, is adaptation itself a form of exploitation?

Scandal and the Ethics of Nonfiction

Ethical concerns are hardwired into the practice of writing creative nonfiction, and serious practitioners of the craft take these concerns seriously. The banner of the prizewinning online magazine *Creative Nonfiction* reads, "True stories, well told" (creativenonfiction.org). This mantra serves as a succinct and evocative definition of the genre: creative nonfiction consists of factual narratives. In defining the genre, Lee Gutkind confronts a problematic misunderstanding about it: "The word 'creative' has been criticized in this context because some people think it implies the writer can pretend or exaggerate or make up facts and embellish details. This is completely incorrect. [...] 'Creative' doesn't mean inventing what didn't happen or reporting and describing what wasn't there. It doesn't mean the writer has a license to lie." Clearly, writers of creative nonfiction bear the responsibility of being honest with their readers. Gutkind goes so far as to call this requirement the "cardinal rule" of the genre. For him, it is "the pledge the writer makes to the reader" and "the anchor" of the genre.[1] When it comes to creative nonfiction, an unwritten but nonetheless vital contract exists between writers and readers: "*You can't make this stuff up!*" (Gutkind, emphasis in original).

The operative distinction that determines the generic conditions of creative nonfiction is between objective and subjective truth. No perfect, wholly objective truth is available to human individuals, who can access truth only partially and in a way that is filtered through their points of view. That said, the subjectivity of a statement or belief or opinion does not in itself render it untrue. I can tell the truth about what I honestly believe I saw happen somewhere or heard someone say. The subjectivity of my limited, fallible perception does not render that perception untrue as long as I am relating it honestly. In short, a statement or a story can be subjective and true at the same time. In this way, we can safely say that a work of creative nonfiction can be true: it can be true insofar as it is an honest account of what the writer genuinely understands to be the case. Lynn Bloom cites Philip Gerard's definition of creative nonfiction as "'stories that carry both literal truthfulness and a larger Truth, told in a clear voice, with grace'" (qtd. in Bloom 278). I take "literal truthfulness" to refer to the factually correct nature of nonfiction stories and "a larger Truth" to refer to that objective truth which can be apprehended only partially. Bloom asserts, "Writers of creative nonfiction live—and die—by a single ethical standard, to render faithfully, as Joan Didion says, [...] '*how it felt to me*'" (278, emphasis in original). She goes on to underscore the relativity of Didion's "how it felt to me" by stating that what writers

---

[1] In this light, serious writers of creative nonfiction would take issue with Kevin Dwyer's statement that "True stories are never quite true" (49), though his subsequent statement that "adaptations of true stories are less so" (49) is accurate. I also find his reasoning problematic when he states, "Once an author is in the process of selecting words to describe a story, he/she could not be engaging in a more manipulative process" (47). Writing about one's experience is not automatically manipulative; it is inherently subjective, but it is also honest if done ethically, and the act of writing honestly is not manipulative.

of nonfiction are rendering is *"their understanding of* both the literal and the larger Truth" (278, my emphasis). For Bloom, while capital-T Truth might exist, what is being shared in the nonfiction narrative is the writer's subjective understanding of it, not unmediated Truth itself. Bloom doubles down on the relativity of nonfictional truth: "There is no question about whose truth gets told in creative nonfiction—it has to be the author's, with all other truths filtered through the authorial rendering" (286). It is a given for practitioners of creative nonfiction not only that nonfiction stories are true but also that they are subjectively true.

Even if nonfiction narratives are written truthfully, they still risk exploiting or appearing to exploit their subjects. Actively working to avoid unfair representations of other people in one's stories is a key element of nonfiction ethics. I call this the "do no harm" approach to nonfictional storytelling. A delicate balancing act is required, as authors strive to speak truthfully while not harming other people in their stories. And yet, according to Bill Roorbach, "Negative emotions and traits, such as jealousy, greed, misery, and meanness, are all part of the story—your story—and shouldn't be left out any more than the good stuff" (qtd. in Bloom 279). Sometimes writing truthfully entails reporting negative information about another person. Even as authors honestly own the truth about something awful someone else did to them, readers who may or may not be personally involved in the events may perceive the story to be exploitative, miscasting its subjects for reasons less than noble. Bronwyn Williams reflects, "when we discuss teaching creative nonfiction, we spend too little time on the effects of our work on those we write about, on the ethics of reportage and observation and representation. It is easy to wrap ourselves in the comforting blankets of the social construction of truth [...] and not feel the chilly breezes of pain and hurt that may come from those we write about" (304). That "pain and hurt" may come *for* as well as *from* those about whom nonfiction writers write. Authors cannot avoid this problem entirely by behaving ethically because they cannot control all readers' perceptions and reactions. What they can do, Williams suggests, is remain mindful of the possible consequences of their work. Then, if they do cause someone pain, at least it will not have been inflicted carelessly.

Despite all of this, it is obviously possible for writers to violate the "do no harm" code of creative nonfiction, whether willfully or accidentally. Celebrities and politicians can use autobiographies as weapons to inflict revenge on those who they feel betrayed them. They can publish tell-all books for their shock value, garnering them attention and money. Even nonfiction authors who approach their craft seriously might exploit, to some degree or another, their readers' interests in sex or in someone else's pain. Anthony Swofford's Persian Gulf War memoir *Jarhead*, for example, is arguably the most important work of American literature to emerge from that conflict; yet Swofford sexualizes aspects of military culture (5–7, 21), describes sex that he or others are having (63–65, 91–93), and recounts instances of suicidal behavior (66–74, 103–6), all of which might arouse or scandalize readers. Writers can push or transgress ethical boundaries in their writing; whether they are doing one or the other might be factually obvious or a matter of the reader's opinion, depending on the situation. The ever-present potential for these contingencies means that we as readers must read nonfiction critically, alert to passages that appear biased or exploitative.

The preceding ethical considerations are equally relevant to documentary filmmaking, much of which is considered nonfiction. Jan Krawitz urges that production students be taught not only how to use a camera correctly but also how "to act responsibly in their relationships with their documentary subjects and audiences" (49). This involves asking from the start, "What is the potential impact of this project, most specifically on the lives of those portrayed?" (49). Krawitz echoes Williams's advice to be mindful of how the nonfiction work may affect the subject being depicted. She states, "Ideally, we will leave those whose lives we have touched none the worse for wear" (51), indicating that the "do no harm" approach similarly applies to documentary production. She asks her students, "By being honest with the subject at the outset," to create a level "playing field so that both subject and filmmaker participate in the project without false assumptions" (50). Directorial integrity is clearly a requirement for ethical documentary production just as authorial honesty is for creative nonfiction; without it, subjects and readers are at risk of being exploited. Documentary production presents "a distillation of the experiences [the filmmakers] encountered in the field, filtered through their own points of view" (50). Documentaries cannot boast unmediated access to objective truth; the truths they present are subjective, like those in a work of creative nonfiction, and the subjectivity of those truths does not in itself render them untrue if they are presented with integrity.

A Readerly Ethics of Adaptation

Should scholars, as Deborah Cartmell has proposed, "relish adaptation studies as 'exploitation'"? Film adaptation typically begins with a financial transaction in which producers purchase an author's literary property, but whether or not copyright is an issue, adapters take an existing text with its own characters, plot, and themes and change that material to fit their own ends. Insofar as the verb *exploit* can mean "to make productive use of" (merriam-webster.com), a film adaptation can indeed be said to exploit its precursor text. However, in the context of this essay, the more relevant meaning of *exploit* is "to make use of meanly or unfairly for one's own advantage" (merriam-webster.com). Film adaptation as a general artistic process is not inherently exploitative in this sense. Yet adaptation does bear the risk of being exploitative in its treatment of the source text. Kevin Dwyer observes, "it is the promise of action, of witnessing human suffering [...] that [...] compels people to read the books and, to a greater extent, to watch the film" (45). There is an exploitative quality to film adaptation in the sense of *using* the source text to make money and of changing it to meet ends for which it was not designed.

If the standard for writing creative nonfiction is to treat the subject matter honestly and fairly, and if so much is at stake for the real-life people depicted in the texts and involved their production, then filmmakers have an ethical responsibility to take due care when adapting a work of nonfiction. To assert this is to extend the "do no harm" approach to adapting nonfiction. Granted, it is futile to insist that film adaptations stick literally to all factual details as they are presented in the book. Filmmakers are readers of texts, and it is a commonplace of poststructuralist theory that all readers of a given text read different texts in the sense that the text gets filtered through different readers' views and backgrounds. Yet we have an ethical obligation to recognize that some people have a stake in the truthfulness of the material being presented. The reputations and careers of individuals represented on screen could be harmed. In this light, filmmakers should not treat the characters in their nonfictional source texts unfairly.

The ethical dimensions of this "do no harm" approach renew questions about fidelity that adaptation scholars have long debated (see, e.g., Raitt, MacCabe et al., de Zwaan, Hermansson, and Johnson). Brian Boyd aptly cautions, "While fidelity should not be seen as the only aim of adaptation, neither should it be dismissed as servile" (597). The problem is not that fidelity as a basic value does not hold up to poststructuralist scrutiny; it is that fidelity as dogma does not.[2] Boyd employs the metaphor of biological evolution to forge a theoretical compromise: "Biological adaptation involves both fidelity and fertility. To be an adaptation, a biological feature must establish itself across the species and must be reliably passed down to subsequent generations: it must be reproduced with fidelity. But to be adaptive, to have solved a new problem, [...] it must have improved in some way on some prior state of the species" (595). As Boyd notes, echoing Linda Hutcheon's definition of adaptation as "repetition with variation" (4), evolution requires some degree of genetic fidelity along with variation. If there is little to no genetic similarity between parents and offspring, the offspring will likely not survive in nature: "Major mutations are usually unenviable and therefore quickly eliminated" (596).

That filmmakers treat their nonfictional literary material fairly should be an expectation of ours as viewers, and we as readers ought to assess whether or not a film adaptation shows signs of being produced ethically. We should also accept that our judgments will inevitably be subjective, shared by some viewers and not by others. This "buyer beware" approach takes a healthy and realistic view of how texts work as texts and how they work socially. We would be better off as scholars and moviegoers if more of us exercised a healthy skepticism toward films that are based on auto/biographical sources. This "buyer beware" skepticism entails keeping one's critical guard up while viewing or studying the film and remembering that there is no way to escape interpretation and mediation when making or viewing nonfiction texts; it also means acknowledging the reality that sufficiently powerful producers and directors will do whatever they decide to do with their films, regardless of what critics and academics think.

This realization shifts the ethics of adapting nonfiction to the jurisdiction of the audience. For example, John McGuigan criticizes Ridley Scott's blockbuster adaptation *Black Hawk Down*, calling it "an especially tragic swindle" (222). Whereas Mark Bowden's nonfiction book, in McGuigan's estimation, employs "journalistic truths and narrative trajectories [that] often force readers to confront and reconcile contradictions," the film

---

[2] Mary Snyder approaches the question of fidelity from the side of the screenwriter: "The goal of honoring or respecting the source text and the question of how best to achieve that goal are fundamental to the work of many screenwriters. Interestingly, this goal echoes the issue of fidelity in film adaptation" (111). While Snyder opts to "nudge screenwriters into feeling less encumbered and freer to be more creative as they embark on a reading of the source text they intend to adapt" (114), she acknowledges that "respecting the text" is a key value held in common among screenwriters.

reduces itself to "simplistic jingoism" (223) by taking "the irreducible complexities of *Black Hawk Down* and convert[ing] them to a simple story that never pauses from the action" (229). Catering to the mainstream Hollywood demand for heart-pounding action might seem like a harmless strategy, but McGuigan finds it exploitative in this case because it takes what is a complex and ambivalent—and truthful—story of the tragic human cost of America's blundering in Somali politics as fuel for the same breed of unthinking, adrenalized patriotism that caused the catastrophe in the first place (237).

Similarly, Oliver Stone's adaptation *Heaven and Earth*, if viewed uncritically, can appear as an uplifting story of a Vietnamese woman overcoming tragedy. Yet, if we viewers practice skepticism in our reading of the film, we find ethically problematic elements in it. Stone built his reputation as an important director on his Vietnam War films, yet his handling of Le Ly Hayslip's memoir *When Heaven and Earth Changed Places* is exploitative in that he uses her book to serve his own agenda in making *Heaven and Earth*. Stone's auteurist appropriation of the text is apparent in the opening credits, which announce that this is "An Oliver Stone Film" (0.00.27). A subsequent credit explains, "This film is based on the true life story of Phung Thi Le Ly Hayslip" (0.00.33). Stone's directorship clearly takes precedent over Hayslip's authorship. The wording of the credit appears strategically ambiguous: that it is "based on" Hayslip's story bestows on Stone plenty of latitude even as the phrase "true life story" promises veracity and authority.

The adaptation is colored by Stone's romanticization of the Vietnam War, the Vietnamese people, and average American soldiers, along with his villainization of the South Vietnamese government and the American military-industrial complex. The nature imagery in the opening of the film—panoramic vistas of lush green fields with mountains on the horizon, Buddhist monks in bright yellow robes, geese waddling along a dirt road, families working cheerfully in the rice fields, and the village community gathered harmoniously around a meal (0.01.05–0.07.50)—portrays Hayslip's village as an agrarian paradise. This idyllic imagery is accompanied by a score featuring soaring stringed instruments, heightening the sense of natural splendor and communal joy. Stone's romanticization of the Vietnamese people oversimplifies them, eliding the realities of exhausting physical labor and casting Hayslip and her fellow villagers as noble savages, one-dimensionally innocent and good (Fig. 1).

Fig. 1 An agrarian vista from the opening minutes of *Heaven and Earth*

While Stone's intentions in bringing Hayslip's story of resilience and healing to a much wider audience were presumably laudable, shifting the text from Hayslip's authorship to Stone's means shifting from a Vietnamese perspective to an American one, from a woman's perspective to a man's, and from a civilian's to a former soldier's. In her memoir, Hayslip speaks as the voice of the powerless who were victimized by the war and by those who wielded the power. Quan Manh Ha observes that Hayslip "admits that the male wagers of war have made her 'their victim,' because men make war. [...] The word *victim* properly implies the power relationship between the exploited and the exploiter, and in a wartime situation, women like Hayslip, [...] can be subdued and subjugated through assault and exploitation by males—by men both from other cultures and from her own culture" (10, italics in original). In relocating the authorial perspective, Stone's film reinstates those cultural and gendered hierarchies that Hayslip subverts. Rebecca Stephens laments, "Though this film purports to be the 'true' story of Hayslip's life and of a Vietnamese-American's experience, the ultimate effect is that, in Stone's hands, Hayslip's story is transformed into a reinscription of the conventional ways that the immigrant 'fits' into American culture" (661). Stephens goes on to argue that while Hayslip wrestles with the complex mingling of the personal with the political in the midst of a civilian woman's struggle to survive physically and psychologically in wartime, Stone reduces her story to a sentimental saga of suffering and rescue at the hands of various white men: "Stone transforms Hayslip's interrogation of national power into collusion with the American national guilt and remorse over the Vietnam War" (668). In this way Stone exploits Hayslip's narrative, treating it not so much as its own story but as part three in his war trilogy and using it as a means to absolve Americans from the destruction they wrought in Vietnam.

Stone's handling of the Steve Butler character is ethically problematic as well. Steve is actually an amalgam of two men in Hayslip's two memoirs (Stephens 664). Ed, a civilian contractor whom Hayslip marries largely to escape the war, dies of an illness a few years after they arrive in the US. Dennis, a Vietnam War veteran, ends up abusing Le Ly, kidnapping her children, and then killing himself. Given the enormity of Dennis's actions and the importance of truthfulness in creative nonfiction and of not doing careless or unnecessary harm to people featured in the story, it is disconcerting to see Stone attribute the one man's destructive behavior to the other man, who was innocent of those actions. If there is a saving grace here, it is that Stone changes Ed's name, thereby offering the real person's reputation at least some protection, however flimsy (Fig. 2).

Stone's exploitation of Hayslip's memoirs, however inadvertent, becomes painfully evident in his handling of sexual violence. *Heaven and Earth* features two scenes, both based on her first memoir, in which Le Ly has consensual sex with a man, once with Anh and once with Steve Butler. The sex scene with Anh is shot with conventional decorum: as soon as the two lie down on her bed, the rest of the scene is restricted to close-ups and medium-close-ups of their faces (0.41.00–0.42.30). The sex scene with Steve is handled similarly, using only medium shots, hiding the lovers' bodies under the bed sheets, and showing them only from the shoulders

Fig. 2 Le Ly Hayslip (Hiep Thi Le, right) meets troubled war veteran Steve Butler (Tommy Lee Jones) in *Heaven and Earth*

up (1.17.50–1.18.40). Yet, the scene in which Le Ly is raped by two Viet Cong soldiers, which is also drawn from her memoir, is handled in a disturbingly different manner (0.34.50–0.35.50). The scene includes several shots in which Le Ly's body is entirely visible, emphasizing the shocking nature of the violence. In addition, the scene includes two shots of female frontal nudity. Given the obviously erotic nature of this kind of imagery and the long and deeply fraught history of the objectification of women in cinema, it is disconcerting to see Stone treat rape as an opportunity to pander to the audience's voyeuristic scopophilia. In Stone's hands, the film becomes complicit in the kind of victimization it seeks to decry.

Adaptation and the Scandal of Genre

The nebulous quality of film adaptations of nonfiction scandalizes the notion of genre, making the following foray treacherous. A genre is a category based on shared similarities (e.g., a combat film typically features combatants of some kind, such as infantry or aviators or sailors, performing their martial duties in a battle environment). The problem with categorizing adaptations of nonfiction is that they share similarities with both fiction and nonfiction. Kevin Dwyer suggests that "it is the very process of adaptation that creates fiction from non-fiction, eroding the latter into the form of a palatable story, fit for dissemination in many forms" (43). If we substitute the verb *transforming* for the more loaded *eroding*, we can say that the process of adaptation, at least in the case of adapting a literary text into a cinematic one, entails a sequence of creative acts performed by a variety of artists ranging from screenwriters and directors to actors and editors, which transforms the nonfictional literary narrative into an audiovisual narrative that exhibits both fictional and nonfictional qualities. In assembling layers of artistic artifacts including scripts, sets, acting performances, and musical scores, the production process inevitably fictionalizes the nonfiction to some degree, resulting in a hybrid of the factual and the fictional.[3]

Of course, every text is a text and not reality itself; even a nonfiction text is subject to the conditions of textuality. In explaining the enduring

---

[3] One might wonder whether the fictionalization of nonfiction that we find in film adaptations in turn problematizes all nonfiction. Though a full-fledged exploration of this question lies outside the scope of this chapter, I would suggest that it ought to involve distinguishing between fiction and narrative.

impact of Mikhail Bakhtin's theory of dialogism on adaptation studies, largely through Robert Stam's influential use of Bakhtin in his scholarship, Dennis Cutchins notes that the Bakhtinian model of intertextuality "suggests that what is being adapted in any particular case cannot be the text alone, nor the essence of the text, but rather a particular understanding of the text that is dialogized, or constantly negotiated along its boundaries" (79). What is being adapted in a film is not the literary text itself but rather an interpretation of the text. To take this a step further, a film adaptation of a text, whether fictional or nonfictional, is really the accumulation of a series of interpretations made by the filmmakers, and these interpretations take the form of visual and aural elements in the film that are not present in the precursor even if their verbal referents are. Hence an adaptation of a nonfiction narrative is itself not nonfiction—or, rather, not simply nonfiction. I draw back from saying not nonfiction *at all* because some factual elements from the precursor text will presumably be retained.[4] When we are dealing with a film adaptation of nonfiction, we could be farther from nonfiction than we realize, as the members of any film's cast and crew will be working from the already adapted script, rather than from the book itself, and many may not even have read the book on which the film is based.[5]

In being based on nonfiction, these films pose as nonfiction, and many are presumably made by filmmakers convinced that they have presented the story and characters responsibly. This leads to the provocative hypothesis that adaptations of nonfiction practice a form of lying, presenting what is not actually the truth as though it were the truth. Put this way, these films do possess an exploitative quality: in some cases, film adaptations present real-life characters doing and saying things they did not actually do or say in real life, and even in scenes in which an adaptation sticks

---

[4] Granted, works of historical fiction will likely contain a certain amount of factual information. However, we can still distinguish between creative nonfiction and historical fiction. According to Gutkind, authors of nonfiction narratives must not invent or change the facts when telling their stories truthfully. In contrast, that the genre label *historical fiction* ends in the word *fiction* immediately signals that the narrative content is largely invented and, therefore, should not be perceived as a necessarily truthful account of real-life persons and events.

[5] In fact, during the studio era, the screenwriter was typically the only one who read the book and did so in the preparation of the treatment that served as the basis for the film's production. There were exceptions, of course, such as producer David O. Selznick, who clearly read the novel *Gone with the Wind*, as well as Selznick and director Alfred Hitchcock, both of whom read Daphne du Maurier's novel *Rebecca* and had a hand in crafting the screenplay.

to the facts presented in the book, the film is displaying shadows of the truth, audiovisual approximations of a truth that was only partially realized in the first place, while earnestly or strategically labeling the film as being true—a claim that is not true. The readerly ethics proposed above practice an active awareness of these contradictions.

So, what should we call this strange, hybrid genre that both is and is not nonfiction, that does and does not tell true stories? Is labeling it necessary or helpful? Should the label end with the word *nonfiction*? If it does, does the label risk reinforcing the persistent misunderstanding of such adaptations? *Non-nonfiction, anti-nonfiction, approximate nonfiction, fictionalized nonfiction,* and *nonfictional fiction* are variously tempting but untenable. Although *dramatic nonfiction* may seem appealing, Lee Gutkind's use of the adjective *dramatic* to describe the work creative nonfiction does in shaping dry facts into an artistic and entertaining story suggests that using the term *dramatic nonfiction* to refer to film adaptations of creative nonfiction would likely lead to confusion, not to mention frustration for authors and scholars of creative nonfiction.

Quasi-nonfiction, which initially seems like a theoretical punt, is more promising. The prefix *quasi-* means (1) "having some resemblance usually by possession of certain attributes," (2) "in some sense or degree," and (3) "resembling in some degree" (merriam-webster.com). In Latin, it means "as if" or "approximately" (merriam-webster.com). Multiple connotations here are useful for describing adaptations of nonfiction: these films possess some but not all of the attributes found in the nonfictional texts they adapt; they approximate nonfiction by taking nonfiction material and combining it with fictional elements; they operate as if they were congruent with the true stories they are retelling; they resemble the books from which they are adapted while also featuring traits that indelibly mark them as different from their precursors, in much the same way an adult child might resemble a parent and yet have distinctive features. Registering adaptations of nonfiction as quasi-nonfiction foregrounds their textual contingency, their condition of being almost-but-not-exactly-nonfiction. *Composite nonfiction* may be the most elegant solution; it signals that the root material is nonfiction and that other ingredients have been added to the adapted text by the inevitable dynamics of transmuting literature into cinema. The term *composite* celebrates the hybridity of adaptations of nonfiction, their condition as a merging of literary and cinematic production and as a blend of fact and fiction. It also signals that various narrative elements such as characters or events may themselves be composites of more than one such element in the book.

Insofar as adaptations of creative nonfiction both are and are not nonfiction, I am compelled to look to quantum physics for help. The famous thought experiment Schrodinger's Cat is a parable designed to illustrate the obscure concept of superposition, the ability of quantum, or subatomic, particles to exist in two or more states at the same time, behaving simultaneously like particles and waves, something impossible for larger objects like baseballs or planets. Observing or measuring this behavior forces the subatomic particle to appear as one or the other, and so scientific observation collapses the superposition, rendering it unobservable, like the cat in Schrodinger's box, which is both alive and dead. In this light, we could think of adapted nonfiction as a *supergenre*, one that hovers in a superposition, behaving like fiction and nonfiction at the same time.

To carry the quantum metaphor one step further, the audience's act of viewing the film forces it to behave as either nonfiction or fiction. Viewers can, and many obviously do, accept a film adaptation as the true story it might claim to be. However, we viewers also have the ability to assess the film skeptically, just as we can read nonfiction critically. Cutchins suggests that the "need for active readers and viewers becomes clear if you imagine yourself in the crowd at an unfamiliar sporting event. Someone who didn't understand the rules and strategies of hockey, for instance, would likely fail to notice exceptional plays and misunderstand fouls" (76). A readerly ethics requires taking on the role of being active, informed readers, knowing the rules and strategies of creative nonfiction and film adaptation, as well as who the "players" are, so that we can recognize "fouls" and appreciate skilled performances. One way to inform ourselves is to read the auto/biographical books on which film adaptations are based. This will help us exercise the ethical skepticism I described above by making us better able to ascertain what has been fictionalized in the film, whereas viewers who have not read the book will not have those references and, therefore, will not be as informed or at least not informed in the same way. Regardless of whether we have read the book, we must consciously and continually remind ourselves that an adaptation of a nonfiction text both is and is not true, that it is a collection of the filmmakers' interpretations and choices, and that even its literary precursor cannot contain the truth in an objective sense and might even be unduly angled in its author's favor.

Conclusion: The Anxiety of Adaptation Studies

One more bit of help I welcome from the field of quantum physics is the lesson of humility. The currently unsolvable mysteries of the universe remind us, physicists and laypersons alike, of the abounding complexity and wonder of the natural world, which humanity has by no means mastered. In this light, I suggest that when we are dealing with the theoretical and critical complexities of transtextuality and adaptation, it is fitting and even beneficial to practice humility. While working on this project, I have wondered if my answers to the questions I was asking amounted to little more than a perplexed, "Yes, and no—and, well, maybe." Could "yes and no" be used strategically to acknowledge that there is not a single answer that applies equally in all possible scenarios for adapting nonfiction literature into film? Could "maybe" serve as an adequate answer in a scholarly work? Perhaps, if "maybe" is used as a springboard for asking further questions.

Thinking about the ethical implications of making film adaptations of war memoirs brings me in a roundabout way to fidelity. Framing my work as an investigation into the ethics of adaptation reminds me of Robert Stam's critique of the moral overtones of the fidelity standard (54–58). Nonetheless, I do not believe that thinking ethically about film adaptation amounts to a refurbishing of the high-toned moralizing of which Stam was rightly critical. Moralizing bears a negative connotation because the people who do it are presuming to occupy an objectively determined and hence unassailable position. Ethics, on the other hand, puts us in dialogue with each other, as ethics are principles that a group of people share precisely because they have agreed to share them. This chapter seeks to enter into dialogue with the work of scholars I have read and to promote further dialogue by other scholars who, I hope, will read it and profit by considering the ways they agree or disagree with specific points it makes.

Thinking ethically about adaptation entails the concept of responsibility. Søren Kierkegaard believed freedom and responsibility to be the defining, existential issues for humanity to unravel. Are filmmakers responsible to or for the texts they adapt? Or are filmmakers perfectly free to do whatever they wish in and with their films, whether or not they are based on factual accounts of real people's lives? In *The Concept of Anxiety*, Kierkegaard characterizes anxiety as the dizziness individuals feel when they look down into the bottomless abyss of freedom. In this light, feeling a little dizzy might be a good sign for scholars as we stand at the edge of the canyon of adaptation studies and contemplate the endless miles of beauty and possibility—and hazard.

References

Bloom, Lynn. "Living to Tell the Tale: The Complicated Ethics of Creative Nonfiction." *College English*, vol. 65, no. 3, 2003, pp. 276–89.
Boyd, Brian. "Making Adaptation Studies Adaptive." Leitch, pp. 587–606.
Cartmell, Deborah. "Adaptation as Exploitation." *Literature/Film Quarterly*, vol. 45, no. 2, 2017, https://lfq.salisbury.edu/_issues/first/adaptation_as_exploitation.html. Accessed 22 Sept. 2021.
Cutchins, Dennis. (n.d.)"Bakhtin, Intertextuality, and Adaptation." Leitch, pp. 71–86.
De Zwaan, Victoria. "Experimental Fiction, Film Adaptation, and the Case of *Midnight's Children*: In Defense of Fidelity." *Literature/Film Quarterly*, vol. 43, no. 4, 2015, pp. 246–62.
Dwyer, Kevin. "True Stories: Film and the Non-Fiction Narrative." *Screening Text: Critical Perspectives on Film Adaptation*. Edited by Shannon Wells-Lassagne and Arianne Hudelet, McFarland, 2013, pp. 43–52.
"Exploit." *Merriam-Webster*, https://www.merriam-webster.com/dictionary/exploit. Accessed 22 Sept. 2021.
Gutkind, Lee. "What Is Creative Nonfiction?" *Creative Nonfiction*, https://creativenonfiction.org/what-is-cnf/. Accessed 17 Sept. 2021.
Ha, Quan Man. "Power and Gender Relations in *When Heaven and Earth Changed Places*." *War, Literature, and the Arts*, vol. 25, 2013, pp. 1–18.
Heaven and Earth. Directed by Oliver Stone, performed by Hiep Thi Le and Tommy Lee Jones, Warner Bros, 1993.
Hermansson, Casie. "Flogging Fidelity: In Defense of the (Un)Dead Horse." *Adaptation*, vol. 15, no. 2, 2015, pp. 147–60.
Hutcheon, Linda, with Siobhan O'Flynn. *A Theory of Adaptation*. Revised ed., Routledge, 2012.
Johnson, David. (n.d.) "Adaptation and Fidelity." Leitch, pp. 87–100.
Kierkegaard, Søren. *The Concept of Anxiety: A Simple Psychologically Oriented Deliberation in View of the Dogmatic Problem of Hereditary Sin*. Narrated by David Rapkin. Audible Studios, 2014. Audiobook.
Krawitz, Jan. "Treading Softly: Ethics and Documentary Production." *Knowledge Quest*, vol. 38, no. 4, 2010, pp. 48–51.
Leitch, Thomas, editor. *The Oxford Handbook of Adaptation Studies*. Oxford UP, 2017.
MacCabe, Colin, et al., editors. *True to the Spirit: Film Adaptation and the Question of Fidelity*. Oxford UP, 2011.
McGuigan, John. "On the Danger of Heroes: *Black Hawk Down*'s Transformation from Narrative Journalism to Cinematic Spectacle." *Midwest Quarterly*, vol. 52, no. 3, 2011, pp. 221–38.

"Quasi." *Merriam-Webster*, https://www.merriam-webster.com/dictionary/quasi. Accessed 22 Sept. 2021.

Raitt, George. "Still Lusting After Fidelity?" *Literature/Film Quarterly*, vol. 38, no. 1, 2010, pp. 47–58.

Snyder, Mary. "Adaptation in Theory and Practice: Mending the Imaginary Fence." Leitch, pp. 101–15.

Stam, Robert. "Beyond Fidelity: The Dialogics of Adaptation." *Film Adaptation*. Edited by James Naremore, Rutgers UP, 2000, pp. 54–76.

Stephens, Rebecca. "Distorted Reflections: Oliver Stone's *Heaven and Earth* and Le Ly Hayslip's *When Heaven and Earth Changed Places*." *Centennial Review*, vol. 41, no. 3, 1997, pp. 661–69.

Swofford, Anthony. *Jarhead: A Marine's Chronicle of the Gulf War and Other Battles*. Scribner, 2003.

Williams, Bronwyn. "Never Let the Truth Stand in the Way of a Good Story: A Work for Three Voices." *College English*, vol. 65, no. 3, 2003, pp. 290–304.

Adaptation and Censorship

Thomas Leitch

Two days after President Donald J. Trump encouraged a crowd of supporters who like him refused to accept the results of the 2020 Presidential election to march on the United States Capitol Building, where many of them overcame security guards and rushed into the building in search of Vice President Mike Pence and the congressional representatives who had refused to support the President's "STOP THE STEAL" movement, and five days before he was impeached for a second time by the House of Representatives, the President suffered perhaps a still greater indignity: his Twitter account, @realDonaldTrump, was permanently suspended, silencing the channel he had used to broadcast his actions, positions, and feelings to some 88 million followers. The President's reaction was swift. On that same evening, 8 January 2021, he or one of his surrogates tweeted on his @POTUS account: "As I have been saying for a long time, Twitter has gone further and further in banning free speech, and tonight, Twitter employees have coordinated with the Democrats and the Radical left in removing my account from their platform, to silence me" (Fung).

T. Leitch (✉)
Department of English, University of Delaware, Newark, DE, USA
e-mail: tleitch@udel.edu

© The Author(s), under exclusive license to Springer Nature
Switzerland AG 2023
T. Leitch (ed.), *The Scandal of Adaptation*, Palgrave Studies in
Adaptation and Visual Culture,
https://doi.org/10.1007/978-3-031-14153-9_11

Although the tweet quickly disappeared, along with the President's access to his Facebook and YouTube accounts, his followers were not silenced. That same evening, Donald Trump Jr. tweeted: "We are living Orwell's *1984*. Free-speech no longer exists in America. It died with big tech and what's left is only there for a chosen few" (Trump, Jr.). Senator Josh Hawley, the Missouri Republican who had aggressively endorsed the President's claims to have won the election and who had been memorably photographed offering a raised fist to the crowd outside the Capitol hours before they stormed the building, greeted the news that Simon & Schuster had canceled the contact for his forthcoming book, *The Tyranny of Big Tech*, with a tweet of his own addressed to "the woke mob at @simonschuster": "This could not be more Orwellian. […] Only approved speech can now be published. This is the Left looking to cancel everyone they don't approve of. I will fight this cancel culture with everything I have" (Hawley). And Marjorie Taylor Greene, a Republican representative from Georgia, appeared on the floor of Congress wearing a face mask emblazoned "CENSORED" to announce on national television that the drive to impeach the President on the grounds that his repeated refusal to accept the results of the election had encouraged a violent insurrection was a "witch hunt scam" (Harvey).

The wide-ranging debates that followed, noting, for example, that the right to every individual's free speech enshrined in the First Amendment does not oblige private corporations to disseminate every speech, that Simon & Schuster's decision to cancel a contract for a book Senator Hawley was free to shop and publish elsewhere was hardly the stuff of *1984*, whose deepest fear was "the perversion of language to mask truth and defend the indefensible" (Beers), and that Representative Greene's claims of censorship were hard to take seriously when they were delivered on the floor of Congress and broadcast across the country, ultimately rested on three assumptions. Everyone involved was against censorship; the question was whether Representative Greene, Senator Hawley, and President Trump were actually being censored. Nobody wanted to be censored, whatever their views, because free speech was their absolute right under the law. And nobody wanted to be accused of censorship themselves; nobody thought of themselves or the gatekeepers whose functions they supported as censors because the assertions they were declining to publish were dangerous attacks on truth and incitements to violence that should be suppressed in ways that could not fairly be called censorship.

Debates over censorship have flared up throughout history from the time of Socrates to the invention of the printing press to the rise of the cinema. But the backlash against censorship, juiced by counter-accusations condemning the spread of cancel culture, became more passionate than ever during the Trump Presidency. The death of George Floyd at the hands of Minneapolis police officer Derek Chauvin had brought the #BlackLivesMatter movement, which had begun in 2013, to new power and prominence. Black Lives Matter (BLM) demonstrators demanded that the United States rename military bases named after heroes of the Confederacy and tear down monuments to Founding Fathers who owned slaves and colonizing explorers like Christopher Columbus, whose national holiday had been overlaid in recent years by Indigenous Peoples' Day. These attempts to rewrite the canon of American history met with varying success and the occasional whiplash. In 2016, Peter Salovey, the president of Yale University, declined the recommendation of an internal advisory committee to rename Calhoun College, which commemorated United States Senator, Secretary of War, Secretary of State, and Vice President John C. Calhoun, a Yale alumnus and ardent defender of slavery, and then ten months later changed his mind, renaming the college Grace Murray Hopper College to honor a more recent alumna who had been a noted computer scientist and a Rear Admiral in the U.S. Navy. In response, conservatives following the website 4chan and encouraged by pundit Ann Coulter launched #CancelYale, a 2020 movement to rename the university itself, whose namesake had been a slaveowner and slave trader.

Cancel culture, the more general term #CancelYale invokes, applies a metaphor drawn from the suppression of contested texts to public figures threatened with the loss of their reputations, their supportive followers on social media, their virtual footprints, or their professional positions when they are publicly called out over revelations of racism, licentious or predatory sexual behavior, political incorrectness, cruelty to animals, or other socially offensive activities. Cancel culture's victims include Senator Al Franken, film producer Harvey Weinstein, writer/director Woody Allen, Fox News chief Roger Ailes, actor Kevin Spacey, comedians Roseanne Barr and Louis C.K., Nobel Prize-winning biologist Sir Tim Hunt, and *New Yorker* staff writer Jeffrey Toobin. The term was taken up by President Trump in his widely publicized Mount Rushmore speech on 4 July 2020, which indicted

a merciless campaign to wipe out our history, defame our heroes, erase our values, and indoctrinate our children.

Angry mobs are trying to tear down statues of our Founders, deface our most sacred memorials, and unleash a wave of violent crime in our cities. [...]

One of their political weapons is "Cancel Culture"—driving people from their jobs, shaming dissenters, and demanding total submission from anyone who disagrees. This is the very definition of totalitarianism, and it is completely alien to our culture and our values, and it has absolutely no place in the United States of America. [...]

In our schools, our newsrooms, even our corporate boardrooms, there is a new far-left fascism that demands absolute allegiance. If you do not speak its language, perform its rituals, recite its mantras, and follow its commandments, then you will be censored, banished, blacklisted, persecuted, and punished. It's not going to happen to us. (Trump)

President Trump, who over the past several years had called publicly for the firing or the resignation of journalists Chris Wallace, Graydon Carter, Bill Maher, Jonah Goldberg, Charles Krauthammer, Rich Lowry, Paul Krugman, and Chuck Todd, seemed to assume that he had a right to cancel his political opponents but that his adversaries did not. Yet his blindness to this contradiction is hardly peculiar to him, or to political conservatives in general. When the *New York Times* forced the July 2020 resignation of editorial page editor James Bennet over his decision to run an op-ed the newspaper had solicited from Senator Tom Cotton advising the use of military force against violent protestors, 153 public figures from Salman Rushdie to J.K. Rowling appeared as signatories to "A Letter on Justice and Open Debate," a column in the October 2020 issue of *Harper's* implicitly supporting Bennet, whom it did not name, by attacking the "censoriousness [...] spreading more widely in our culture: an intolerance of opposing views, a vogue for public shaming and ostracism, and the tendency to dissolve complex policy issues in a blinding moral certainty" ("A Letter" 3). The counter-backlash against the backlash of "the Harper's Letter" was equally dramatic. Its most notable product was "A More Specific Letter on Justice and Open Debate," a document signed by over 160 figures in the media and the academy, who charged: "The signatories [to the Harper's Letter], many of them white, wealthy, and endowed with massive platforms, argue that they are afraid of being silenced, that so-called cancel culture is out of control, and that they fear for their jobs and free exchange of ideas, even as they speak from one of the most prestigious magazines in the country." Ignoring the fact that "cis white intellectuals [have] never been under threat en masse," this response argued, the

Harper's signatories "championed the free market of ideas, but actively ensured that it is free only for them" ("A More Specific Letter"). Cary Nelson, a professor at the University of Illinois at Urbana-Champaign and former president of the American Association of University Professors (AAUP) who had signed the Harper's Letter, was called out by name in the response as someone "whose support of free speech, apparently, does not extend to everyone"—a reference to Nelson's support for his university's decision to withdraw a job offer to American Studies scholar Steven Salaita, an outspoken advocate of the BDS (boycott–disinvest–sanction) movement against Israel, a movement Nelson had led the Modern Language Association to reject despite his earlier support for Norman Finkelstein and Neve Gordon, two other controversial academics sharply critical of Israel. John K. Wilson, an AAUP colleague of Wilson's, announced, "To endorse the firing of a scholar based on the politics of his tweets is not only absolutely intolerable, but it goes against everything Cary has stood for his entire career" (Flaherty). Once again, all parties agreed that censorship was bad—as the comment by one Parry Hotter archived on the Objective Journalism website put it, "Let people be people and have debates, but DON'T YOU DARE TO CENSOR, that's all" (Hotter)—while disagreeing vociferously about who was being or had been or was in danger of being censored and which comments merited strong countermeasures that did not amount to censorship.

In an effort to put calls for the destruction of public monuments in a broader historical context and demonstrate that it was "not a frivolous exercise in cancel culture" [2], legal scholar Alex Zhang has compared them to the Roman legal practice of *damnatio memoriae*, "the erasure of public figures—usually once-powerful politicians—from all public memory by negating their presence in monuments, statues, and records" (1–2). Reviewing "four values potentially served by memory condemnation: retribution, deterrence, expression of moral disapproval, and rehabilitation of the public space," Zhang concludes that "rehabilitation provides the best lens through which to view the debate about public memory and the most promising approach for the current progressive social movement to effect transformative change" (2). The rehabilitation Zhang describes refers not to disgraced public figures but to the statues that had memorialized them (8), whose "transformations included superimposing the new emperor's head onto an old, decapitated statue, tossing the mutilated monuments into the Tiber river, and recycling images as pavestones to accentuate the message of condemnation as carriages and pedestrians trampled the punished underfoot" (8). Observing that "[w]hat the Trump administration and other anti-BLM commentators have failed to recognize is not *whether* but *how* we should remember our country's past or commemorate its legacy in public," Zhang suggests: "Black Lives Matter presents a unique opportunity for carrying out this transformative change in our public space, using monuments and symbols not to communicate the power of past racism, but to communicate hope for the justice of the future. This rehabilitative approach obviates another criticism of memory erasure—that history should be preserved rather than destroyed—by recognizing the insight that preserving history need not involve commemorating the offender" (9).

The rehabilitation Zhang recommends might seem to replace censorship or cancelation with adaptation, whose both/and logic produces new texts, monuments, and histories instead of using the either/or logic of censorship or cancelation to suppress or obliterate histories, monuments, and messages to which it objects. A particularly powerful recent example of this both/and logic is Caroline Randall Williams's *New York Times Magazine* essay "You Want a Confederate Monument? My Body Is a Confederate Monument," whose offer to add her own body to the gallery of monuments commemorating the Confederacy is supported by the observation, "I am a black, Southern woman, and of my immediate white male ancestors, all of them were rapists. My very existence is a relic of slavery and Jim Crow," and the argument: "What is a monument but a standing memory? An artifact to make tangible the truth of the past. My body and blood are a tangible truth of the South and its past" (Williams). More generally, adaptation study invites observers to look farther afield for monuments to their collective past and to be more alert to specific adaptations that memorialize that past, often in shockingly illuminating ways. A great deal of the lively debate over the *New York Times*'s 1619 Project, which seeks "to reframe American history by considering what it would mean to regard 1619 as our nation's birth year" (Silverstein), has focused on whether it makes more sense to date the birth of the nation from 1776, the year of the Declaration of Independence, or 1619, the year the first African slaves were imported to Virginia. Indeed, one of the last acts of the Trump presidency was the publication of *The 1776 Report,* which declared, "The facts of our founding are not partisan" (*The 1776 Report* 1), announced that "the American people have ever pursued freedom and justice" (1), and warned "against pressing partisan claims or utopian agendas too hard or too far" (1)—for example, the charge that since so many of the Founding Fathers owned slaves, "they were hypocrites who didn't believe in their stated principles, and therefore the country they built rests on a lie. This charge is untrue" (10). In "Orwell's *1984* and Today," Larry P. Arnn, the Hillsdale College president who chaired the commission that produced *The 1776 Report*, went still further in comparing the 1619 Project, which "promotes the teaching that slavery, not freedom, is the defining fact of American history," to *1984*, whose Ministry of Truth "exists precisely to repeal the past" (2, 5). Ironically, Arnn's essay appeared too early to note the most Orwellian turn in the fate in *The 1776 Report*: on the day of Joe Biden's inauguration as President, it was removed without explanation from the whitehouse.gov website.

Instead of taking sides in the question of who had the authority to cancel or overwrite which views of history without being accused of censorship, adaptation scholars would point out that the question at issue is not whether 1619 or 1776 marks the single defining event in American history but rather which historical events we most want to identify as historical sources or frames or scripts, and whether we want to choose only events in which we can take pride—"patriotic education," as President Trump has called it (Wise), or "a sense of enlightened patriotism," as *The 1776 Report* calls it (17)—or add events we are bound to commemorate, as contemporary Germany continues to commemorate the Second World War and the Jewish Holocaust, lest their shameful legacy be forgotten. After all, patriotic education amounts just as clearly as historical revisionism to censorship: partisans on both sides of the debate accept their own censorship as reasonable and perhaps civically necessary even as they condemn the other party's censorship as negation or cancelation.

As Zhang's own analysis makes clear, adaptation represents not an alternative to censorship but a particular rehabilitative approach to censorship. The complicated relationship between adaptation and censorship, and the continued confusion surrounding the nature of that relationship, is illuminated by the dialogue surrounding HBO Max's decision in June 2020 to remove *Gone with the Wind* from its streaming catalogue in the light of the nationwide racial unrest associated with Black Lives Matter, and in immediate response to a *Los Angeles Times* op-ed by Academy Award-winning *12 Years a Slave* screenwriter John Ridley. Acknowledging that "movies are often snapshots of moments in history" and that "even the most well-intentioned films can fall short in how they represent marginalized communities," Ridley described *Gone with the Wind* as "its own unique problem" because "it is a film that, when it is not ignoring the horrors or slavery, pauses only to perpetuate the most painful stereotypes of people of color," a film that "has helped to perpetuate the racism that's causing angry and grieving Americans to take to the streets." Noting that "[c]urrently, there is not even a warning or disclaimer preceding the film," he added tellingly (Fig. 1):

> Let me be real clear: I don't believe in censorship. I don't think "Gone with the Wind" should be relegated to a vault in Burbank. I would just ask, after a respectful amount of time has passed, that the film be re-introduced to the HBO Max platform along with other films that give a more broad-based and complete picture of what slavery and the Confederacy truly were. Or, perhaps it could be paired with conversations about narratives and why it's important to have many voices sharing stories from different perspectives rather than merely those reinforcing the views of the prevailing culture. (Ridley)

Fig. 1 Marvin Davis, Oscar Polk, and Dawn Dodd are among the Black performers who are cast in offensively stereotypical roles in *Gone with the Wind* (1939)

Bob Greenblatt, the entertainment and direct-to-media chair of WarnerMedia, echoed Ridley's language in his announcement that the film would no longer be streamed on HBO Max when he told Jess Cagle in an interview on Sirius XM that "the decision to temporarily pull *Gone with the Wind* [was] 'a no-brainer' but said it would be restored because 'we can't censor these films'" (Hayes). Despite the shared insistence of Ridley and Greenblatt that they didn't believe in censorship, right-wing commentators were quick to condemn HBO Max's action as censorship. Their reactions are aptly summarized by an outraged tweet Megyn Kelly posted on 10 June 2020 arguing that "you can loathe bad cops, racism, sexism, bias against the LGBTQ community, and not censor historical movies, books, music and art that don't portray those groups perfectly. Ppl understand art reflects life ... as we evolve, so do our cultural touchstones" (Kelly). If Ridley found the continued availability of *Gone with the Wind*'s portrayal of the antebellum South scandalous and Greenblatt thought pulling it from circulation a no-brainer, Kelly found its sudden unavailability even more brainless and scandalous.

Two weeks after pulling *Gone with the Wind* from circulation, HBO Max returned it to its library with two notable additions. One was a new four-and-a-half-minute introduction by University of Chicago film professor and Turner Classic Movies (TCM) commentator Jacqueline Stewart that supplemented its overview of the film's background, production, and ten Academy Awards with a consideration of the offensive racial stereotypes that had made the film controversial, especially among Black viewers, ever since its first release. The second was a supplemental video recording of "*Gone with the Wind*: A Complicated Legacy," an hour-long panel discussion of the film TCM had staged the year before to commemorate the film's 80th anniversary. The implication of these two additions, in the words of the *Washington Post* headline of its story on the film's return, was that "HBO Max isn't censoring *Gone with the Wind*. It's reframing it" (Hornaday). These two reframings, however, carried revealingly different charges. Stewart's brief introductory remarks, which described the film as presenting "the Antebellum South as a world of grace and beauty without acknowledging the brutalities of the system of chattel slavery upon which this world is based," so that its "treatment of this world through a lens of nostalgia denies the horrors of slavery, as well as its legacies of racial inequality," were apparently deemed mandatory viewing by audiences who didn't fast-forward through them. The much longer panel discussion moderated by Black film scholar Donald Bogle, whose "length and utilitarian photography," as Jason Bailey reported in the *New York Times*, "may render it of greater interest to cinephiles than casual viewers," was presented as an optional extra that audiences could watch or skip at their pleasure. However many drafts Stewart's introduction had gone through in consultation with TCM and HBO Max, in the end it presented itself in her own individual voice, enclosing the film's television presentation in a single authoritative frame, whereas the panel discussion presented itself frankly as an unresolved dialogue among different viewpoints about how best to frame *Gone with the Wind* for contemporary audiences.

HBO Max's tango with *Gone with the Wind* is reminiscent not only of America's love/hate relationship with D.W. Griffith's more floridly racist 1915 Civil War epic *The Birth of a Nation* but, more generally, of the intricate dance between censorship and adaptation over the years. Although none of the commentators whose accounts of HBO Max's now-you-see-it handling of *Gone with the Wind* treated it as an exercise in adaptation, its newly emergent status as what Zhang calls rehabilitative *damnatio memoriae* suggests that that is exactly what it is. For what, after all, is adaptation but a mode of reframing or recontextualizing that chooses certain textual details to emphasize and systematically suppresses other details that might have been equally important in the adapted text in the interest not only of social mores but of other exclusionary scripts like brevity, generic decorum, and the brand identities of particular stars and studios? Although film scholars are used to thinking of adaptations as abridgments, especially when the texts adapted are as long as *Gone with the Wind*, HBO Max's recontextualization presented its restored version of the film as *Gone with the Wind*–Plus or *Gone with the Wind*–Max, a new presentation of the film with additions, at least one of which, Stewart's introduction, was deemed so authoritative that its account of the film's racial politics was more trustworthy than the film itself.

Observers dizzied by the double, or triple, standard behind HBO Max's attitude toward one of its most prized properties might take example from adaptation scholars, who have persistently attempted to reframe the question most often raised by defenders of suddenly problematic heroes—"Do we want to preserve our common history or bury it?"—with a pair of meta-questions: "Given that history is always constructed by present-day scholars, how do we propose to construct, transform, maintain, and police it?", and ultimately, "What do we want our history to say about us, and to do for us?" Instead of asking, "should there be memorials to equivocal figures from our past?", adaptationists join Zhang's rehabilitators in asking, "Which specific past events and people do we most want to memorialize? What sorts of memorials do we want to create? Should these memorials take the form of statues that honor particular heroes, monuments like the Vietnam War Memorial that identify thousands of casualties from a long-running war, or more abstract structures that commemorate other historic events? Where should these memorials be located, and how should they be introduced, framed, and contextualized?" When the American Museum of Natural History announced its plan to remove the statue of Theodore Roosevelt at its door, Roosevelt biographer David Gessner wrote: "[T]hough I fully support taking the statue down, my hope is that we don't take Roosevelt down with it."

It is tempting to argue that adaptation is categorically different from censorship because, following its both/and logic, particular adaptations always seek to supplement rather than erase the texts they are adapting. But this temptation can be resisted by considering the adaptations that present themselves as more authoritative or definitive than the texts they adapt. Think of George Cukor's 1944 film *Gaslight*, a remake of Thorold Dickinson's 1940 film adaptation of Patrick Hamilton's 1938 play, whose producers at MGM sought to purchase and destroy all copies of Dickinson's film before releasing their own. Think of *The Wizard of Oz*, which most audiences recall most vividly in its 1939 film adaptation, or all those Disney cartoons like *Bambi* (1942), *Lady and the Tramp* (1955), and *101 Dalmatians* (1961) based on stories or novels deliberately eclipsed by what Richard Schickel has tellingly called the Disney version. Or think of what Jerod Ra'Del Hollyfield calls BuzzFeed Theory, "Internet writing aiming for optimal dissemination that acts as full-fledged adaptations of the texts it discusses in order to curtail the web of intertextuality by deposing and replacing source texts via scandal, a strategy that protects it from resistant scholarly interventions" (104). Zhang's rehabilitative examples do not graft the images of new emperors onto statues of old, disgraced emperors; they lop off the statues' heads or recycle them as pavestones to be trampled underfoot. More often, adaptations are versions of stories whose struggles to compete with the versions they nostalgically salute, abridge, update, satirize, or embalm often adopt the techniques, while refusing the label, of censorship. Even though seven million copies of *Gone with the Wind* had already been sold in the three years before its film adaptation was released, the film attempts to establish itself as a more acceptable, if no more definitive, *Gone with the Wind* in large part by moderating Margaret Mitchell's combination of condescension toward and fear of African Americans and her glorification of the white supremacism embodied in the Ku Klux Klan. David O. Selznick, the producer behind *Gone with the Wind*, sought to make its racism more palatable to the mass audience he hoped to attract to its fantasy of a proud antebellum South brought low precisely by strategically censoring any references to the Klan. Two generations later, Alice Randall would censor the novel's racism in *The Wind Done Gone* not by eliminating it but by examining it from a new point of view that sought to invert its privilege, displacing Scarlett O'Hara as heroine by her slave and half-sister Cynara, who refers to Scarlett only as "Other" and Rhett Butler, Scarlett's husband and Cynara's lover, as "R." Randall, who doubtless thought of her novel as exposing *Gone with the Wind*'s racism rather than censoring it, never called her rewriting of Tara's history an exercise in censorship for the same reason Selznick did not call his film adaptation of Mitchell's novel an act of censorship. As it turned out, the only connection in which the term arose when Randall's novel was published concerned the question of whether and under what circumstances the American justice system, prompted to action in this case by a lawsuit Mitchell's estate filed to prevent the publication of *The Wind Done Gone* on the basis of copyright infringement, had the right to censor what Houghton Mifflin, Randall's publisher, insisted was a parody entitled to legal protection from legal censorship (see, e.g. Murphy, Schur). When the dust had settled, the Court of Appeals for the Eleventh Circuit ruled that *The Wind Done Gone* "is principally and purposefully a critical statement that seeks to rebut and destroy the perspective, judgments, and mythology of *Gone With the Wind*" (*Suntrust v. Houghton Mifflin*, at 1270). Despite the fears the plaintiffs' attorneys had expressed that the publication of Randall's novel might harm the future commercial prospects of Mitchell's, none of this kerfuffle dampened readers' enthusiasm for reading *Gone with the Wind*, which Amazon currently lists as the 55,372nd best-selling book it sells (*The Wind Done Gone* comes in at #955,574). The considerable success of *The Wind Done Gone*'s censorship depends not on annihilating *Gone with the Wind* but on recontextualizing its story by presenting an alternative, corrective, supplementary version of it that a critical mass of readers have found worth taking seriously.

Although adaptation theory in principle supports the publication of revisionist adaptations like *The Wind Done Gone*, it does not oblige us to choose between Randall's and Mitchell's novels, or between their views of slavery, or between opposing parties who reject calls for cancelation or censorship of their own speakers. Instead, it encourages us to ask another series of meta-questions about adaptation, cancelation, and censorship. What does, or should, it mean for one party to cancel another—murdering them, boycotting them economically, depriving them of their voice or their privilege or their platform, grinding their statues into paving stones? If we choose not to accept structural inequality and oppression but rather to identify and brand them, should we concentrate on calling out individuals, groups, or whole subcultures? On what basis should individuals be branded or exempted from branding? Once they have been branded, should they be canceled? How should we weigh their virtues against their vices in answering these questions? More generally, the practice of adaptation studies routinely moves from reductive dualities like "cancel or condone?" to more thoughtful meta-questions like "on what basis are we prepared to accept this person or these people as individuals or representatives, and on what basis are we prepared to accept whatever changes or adaptations they are willing to make?" Reflecting on questions like these suggests that what adaptation does with real-world problems, and indeed with texts and canons, is not solve them but reconsider, reframe, reformulate, police, and otherwise manage them. And it suggests three conclusions strikingly at odds with the assumptions baked into so much contemporary debate about censorship: that censorship is bad, that no one wants to be censored, and that no one wants to censor anyone else.

The first of these conclusions should be obvious by now: whether or not everyone subscribes to cancel culture, everyone really does believe in censorship, no matter how vigorously they condemn the label or disavow the practice. Different parties and cohorts simply make different assumptions about what ought to be censored when, why, and by whom.

The second conclusion is that adaptation is not an alternative to censorship, as some of my examples might have seemed to suggest. It is more accurately described as a mode of censorship that feels acceptable because we don't perceive it as censorship. By choosing which features of its adapted texts to preserve, revise, transform, and eliminate, adaptation takes its place among other invisible modes of censorship like the operations of the Hays Office, which allowed Hollywood studios to keep government censors at bay by voluntarily and preemptively censoring their own product; the division of many public libraries into rooms for adults and children, which promote the legal fiction that small children should be insulated from materials about questionable subjects because they aren't interested in them; and social media, which were largely successful in keeping their equally problematic experiments with censorship and non-censorship out of the mainstream news for years before the roof fell in, in this as in so many areas, in 2020.

The third conclusion is the most challenging: just as we can see adaptation as a mode of censorship, we can also see censorship as a mode of adaptation, a way of recontextualizing the textual particulars of scandalous texts by providing paratextual scripts that police those texts, from Hays Office memos to the *Index Librorum Prohibitorum*. Even the *Index*, the centuries-old list of writings condemned by the Catholic Church, did not succeed in preventing the publication of more than a fraction of these writings because its temporal power did not extend beyond the Papal States. Instead, the Congregation for the Doctrine of the Faith encouraged authors to submit drafts of their books before they were published, allowed the authors to defend them, encouraged revisions that would bring them into accord with Church teaching, took issue with the doctrinal errors of many published books, forbade the faithful from reading them, and, after 1897, "graded authors according to their supposed degrees of toxicity" and "marked specific passages for expurgation, rather than condemning entire books" (Lyons, quoted in "*Index Librorum Prohibitorum*") before it was disbanded in 1966 because, as Cardinal Alfredo Ottavini acknowledged, there was simply too much contemporary literature to review. The history of the *Index* reminds us that censorship is not reducible to a process of subtraction and negation on the model of the book-burning firemen Ray Bradbury presents in his twice-filmed 1953 novel *Fahrenheit 451* but rather a series of processes for producing, altering, policing, and managing texts (Fig. 2).

Roxane Gay, justifying her decision to remove her podcast "The Roxane Gay Agenda" from Spotify to protest the platform's continued hosting of provocateur Joe Rogan's podcast "The Joe Rogan Experience," whose broadcasts she found peppered with conspiracy theories, racism, and misinformation about COVID-19, announced: "I would never support censorship. [...] There's a difference between censorship and curation. [...] To say that maybe Mr. Rogan should not be given unfettered access to Spotify's more than 400 million users is not censorship, as some have suggested. It is curation" (A21). According to this logic, the *Index Librorum Prohibitorum*, the most famous censorship project in history, is an exercise in curation, not censorship. But in fact censorship is not an alternative to curation; it is a process inextricably intertwined with curation.

Fig. 2 Michael B. Jordan and Michael Shannon's unapologetic approach to censorship in *Fahrenheit 451* (2018)

In the same way, it would be a mistake to think of adaptation as a process of simply multiplying texts or versions of texts; like curation and censorship, with which it is deeply intertwined, it is a series of processes for managing texts whose reframings more or less explicitly suppress some readings of these texts (e.g. *Gone with the Wind* as an apologia for slavery) in favor of others (*Gone with the Wind* as the product of a less enlightened time). Even though adaptation by its very nature multiplies texts and ways of interpreting texts, it will never end the dualities, binaries, and drive to cancelation associated with censorship for at least two reasons: because censorship is far more complicated than cancelation—even cancel culture is more complicated than cancelation—and because, just as an indefinitely expanded canon would lose the ability to function as a canon, the limits of canons, archives, search engines, human patience, and individual and collective memory will prevent anyone from accessing or retaining more than a fraction of these texts and interpretations. Instead of laboring to oppose adaptation to censorship, scholars in the field would do better to acknowledge its deep mutual implication with censorship, a generative process that is also risky, dangerous, and often unavoidably scandalous.

Whatever a given adapter's motives, adaptation inevitably involves censorship. So adaptation can neither align itself against censorship nor opt out of censorship. The best adapters and adaptation scholars can do is to be mindful about choosing how they want to censor which texts and whom they want to authorize to censor those texts under which circumstances. In the process, they would do well to appreciate the generative, productive possibilities of censorship, as opposed to canceling—just think of all those sublime moments of Hollywood innuendo encouraged by the Hays Office, or the proliferation of censor-baiting films that followed Twentieth Century Fox's adaptation of *Peyton Place* in 1957, marketed as sensational even though they had eliminated the most scandalous moments in the novels they adapted—and align themselves not with HBO Max's obligatory introduction to *Gone with the Wind*, which purports to define the film's historical significance once and for all, but with the platform's supplementary, thoroughly inconclusive roundtable.

References

"A Letter on Justice and Open Debate." *Harper's*, vol. 341, no. 2045, Oct. 2020, p. 3. https://harpers.org/a-letter-on-justice-and-open-debate/, 7 July 2020. Accessed 25 Jan. 2021.

"A More Specific Letter on Justice and Open Debate." *The Objective*, 10 July 2020, https://www.objectivejournalism.org/p/a-more-specific-letter-on-justice. Accessed 25 Jan. 2021.

Arnn, Larry P. "Orwell's *1984* and Today." *Imprimis*, vol. 49, no. 12, Dec. 2020, pp. 1–7.

Bailey, Jason. "'Gone with the Wind' Returns to HBO Max With a Few Additions." *New York Times*, 25 June 2020, https://www.nytimes.com/2020/06/25/movies/gone-with-the-wind-hbo-max.html?searchResultPosition=2. Accessed 25 Jan. 2021.

Beers, Laura. "What Josh Hawley doesn't get about George Orwell." *CNN Opinion*, 15 Jan. 2021, https://www.cnn.com/2021/01/15/opinions/trump-and-allies-invoke-george-orwell-orwellian-beers/index.html. Accessed 25 Jan. 2021.

Court of Appeals, (n.d.) Eleventh Circuit. *Suntrust v. Houghton Mifflin*. 268 F. 3d.

Flaherty, Colleen. "'In a Hurricane.'" *Inside Higher Ed*, 15 Aug. 2014, https://www.insidehighered.com/news/2014/08/15/cary-nelson-faces-backlash-over-his-views-controversial-scholar. Accessed 25 Jan. 2021.

Fung, Brian. "Twitter bans President Trump permanently." *CNN Business*, 8 Jan. 2021, https://www.cnn.com/2021/01/08/tech/trump-twitter-ban/index.html. Accessed 25 Jan. 2021.

Gay, Roxane. "Why I've Taken My Podcast Off Spotify." *New York Times*, 4 Feb. 2022. A21.

Gessner, David. "Taking Down Teddy." *American Scholar*, 10 Sept. 2020, https://theamericanscholar.org/taking-down-teddy/. Accessed 25 Jan. 2021.
Harvey, Josephine. "GOP Lawmaker Mocked for Wearing 'CENSORED' Mask ... on National Television." *Huffington Post*, 13 January 2021, https://www.huffpost.com/entry/marjorie-taylor-greene-censored-mask_n_5fff5f1fc5b6c7 7d85ec85bc. Accessed 25 Jan. 2021.
Hawley, Josh. *Twitter*, https://twitter.com/HawleyMO/status/ 1347327774300499585. Accessed 25 Jan. 2021.
Hayes, Dade. "Pulling 'Gone With The Wind' Was A 'No-Brainer,' But It Will Return To HBO Max Because 'We Can't Censor' It, WarnerMedia's Bob Greenblatt Tells SiriusXM." *Deadline*, 12 June 2020, https://deadline.com/2020/06/pulling-gone-with-the-wind-was-a-no-brainer-but-it-will-return-to-hbo-max-because-we-cant-censor-it-warnermedias-bob-greenblatt-tells-siriusxm-1202957806/. Accessed 25 Jan. 2021.
Hollyfield, Jerod Ra'Del. "'We Need More Input!': John Hughes's *Weird Science* (1985) and Scandals from the Red Scare to the Twitter Mob." *The Scandal of Adaptation*. Edited by Thomas Leitch, Palgrave Macmillan, 2022, pp. 99–118.
Hornaday, Ann. "HBO Max isn't censoring 'Gone with the Wind.' It's reframing it." *Washington Post*, 10 June 2020, https://www.washingtonpost.com/lifestyle/style/hbo-max-isnt-censoring-gone-with-the-wind-its-reframing-it/2020/06/10/d78544ec-ab3e-11ea-94d2-d7bc43b26bf9_story.html. Accessed 25 Jan. 2021.
Hotter, Parry. Comment on "A More Specific Letter on Justice and Open Debate." *The Objective*, 11 July 2020, https://www.objectivejournalism.org/p/a-more-specific-letter-on-justice/comments. Accessed 25 Jan. 2021.
"*Index Librorum Prohibitorum*." *Wikipedia*, https://en.wikipedia.org/wiki/Index_Librorum_Prohibitorum. Accessed 25 Jan. 2021.
Kelly, Megyn. *Twitter*, https://twitter.com/megynkelly/status/ 1270680902943858689?ref_src=twsrc%5Etfw%7Ctwcamp%5Etweetembed% 7Ctwterm%5E1270680902943858689%7Ctwgr%5E%7Ctwcon%5Es1_&ref_ url=https%3A%2F%2Fwww.yahoo.com%2Fentertainment%2Fmegyn-kelly-rails-against-censorship-amid-gone-with-the-wind-being-pulled-161742326. html. Accessed 25 Jan. 2021.
Lyons, Martyn. *Books: A Living History*. Los Angeles: Getty, 2011.
Murphy, Barbara S. "*The Wind Done Gone*: Parody or Piracy? A Comment on Suntrust Bank v. Houghton Mifflin Company." *Georgia State University Law Review*, vol. 19, no. 2, 2002, pp. 567–601. https://readingroom.law.gsu.edu/cgi/viewcontent.cgi?article=2301&context=gsulr. Accessed 25 Jan. 2021.
Ridley, John. "Op-Ed: Hey, HBO, 'Gone with the Wind' romanticizes the horrors of slavery. Take it off your platform for now." *Los Angeles Times*, 8 June 2020, https://www.latimes.com/opinion/story/2020-06-08/hbo-max-racism-gone-with-the-wind-movie. Accessed 25 Jan. 2021.

Schickel, Richard. *The Disney Version: The Life, Times, Art and Commerce of Walt Disney.* Revised ed., Pavilion, 1986.
Schur, Richard. "*The Wind Done Gone* Controversy: American Studies, Copyright Law, and the Imaginary Domain." *American Studies,* vol. 44, no. 1/2, Spring/Summer 2003, pp. 5–33.
Silverstein, Jake. "Why We Published The 1619 Project." *New York Times Magazine,* 20 Dec. 2019, https://www.nytimes.com/interactive/2019/12/20/magazine/1619-intro.html. Accessed 25 Jan. 2021.
The President's Advisory 1776 Commission. *The 1776 Report,* Jan. 2021, https://www.whitehouse.gov/wp-content/uploads/2021/01/The-Presidents-Advisory-1776-Commission-Final-Report.pdf. Accessed 16 Jan. 2021; since removed.
Trump, Donald. "Remarks by President Trump at South Dakota's 2020 Mount Rushmore Fireworks Celebration | Keystone, South Dakota," 4 July 2020, *Perma.cc.* https://perma.cc/NWP5-TECB. Accessed 25 Jan. 2021.
Trump, Donald, Jr. *Twitter.* https://twitter.com/DonaldJTrumpJr/status/1347697226466828288. Accessed 25 Jan. 2021.
Williams, Caroline Randall. "You Want a Confederate Monument? My Body Is a Confederate Monument." *New York Times Magazine,* 26 June 2020, https://www.nytimes.com/2020/06/26/opinion/confederate-monuments-racism.html. Accessed 25 Jan. 2021.
Wise, Alana. "Trump Announces 'Patriotic Education' Commission, A Largely Political Move." *NPR,* 17 Sept. 2020, https://www.npr.org/2020/09/17/914127266/trump-announces-patriotic-education-commission-a-largely-political-move. Accessed 25 Jan. 2021.
Zhang, Alex. "*Damnatio Memoriae* and Black Lives Matter." *Stanford Law Review,* vol. 73, Sept. 2020, https://www.stanfordlawreview.org/online/damnatio-memoriae-and-black-lives-matter. Accessed 25 Jan. 2021.

Cinematic Contagion: *Bereullin* (*The Berlin File*, 2013)

William Mooney

In her seminal book on outbreak narratives, Priscilla Wald writes that "one of earliest usages [of the word *contagion*], in the fourteenth century, referred to the circulation of ideas and attitudes" (12). Before the identification of microbes, diseases seemed to move by way of some mystical force; yet even after an awareness of the biological basis of contagion, the concept has been employed metaphorically, frequently applied to ideas labeled revolutionary or as religious heresies.

As a metaphor for a process of adaptation, contagion implies an equivalence between texts and bodies, virus-like elements passing from one textual body to another, transmissible units that find opportunities to thrive, perhaps in a new way, in a vulnerable host. Obviously, there are human agents involved, people who come in contact with an idea, consciously or unconsciously adopting it so that it finds expression in one or more new entities. This is hardly a ground-breaking notion: "going viral" is the most common phrase we are likely to hear for an explosive spread of

W. Mooney (✉)
Fashion Institute of Technology, New York, NY, USA
e-mail: william_mooney@fitnyc.edu

© The Author(s), under exclusive license to Springer Nature
Switzerland AG 2023
T. Leitch (ed.), *The Scandal of Adaptation*, Palgrave Studies in
Adaptation and Visual Culture,
https://doi.org/10.1007/978-3-031-14153-9_12

information of any kind. In its root sense of "touching together," contagion indicates communicability through contact, though, as we all know, contagious elements can also be "airborne," passing among hosts indirectly and over a distance. Bodies' responses to them vary widely. The transmissible element can have little impact on the host; indeed, some can become "carriers" without becoming infected. Other hosts are transformed, their life trajectories altered, their bodies perhaps ravaged and destroyed. Many such germs pass through bodies regularly, sometimes combining among themselves or as a function of the new biological environment to produce new results. A host might throw up defenses, attempting to fend off or neutralize the intruder. Or the new element might find itself so completely integrated into the functioning of the host body that it becomes unremarkable, even part of organism's genetic makeup, and is passed on to new generations.

If we think of narrative and other elements as transmissible in this way, we are not far from Richard Dawkins's coinage, the now ubiquitous term "meme." "Examples of memes," wrote Dawkins, "are tunes, ideas, catchphrases, clothes fashions, ways of making pots or of building arches" (249). For Dawkins, memes function like genes, but in a process of *cultural* evolution. Memes spread throughout the "meme pool" depending on qualities similar to those of successful genes: *replicability, fecundity,* and *longevity*. Unlike genes, memes do not depend on the mechanisms of sexual reproduction, as Dawkins explains. Indeed, memes become very like replicated viral or microbial elements, the spread of which, rapid or slow, depends—as with genes—on how frequently they are copied and how long the copies that are distributed persist. It is not difficult to identify elements of literary or cinematic texts—narratives or fragments of them, characters, images, bits of dialogue, and so forth—that are replicated and deployed, more or less widely, in various media through a process much like contagion. It is the fear that this process will overwhelm us that leads to a sense of scandal, the outbreak narrative.

At the heart of this fear is the process's further devaluation of textual integrity and authorship, central to adaptation studies in the field's formative, mid-twentieth-century manifestation. Since then, from a tradition of book-to-film comparison when the cultural status of the two media were contrasted as high and low, and when a culture of "remaking" fostered commercial exploitation of titles already owned by a particular studio, we have moved into a postmodern age of serialities and multiplicities. This shift, while one of critical focus, is also a transformation of filmmaking practice. Among other things, it is a consequence of digital reproduction and storage for "home video" (eventually in the form of DVD, streaming, YouTube, internet ubiquity, and so forth) which has allowed audiences to develop a database in their minds as an enabling condition for infinite reference to recycled images and fragments of intellectual/entertainment consumables.[1] This very fact encourages piecemeal recycling over adaptation of a single well-wrought text. Thus it fans the flames, we might say, of a fragmenting textual and cinematic contagion. To follow the metaphor, it promotes an "outbreak" of what might be seen by some as a fearful disease, a plague in the face of which even the survival of many earlier practices of adaptation is threatened, along with the sacrosanct paradigm of authorship and individual artistic creation.

In this essay, I would like to look at Ryoo Seung-wan's 2013 film *The Berlin File* as a site of such contagion, a typical rather than an extreme case, in which elements from the cultural flow, Dawkins's "meme pool," become part of the formation of this new textual *body*. These interact to form the new work, porous, heterogenous, and transitory like all such cultural products, yet identifiable as a host, or "vehicle," for the viral entities that inhabit it. Texts teem with such preexisting materials, of course, which make up most what we know and think: this analysis of *The Berlin File* limits itself to some of the broadest migratory elements that traverse the text and those most visible to international audiences. One open question is the *function* of each replicated, adapted element in a film which, however porous, proceeds with an internal economy on which its communicative success and its nature as host and vehicle depend. In speaking of these viral invaders, should we condemn them as heretical or embrace the process as evolutionary or revolutionary? Does it foreshadow doom or simply lead to a transformed relationship with media and society?

The Berlin File is a South Korean spy and action thriller sharing kinship with many films from various national and global traditions. Its generic identity is one dominant feature, yet generic processes do not exclude contagion by additional elements: ideas associated with the city of Berlin, the fraught relationship between North and South Korea, the evocation of the Jason Bourne movies, and the appropriation of material from *Das Leben der Anderen* (*The Lives of Others*, 2006). The film's Korean title, *Bereullin* (Berlin), identifies the film's key element accurately: all aspects of the film build on the reputation of Berlin as a hub of Cold War spy activity

---

[1] For a fuller description of this, see Verevis, 18.

and—addressing the open question of a divided Korea—on the fall of the Wall in 1989 as a dramatization of German reunification. Evoking the Bourne franchise situates Ryoo's film in a context of global cinema, while specific appropriations from *The Lives of Others* enrich *The Berlin File*'s representation of repression by communist and capitalist governments and of national division and reunification, while they also anchor the film firmly within Korean cinema's tradition of melodrama.

The Berlin File's baroque complexity is a fundamental dimension of its design and meaning. Its action, unfolding during the transition of power after the death of Kim Jong-il in December 2011, occurs in the shadow of an uncertain future. In Berlin, an arms sale by agents of the North Korean Democratic People's Republic (DPRK) goes wrong, raising suspicions of betrayal for the authorities in Pyongyang and alarms in spy agencies across the globe. DPRK agent Pyo Jong-sung (Jung Woo Ha) and his wife Ryun Jung-hee (Jun Ji-Hyun), an embassy employee, are the principal focus of the story, along with Dong Myung-soo (Seung-bum Ryoo), an agent sent by Pyongyang to investigate them. Yet this intrigue on the North Korean side is balanced by division among the South Koreans: agent Jung Jin-soo (Suk-kyu Han), surveilling Pyo, is similarly blamed and distrusted by his government. Eventually the audience learns that Dong is trying to frame Pyo and others to conceal wholesale embezzlement by his father, who is a prominent DPRK official repositioning himself in the new regime. Dong's pursuit of Pyo and Ryun ultimately leads to a confrontation in which Pyo kills Dong, though in this battle, motivated by an attempt to rescue her, Ryun also dies.

Much of *The Berlin File* is familiar to audiences because its spies, betrayals, melodrama, chases, and martial arts fight scenes have all been part of many films, not only from Korea, but from Hong Kong, Hollywood, and elsewhere. If genre once reinforced boundaries of national cinema, for example, classical Hollywood's westerns and musicals, this is no longer the case. In a contemporary context, as Hye Seung Chung and David Scott Diffrient have argued, genre is more likely to foster transnational cinematic "migrations." East Asian cinema since the 1980s, they argue, cannot be "fully grasped within the traditional frameworks provided by 'national cinema'" (6). Korean cinema especially "has long gravitated toward non-Korean sites (and sights) as sources of localized discourse" (3).

One such "non-Korean site" exploited by *The Berlin File* is the determinedly global Jason Bourne franchise, especially *The Bourne Supremacy*, which is set in Berlin. The Bourne narratives, production, and distribution—as distinct from the films' perspective—are all international in obvious ways. The narratives travel the globe, *The Bourne Identity*, for example, moving from a Portuguese fishing boat to Marseille, Zurich, Paris, and New York. The source material and scripts are American, the director, music director, and cinematographer British, with non-U.S. actors such as the German Franka Potente, best known previously from *Lola rennt* (1998). In addition to Berlin, where a German film crew was involved in the shooting, *The Bourne Supremacy* was shot on location in Moscow, Naples, and Goa, India, and a significant part of *The Bourne Ultimatum* is set in Tangiers. Distribution and marketing were equally global in design, producing a particularly successful instance of a global blockbuster in the spy/action genre, the three films achieving worldwide box-office grosses of $214 million, $291 million, and $444 million. The Bourne films participate in, rather than initiate, this globalizing trend of action blockbusters, of course, whether they originate in Asia, the United States, Australia, or elsewhere: the extraordinary capabilities of the protagonist, exaggerated and stylized action, and carefully orchestrated fight scenes build especially on martial arts film traditions. Yet the Bourne franchise is more than just one among many influences absorbed anonymously into *The Berlin File*; echoes of its camerawork, sound, and other elements are foregrounded as if to announce: "I am making a film *in the tradition of* the Bourne trilogy." Thus, Ryoo emphasizes the connection especially during an opening ten-minute sequence, before *The Berlin File*'s credits, after which he keeps references to the franchise more at arm's length.

From the beginning, *The Berlin File* feels like a Bourne film, focusing on a beleaguered yet resilient agent betrayed by his government, working to discover the truth while at the same time trying to prevent his romantic partner and their love from being destroyed by international intrigue and the secret operations of governments further corrupted by individual ambition and greed. *The Berlin File* and *The Bourne Supremacy* both begin with botched clandestine transactions, a common spy- or crime-film opening that nonetheless is a significant similarity between them. In *The Bourne Supremacy*, the disruption occurs when Pamela Landy (Joan Allen) of the CIA is engineering payment to an unnamed Russian source for the "Neski files," documents concerning a theft of 20 million dollars seven years prior. As in the later *Berlin File*, each side in the confrontations that unfold is riven by internal divisions, so that the number of competing agents is multiplied by betrayals from within. In both films, the high-level traitors are motivated by ambition and money, in *The Bourne Supremacy* over a deal for oil, in *The Berlin File* over a gas pipeline.

As opening statements, both films present a puzzle for the film's protagonist and for the audience. In *The Bourne Supremacy*, fragments that make up a rapid montage are flashes of memory from Jason's initial assignment as an assassin, which had transpired in Berlin. In *The Berlin File*, the comparable swirl of images is a remix largely from a three-hour period we will shortly be shown in flashback, though at least two images—of the Brandenburg Gate and of a younger Dong Myung-soo in uniform—refer to moments later in the narrative. This rapid montage of shots to a driving beat includes agitated handheld camera, disorienting pans, and zooms, reiterating the Bourne experience of a puzzle that must be solved by the agent trying to understand his situation and by the viewer who experiences the film largely from the protagonist's perspective.

The opening montage of *The Berlin File* is followed by an action scene that stands out as an example of the widely imitated Bourne mode. Pyo is confronted by an anonymous South Korean agent in a stairwell, where close camerawork against bare walls in the confined space exaggerates the hectic movement and fast cutting that already amplify the excitement of the fight. The Bourne films are stylistically marked by this technique, DP Oliver Wood's whipsaw camera movements further ramping up fast action, including shifts among objects while the editing constantly disrupts and connects, disrupts and reconnects. When Pyo reaches the rooftop, we have immediate evidence of Ryoo's skill as a director: we experience viscerally the instant relief from the violence compressed within close spaces, a chance to breathe. A first confrontation between Jung and Pyo is presented against the open sky, the two characters alone in space, a moment which offers another hallmark of the Bourne films, a kind of movie tourism in expansive views of the city.

Ryoo also adopts the Bourne films' approach to market and crowded street scenes, which put the viewer in the position of an objective yet harried spectator who must work hard to locate what is significant and keep from losing the protagonist within the scene. Again, this is a commonplace of spy and detective films, public spaces that challenge surveillance and the sleuth. These films, however, also emphasize new technologies, especially ubiquitous cameras and microphones and the databases built from their recordings. One moment in the early montage of *The Berlin File* evokes a scene in *The Bourne Supremacy* in which Bourne (Matt Damon) meets Nicky (Julia Stiles) by the *Weltzeituhr* (World-time Clock) in Berlin's Alexanderplatz under cover of confusion created by chanting political demonstrators who flood the square amidst moving S-Bahn trains and trollies. Such scenes occur throughout the Bourne films, a noteworthy one, for example, in London's Waterloo Station in *The Bourne Ultimatum*. The most significant crowd moment in *The Berlin File* occurs when North Korean Ambassador Ri (Lee Kyung-young), on his way to defect to the Americans, is followed by agents of the narrative's many competing factions. This scene reaches its climax through an orchestration of multiple points of view, including those of agents Pyo and Jung immersed in the crowd, executed with the skill and sophistication typical of the Bourne films.

A further evocation of the Bourne films, in this case *The Bourne Identity*, occurs during the closing showdown between Pyo and Dong, set in a rural compound surrounded by fields where the high grasses allow the adversaries to circle each other before finally coming together so that the protagonist can kill his enemy. In *The Bourne Identity*, Jason and Marie have fled to the property of a former friend of hers. In *The Berlin File*, Ryun is taken to the rural setting as Dong's hostage. Like Bourne and the "asset" pursuing him, Pyo and Dong have their final battle after a game of cat and mouse in the fields. In *The Bourne Identity*, Jason separates from Marie for her safety while he goes on the attack. Marie will be killed in the opening scenes of the sequel, *The Bourne Supremacy*, her death offering new motivation for Bourne's revenge. In *The Berlin File*, Pyo is similarly motivated by Ryun's death. According to producer Frank Marshall, the idea for a sequel to *The Bourne Identity* arose out of Jason Bourne's threat to go after those in the CIA responsible for what happened to him. *The Berlin File* ends with a similar threat of revenge: Pyo calls Dong's father in Pyongyang to announce that he is coming after him. The screenplay for a sequel to *The Berlin File* has apparently been written, though the film remains unproduced.

Over and above formal and narrative similarities, the trigger for a specific engagement between *The Berlin File* and *The Bourne Supremacy* is their location. Both *The Bourne Supremacy* and *The Berlin File* build on Berlin's celebrity as a point of contact during the Cold War, and consequently as the site of conflict and spying so eloquently pursued by writers like John le Carré and in a list of films that includes the 1965 adaptation of his *The Spy Who Came in from the Cold*.[2] Berlin for Ryoo, however, symbolizes not only the post-World War II division of a nation based on conflicts among the victors and their ideologies; since the fall of the Wall in 1989, the city also represents a possible end of such divisions. South Korean fears of North Korea were greatly inflamed by the DPRK's development of nuclear weapons in the 1990s, eventually confirmed when underground tests were conducted in 2006. This existential threat to South Korea and the resulting diplomatic tensions are inevitably reflected in its popular films. In fact, war scenarios and narratives that advocate reconciliation between the North and South have been an obsessive theme, as in *Shiri* (1999), *Joint Security Area* (2000), *Secret Reunion* (2010), and *Steel Rain* (2018). *The Berlin File* marks itself off from these other films precisely by transporting the rivalry of governments on the Korean peninsula to the German city so redolent of Cold War history.

In *The Berlin File*, the DPRK is presented as hostile, aggressive, repressive, and in league with caricatured "anti-imperialist Arab" terrorists. But actions by the powerful on both sides ultimately dramatize an argument that power corrupts and that the forms of government—authoritarian communism on the one hand and capitalist democracy on the other—merely determine the form that corruption will take. Money would seem to be the root of all evil, exemplified by the Dong family's self-enrichment in North Korea and the energy sales by South Korean officials regardless of principle. That a final pipeline deal is made specifically between unseen South Korean leaders and the corrupt Dong Jung-ho (Gye-nam Myeong) establishes their equivalence in amoral conduct. Costuming, décor, and a gestural flamboyance contrast the consumerist South with the more austere North, yet moral laxity and betrayal are the common ground of their elites, despite their ideological differences.

Pyo, the film's primary protagonist, embodies the stoicism and loyalty of ordinary North Koreans, admirable traits even if their allegiance is misplaced. Jung, representing the South in this allegory, appears good-natured and self-indulgent, if a somewhat inflexible holdover from the Cold War who is insufficiently committed to the contemporary capitalist state. A rabidly anti-communist devotion to the United States is dramatized in his personal bond with the aging CIA agent Marty (John Keogh).

[2] Beyond the well-known titles *Torn Curtain* (1966), *Octopussy* (1983), *The Man from U.N.C.L.E.* (2015), Steven Spielberg's *Bridge of Spies* (2015), and episodes of *Homeland*, season 5 (2015), there are many others.

The film presents the trust developed between Pyo and Jung as transcending a North/South division that is upheld by forces of greed and ideology against natural human sympathy. The third in the trio of principal characters is Ryun, whose subservience and sacrifice are doubly determined by her situation as a (North) Korean woman and by generic patterns in melodrama. In the allegory, she defends love, the unborn child, and the idea of family against the corrupt authoritarian state. Ryun's demonstrations of strength come in confronting Pyo with his mistake of choosing the state over love and family.

I would underscore at this point how little of *The Berlin File* is unique. It borrows heavily from the spy/thriller genre generally, and from *The Bourne Supremacy* specifically; it leans on a long-standing identification of the city of Berlin with Cold War conflict, and it dwells on the common divided-nation theme in Korean cinema. By contrast, Ryoo's adopting and adapting of *The Lives of Others* might seem less predictable because Florian Henckel von Donnersmarck's film circulated more as an art film than as popular entertainment. It is hardly free of genre elements, as critics have noted. Paul Cooke even argued, for example, that Donnersmarck's work promotes "the core values of the Hollywood genre cinema" (223). David Bathrick discussed East/West intrigue in the film to place it in relation to the espionage genre, while Rüdiger Suchsland denigrated it as "a palatable melodrama, from the brown dusty days of the GDR, seasoned with some sex and art, [and] lots of horrible repression" (Cooke 8). Commentators in the circle of Berlin School filmmakers viewed it as a "heritage film," in Eric Rentschler's words, seeking "consensus" at the cost of accountability (Rentschler 323; Cooke 242). Yet while Donnersmarck's film does embrace conventions of popular cinema, it stood apart from the mainstream at the time of its release because of subject matter that was doubly taboo: it emphasized German-on-German tyranny and complicity in the GDR, and it indirectly once again invoked the involvement of ordinary Germans in Nazi crimes.

The mixture of genre and art-film appeal in *The Lives of Others* would hardly disqualify it for attention in South Korea, especially in an industry where box-office favorites from *Old Boy* (2003) to *Parasite* (2019) also win prestigious festival awards internationally. In fact, in combination with the issue of division and reunification that drew *The Berlin File* to Berlin in the first place, melodrama—a staple of South Korean cinema since the 1950s—would have greatly supplemented the appeal of *The Lives of Others*. Melodrama is the reason that we find the story of Christa-Maria Sieland

(Martina Gedeck) and Georg Dreyman (Sebastian Koch), under pressure from Stasi agents, reenacted by Ryun and Pyo under pressure from the DPRK. As in *The Lives of Others*, the political pressures of the spy drama and a divided country are played out as distrust within a couple.

The Lives of Others and *The Berlin File* have the same structure: a political spy plot that is paralleled and illuminated by the story of a couple's relationship. In *The Berlin File* as in Donnersmarck's film, a woman violated by a powerful figure in the government becomes isolated by mutual distrust from a partner who learns of her actions without understanding the circumstances. In the end, the woman dies, herself a victim but also denying her partner the possibility of redemption for his failure of trust. The parallels, however, go well beyond a close, if general, similarity in the narratives. Specific visual framings, mise en scène, actions, and dialogue combine as direct citations of *The Lives of Others*, a recognition of the film's importance in elaborating *The Berlin File*. One image, for example, replicates the most widely used publicity still for *The Lives of Others*, Gerd Wiesler (Ulrich Mühe) in headphones, intensely concentrating at his listening post in the attic of Sieland and Dreyman's apartment building. In *The Berlin File*, Pyo, Wiesler's counterpart, who has installed cameras to watch Ryun and her boss at the embassy, is similarly shown in headphones, hunched over his computer screen as he listens intensely and watches Ryun and the Ambassador. Furthermore, as if to flag the films' interrelationship, Ryoo casts Thomas Thieme, who plays the reprehensible Minister Hempf in *The Lives of Others*, as the corrupt German official, Sigmund, who forces himself on Ryun. Rape is the central fact in the melodrama of each film, a long-standing trope of the genre. It might not be an exaggeration to see rape as the central metaphor in these films for violation of a (national) community by those lusting for power (Figs. 1 and 2).

The crucial scenes in this appropriation are those in which the couple, divided by the woman's experience and its misrepresentation to her husband, are in the same living space yet cannot connect with each other. In *The Lives of Others*, after Sieland is raped by Hempf and Dreyman has been put in a position to observe her getting out of Hempf's car, she enters their apartment. Both characters are frozen at this moment, incapable of communicating what they are experiencing. As Sieland takes a shower, a cleansing ritual, the filming emphasizes her inner pain and isolation. Dreyman sits stunned at his desk, while in silence Sieland goes to the bedroom in the background. An ensuing shot shows her in bed, curled in a fetal position. Eventually Dreyman comes to her and speaks her name,

Fig. 1 Hempf (Thomas Thieme) assaults Christa-Maria Sieland (Martina Gedeck) in *Das Leben der Anderen*

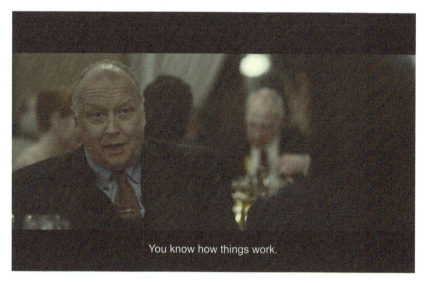

Fig. 2 Siegmund (Thomas Thieme) explains "how things work" in *Bereullin*

attempting contact. "Just hold me," she says. The pain between them is palpable, and Dreyman's response—he does hold her—answers the question raised in the mind of audiences about the strength of the characters' bond in the face of such a trauma.

The encounters in *The Berlin File* unfold similarly, though across several scenes. The first follows the meeting in the restaurant where Ryun is told by Ambassador Ri that she must have sex with Sigmund (Thieme). Her violation occurs offscreen; meanwhile, the narrative follows a waitress from the restaurant who passes a recording of the dinner conversation to NIS agent Jung. We are brought back to Ryun as she arrives home looking weak and depressed, carrying groceries in an attempt to maintain the façade of a normal day. Pyo is seen from behind seated at a small table, like Dreyman at his desk. Then we see Ryun in the shower, the water falling on her head and face, a familiar trope, yet pointedly echoing the scene with Sieland. Like Sieland's, Ryun's attention is inward, in her case including brief flashbacks of the faces of Ri and of Sigmund as the shower continues. Earlier, in order to escape the embassy and Ri's control, Ryun had asked Pyo about the possibility of returning to Pyongyang. "Any news from Pyongyang?" she now says, and when he rebukes her, Ryun's emotions surface in a way comparable to Sieland's. "Can't you just ask me *why* I want to go back?" she asks Pyo. The shot following this scene shows Ryun in bed in the same position as Sieland in *The Lives of Others*, though the framing is tighter. As if for emphasis, when Pyo and Ryun are next alone together this shot is repeated, even more closely replicating that of Sieland in her moment of despair.

In *The Lives of Others*, Dreyman gains the courage to address Sieland directly only after his friend Jerska's suicide. Finally willing to face the truth, he tells her: "You don't need [Hempf]." Pyo has a comparable, if somewhat less direct line appealing to his wife's character to resist the pressures she faces: "We can live with our heads held high even if we are poor." Like Sieland, however, Ryun has lost faith in her husband's support. Pyo too will have to prove himself personally and politically.

A final scene of confrontation echoes Sieland's calling out Dreyman for his own compromises with the GDR government. One of *The Berlin File*'s subplots is that Pyo and Ryun have previously lost a child to an unspecified illness; Ryun has kept secret from her husband not only that she is being forced by the Ambassador to "entertain guests," but also that she is pregnant with Pyo's child. A visit to her obstetrician's office near the U.S. Embassy has fanned suspicions that she is involved in Ambassador

Ri's plan to defect. Now, after Pyo has torn their apartment apart searching for evidence of her treachery, Ryun enters to stand among a material disarray that perfectly expresses her state of mind. In response to Pyo's angry questioning, she reveals first her forced prostitution, then that she is pregnant with his child. If she is concerned that he might believe the child is not his, he is too locked in his obsession with loyalty to the state to notice. "What I believe does not matter," Pyo rages. "Tell me the truth!" Ryun digs into her bag, and hands him her sonogram. "*This*," she says, "is the truth!" It is one high point of the film's melodrama, yet it also serves to endorse a major theme in the film, the central role in life played by values of love and family.

As with Sieland and Dreyman, once all is in the open, the couple seem closer to bridging the divide between them. Yet like Sieland, Ryun resists an unsatisfactory reconciliation. Earlier, Ryun's words had underscored a key dichotomy in the film: "I forgot you're the Republic's hero before you're my husband." She can forgive Pyo's being caught up in the intrigues and betrayals of the government, but she cannot forgive his failure to trust her. "You should have believed me," she tells him. Pyo has failed Ryun as Dreyman failed Sieland.

Pyo and Ryun are pursued further. She will be held hostage by Dong, dying during the rescue attempt, a death comparable to Sieland's, both women sacrificed so that their men can learn what they need to learn about life. Dreyman escapes the collapsed GDR and becomes a fulfilled artist; Pyo escapes his fealty to the DPRK and becomes his own person, ready to take revenge against the corrupt and powerful man responsible for Ryun's death.

The parallels between the films could be parsed in even greater detail. Both films, for example, carefully develop the idea of austere and repressive communist societies hostile to children. At the same time, neither film emphasizes the superiority of the capitalist society over the communist one, arguing rather that there is an underlying human commonality that is more important than ideology. In *The Lives of Others*, the Stasi agent is the "good man" in the film, discovering in the lives of Dreyman and Sieland a sympathy more important than his affiliation with the state. *The Berlin File* emphasizes the personal bond between Jung and Pyo, South and North Korean agents, which transcends their ideological differences. Jung is the good man who, like Wiesler, sympathizes with his adversary during surveillance and ultimately tries to rescue him. Jung stands over Pyo as he holds the body of his dead lover just as Wiesler, in the earlier film, is the witness of Dreyman holding Sieland. When Jung turns Pyo loose to attempt revenge on Dong, Jung's human feelings have overcome South Korea's official postures and policies just as Wiesler's feelings inspired his attempt to protect Sieland and Dreyman at the cost of his own career. Of course the villains, like the heroes, traverse ideological boundaries. Hempf, the personification of GDR corruption in *The Lives of Others*, finds himself equally at home in the democratic and capitalist reunified Germany. In *The Berlin File*, the pipeline deal between the South Korean leaders and arch-villain Dong Jung-ho is shown to be more than clever policy; it is presented as the corrupt reason that Jung is ordered to betray both his professional commitment and his sentimental bond with Pyo. One might criticize *The Berlin File* as some did *The Lives of Others*, as Rentschler does in describing Donnersmarck's film as a "tale of consensus for a unified Germany" (316). *The Berlin File* similarly downplays accountability for crimes of the authoritarian state in favor of advocating, based on kinship and common human feeling, for a unified Korea.

As a site of contagion, *The Berlin File* exhibits a range of borrowed materials only sampled here, as are the range of functions they can come to serve within the new textual body. The ideas associated with Berlin are global commonplaces of twentieth-century history, while the future of the two Koreas is more germane to those experiencing the peninsula's conflict. *The Bourne Supremacy* is a specific media and entertainment product that conveys, and through which pass, formulaic geopolitical tropes; it participates in the modalities of the international action/spy thriller, including its theme of the dangers and corruption of government power, which provide generic scaffolding for *The Berlin File*. In a very different way, awareness of *The Lives of Others*, a European art film distinguished from Germany's commercial mainstream by its subject matter if not its narrative form, encourages reading Ryoo's film against both the backdrop of Cold War history and that of recent European cinema. Donnersmarck's film is mined for its central dramatic relationship, providing Ryoo with granular materials of thought and specific language through which, within the generic framework of melodrama, he can extrapolate and articulate his story.

The English title of *Bereullin—The Berlin File*—inadvertently underscores this film's composite nature as a *file*, containing separate documents that relate to a particular subject, but which are yet to be integrated. For us, furthermore, the film raises the question of the extent to which much adaptation today functions through a similar recombinatory process. And if adaptation, like translation in Lawrence Venuti's analysis, was always and already scandalous for—as R. Barton Palmer puts it in this volume—rejecting the neoromantic notion of literary expressions as linked to their ostensible authors, then what is an appropriate descriptor for works compiled from the fragments of dismembered textual bodies and other artifacts adrift in the meme pool?

The creator of such works becomes, at most, one who *discovers* rather than one who *invents*, one who observes affinities among elements in a reservoir of cultural consciousness that invite recombination. Authors or directors become enablers in a less egocentric, more mechanistic universe, in some respects echoing their role in the collaborative production of classical Hollywood. In our time the position is imposed on filmmakers not by a studio boss or factory approach to mass-produced and consumed entertainment, but rather by their being engulfed in media that have fostered a new idealism. The author or *auteur* is reduced to a role as facilitator in a collective cognition that animates the very material environment on which life as we know it depends. Adaptation studies has learned to *read* the serialities and multiplicities in which texts have always participated. Now, however, as in *The Berlin File*, adaptation frequently *foregrounds* its diverse materials and interrelationships as fundamental in its recombinatory creative processes.

There can be no question that such adaptation shares characteristics of contagion, but where does understanding this lead us? The evolutionary paradigm, to return to Dawkins, is descriptive rather than evaluative, attempting to neutrally delineate a non-teleological process of the material universe. *Contagion*, by contrast, cries scandal; it laments a snowballing loss of authorial importance and control, even industrial control, illusory as these might ever have been. Invoking fear of disease and destruction of the old order, it fans the scandal of fragmentary adaptation into an outbreak narrative and the fear of a species-ending plague. One might take either side in a controversy over heresy or the value of a revolution. Ultimately, however, we must accept the fact that a process of contagion is fundamental to adaptation; cinematic and otherwise, it is at the heart of the process. Adaptation *is* contagion, the spread of which cannot be contained.

References

Bathrick, David. "*Der Tangospieler* Coming in from the Cold Once and for All? *The Lives of Others* as Cold War Spy Film." Cooke 121–38.

Chung, Hye Seung, and David Scott Diffrient. *Movie Migrations: Transnational Genre Flows and South Korean Cinema*. New Brunswick, NJ: Rutgers UP, 2015.

Cooke, Paul, ed. *The Lives of Others and Contemporary German Film*. Berlin: de Gruyter, 2013.

Dawkins, Richard. *The Selfish Gene* (40th Anniversary Edition). Oxford: Oxford University Press, 1989 (first published 1979). Kindle edition.

Rentschler, Eric. *The Use and Abuse of Cinema: German Legacies from the Weimar Era to the Present*. New York: Columbia UP, 2015.

Verevis, Constantine. *Film Remakes*. Edinburgh UP, 2017.

Wald, Priscilla. *Contagious: Cultures, Carriers, and the Outbreak Narrative*. Durham, NC: Duke UP, 2008.

Periphery and Process: Tracing Adaptation Through Screenplays

Jonathan C. Glance

When Thomas Leitch proposed a roundtable discussion for the 2020 South Atlantic Modern Language Association (SAMLA) on "The Scandals of Adaptation," inspired by Lawrence Venuti's *The Scandals of Translation*, I immediately remarked a parallel between Venuti's call for a revaluation of translation—which he characterizes as "stigmatized as a form of writing, discouraged by copyright law, depreciated by the academy, [and] exploited by publishers and corporations" (1)—and my own experience conducting scholarship concerning adapted screenplays. Venuti's characterization of translation applies to these texts too: screenwriting has been notably stigmatized within the film industry and until recently within the academy; copyright for screenplays resides with the studio, not the screenwriter, hindering scholarship and reproduction; only very recently have scholars, notably within the field of screenplay studies, considered screenplays as works of interest in themselves; and even when published, "screenplays" are frequently misrepresented transcriptions produced after the

---

J. C. Glance (✉)
Mercer University, Macon, GA, USA
e-mail: GLANCE_JC@mercer.edu

© The Author(s), under exclusive license to Springer Nature Switzerland AG 2023
T. Leitch (ed.), *The Scandal of Adaptation*, Palgrave Studies in Adaptation and Visual Culture,
https://doi.org/10.1007/978-3-031-14153-9_13

film. Moreover, the screenwriting process, by means of which adaptation occurs and through which adaptations are created, is restricted to a marginal niche within the already marginalized field of adaptation studies. This process is a fundamental and essential component in film adaptations, yet it is too often neglected or ignored in our scholarship, an oversight I believe is a scandal. This chapter reviews the nature and treatment of screenplays, considers their role in understanding the process of film adaptation, and calls for much greater attention to them within adaptation studies. It uses Billy Wilder's *Double Indemnity* (1944) and John Huston's *The Man Who Would Be King* (1975) to illustrate how screenwriters approach adaptation and how multiple variant drafts document creative and essential aspects of that process. These documents can deepen and even transform our understanding of movies and adaptation.

Screenplays, although essential to any film, have been stigmatized and depreciated as a form of writing within the film industry, which has often treated script drafts "as little more than industrial waste products" (Price and Pallant 2). The collaborative art of film, in which many people contribute to create a product and jostle for the credit, has long led to animosity and suspicion between competing parties. Emblematic of this tension are two oft-recycled quips. A remark most often attributed to Jack L. Warner derided Warner Brothers' hired writers, who at the time included William Faulkner, as "schmucks with Underwoods," interchangeable cogs scarcely worth the mogul's notice. Writer Burt Kennedy, by contrast, ridiculed the notion that a producer or director is the creator of a film: "I was driving by Otto Preminger's house last night—or is it 'a house by Otto Preminger'?" (qtd. in Corliss xvii). For Kennedy, Preminger is no more the creator of a film than he is the architect of his house.

Surprisingly, Hollywood's stigmatization of screenwriters was for too long echoed in the dismissal of screenplays as subjects of interest. In 1984 Gary Davis observed that "the literary community, like the business world of Hollywood, views the screenplay only as a means to an end rather than an entity in itself" (90). Instances of this disregard are easy to find. Roger Manvell, for example, denigrated the genre out of hand in his monograph *Theatre and Film*: "Film scripts, especially today, are frequently published, but it is evident from the very appearance of the printed page that very few of them can rank as literature; the description of the action is very evidently a secondhand affair, losing visual impact through the referential nature of the words. It is like a description of a painting instead of the painting itself" (25). Manvell contrasts stage play scripts with screenplays, asserting that while the former is a form of literature, a screenplay is like a description of a superior and more artistic visual form, the completed film. Viewed in this way, scripts are merely an intermediary verbal stage of a visual art. To borrow Pier Paolo Pasolini's phrase, a screenplay is "a structure that wants to be another structure" (53) and not a complete artistic work on its own. If a screenplay is just a blueprint for a film, to use a widely repeated metaphor, then once the film is completed the script has served its function and is superfluous. Isabelle Roblin and Shannon Wells-Lassagne emphasize this superfluity: "For a very long time, screenplays were considered as invisible texts: torn, crumpled, dirtied and eventually thrown into the studio dustbins at the end of the shoot, as Jean-Claude Carrière remarked" (5). Moreover, an unproduced script—that is, one never shot or never completed—would be of no interest for scholars, languishing instead as "a kind of textual other, the exiled abject of mainstream film and theatre discourse" (Boon 1–2).

Various explanations have been offered for this neglect of screenplays. The script's preliminary status, noted above, is a common suggestion. Jill Nelmes, for instance, notes, "Even though the screenplay has been in existence since the first scenarios of the early twentieth century the form has received little academic attention [...] mostly because film has been seen as part of an industrial and technological process, in which the screenplay is considered merely the first stage towards the final product, the feature film" (*Analysing* 1). Contrasting this critical indifference to the wealth of studies of film directors, she adds that while "there are a plethora of publications on the subject of how to write a screenplay [...] there has been a meagre amount of published academic work which analyses the screenplay itself" (2). Another suggestion, explored by Steven Price, is the contractual nature of screenwriting, which vests copyright with the studio, not the screenwriter: "Especially in Hollywood, the writer lacks the legal status of an author, and unlike the playwright, the screenwriter has little or no copyright or other legal authority in matters relating to the text. Under the US copyright law, films are ordinarily described as 'works made for hire'" (13). Critical assumptions of authorship are even more problematic when the text has been produced, as screenplays commonly are, by multiple writers working together or sequentially, with credit determined within industrial parameters (specifically, the Writer's Guild of America's codified Minimum Basic Agreement guidelines) but often omitting many of the writers involved. Price adds, "A short answer to the question of why the auteur theory has attached itself to the directors, but not at all to the screenwriters, is that the latter are not authors but writers" (13). A literary author, that Romantic and romanticized figure who creates worlds out of his imagination, receives plaudits and more importantly ownership of his intellectual property; writers, contracted to contribute words and pages which become the intellectual property of their employer, dissolve into unseen schmucks with Underwoods.

It is certainly true that some critics have recognized the significance of screenplays. Ninety years ago, Béla Balázs celebrated the film script as "no longer a technical accessory, not a scaffolding which is taken away once the house is built, but a literary form worthy of the pen of poets" (246). Within the field of adaptation studies, Jack Boozer has insisted on the screenplay's "centrality to the collaborative authorship that is at the heart of film adaptation" (1); it supplants the source text as the "foundation and fulcrum for any adapted film" (40). Ian MacDonald concurs, emphasizing the screenplay as "the point at which basic decisions are made" as well as an invaluable record of "certain kinds of decisions—often political or thematic, and economic" which "can explain choices, preferences and dispositions in relation to the whole field of production" (13). More recently, Jamie Sherry has echoed Boozer's call, asserting that the "lack of attention to the crucial processes of adaptation, and the transitional mode of adaptation screenwriting [...] illustrates a fundamental gap in adaptation studies" (15). Sherry differs from Boozer, though, in arguing that it is not the final adapted screenplay but rather the preceding script drafts which are most important: "In opposition to Boozer's view that the adapted screenplay is the most complete document of the adaptation process, it is actually the diverse, unstable and incomplete nature of the screenplay that can offer us some of the most profound insights into remediation" (26). Simone Murray asserts that "the contribution of screenwriters has been systematically marginalized" (132) by adaptation studies, despite the fact that "all adaptation industry traffic necessarily passes through the nodal point of the screenwriter" (133–34). Peter Lev adds, "Without this kind of primary source research, which is very much the exception in adaptation studies, our field is missing a vital tool" (672). Adaptation studies has mostly ignored the rich resources of the screenplay record. At the 2020 annual conference of the Association of Adaptation Studies (eventually canceled because of the pandemic), for example, of the seventy-four presenters selected to represent the current state of the discipline, only six mentioned screenplays in their abstracts, and even fewer indicated any attention to multiple draft scripts.

Given the central role screenwriting occupies in adaptation and the burgeoning recognition of the value screenplays hold for understanding the adaptation process, why has adaptation studies been remiss in exploring this resource? Perhaps the reason is rooted in theoretical issues tied to the development of adaptation studies itself. Murray speculates that "the adapted screenplay's status as both explicitly unoriginal as well as implicitly intermedial" magnifies "both of the problems with which adaptation studies was already wrestling" (132). Yet the discipline's concerns may make an even stronger case for further attention, as Roblin and Wells-Lassagne insist: "By striking at the heart of some of the central paradoxes of filmmaking in general and adaptation in particular—the notion of authorship, the specificity of media, the protean nature of 'story'—screenwriting becomes a crucial aspect of the production practices that hold increasing sway in adaptation studies" (8).

A still more compelling reason for the paucity of scholarly attention may be methodological. Andrew Horton and Julian Hoxter make a persuasive case for this hypothesis, noting that for many films only an incomplete record of the script stage is extant: "Much of the difficulty of writing the history of screenwriting lies in gaining access to the appropriate primary sources. Developmental (and even 'final') screenplay drafts are disposable artifacts. They may not be kept and are rarely offered by studios, much less by writers, for study either for contractual reasons or due to the formative nature of the documents" (3). Arguably the best archival resource for screenplays is the Margaret Herrick Library, the reference and research site for the Academy of Motion Pictures Arts and Sciences (AMPAS). This library houses screenplays for over 15,000 films produced since 1910, albeit predominantly "late drafts or shooting scripts, formatted and prepared for production. However useful these documents are in their own right, they conceal much of the development process that predates them" (Horton and Hoxter 3–4). Complicating the matter further for scholars who wish to utilize this library are two problems. One problem stems from studio ownership of screenplays as intellectual property. As a result, unpublished scripts (including all preliminary script versions and drafts) may not be photocopied, thus requiring the scholar to transcribe all scripts that might later prove relevant to a research project. Even after having completed this time- and labor-intensive step, all quoting for publication of these scripts necessitates negotiations with the Intellectual Property division of the studio (or whichever conglomerate entity currently owns that IP) for permission to publish and payment of a licensing fee. A second problem is that the Herrick library closed in March 2020 because of the COVID pandemic, reopening only in April 2022.

Despite these drawbacks, however, the Herrick Library is an invaluable resource for adaptation studies because it houses special collections of considerable interest. These collections can be haphazard, often dependent on which film industry individuals (e.g. producers, directors, actors) compiled the materials and donated them to the Academy. Frequently the screenplays within these collections are final or late-stage versions, although sometimes these are annotated. Some of these collections, however, contain multiple screenplay drafts revealing and documenting the script stages of a film production from beginning to end. Directors most involved with these script stages—either directly in the case of writer-directors Billy Wilder and John Huston or in collaborative but uncredited roles, as in the case of Alfred Hitchcock—tend to have these more complete records among their papers.

Yet even a scholar who has been able to locate and access such a beginning-to-end record of the screenwriting process for a given film faces considerable difficulty, especially if that scholar innocently assumes that a screenplay is a blueprint for a film. The metaphor of the blueprint, often "used to characterize the function and the significance of the screenplay during the production process" (Sternberg 50), suggests "that the script is a completed conception awaiting execution at the filming stage" (Price 63). Publication of final or late draft scripts that closely resemble the released film or, even worse, transcripts of the film dialogue printed in screenplay format serve only to perpetuate this notion. As many critics now agree, however, the blueprint is an "outdated and simplistic model" (Horton and Hoxter 1–2) that inadequately captures the fluid process or industrial practice of screenwriting: "Unlike the manufacturing of a dress or car, where the end product conforms closely to a drawing or blueprint and the cost estimates are reliable, a film script evolves during the process of making the film" (Acheson and Maule 315). Steven Price argues in *The Screenplay* that a screenplay is "not so much a blueprint as an enabling document, necessary for the production but transformed by directors, actors, vagaries of the weather, and a multitude of other factors" (xi), and in *A History of the Screenplay* suggests that instead of a blueprint "we might think of a screenplay as a kind of conversational gambit: an accumulated set of suggestions, usually the product of multiple dialogues between different contributors" (19). The seemingly neutral metaphor of the blueprint perpetuates the stigmatization of the screenwriters, obscures their creative contributions, and misrepresents the process of screenwriting; what is required is another way of thinking about a form that is characteristically unstable, fluctuating, tentative, and recursive.

How do screenwriters practice adaptation, and what issues do they consider as part of this practice? What do they think they are doing when they adapt a source text? Recognizing that there is much variability across individual approaches to a creative process, we can still note broad practices. Fidelity to the source text may be one consideration, especially for recent bestsellers with a fanbase of devoted readers who expect or demand fidelity. A more crucial consideration, though, is the structural viability of the narrative and the conventions and demands of the film medium. No matter how popular a novel is, its film adaptation is likely to reach a wider audience, including many who have not read the book. Hence the film adaptation must stand on its own as a cohesive and satisfying work. For that reason much of the adapter's preliminary work is, to use Joseph McBride's term, to "break the back of the book" (83)—to determine its structural elements and analyze how they work. In his guide to screenwriting, McBride asserts, "Rigorously analyzing the structure to decide what works and what doesn't, and ruthlessly discarding scenes that don't advance the story line, is the basic task of adaptation" (91). This work is rarely straightforward and often entails much trial and error, generating multiple versions of the same scene. Emphasizing the "continual testing of and discarding of ideas as to their suitability for the story" as crucial to the process, Jill Nelmes notes that these testing and discarding decisions are formative because "[a]ll decisions about character and plot take the story along particular paths" ("Some Thoughts" 111). The process of adaptation in screenwriting is not as a linear path connecting the source text to the final adapted product. Although the final screenplay may create that impression, the preceding test scenes, variant scripts, and discarded pages reveal instead a host of forking paths, some followed and others curtailed. "This process of asking questions and making decisions," Nelmes observes, "particularly [regarding] the consequences of an action by a character [and] the cause and effect direction of the story, is crucial to the development of the narrative" ("Some Thoughts" 111).

To reveal and explore salient characteristics of the screenwriting process, I wish to discuss two adapted films: Billy Wilder's *Double Indemnity* (1944) and John Huston's *The Man Who Would Be King* (1975). Both films were made by writer-directors actively engaged in a collaborative screenwriting process, both received Academy Award nominations for

Best Adapted Screenplay, both are represented by a published screenplay,[1] and both underwent a prolonged process of composition recorded in multiple drafts. These drafts are extant because these directors retained them and donated them to the Herrick as part of the Billy Wilder Papers and the John Huston Papers, presumably under the impression that studying them might generate valuable insights. They prompt us to re-examine our assumptions about these movies and adaptation more broadly. We might assume that the screen adapter strives to maintain the intrinsic aesthetic and narratological elements from the source while battling extrinsic factors like limited budgets, meddling producers, and restrictive guidelines imposed by the Motion Picture Production Code. Tales of such battles by writers or auteur directors against these obtruding forces are common in Hollywood lore. The archival records suggest, however, that these apparently intrinsic and extrinsic pressures are in fact intertwined throughout the pre-production stage of filmmaking whether or not the films in question are adaptations. Concerns of budget, censorship, and audience expectations are as intrinsic to the process of adapting *Double Indemnity* or *The Man Who Would Be King* as Cain's or Kipling's words and scenes in the source texts.

DOUBLE INDEMNITY

James M. Cain clearly intended his novella *Double Indemnity* to be adapted by Hollywood and actively sought a film deal. Even before he serialized it in *Liberty Magazine* in February–April 1936, Cain sent mimeographs of the manuscript to the major studios, and several bid for the film rights. Cain's story of an insurance salesman who has an affair with an oilman's wife and murders him to collect the insurance money violated multiple principles of the Motion Picture Production Code, however, and Production Code Administration chief Joseph Breen sent a letter in October 1935 to Louis B. Mayer at MGM (with copies subsequently sent to Jack Warner at Warner Brothers and to David O. Selznick, and also shared with a representative from Columbia) categorically warning off all would-be adapters: "the story under discussion is most objectionable and,

---

[1] A *Double Indemnity* script dated 25 November 1943 was published by the University of California Press in 2000 with an introduction by Jeffrey Meyers. A script for *The Man Who Would Be King* dated 15 November 1974 has also been published, but that facsimile printing does not list a press or publication date.

unless it can be materially changed, both in the structure and in detail, all consideration of it for screen purposes should be dismissed" (PCA Records).

That warning held until 1943, when Billy Wilder convinced Paramount to attempt the adaptation. Wilder intended to collaborate on a screenplay with Cain, but the novelist was under contract to Fox for another script, so Paramount brought in Raymond Chandler to cowrite the screenplay with Wilder. While Chandler was an experienced author who had published four novels and a score of stories (mostly in *Black Mask* and *Dime Detective* pulp magazines), he had never written a screenplay. In later years Wilder often regaled journalists and biographers with conflicting accounts of how he schooled Chandler in screenwriting (see, e.g. Zolotow, Sikov, and Phillips), but archival records discredit his stories. Twenty-nine separate documents—partial and complete script drafts and variants dated between May and December 1943—chronicling the planning and drafting of the screenplay are available in the Herrick Library, chiefly in the Billy Wilder Papers. (Excerpts from documents relating to *Double Indemnity* granted courtesy of Universal Studios Licensing LLC.) These drafts and variants provide documentary evidence of this adaptation's process of composition.

First, the archived documents indicate that Chandler worked alone for nearly a month on significant elements of the adaptation. Rather than the overeager blunderer of Wilder's later accounts, however, we see that Chandler from the start was a careful and methodical planner. He created a "Rough Scheme of Scenes" (dated 1 June)—a detailed list of forty-six story beats and the developments required for each scene of the plot's narrative sequences, labeled A through E, debating possible motivations for Walter's crime and confession, and pointing out holes in Cain's narrative to be addressed in the film (Billy Wilder Papers 1.f-14). These notes illustrate how Chandler planned where to be faithful to or diverge from his source text, identified which scenes not in the book needed to be created, invented the structural device of interspersing Walter's recording of his confession onto a dictaphone with flashbacks to the action, and envisioned a significantly different ending than Cain's double suicide by drowning. In Chandler's earliest work, a seven-page test scene (dated 24 May), Phyllis Nirdlinger invites Walter Huff to her house ostensibly to renew her husband's auto insurance, but really to learn whether she can acquire accident insurance on her husband without his being aware of the policy.[2] In tight, rapid dialogue, Phyllis and Walter progress from casual small talk to avid flirtation to wary scheming to jaded accusations to feigned outrage to sexual blackmail (Billy Wilder Papers 1.f-12). The first script attributed to both Chandler and Wilder (dated 15 June–15 July) retains many elements from Chandler's initial pages before evolving toward the screenplay used in the film.

Some scenes that seemed particularly problematic required the greatest number of drafts. The opening scenes—the beginning of Walter's confession, the first meetings of Walter and Phyllis—are clearly crucial to the foundation of the plot and therefore repeatedly and thoroughly revised in multiple drafts. These revisions tested variations in pacing and wording, and ultimately developed the punchy, quippy dialogue of the film. Similarly, Chandler's original ending was thoroughly revised. In his "Rough Scheme of Scenes" Chandler waves vaguely toward an ending while explicitly acknowledging the Production Code's dominion: "Tag scenes, etc., as we have to have them for the benefit of the Hayes [sic] Office" (4) Later, the screenwriters planned to show the execution of Walter in the San Quentin gas chamber (Sequence E of the screenplay). Wilder seems to have envisioned this ending early on: he sent thirty-eight questions to the San Quentin warden asking about the precise details of execution protocols and traveled with Chandler to San Francisco to see the prison's gas chamber in July 1943. Breen adamantly opposed that ending, calling the execution sequence "unduly gruesome from the standpoint of the Code" (Breen letter, 1 Dec. 1943). Although Wilder had constructed the execution chamber and filmed the death scene, he relented to Breen's pressure in the edit submitted for the PCA's final judgment. That final cut of *Double Indemnity* received Certificate Number 9717, clearing it for public exhibition.

A less obviously pivotal scene (designated C-12) occurs after Barton Keyes, the insurance company's claims adjustor, confides in Walter that

---

[2] At this stage the characters used Cain's names, but their surnames were eventually changed in the film to Walter Neff and Phyllis Dietrichson. The archives establish when and why those changes occurred. There was a Walter Huff listed in the Los Angeles phone book, and moreover he was an insurance salesman, so to protect the studio from possible lawsuits, the Paramount legal office instructed the screenwriters to change his surname (which they did by 11 October). There was also a single Nirdlinger household in the LA city directory, so the lawyers required a name change for Phyllis too. A memo dated 24 September approved Dietrichson from a list of names Wilder submitted (Paramount 100.f-1264).

the death was no accident and that he suspects Phyllis murdered her husband. Between 15 September and 18 October, Chandler and Wilder composed five distinct scenes (all contained in the Billy Wilder Papers 1.f-16) exploring Walter and Phyllis's reactions to this development, revealing the screenwriters' efforts to calibrate the main characters and determine the trajectory of the plot. In the first version, dated 15 September, Phyllis seeks comfort: "Phyllis comes very close to him. She puts her arms around him. 'Hold me, Walter. I'm scared.'" In the second version (15 October), Phyllis is resolute—exclaiming, "'I'm not scared. I've never been scared in my life. I'm not scared now'"—while it is Walter who seems shaken and wavering; she says she loves him, but he embraces her "as if unwillingly," says nothing, and "bends his head slowly, his face almost tortured as they go into the kiss." In the third version (16 October), he is the one who says he loves her, and they kiss without reluctance. In the fourth version (18 October), Phyllis exclaims, "Yes, I'm afraid. But not of Keyes. I'm afraid of us. We're not the same any more. We did it so we could be together, but instead of that it's pulling us apart, isn't it, Walter?" When she accuses him of not caring whether they see each other again, he replies, "Shut up, baby," then "pulls her close and kisses her." The fifth version returns to resolute and fearless Phyllis and mutual expressions of love as they kiss. Ultimately, the fourth version appears in the film (Fig. 1).

As David Bordwell points out in *The Classical Hollywood Cinema*, a film scene "is both a detachable segment and a link in a chain" of scenes; as such, a given scene "develops or closes off lines of cause and effect" from previous scenes while "open[ing] and perhaps develop[ing] at least one new causal chain" (63–64). Those five variants of C-12 illustrate the two screenwriters feeling their way through this process, determining and selecting the precise causal chain that will bind subsequent scenes; each of their choices forestalls some paths and necessitates others. The process exhibited in *Double Indemnity* of adapting through finding a workable structure, imagining scenes, exploring significantly diverse narrative paths, and internalizing the seemingly external constraints recurs throughout the production history of Huston's film to an even greater degree than in Wilder's.

Fig. 1 Realizing that their murder of her husband may soon be discovered, Walter Neff (Fred MacMurray) and Phyllis Dietrichson (Barbara Stanwyck) connive what to do next in *Double Indemnity (1:10:01)*

THE MAN WHO WOULD BE KING

Rudyard Kipling's short story "The Man Who Would Be King," written when he was twenty-two, was first published in 1888 in *The Phantom Rickshaw and Other Eerie Tales*. The first-person narrator tells of his encounter with two British ex-soldiers and fellow Freemasons, Peachey Carnehan and Daniel Dravot, who travel from Lahore to Kafiristan to seek their fortune. This narrator's account frames the heart of the story, the rise and fall of the two adventurers, told by the shattered ruin of Carnehan, who returns three years later. Carnehan tells how they succeeded in reaching and ultimately ruling Kafiristan, how Dravot was acclaimed as king and god, but how he overreached and pursued a dynasty through marriage to a Kafiri girl. At their wedding ceremony, the terrified girl bit him, drawing blood and thus disproving his divinity. Enraged priests cast Dravot from a rope bridge into the ravine a thousand feet below, crucified Carnehan, and, when he survived the ordeal, sent him back home. Proof of Carnehan's tale are the "dried, withered head of Daniel Dravot" and his battered crown, which Peachey displays as he eulogizes his comrade: "You behold now [...] the Emperor in his habit as he lived—the King of Kafiristan with his crown upon his head. Poor old Daniel that was a monarch once!" (Kipling 278). The story is one of Kipling's most celebrated tales.

So memorable was "The Man Who Would Be King" to Huston, who first read the story at age twelve (Bachmann and Huston 3–4; Madsen 244), that he attempted for twenty years to adapt it. Madsen's biography of Huston details aborted projects in 1955 for Allied Artists, with a screenplay by Peter Viertel (151–52); in 1959 for Universal Studios, with a screenplay by Aeneas MacKenzie (223); and in 1963 for Seven Arts, with a screenplay by Tony Veiller (196). Finally, in 1973 the draft screenplays came to the attention of John Foreman, who ultimately produced the 1975 film. In his autobiography *An Open Book*, Huston recalls that, working with his assistant Gladys Hill and "[u]sing such material as springboards, we did a lot of invention, and it turned out to be good invention, supportive of the tone, feeling and spirit underlying the original short story" (351). Huston and Hill utilized elements from the three prior writers' scripts to create the final screenplay, which would be nominated for an Academy Award, and on which neither Viertel, MacKenzie, nor Veiller was credited. The creative choices made by these screenwriters and the variant drafts they produced—the Herrick Library's collection includes 14 variant scripts and approximately 165 loose discarded pages and "screenplay scraps" for the film—provide a vital record of their attempts to translate a famous but problematic source text into a successful feature film. (Excerpts from documents relating to *The Man Who Would Be King* granted courtesy of Warner Bros. Entertainment Inc.)

Kipling's text creates specific problems for an adapter. Aeneas MacKenzie's story treatment, from April 1956, identifies a major problem: "The story itself would seem to have a paucity of substance for a full length film [...] especially as considerable stretches of it are more narrative than dramatic in their nature" (*Report* 1). In other words, the story tells more than it shows, and the events in Kafiristan, the most interesting and cinematic portions of the story, are related only after the fact by Carnehan. Although key scenes from Kipling's narrative appear throughout the screenplay drafts, the screenwriters have to invent transitional scenes, dialogue, and characterizations. MacKenzie concludes that while the challenge of handling the polyglot communication (entailing English, Pushtu, and Kafiri) is "a bitch of a prospect to contemplate" (29), "the vital issue is expansion or additional material" to expand a short story, "limited by a single line of action to a single incident" (40), into the more complex story arc and character development required for a feature film.

All the draft screenplays present Kipling's unnamed narrator as Rudyard Kipling himself. The screenwriters tend toward fidelity, as does Huston's film, and all variants dramatize the source text's key plot points. In the interplay of repetition and invention that characterizes adaptation, however, those points are worked out in strikingly different ways. To take one example, the Kafiri girl whom Dravot takes as his bride is in Kipling's source text a blank slate, nameless and voiceless. Her plot function is crucial—she provides a manifestation of Dravot's hubris, a wedge between the comrades, and the catalyst for the collapse of their scheme to acquire loot and power—but Kipling's characterization of her is negligible. Audiences understandably expect a significant character to have a larger presence, and Hollywood exigencies demand a "love interest" to play a significant role. According to Huston, "in those days you had to have a boy-girl romance in it" (quoted in Madsen 245). The screenwriters therefore felt obliged to invent a screen character for her. She receives a name, a backstory, a personality, some dialogue, and a smattering of character development. Dravot's bride appears as Viertel's sweet villager Madora, MacKenzie's exotic snake priestess Roxana, and Veiller's Cinderella-like Roxane before culminating in Huston and Hill's lovely, objectified, and once again silent Roxanne (Fig. 2).

The scripts clearly indicate that Huston intended to follow Kipling's lead in emphasizing the whiteness of the Kafiris and their Greek ancestry. As a procession of worshippers file past Dravot in a July 1974 script, he is "stunned by [Roxanne's] beauty"; she looks "like a figure from an Attic vase" with "lapiz blue eyes" and "auburn hair" in ringlets (John Huston Papers 30-f.288 79). The 15 November draft extends the description of her Greek beauty and concludes, "Taller by a head than any man present, she is, pound by beautiful pound, an exceeding armful" (80). Dravot's amazed response epitomizes Huston's characteristic blend of the tasteful, the tasty and the titillating: "Venus de Milo, in the flesh—if flesh it is—and not cream and honey and pink champagne" (80). A casting memo from 8 August 1974 that authorizes a search for women to play Roxanne's family and attendants specifies that they "must be pale skinned and rinses may have to be applied to their hair in order to keep 'the Alexander Strain'

Fig. 2 Daniel Dravot (Sean Connery) weds Roxanne (Shakira Caine) moments before his kingdom crumbles in *The Man Who Would Be King (1:56:00)*

evident throughout the story" (Batt). Huston originally cast Tessa Dahl, daughter of writer Roald Dahl and actress Patricia Neal, to play Roxanne, but after filming began in Morocco, he cut her from the production for pragmatic and budgetary reasons. On 6 February 1975 he wrote to her to explain his dilemma: "The only way that the original concept of Roxanne might be used in the film would require that we send for at least a hundred other tall, fair-skinned people to support her and to make her presence among these smaller, darker-skinned tribespeople believable" (31-f.299). Huston wrote on that same day to placate Tessa's furious father, emphasizing the "prohibitive" cost of trying to locate tall, pale extras in Morocco and regretting that as a result "this important story point must be abandoned" (31.f-299). In the end, the film presents Shakira Caine, the Guayanese wife of co-star Michael Caine, in the role of Roxanne, primarily because she was beautiful, appropriately dark, and already available on the set. Perhaps because Shakira Caine was not a trained actress, however, the film gives her no dialogue to speak.

Similarly, the scripts reveal manifold approaches to adapting Kipling's dramatic climax when Carnehan returns and relates his tale, producing Dravot's head and crown. Huston's ending in the completed film suggests a conventional fidelity—Carnehan displays Dravot's head and crown—but the earlier variants disclose prolonged struggles to shape or control the ending. These documents record a recurring conflict over whether to display the head and the crown, or merely the crown, or whether to have both adventurers die in Kafiristan and cut the narrative frame entirely to save money. Pages from a single week in September 1974, for example, record six different attempts by Huston to compose an ending. Clearly the image of a severed head with a golden crown has irresistible power as a grisly monument to hubristic overreach. Urging against its use, though, are legitimate fears about the reactions of both censors and audiences. The Motion Picture Production Code of 1930 lists "Brutality and possible gruesomeness" under the category "Repellent Subjects" that "must be treated within the careful limits of good taste." A severed, decaying head runs afoul of this section of the Code. Even in 1975, with the Production Code no longer in effect, Huston faced opposition from the film's backers, and the final image was not settled until very late. Clearly, as Jamie Sherry observes, "decisions made by adapters of source material at script stage are multifarious and informed by as many practical issues as conceptual" (26). These fluid, interstitial drafts tell us far more about the adaptation process than we can learn from considering only the source text and the completed film.

As with Roxane, the screenplays display multiple attempts to depict the protagonists; here, however, the causes are different. As Aeneas MacKenzie notes in his 1956 treatment, Kipling creates several problems for adapters. The author dramatizes only a few scenes, chiefly one in which the unnamed narrator interacts with Dravot and Carnehan before they depart on their adventure, and one presenting Carnehan when he returns. Over half of the story presents an addled, traumatized Carnehan reporting bits and pieces of what happened in Kafiristan. Moreover, Dravot and Carnehan split up for a time, limiting what Carnehan can report. MacKenzie cannot hide his irritation at Kipling's narrative "sleight of hand": "he parts the pair and centers the interest on Carnehan to avoid having to tell what Dravot is doing and—more particularly—how he is doing it. But what Dravot is doing, and how Dravot is doing it happens to be the story! [...] All this off scene and narrated as a fait accompli in a single speech without detail or explanation!" (*Report* 30) Further, MacKenzie complains that

"Kipling failed to isolate his two major characters effectively, since each could be the other" (1). Kipling's protagonists are both decommissioned soldiers, surviving in India on the fringes of the law and making repeated forays into gun-running and extortion schemes; they are both Freemasons, loyal to the Craft and to each other; and they both sign a "contrack" to swear off women and alcohol until they become kings of Kafiristan. Given Kipling's lack of character differentiation, MacKenzie notes, the screenwriter must distinguish the characters further—for example, by "transferring or splitting the author's dialogue to make Carnehan a man of action and decision, and Dravot one of mind and imagination" (1). In his earlier script, Peter Viertel had accentuated Dravot's weakness for women and Carnehan's greed to differentiate their characters. But Viertel had the benefit of knowing that Huston envisioned Clark Gable and Humphrey Bogart in these roles, and his dialogue often seems written with those stars in mind. That was no longer possible for MacKenzie or Veiller, as numerous actors from Cary Grant to Marlon Brando were considered to play the roles. While recognizing Huston's "disinclination to depart in any marked degree from the original material, or to make any major interpolations" (*Report* 1), MacKenzie emphasizes the challenges in producing a faithful adaptation that succeeds as a film.

Even after a screenwriter has created additional scenes, added thematic elements, fleshed out barely described incidents, and differentiated the protagonists, a further issue remains. Kipling's story is deeply ambiguous about whether Dravot and Carnehan are heroes or scoundrels and whether the disastrous ruin of their kingdom amounts to their tragic fall or their just deserts. Kipling scholars continue to debate whether the story is a celebration of British imperialism or a condemnation of it. One notable plot device that illustrates the ambiguity is the scene in which Dravot first becomes worshipped as a god in Kafiristan. In Kipling's story, Dravot's knowledge of the Third Degree of Masonic rituals impress the priests who had retained only the first two degrees. While Viertel follows Kipling's scene, MacKenzie creates a much more visually dramatic cause in his scripts. Leading a charge against a native army, Dravot is struck in the chest by an arrow which sticks in the bandolier under his tunic. Unharmed, he pulls out the arrow and is perceived as the divine Son of Sikander. Huston and Hill retain this scene, describing the moment in their November 1974 draft: "He jerks the arrow free—holds it aloft. It might be Ahab's harpoon, or Excalibur, or a splinter from the True Cross. His troop follows him" (71). This tangled cluster of allusions at once suggests doomed obsession, rightful sovereignty, and holy sacrifice. Dravot accepts this fake divinity reluctantly at first, then brazenly, finally succumbing to the lure of power and embracing his destiny, half-believing his own spurious godhood. In Huston's scripts and film, the arrow, later gilded, serves as an index of Dravot's rise and fall.

A brief scene illustrates how the scripts test ways to calibrate characterization for Dravot and Carnehan. This incident occurs on their journey to Kafiristan, after they have split off from a caravan. They have twenty Martini rifles and ammo—their tools to conquer a kingdom—hidden in the packs of two camels. As they climb the Hindu Kush mountains, though, their camels can no longer tolerate the altitude. They kill the camels and look for a way to switch to mules. Kipling handles this necessity, as so often in "The Man Who Would Be King," with the barest sketch of a scene:

> [T]wo men came along driving four mules. Dravot up and dances in front of them, singing, 'Sell me four mules.' Says the first man, 'If you are rich enough to buy, you are rich enough to rob'; but before ever he could put his hand to his knife, Dravot breaks his neck over his knee, and the other party runs away. (260)

From this scant source material, the screenwriters produced over a dozen variant scenes, most of them three to four pages long. Every version has tribesmen and mules, but the numbers vary. Most versions include Kipling's line "If you are rich enough to buy, you are rich enough to rob," but invent additional dialogue. Finally, the details seem quite fungible. The scene can cast Dravot and Carnehan as heroes or scoundrels or somewhere in between. In different drafts the protagonists kill the camels, or sell them in a village, or release them to find their way home. They defeat the bandits and rescue a captive maiden who later marries Dravot or make a good faith offer to purchase the mules and kill only in self-defense or resist the temptation to shoot the strangers and steal the mules or murder the sleeping Afghans, loot their corpses, and seize their animals. The drafts follow typical screenplay practice, closing each scene with a character's declaration that amounts virtually to a punch line. For example, Dravot remarks: "Well, there's a lesson learned in any case" (Viertel 73), and MacKenzie's undated revision of pages for his May 1960 draft has Dravot ask, "You don't suppose it would've been polite to have woken 'em up first?" to which Carnehan replies, "No, if we're going to be Kings we can't afford to be gentlemen, too" (36). These variants show the different ways in which the adapters characterize the protagonists. The last example strongly suggests MacKenzie's disdain for these dubious heroes. Several of his scripts depict them as reprobates and blunderers, and one portrays Dravot haranguing the Kafiris "like Hitler at a Nazi rally" (*Report* 36). Veiller and Huston, on the other hand, generate a proliferation of details that mitigate the protagonists' culpability for the deaths of the Afghans and emphasize Dravot's and Carnehan's resourcefulness. Huston's film, for example, increases the number of Afghans to five to raise the threat level, strips Dravot and Carnelian to their underwear to increase their apparent vulnerability, and contrasts the Afghans' belligerence with the protagonists' passivity, diminishing the latter's culpability in the deaths.

Conclusions

Screenplays, these "vital tools" in the production process, have much to contribute to our understanding of adaptation. They provide an important record of the translation of a source text into a film, with successive drafts and discarded pages revealing the fluidity of the process. They document the intermedial space between the source text and the final adapted product and highlight the myriad forking paths into alternative possibilities overridden by the final version. Ultimately, these screenplay drafts and production notes underline the fluidity of the process of adaptation as it finds its way through individual scenes, not so much scaffolding each draft on the preceding draft as using each draft to explore different, sometimes mutually exclusive possibilities. They suggest that the process inherently entails not only aesthetic and narratological questions of how best to translate a story to another medium but equally exigent industrial pressures involving budget, censorship, and audience expectations. These "mechanisms by which adaptations are produced" (Murray 4) document the creative play and flux of adaptation as an incremental process and expand our understanding of adaptation to include the how and why of that process. The screenwriters' transitional conceptions reveal and document the fluid creative process of adaptation; the final film possesses whatever special authority it has, not because it is the best version but because it is the last. In his autobiography Huston writes of *The Man Who Would Be King*, "I liked this script as well as any I ever wrote" (351), but his script perches atop uncredited screenplays by Viertel, MacKenzie, and Veiller; like a palimpsest, the film retains traces of their work. Just as significant as these visible traces are the effaced variants, the paths not taken, which are visible only in draft screenplays and production notes. For the field of adaptation studies, these documents, a physical record of the actual process of adaptation, bid adaptation scholars to turn our attention toward the process that everywhere shapes and informs the ultimate product.

References

Acheson, Keith, and Christopher J. Maule. "Understanding Hollywood's Organisation and Continuing Success." *An Economic History of Film.* Edited by John Sedgwick and Michael Pokorny, Routledge, 2005, pp. 312–46.
Balázs, Béla. *Theory of the Film; Character and Growth of a New Art,* Dover, 1970.
Batt, Bert. Production memo to John Huston et al. John Huston Papers, Margaret Herrick Library, 32-f.305, 8 Nov. 1974.
Bernardi, Daniel, and Julian Hoxter. *Off the Page: Screenwriting in the Era of Media Convergence,* U of California P, 2017.
Boon, Kevin Alexander. *Script Culture and the American Screenplay,* Wayne State UP, 2008.
Boozer, Jack, editor. *Authorship in Film Adaptation,* U of Texas P, 2008.
Bordwell, David, et al. *The Classical Hollywood Cinema: Film Style and Mode of Production to 1960,* Columbia UP, 1985.
Corliss, Richard. *Talking Pictures: Screenwriters in the American Cinema,* Overlook, 1985.
Davis, Gary. "Rejected Offspring: The Screenplay as a Literary Genre." *New Orleans Review,* vol. 11, no. 2, 1984, pp. 90–94.
Double Indemnity. Directed by Billy Wilder, performed by Fred MacMurray and Barbara Stanwyck, Paramount, 1944.
Horton, Andrew, and Julian Hoxter. *Screenwriting,* Rutgers UP, 2014.
Huston, John. *The Man Who Would Be King* Correspondence. John Huston Papers, Margaret Herrick Library, 31-f.299, 6 Feb. 1975.
Huston, John. *An Open Book,* Knopf, 1980.
Huston, John, and Gladys Hill. *John Huston's The Man Who Would Be King* [screenplay]. N.p., 1974a.
Huston, John, and Gladys Hill. Script for *The Man Who Would Be King.* John Huston Papers, Margaret Herrick Library, 30-f.288, 5 June 1974b.
Hutcheon, Linda, with Siobhan O'Flynn. *A Theory of Adaptation.* Revised ed., Routledge, 2012.
Kipling, Rudyard. "The Man Who Would Be King." *The Man Who Would Be King, and Other Stories,* Oxford UP, 1999, pp. 244–79.

Lev, Peter. "How to Write Adaptation History." *The Oxford Handbook of Adaptation Studies*. Edited by Thomas Leitch, Oxford UP, 2017, pp. 661–678.
MacDonald, Ian W. *Screenwriting Poetics and the Screen Idea*, Palgrave Macmillan, 2013.
MacKenzie, Aeneas. Report on *The Man Who Would Be King* for Film Production. John Huston Papers, Margaret Herrick Library, 28-f.275, 24 Apr. 1956.
MacKenzie, Aeneas. Revised pages for 2 May, 1960 script for *The Man Who Would Be King*. Undated. John Huston Papers, Margaret Herrick Library, 29-f.281.
Madsen, Axel. *John Huston: A Biography*, Doubleday, 1978.
Manvell, Roger. *Theater and Film: A Comparative Study of the Two Forms of Dramatic Art, and of the Problems of Adaptation of Stage Plays into Films*, Associated UP, 1979.
McBride, Joseph. *Writing in Pictures: Screenwriting Made (Mostly) Painless*, Vintage, 2012.
Murray, Simone. *The Adaptation Industry: The Cultural Economy of Contemporary Literary Adaptation*, Routledge, 2012.
Nelmes, Jill. "Some Thoughts on Analysing the Screenplay, the Process of Screenplay Writing and the Balance between Craft and Creativity." *Journal of Media Practice*, vol. 8, no. 2, Sept. 2007, pp. 107–13. *EBSCOhost*, https://doi.org/10.1386/jmpr.8.2.107_1.
Nelmes, Jill. *Analysing the Screenplay*, Routledge, 2011, *EBSCOhost*, http://proxy-s.mercer.edu/login?url=http://search.ebscohost.com/login.aspx?direct=true&db=nlebk&AN=340034&site=ehost-live.
Paramount Pictures production records. (n.d.) Margaret Herrick Library, 100.f-1264.
Pasolini, Pier Paolo. "The Screenplay as a 'Structure That Wants to Be Another Structure.'" *American Journal of Semiotics*, vol. 4, no. 1/2, 1986, pp. 53–72.
Phillips, Gene D. *Some Like It Wilder: The Life and Controversial Films of Billy Wilder*, UP of Kentucky, 2010.
Price, Steven. *The Screenplay: Authorship, Theory and Criticism*, Palgrave Macmillan, 2010.
Price, Steven. *A History of the Screenplay*, Palgrave Macmillan, 2013.
Price, Steven, and Chris Pallant. *Storyboarding: A Critical History*, Palgrave Macmillan UK, 2015. *ProQuest Ebook Central*, https://ebookcentral.proquest.com/lib/merceru/detail.action?docID=4082180 .
Roblin, Isabelle, and Shannon Wells-Lassagne. "Screenwriting, Adaptation and the Screen Idea." *Journal of Screenwriting*, vol. 7, no. 1, 2016, pp. 5–9.
Sherry, Jamie. "Adaptation Studies through Screenwriting Studies: Transitionality and the Adapted Screenplay." *Journal of Screenwriting*, vol. 7, no. 1, 2016, pp. 11–28.

Sikov, Ed. *On Sunset Boulevard: The Life and Times of Billy Wilder*, UP of Mississippi, 2017, *ProQuest Ebook Central*, http://ebookcentral.proquest.com/lib/merceru/detail.action?docID=4908131.

The Man Who Would Be King. Directed by John Huston, performed by Sean Connery and Michael Caine, Columbia, 1975.

Veiller, Anthony. Script for *The Man Who Would Be King*. John Huston Papers, Margaret Herrick Library, 30-f.286, 9 Mar. 1964.

Venuti, Lawrence. *The Scandals of Translation: Towards an Ethics of Difference*, Taylor and Francis, 1998. *ProQuest Ebook Central*, https://ebookcentral.proquest.com/lib/merceru/detail.action?docID=169424.

Viertel, Peter. Script for *The Man Who Would Be King*. John Huston Papers, Margaret Herrick Library, 28-f.274, 19 July 1954.

Zolotow, Maurice. *Billy Wilder in Hollywood*, Limelight, 2004.

The Narcissistic Scandal of Adapting History

Kristopher Mecholsky

On 25 February 2022, Twitter user @firastopher adapted a phrase that well-off American social media users had been posting since 21 March 2020, a couple of weeks into their experience of the initial coronavirus lockdown: "I'm tired of living through historic events" (Philipp). The statement itself is understandable. Those following the news have been overwhelmed in recent years by the apparent record-breaking historicity of headlines: pandemics, impeachments, Capitol storming, European land wars, and more. But the statement is also a kind of humble-brag. Firastopher's post, which became a massive enough viral hit to make it his pinned tweet, provides a privilege-check gut-punch through two simple additions: quotation marks around the phrase itself and an accompanying photograph. The image he added is an idyll of upper-middle-class Western aspiration: a white woman working from home in comfort (untucked Oxford, jeans, socks) at a health-conscious standing desk, bathed in sunlight streaming in from the many windows of her spacious home office, and framed by a plant-enthroned couch and a record player sitting on

K. Mecholsky (✉)
Savannah College of Art and Design, Savannah, GA, USA
e-mail: kmechols@scad.edu

© The Author(s), under exclusive license to Springer Nature Switzerland AG 2023
T. Leitch (ed.), *The Scandal of Adaptation*, Palgrave Studies in Adaptation and Visual Culture,
https://doi.org/10.1007/978-3-031-14153-9_14

shelves of LPs. The image is one of complete insulation from history. Indeed, the houseplants and vinyl suggest the subject's ability to craft whatever time and space she desires.

Firastopher's adaptation of a common, often honest lament when even more bad news fills the feeds of the fortunate highlights a scandalous adaptation pervading the twenty-first-century West as it endeavors to situate and make sense of its place in history: Are things really that bad? To what can our situation be compared? In fact, Firastopher's post draws back the curtain on everyday conversations and social media posts to reveal insulated Westerners who are not, in fact, tired of living through historic events but who are instead charged and challenged by the experience. We turn to rereadings in times of apparent historical crisis because they are adaptations that reveal and ensure our entanglement with the past. But then how do we distinguish ourselves from those readings and those times?

Linking adaptation and history is certainly not a new idea, and in recent years, adaptation studies has zeroed in on it. Laurence Raw and Defne Ersin Tutan's 2013 collection *The Adaptation of History: Essays on Ways of Telling the Past* was followed in 2015 by Thomas Leitch's essay "History as Adaptation" and in 2017 by Tutan's essay "Adaptation and History" that narrows Leitch's basic argument by asserting that "all historical representations are radically adaptive" in ways that "tell us more about the present than about the past they refer to" (577). Across these meditations and others like Frans Weiser's 2017 "Contextualizing History-as-Adaptation," a thread surfaces that Tutan aptly summarizes: "As we try to come to terms with the present and the future, we are obliged to come to terms with the past. [...] It is by way of our negotiation with the past that we reclaim the present and move on to the future" (579). Instead of focusing on history as adaptation, I want to explore living the present as an adaptation of the past. In doing so, I hope to uncover and inhabit a scandal of adaptation: despite Tutan's optimistic claim that our negotiation with the past helps us reclaim the present, I suspect that in living out the present in intimate relation to the past we are deceiving ourselves about the historical moments we live through. Perhaps they are less prestigious than the past; perhaps they are more. What do we lose and gain when we compare our experiences to past experiences we take as their pattern?

A primary mode of this phenomenon of situating the present historically involves rereading: rereading past history, its literature, and literary responses to it—what together I will call historical–poetic interpolation.

In the early 2020s, for instance, references to Defoe's *Journal of the Plague Year*, Boccaccio's *Decameron*, Poe's "Masque of the Red Death," and Camus's *The Plague* spread feverishly through the news cycle of the COVID-19 pandemic, recalling a similar trend of references to Orwell's *1984*, Atwood's *The Handmaid's Tale*, and Lewis's *It Can't Happen Here* during and after the 2016 election cycle. Even while revisiting seemingly unrelated works, as in a 2019 documentary on *Fiddler on the Roof*, participants connected the material to current events. Just five minutes into the documentary, Samantha Massell, the actress who played Hodel in the Trump-era Broadway revival suggests in reference to the pogroms in the musical that "in those moments of darkness and reality, like the ones we live in now, we have pieces of theater like this to remind us that we're not alone in the world and in history."

This impulse is not unique to the present. Humanity has long relied on historical–poetic interpolation, engaging with art and the past to navigate its responses to personal and historical moments. Indeed, *Fiddler on the Roof*, a midcentury musical adaptation of the Yiddish writer Sholem Aleichem's stories of Ukrainian shtetl life in the latter days of the Russian empire, arguably connects the pogroms to the Holocaust as well as the feminist and Civil Rights movements of the 1960s, when it was developed (*Fiddler*). Alternatively, one might choose at random any of a number of other examples from history. One that serves to indicate the longevity and cyclic nature of revisiting "classics" to make sense of the present, thus steering humanity forward in hope, is the life and work of Samuel Taylor Coleridge.

As the eighteenth century drew to a close, young Coleridge devoted much time reflecting on the tumultuous French Revolution, following with keen anticipation its changing fortunes and aftermath. Like many other young Europeans inspired by the Enlightenment, Coleridge cultivated radical, utopian visions for France and England, substantiated not only by contemporary writings like Thomas Paine's *Rights of Man* but also by writers from a century earlier like Algernon Sidney, James Harrington, and John Milton (Mee 179 and Kitson, "Sages" 206–7). Coleridge wrote in his notebooks, book margins, and lectures his musings on work Milton had published over a hundred years before that meditated on the promises and disappointments of the English Civil War. Peter Kitson observes that like Coleridge, "the poet of *Paradise Lost* had witnessed the complete wreck of his own hopes for a regenerated nation" (197). And indeed, reflections on that English Revolution by Milton and his ilk directly inspired the French Revolutionaries as well as English Jacobins like Coleridge (Kitson, "Sages" 206). Kitson argues that those English radicals "[engaged] in the English political struggle by emplotting the 150-year-old English Revolution and the contemporary French Revolution in various ways to substantiate and differentiate their own dissent," none more consistently and enthusiastically than Coleridge ("Sages" 207). Coleridge, who had hoped to advertise the revolutionary Channel connection, planned a series of lectures in 1795 explicitly linking the English and French Revolutions, intending to focus directly on writers like Milton. But Milton and other radical forebears loomed large even in the lectures he delivered in Bristol that year. Coleridge seems to have organized his "Moral and Political Lecture" around quotations from *Samson Agonistes*, *Paradise Lost*, and *Paradise Regained*, invoking Milton in order to inspire his audience to use the example of France to secure more freedom in Britain, and he rhapsodized in a later lecture on two restrictive bills introduced and passed that year: "Sages and patriots that being dead do yet speak to us, spirits of Milton, Locke, Sidney, Harrington" ("Plot" 290). Time and again, literary idols, Milton especially, were his guides. "Not the poem which we have *read*," he later writes in *Biographia Literaria*, "but that to which we *return* [...] possesses the genuine power, and claims the name of *essential poetry*" (167, emphasis in original).

Historical–poetic interpolation is multidirectional. Coleridge not only relied on rereading classic works to make sense of the historical upheavals of the advent of the nineteenth century but used them in concert with his imagination to craft a philosophical response to them. As Marija Reiff contends, Coleridge's play *Zapolya*, written around the end of Napoleon's reign and his subsequent exile, adapts the plot structure of Shakespeare's romance *The Winter's Tale* "to demonstrate the malign traits of commanding genius, to show the disastrous nature" of a Napoleonic reign, "and to further allegorize Napoleonic rule" (96). Reiff specifically asserts that "Coleridge is simultaneously apologizing for and indicting the positive early Romantic view of the Revolution and its incipient 'democracy'" that he realized had not come to pass (96). But *Zapolya* was certainly not Coleridge's only poetic response to the French Revolution. Kitson claims that even Coleridge's most famous (and famously abstract and supernatural) poem is indelibly tied to the French Revolution and reveals Coleridge's absorption of the revolution's failure, much as *Paradise Lost* reflects Milton's own absorption of political failure. He shows how Coleridge's reading of Milton's response to the English Revolution convinced him that a concurrent moral revolution was necessary for any political revolution to succeed ("Coleridge" 198). In the service of that revolution, Kitson suggests, Coleridge turned his attention away from political action to internal, moral action: "In a sense, the Revolution has been both naturalized and internalized. The millennium takes place in the mind of man and paradise becomes not a place on earth but a state of mind, 'the paradise within' of *Paradise Lost*. 'The Ancient Mariner' shows us the moral revolution, the necessity for which Coleridge has consistently pleaded" (207).

If turning to older narratives to understand the present and prepare for the future is not a new phenomenon, it has increased recently. And it appears the Mariner still hath our will. As our sense of the past two decades' place in history develops further, rereadings of older stories, real or imagined, that seem to reflect our own have accelerated. For the past several years, the *Atlantic* and the *New York Times* have repeatedly examined our present calamities, misfortunes, and polarizations in light of centuries of history and culture. In the conclusion of an April 2020 *Atlantic* article exploring the confusion of COVID-19, Ed Yong likened our foray into the nightmare of the pandemic as a classic hero's journey, wherein "the protagonist reluctantly departs from normal life, enters the unknown, endures successive trials, and eventually returns home, having been transformed. [...] If such a character exists in the coronavirus story, it is not an individual, but the entire modern world." In May of that year, James Parker drew on Yong's archetypal reference to emphasize how a collaborative "Big Read" rendering of Coleridge's "Ancient Mariner" by celebrities such as Willem Dafoe, Marianne Faithfull, Iggy Pop, and Tilda Swinton—coincidentally premiering at a time when many had been ordered into lockdown—reflected a modern hero's journey par excellence. "The Ancient Mariner," Parker argues, both presages our ongoing "ecological catastrophe" and "speaks of the sea-moment, the liminal state: the treacherous zone between a ruined world and a new one" that especially defined the early months of the pandemic: "The ship drives on, crewed by dead men. The sea is alive. Dreams and terrors await, and then a turn for home. How can you not listen?" (Fig. 1)

As Kitson himself admitted when advancing his argument regarding "Rime" and the French Revolution, "there have been almost as many readings of 'The Ancient Mariner' as there are critics" ("Coleridge" 204). Jerome McGann concurs in his landmark essay "The Meaning of the Ancient Mariner": "A poem like the 'Rime' encourages [...] the most

Fig. 1 The *Atlantic* used this image from Gustav Doré's illustrations for Samuel Taylor Coleridge's "Rime of the Ancient Mariner" to accompany James Parker's reflection on the Ancient Mariner Big Read in order to reflect humanity as a collective navigating the pandemic

diverse readings and interpretations" (66). Indeed, he claims, the poem itself "illustrates a special theory of the historical interpretation of texts" (50). Coleridge means to convey the very sense of stories being passed along, generation after generation, for future interpretation and retelling. "The Rime of the Ancient Mariner" is historical–poetic interpolation made manifest, in form and in content. It is an "ideological commitment to a preconditioned ground of processive truth," sanctioning "in its readers a diversity of interpretations based upon their particular lights" (52). Coleridge, McGann hints, would endorse historical–poetic interpolations like the *Atlantic*'s use of the "Rime" to help us through the pandemic.

As fanciful or self-indulgent as some may first appear, such reflections on our ongoing historical calamities drive policy as well as new artistic endeavors. The Delta Center, a Robert Wood Johnson Foundation initiative to promote equitable health policy, employed Yong's metaphor of the hero's journey in the *Atlantic* at a 2020 convention to explain the modern world's experience of the pandemic and encourage stakeholders to recognize the opportunity for shaping future action. Additionally, across the country, numerous organizations—local library and art communities, theater companies, an opera coalition spanning the United States, and, most recognizably, the *New York Times*—turned to the example of Boccaccio's *Decameron* to inspire adaptations and/or craft "hypertexts" over it as a means to reflect on and provide diversion from the pandemic, much as Boccaccio's storytellers took refuge from the Black Death. Turns to the past even seem to be steering world events. When the Russian army invaded Ukraine at Vladimir Putin's direction, headlines were filled with comparisons to Hitler's invasion of Czechoslovakia as well as exhortations to turn to Melville's Ahab (Bailey) or Auden's wartime poetry (Balakian) to make sense of a self-absorbed madman's quest for historical "greatness" and unending human suffering. And world leaders found themselves (re)reading to make sense of it all, as Ukrainian president Volodymyr Zelensky demonstrated when he quoted *Hamlet* in an 8 March 2022 speech to the UN Drew Lichtenberg, the Shakespeare Theater Company dramaturge, asserts that "there's a long tradition in Central European countries, such as [...] Ukraine, of embracing Shakespeare and especially *Hamlet* as a kind of metaphor for the broader political situation" (qtd. in Dowd).

"That to Which We Return"

These examples suggest that we seek our understanding from the past and literature of its time because the past is demonstrably memorable and important. If memories and reflections on those events have survived in our own time, we reasonably reckon that our own existential entanglement with them may carry us forward, too. By implicating ourselves in already important events, we hope to ensure our own remembrance. If our pandemic is like others we have remembered, we may be remembered. If political upheavals and polarizations are like others that we recall, ours will be remembered in their lineage. While we often look to the past for wisdom on how to handle similar predicaments, the sheer number and variety of parallels that we invoke indicate not only a desire to learn how to plan our next steps but a more general desire to assert our importance.

In addition to using history to anchor our unmoored lives, historical–poetic interpolation prompts active narrative emplotment. By connecting present to previous events, we engage with the past in a way that indelibly ties our own narrative to anchors within ongoing historical narratives. Through the example of new revelations introduced into Balzac's *Le Colonel Chabert*, Peter Brooks explains how new tales introduced within the context of a larger story fundamentally transform it by resolving information with respect to events only partially disclosed before (229). Past narratives, then, must be reordered and integrated with present information. Relying on Brooks's conception of narrative as an interplay of desire and rest, which he likens respectively to metonymy and metaphor, we can conceive how the present can become a vital part of the narrative of history if it is indelibly and transformationally connected to the past, metonymically connected to previous moments in history and thus part of the greater collapsed metaphor of an historical narrative.

Within the historical–poetic interpolation of the English Revolution that inspired French Revolutionaries who inspired new English radicals, the Reign of Terror was contemporaneously conceivable because despite the limited aims of its national precursor, the mid-seventeenth-century Fronde, the English had beheaded their own monarch just a century before. Across the Atlantic, another revolution had also served as an inspiration. The activities, ideas, and methods of the American revolutionary colonists, who declared independence from Great Britain in 1776, continue to serve as an inspiration for would-be revolutionaries nearly 250 years later. On 6 January 2021, groups of protestors directly inspired by

Donald Trump's forceful denials that he had lost the 2020 Presidential election stormed the United States Capitol with the apparent intent of changing the election's outcome. The numerology of the nation's history held sway over the event, as it has over so much ideology in the past five years. Thomas Cryer, pointing out that "the mere number '1776' adorned numerous flags during the January 6th Capitol riots," notes that the year "has become a slogan in campaigns against critical race theory. Indeed, one of President Trump's last acts in office was to rekindle calls for 'patriotic education' through his own 1776 Commission" in response to the *New York Times*'s 1619 Project, which weighs the traditional 1776 year of origin against the year when the first enslaved Africans were brought to the colonies. More than a rallying cry, the events of 1776, real or imagined, directly inspired attendees of the protest. Enrique Tarrio, national chairman of the Proud Boys in early 2021, received a nine-page plan titled "1776 Returns" to overrun several buildings in Washington, D.C. on 6 January, in a spirit of intended revolution ("Second Superseding Indictment"). As the examples of Robespierre, Napoleon, and Stalin, all heroes in their own and others' stories, attest, much havoc can be wrought in the name of the general welfare.

While history can provide a frame or guide, classic literature acts powerfully as blood and ballast in the burgeoning of new revolutionary-adjacent events. The works of Burns, Milton, Shelley, and Shakespeare "dignified and elevated the struggle for reform" for radicals and Chartists in nineteenth-century Britain, Antony Taylor observes, providing "a historical and constitutional pedigree" for politics of the time (358). John Wilkes Booth quoted Shakespeare, invoking the spirit of the liberal Brutus, when he leapt from Lincoln's box at Ford's Theatre. Zelensky invoked Hamlet's existential question when addressing the European Union following Putin's invasion. In a similar vein, but with much more force, resolve, and intention, V.I. Lenin was so inspired by Nikolay Chernyshevsky's mid-nineteenth-century utopian novel *What Is to Be Done?* that he penned a pamphlet of the same name to promote his Bolshevik program in the early years of the twentieth century. Later, in the midst of a faltering revolution he was driving, Lenin wrote an essay exploring how "the contradictions in Tolstoy's views are indeed a mirror of those contradictory conditions in which the peasantry had to play their historical part in our revolution." Tolstoy's work, Lenin suggests, "reflected the pent-up hatred, the ripened striving for a better lot, the desire to get rid of the past—and also the immature dreaming, the political inexperience, the revolutionary flabbiness." He goes on to assert that if "beaten armies learn well [...] there is one gain from the first years of the revolution. [...] It is the mortal blow struck at the former softness and flabbiness of the masses [...] who will be less capable of falling into our historical sin of Tolstoyism!" Lenin relied on literature to convince his followers of a new direction. In our own century, Donald Trump, Jr. likened his father's social media ban after 6 January to "living Orwell's 1984" (qtd. in Leitch, "Adaptation and Censorship" 196), a comparison that encourages and justifies the fiercest and staunchest of oppositional measures.

Examples like these become specifically uses or abuses of the past only in the judgment of later historians. Strictly speaking, they all begin as abuses of the past. In the living and making of those moments, through historical–poetic interpolation, the present becomes a masquerade, foppish or grotesque, depending on the outcome. Later historians might then choose to interpret from a variety of types of primary evidence to weave together any of a number of narratives. To generalize from what Leitch observes in "History as Adaptation" about legal disputes, "any new selection of facts, any new emphasis, any new interpretation, produces a new story" enabling "competing stories" that remain in conflict until one is "sanctified" (14) by the prevailing zeitgeist. The attempts of Booth, Coleridge, Milton, Lenin, Trump, and ourselves to make our present moments mean what we hope them to mean—our historical–poetic interpolations—are, like the Ancient Mariner's wandering storytelling, ceaseless.

In *Time and Narrative*, Paul Ricoeur suggests why competing interpretations of history multiply by explaining the power of condensing the aporatic complexity of time into the metaphorical package of a tidy narrative. He likens our historical–poetic tendency to our sense of clarification and understanding toward the end of a complex story—the process, he argues, that Aristotle called catharsis. Following Hans Robert Jauss, who defines allegorization as an attempt "to translate the meaning of a text in its first context into another context" (qtd. in Ricoeur 176–77), Ricoeur relates our ability to see ourselves in the past to our ability to make sense of literature. Borrowing from Jauss's "*Gegenüber Gewesenen*," the term *Gegenüber* (the Now [i.e., not then] Writing of the "Then"—or the "'Been' that is Across From 'Having Been'"), Ricoeur writes, "is ultimately this allegorizing power, related to catharsis, that makes literary application the response most similar to the analogizing apprehension of the past in the dialectic of the *Gegenüber* and of indebtedness" (177). We see ourselves in the past much as we see ourselves in stories. Moreover, we seek to reconstruct the past because we owe our existence to those who lived in it, and we hope that those who follow us will continue to carry a sense of our own time into the future. It is natural, then, that we begin to see ourselves in history *as* we see ourselves in stories (and vice versa). "Once we have admitted that the writing of history is not something added from outside to historical knowledge, but is one with it," Ricoeur writes in *Time and Narrative*, "nothing prevents us from admitting as well that history imitates in its own writing the types of emplotment handed down by our literary tradition" (185). The cathartic experience is likewise handed down as "we learn to see a given series of events as tragic, as comic, and so on" (185).

This desire for emplotment amounts to a desperation for narratives when we encounter what we know will be historic moments. We turn to rereadings of anointed classics when we don't understand a historical moment but have a notion that we need to—and might be able to. Aristotle, for instance, asserts in *Poetics* IX that "poetry tends to express the universal, history the particular" (1451b). In the weeds of the particular of history, we ache for universal patterns. Just a week after Putin invaded Ukraine, Kaitlyn Tiffany argued in the *Atlantic* that some idle social media chatter about the war—from joking complaints about its not being the "vibe shift" the world was looking for to insensitive attempts to cast a future action film about it—reflects a collective restlessness of aimless activity in the wake of disaster called "milling." Sociologists have defined milling as "a search for socially sanctioned meaning in a relatively unstructured situation" in the specific context of seeking action (Turner and Killian 59). For Tiffany, milling especially fits the mood around trying to understand the invasion of Ukraine: "we're emoting, lecturing, correcting, praising, and debunking. We're offering up dumb stuff that immediately gets swatted down. […] We're being aimless and embarrassing and loud and responding to each other's weird behavior."

Tiffany's argument is strenuously critical of the ways the West is going about this milling, even as she explains its utility and necessity. But her adoption of the sociological idea of milling illustrates the kind of historical–poetic interpolation I have been describing here. Milling, as "a search for socially sanctioned meaning" (59), reveals our ongoing process of writing history as we live it—and we clearly require literature to do it, as both Jauss and Ricoeur contend. Historical–poetic milling happens when there is a failure of what Coleridge calls "secondary imagination." In

Biographia Literaria, Coleridge axiomatically divides imagination as primary, "the living power and prime agent of all human perception," and secondary, "an echo of the former, coexisting with the conscious will. [...] It dissolves, diffuses, dissipates, in order to re-create" (313). As many of Coleridge's commentators have stated, the secondary imagination involves a conscious working of the mind on its sensory impressions to comprehend and understand them. Milling and historical–poetic interpolation occur, I suggest, when a progression from primary imagination to its secondary organization falters. Instead, the mind falls back on fancy, which Coleridge calls "a mode of memory emancipated from the order of time and space," working with "materials ready made from the law of association" (313). Coleridgean fancy is a spontaneous mental process that reassembles elementary images into a different arrangement to aid allegorization and catharsis in order to prompt the secondary imagination to make sense of confusing and complicated times. It is a background operation. Our retreat into fancy promotes a kind of sensual intuition over and against the intellectual working-on defined by Coleridge's "secondary imagination," a casting about for any memory of a port in the storm in the midst of a new storm on a completely different coastline.

Sic Semper

The casting about in times of crisis that is historical–poetic interpolation offers solace because it ensures connection with the demonstrably memorable past. It not only offers solace, but proudly insists upon its necessity. As we are faced with moments in history we know will somehow be bound up in one or more historical narratives, our collective unconscious, through fancy, seeks historical and literary models to offer patterns of the events and our reactions to them. Despite our concerns for the present, we are excited to know that what we live will be remembered because our posterity in history is assured. Further, we instinctively seek historical–poetic interpolations because—insofar as they are rereadings and thus adaptations—they persistently conjure former narratives in our minds. In doing so, we become implicitly tied up in a narrative network when we turn to rereadings because adaptations are always inexorably in dialogue with the past. In watching Bergman's *Seventh Seal* or reading Poe's "Masque of the Red Death," we entangle our narrative experience with both the time of their composition and our own time of engagement.

What is the scandal, then? It makes perfect sense to seek out like conditions, characters, causes, and effects. Metaphorically yoking past events with a present not yet concluded, however, inevitably involves self-deception. Past events and cultural reflections on them are usually contextualized through what Frank Kermode influentially called the sense of an ending, but we live with no certainty of any particular ending. We know that the Declaration of Independence and the American revolution were successful, but Coleridge did not know in 1795 what the end result of the French Revolution would be, and Beethoven did not know Napoleon's arc when, with the republican consuls of Rome in mind, he dedicated his Third Symphony to him. We know that Brutus's plans after his assassination of Caesar ran aground, as Booth's did following Lincoln's murder, but we do not yet know what the lasting legacy of the 6 January attempts on Mike Pence's life will be. Linking the three moments like this casts metonymic shadows on each that can shade them in dangerous directions, aggrandizing or denigrating each of them. How patriotic these revolutionary acts are is a matter of time and shifting historical perspective.

A sense of an ending suggests a root scandal of historical–poetic interpolation: narcissism. Are our attempts to link our ongoing emplotment of our unfolding historical moments merely self-indulgent gazing at imagined reflections in idealized works, such as *Julius Caesar* or *1984*, or even relatively ahistorical works, such as Poe's "Masque" or Bergman's *Seventh Seal*? Are we simply seeking catharsis and reaching for works that flatter us in doing so? What if we aren't giving ourselves enough credit for agency and originality?

Before the historical turn of adaptation studies, a number of thinkers had critiqued history as a discipline. Leitch (2015) and Tutan (2017) both draw on Hayden White, and I have invoked Paul Ricoeur's work here to demonstrate how history is an extension of humanity's narrative impulse to find some similarities among different events. Considering our potential narcissism or forced humility in relying on historical–poetic interpolation brings an even earlier thinker to mind: Friedrich Nietzsche. In "History in the Service and Disservice of Life," Nietzsche meditates on the ability of historical knowledge to make us happy, even though some balance of forgetfulness is necessary since "the man who cannot pause upon the threshold of a moment, forgetting the entire past [...] will never know happiness. [...] *The unhistorical and the historical are equally necessary to the good health of a man, a people, and a culture*" (*Unmodern Observations* 89, emphasis in original). He forcefully denounces history as a pure science, a judgment both White and Ricoeur echo in their fundamental agreement that history requires a creative, imaginative component (see Pelluer). In arguing that "life needs the services of history" (94), Nietzsche asserts that humans rely on three aspects of history to create their lives in time: "*exemplary* or *monumental, antiquarian*, and *critical* history" (95, emphasis in original). We use history in an exemplary way to find models to emulate; we rely on history in an antiquarian way when we revere the past and attempt to preserve tradition; and we resort to critical history when we suffer or rebel against traditions we consider outdated, antithetical, and harmful. Coleridge clearly relied on monumental and antiquarian approaches to history in his own approach to the French Revolution, emulating Milton's response to the English Civil Wars in his lectures and his use of arguments and archaic forms in his poetry, as well as exalting Shakespeare and adapting his *Winter's Tale* to criticize Napoleon. At the same time, much of the Romantic period in English literature was driven by a conscientious abandonment of the hierarchical thinking inherent in monarchies and traditional Christian contexts.

Although Nietzsche hints at the potential narcissism of historical–poetic interpolation, his argument does not at first seem to explain why we would want to pattern ourselves after historical periods no one would want to relive, like the Great Plague or the fall of the Roman Empire. My own argument depends on Ricoeur's insistence that history relies inherently on narrative: the closure it promises and the memorability, and thus possible immortality, it offers. We may not want to emulate or repeat calamitous moments in history, but our narrative intuition reminds us that a primary feature of any story is that it is memorable by virtue of the fact that it is a connected series of events worthy of being repeated. If something is important enough to be repeated, it is important enough to be remembered. To Nietzsche's three uses or types of history, then, I would add a fourth one, *memorable history*, that logically precedes the other three. An apparent tautology, the term is meant to indicate a crucial aspect of our privileged relation with history. We seem to seek importance first. Perhaps we would rather be a part of a story vividly remembered than live in unmemorable tranquility. For instance, while our society should logically have compared the COVID-19 outbreak to the more recent flu pandemics of 2009 or 1968, both of which remain in living memory, most cultural reflections on it harkened back to the more historically memorable 1918 pandemic or even the Black Death. In addition, the United States has been living through an historic moment for the past two decades that thoroughly conveys the urgency of the memorable history motive: the increasing number of copycat mass shootings that emphasize each time that no other factor matters more than sheer memorability.

"FANCY ... MISJOINING SHAPES, WILD WORK PRODUCES OFT"

The frantic grasping of our historical fancy, to borrow from Coleridge, for memorable plots and genres to make sense of unfolding events recalls Adam's response to Eve's dream of Satan in *Paradise Lost*:

> Oft in [Reason's] absence mimic Fancy wakes
> To imitate her; but misjoining shapes,
> Wild work produces oft, and most in dreams,
> Ill matching words and deeds long past or late. (V.111–113)

The misjoined shapes and wild work of ill-matched words and deeds long since gone that some have wrought to make sense of the past several years are the price of the scandals of historical–poetic interpolation. What happens to us if we wear a mantle of the past and dress in the trappings of other narratives and times of historical import? Do we threaten to erase our particularity in favor of memorability? Do we risk making monumental what should be a molehill? If we must make sense of the present by connecting it somehow to the past, do we run the risk of letting the past's themes run rampant and "contaminate" the narrative? As William Mooney suggests in his contribution to this collection, "Adaptation *is* contagion, the spread of which cannot be contained" (227). Recalling the compelling arguments that insist that history is adaptation, an echoing collection of narratives passed down from generation to generation, history becomes not a science but a perpetually infected Ancient Mariner.

Yet Nietzsche's life-affirming philosophies remind us that action and manifestations of will often require models to ensure self-assertion. The achievement of Milton may prepare the emergence of Coleridge; an American Revolution may follow an English Civil War. Without greatness to follow or imagine, we might be too cautious in our actions. Perhaps the essentialism sometimes believed to inhere in the idea of classical canons or historical progressions is no more than a case of repeated tropes and motifs. What we take as universal truths might simply be motifs repeated for continuity's sake. History doesn't repeat, they say; it rhymes. If so, the rhyme is always a little forced and contaminated.

The exploitative nature of obsessions like that of Coleridge for Shakespeare and Milton may not be fully appreciated. The tragic, beautiful weight of history is enticing as not only a pattern but a narrative anchor, like the *Iliad* for the *Aeneid*, because it offers credibility and memorability. In her examination of Holocaust memoirs, Amy Hungerford suggests that in an effort to wrestle with the fact that he doesn't feel he can compete with his father's trauma from the Holocaust, Art Spiegelman in *Maus* envelops his father's story and trauma into his own, thereby perpetuating it and passing it forward. Similarly, she argues, Jonathan Safran Foer appropriates his ancestor's Holocaust experiences in order to substantiate his own memoir. Neither lived through the trauma, but it weighed so heavily on them that they felt the need to convey it. As Hungerford puts it, each sought a way to transcend "the limits of [...] current experience and personal past to encompass experiences [...] that are historically remote from the individual" (90).

In his contribution to this volume, Geoffrey A. Wright asks whether "adaptation [is] itself a form of exploitation" (178), and I wonder whether the unfolding of our history and our lives may be a form of exploitation as well. Although Wright notes that a memoir, like Spiegelman's, "can be true insofar as it is an honest account of what the writer genuinely understands to be the case" (179), he points out that "even if nonfiction narratives are written truthfully, they still risk exploiting or appearing to exploit their subjects" (180). Then what do we do about the possibility that we are driven by the structure of narratives themselves to make things more important than they may really be? To put it another way, what do we do about the possibility that we have inflated ourselves in a good-faith effort to make an account of our lives that meets our own understanding of how important our lives are? Wright rightly focuses on the nonfiction author's responsibility to depict honestly and accurately others' roles in the author's story, but he does not explore the ethical conundrum of telling another's story, perhaps subconsciously, in a way that slyly envelops it within one's own story. Does this self-inflation do violence to the other's story? By using another's story to inflate the value of your own, do you act dishonestly even if you act in sincere good faith?

In the end, with apologies to Elvis, we are caught in a trap. Memory partially defines itself as a struggle against forgetting, and the past implicitly exhorts us not to forget. We feel that exhortation viscerally as we live out the writing of our own history. It pleases and satisfies us when we reference and pattern ourselves after classic periods and works because (1) we are paying respect to the past and fulfilling our indebtedness to it, (2) we are placing ourselves in time and making sense of it, and (3) we are passing forward an exhortation and debt to descendants and students of history that we hope ensures the longevity of our narrative.

But humankind "struggles under the great and ever-growing burden of the past, which weighs him down and distorts him" (Nietzsche 89). In a recent interview on Putin's invasion of Ukraine, historian Yuval Noah Harari was asked to reflect on the historical repercussions of the trauma and suffering of within Ukraine and in Europe more broadly. "These are the seeds of hatred and fear and misery that are being planted right now in the minds and the bodies of hundreds of millions of people" that "will give a terrible harvest [...] in decades to come," he responded:

> This war now, its seeds were, to a large extent, planted decades and even centuries ago. Part of the Russian fears that are motivating Putin [...] is memories of past invasions of Russia. [...] And, of course, it's a terrible mistake. [...] They are recreating again the same things that they should learn to avoid. [...] Some of the seeds of this war were planted in the siege of Leningrad. And now it gives fruit in the siege of Kyiv, which may give fruit in 40 or 50 years. We need to cut this, we need to stop this. As an historian, I feel sometimes ashamed or responsible, I don't know what, about what the knowledge of history is doing to people. [...] I know it for my own country. In Israel, we also suffer from too much history. I think people should be liberated from the past, not constantly repeating it again and again. Everybody should kind of free themselves from the memories of the Second World War. It's true of the Russians, it's also true of the Germans.

Perhaps the deepest irony of the inherently exploitative nature of rereading past history, its literature, and literary responses to it through historical–poetic interpolation in order to write ourselves into history is that we might do more to elevate ourselves, and our place in history, if we simply took Harari's and Nietzsche's advice: fuhgeddaboudit.

References

Ali, Tariq. "How Lenin's love of literature shaped the Russian Revolution." *Guardian*, 25 Mar. 2017, https://www.theguardian.com/books/2017/mar/25/lenin-love-literature-russian-revolution-soviet-union-goethe. Accessed 21 June 2022.

Aristotle. *Aristotle's Theory of Poetry and Fine Art (With a Critical Text and Translation of The Poetics)*, translated by S.H. Butcher, fourth edition, Macmillan, 1923, *Google Books*, https://www.google.com/books/edition/Aristotle_s_Theory_of_Poetry_and_Fine_Ar/zFMNAAAAIAAJ?hl=en&gbpv=1. Accessed 21 June 2022.

Bailey, James R. "Vladimir Putin's search for 'Moby Dick.'" *The Hill*, 6 March 2022, https://thehill.com/opinion/international/596835-vladimir-putins-search-for-moby-dick/.

Balakian, Peter. "Auden's Foreboding Poem 'September 1, 1939,' Captures Today's Mood, Too." *Washington Post*, https://www.washingtonpost.com/outlook/2022/02/28/wh-auden-poem-1939-invasion-poland/. Accessed 21 June 2022.

Beers, Laura. "What Josh Hawley doesn't get about George Orwell." *CNN Opinion*, 15 Jan. 2021, https://www.cnn.com/2021/01/15/opinions/trump-and-allies-invoke-george-orwell-orwellian-beers/index.html. Accessed 21 June 2022.

Brooks, Peter. *Reading for the Plot: Design and Intention in Narrative*, Harvard University Press, 1984.

Coleridge, Samuel Taylor. *Lectures 1795: On Politics and Religion*. Edited by Lewis Patton and Peter Mann, 1971. *The Collected Works of Samuel Taylor Coleridge*, Kathleen Coburn, general editor, volume 1, Bollingen Series LXXV, Princeton University Press, 1971–2002.

Coleridge, Samuel Taylor. Biographia Literaria. *Samuel Taylor Coleridge: The Major Works*, edited by H.J. Jackson, Oxford World's Classics, Oxford University Press, 1985, pp. 155–482.

Coleridge, Samuel Taylor. (n.d.-a) "A Moral and Political Lecture." Patton and Mann, pp. 1–19.

Coleridge, Samuel Taylor. (n.d.-b) "The Plot Discovered: or, An Address to the People, Against Ministerial Treason." Patton and Mann, pp. 277–318.

Cryer, Thomas. "As America looks ahead to its 250th anniversary, the nation's past is likely to be just as contested as its present." *USAPP blog*, London School of Economics' (LSE) Phelan United States Centre, 30 Nov. 2021, https://blogs.lse.ac.uk/usappblog/2021/11/30/as-america-looks-ahead-to-its-250th-anniversary-the-nations-past-is-likely-to-be-just-as-contested-as-its-present/. Accessed 21 June 2022.

Dowd, Maureen. "Zelensky Answers Hamlet." *New York Times*, 12 Mar. 2022, https://www.nytimes.com/2022/03/12/opinion/zelensky-ukraine-russia-biden.html. Accessed 21 June 2022.

Fiddler: A Miracle of Miracles. Directed by Max Lewkowicz, performed by Sheldon Harnick and Lin-Manuel Miranda, Roadside Attractions, 2019.

Harari, Yuval Noah. "The War in Ukraine Could Change Everything." *TED Membership Event*, interview conducted by Bruno Giussani, 1 March 2022, *YouTube*, uploaded by TED, https://www.youtube.com/watch?v=yQqthbvYE8M, 24 May 2022. Accessed 21 June 2022. Accessed 21 June 2022.

Hungerford, Amy. *The Holocaust of Texts: Genocide, Literature, and Personification*, Harvard University Press, 2003.

Jauss, Hans Robert. "Limits and Tasks of Literary Hermeneutics." *Diogenes*, translated by Johanna Picks Margulies, vol. 28, no. 109, 1980, pp. 92–119, https://doi.org/10.1177/039219218002810907.

Kermode, Frank. *The Sense of an Ending: Studies in the Theory of Fiction, with a New Epilogue*. Oxford University Press, 2000.

Kitson, Peter. "Coleridge, the French Revolution, and 'The Ancient Mariner': Collective Guilt and Individual Salvation." *Yearbook of English Studies*, vol. 19, 1989, pp. 197–207.

Kitson, Peter. "'Sages and patriots that being dead do yet speak to us': Readings of the English Revolution in the Late Eighteenth Century." *Prose Studies: History, Theory, Criticism*, vol. 14, no. 3, 1991, pp. 205–230, https://doi.org/10.1080/01440359108586452.

Leitch, Thomas. "History as Adaptation." *The Politics of Adaptation: Media Convergence and Ideology*. Edited by Dan Hassler-Forest and Pascal Nicklas, Palgrave Macmillan, 2015, pp. 7–20.

Leitch, Thomas. "Adaptation and Censorship." *The Scandal of Adaptation*. Edited by Thomas Leitch, Palgrave Macmillan, 2022, pp. 195–212.

McGann, Jerome. "The Meaning of the Ancient Mariner." *Critical Inquiry*, vol. 8, no. 1, 1981, pp. 35–67, *JSTOR*, https://www.jstor.org/stable/1343205.

Mee, Jon. "Anxieties of Enthusiasm: Coleridge, Prophecy, and Popular Politics in the 1790s." *Enthusiasm and Enlightenment in Europe, 1650–1850*, special issue of *Huntington Library Quarterly*, vol. 60, no. 1/2, 1997, pp. 179–203, *JSTOR*, http://www.jstor.org/stable/3817836.

Milton, John. *Paradise Lost*. Edited by Merritt Y. Hughes, Odyssey, 1962.

Mooney, William. "Cinematic Contagion: *Bereullin* (*The Berlin File*, 2013)." *The Scandal of Adaptation*. Edited by Thomas Leitch, Palgrave Macmillan, 2022, pp. 213–28.

Morehead, Craig. "Monument Films and The Politics of Tragic Public Emotions." Only Connect: Virtual Joint Symposium of LFA and AAS, 18 Feb. 2022.

Nietzsche, Friedrich. "History in the Service and Disservice of Life." *Unmodern Observations (Unzeitgemäße Betrachtungen)*. Translated by Gary Brown, edited by William Arrowsmith, Yale University Press, 1990, pp. 73–145. *Internet Archive*, https://archive.org/details/unmodernobservat0000niet.

Pellauer, David. "Ricoeur and White on the Historical Imagination." *Archivio Di Filosofia*, vol. 81, no. 1/2, 2013, pp. 261–70, *JSTOR*, http://www.jstor.org/stable/24488500.

Philipp. "Tired of Living Through Major Historical Events." *Know Your Meme. Literally Media*, 2022, https://knowyourmeme.com/memes/tired-of-living-through-major-historical-events, 30 Apr. 2022. Accessed 21 June 2022.

Reiff, Marija. "Napoleon's Historic and Aesthetic Threat: Commanding Genius and Shakespearean Allusion in Samuel Taylor Coleridge's *Zapolya*." *Coleridge Bulletin: The Journal of the Friends of Coleridge*, vol. 44, Winter 2014, pp. 89–96, *The Friends of Coleridge*, https://www.friendsofcoleridge.com/images/12_Reiff_Marija_-_Zapolya_prnt.pdf. Accessed 21 June 2022.

Ricoeur, Paul. *Time and Narrative*. 1985. Translated by Kathleen Blamey and David Pellauer, vol. 3, U of Chicago P, 1988.

Taylor, Antony. "Shakespeare and Radicalism: The Uses and Abuses of Shakespeare in Nineteenth-Century Popular Politics." *Historical Journal*, vol. 45, no. 2, 2002, pp. 357–79, *JSTOR*, http://www.jstor.org/stable/3133649.

Tiffany, Kaitlyn. "The Ugly, Embarrassing Spectacle of 'Milling' Around Online." *Atlantic*, 3 Mar. 2022, https://www.theatlantic.com/technology/archive/2022/03/russia-ukraine-invasion-twitter/624168/. Accessed 21 June 2022.

Turner, Ralph H., and Lewis M. Killian. *Collective Behavior*, vol. 3, Prentice-Hall, 1957.

Tutan, Defne Ersin. "Adaptation and History." *The Oxford Handbook of Adaptation Studies*. Edited by Thomas Leitch, Oxford University Press, 2017, pp 576–86.

United States Department of Justice, United States Attorney's Office for the District of Columbia. "Second Superseding Indictment." *United States of America v. Ethan Nordean, Joseph Biggs, Zachary Rehl, Charles Donohoe, Enrique Tarrio, and Dominic Pezzola*, 8 Mar. 2022, https://www.justice.gov/opa/press-release/file/1480891/download. Accessed 21 June 2022.

Wright, Geoffrey A. "(Re-)Writing the Pain: War, Exploitation, and the Ethics of Adapting Nonfiction." *The Scandal of Adaptation*. Edited by Thomas Leitch, Palgrave Macmillan, 2022, pp. 177–93.

Zelensky, V. "User Clip: Zelensky To Be Or Not to Be." *C-Span*, 8 Mar. 2022, https://www.c-span.org/video/?c5005151/user-clip-zelensky. Accessed 21 June 2022.

Index[1]

A
Abuse, 84
Academic industry, 171
Academy of Motion Pictures Arts and Sciences (AMPAS), 233
Adaptation process, 244
 adaptability, 5–7, 26
 adaptation(s), 44, 63, 81–96, 100, 104, 119–134, 140, 165, 173, 177–178, 187–190, 200, 204, 207, 227, 229–248
 adapts, 110
 and censorship, 201
 contagion, 227, 265
 and history, 252
 and incest, 93
 industry, 5, 104
 inevitably involves censorship, 209
 itself a form of exploitation, 178, 266
 of nonfiction, 188
 of a nonfiction narrative, 188
 scandalous, 160
 studies, 3, 157
 theory, 7
 to censorship, 209
 and translation, 2
 of war memoirs, 191
Adorno, Theodor, 170, 171
Adulteress, 22
Adultery, 19–40, 48
Aeneid, 266
Aesthetics, 3, 7
Ailes, Roger, 197
Akira, 148
Aleichem, Sholem, 253
Allen, Joan, 217
Allen, Woody, 197
Allied Artists, 241
Almachar, Allen, 132
Alonso, Mejías, 82
An American Tragedy, 15, 158, 159, 161, 162, 165, 168, 170, 171

---

[1] Note: Page numbers followed by 'n' refer to notes.

A

Amory, Cleveland, 70
Andrew, Dudley, 5
Animal Crossing: New Horizons, 139
Anna Karenina, 12, 13, 19–22, 24, 26–28, 30–32, 33n8, 35
Anna Karenina-2, 30
Anninskii, Lev, 24
Anti-nonfiction, 189
Appropriation, 3, 52, 54, 158
Approximate nonfiction, 189
Archives, 7, 209
Arenas, Reinaldo, 82, 89, 91, 92
Arias, Imanol, 85, 86
Aristotelian aesthetics, 100
Aristotle, 5, 260, 261
Arnn, Larry P., 201
Aronofsky, Darren, 34
Asheim, Lester, 163
Association of Adaptation Studies, 1
Atonement, 35
Atwood, Margaret, 253
Auden, W.H., 257
Austin, Elisabeth L., 13, 81
Author, 227
Authorship, 3, 16, 66, 214, 233
Aves sin nido (Birds without a Nest), 83

B

Backstein, Karen, 36
Back to the Future, 101, 112
Bacterial infection, 108
Bacterial logic, 107
Bailey, Jason, 204
Bailey, Laura, 145
Bailey, Steve, 111
Baker, Troy, 141
Bakhtin, Mikhail, 7, 188
Bakunin, Mikhail, 115
Balázs, Béla, 232
Baldur's Gate: Dark Alliance, 146
Baldwin, James, 76

Ballet, Joffrey, 26
Balzac, Honoré de, 258
Bambi, 205
Barr, Roseanne, 197
Barthes, Roland, 22
Bathrick, David, 221
Bazin, André, 163
Beasley, Tom, 131
Beethoven, Ludwig van, 263
Bell, John, 94
Bemelmans, Ludwig, 47
Benavides, Miguel, 87
Benjamin, Walter, 129
Bennet, James, 198
Bennett, Joan, 45, 47, 49, 50, 54, 55, 61
Benny, Jack, 8, 9
Bereullin (The Berlin File, 2013), 16, 213–227
Bergman, Ingmar, 262, 263
Berman, David Elliot, 104
Bernstein, Elmer, 72, 73
Bernstein, Matthew, 47, 55
Bestseller, 3
Beyond a Reasonable Doubt, 52
Bhabha, Homi, 101
Biden, Joe, 201
The Big Knife, 75
The Birth of a Nation, 204
Black Hawk Down, 183, 184
Black Lives Matter (BLM), 197, 200, 201
The Black Swan, 34
Blade Runner, 140, 146, 148, 150
Blair, David, 22
Bloom, Harold, 5, 32, 165
Bloomian, 158
Bloom, Lynn, 179, 180
Bluestone, George, 6, 164
Boccaccio, Giovanni, 253, 257
Bogart, Humphrey, 75, 245
Bogle, Donald, 203

Boingo, Oingo, 109
Bonaparte, Napoleon, 259, 263, 264
Booth, John Wilkes, 17, 259, 260, 263
Boozer, Jack, 232
Bordwell, David, 239
Borges, Jorge Luis, 96
Bosch, Hieronymus, 120
The Bourne Identity, 219
The Bourne Supremacy, 16, 216–219, 221, 226
The Bourne Ultimatum, 217
Bowden, Mark, 183
Bowdlerization(s), 14, 158–163, 165, 168, 170–172
Bowdlerizing, 157–173
Boyd, Brian, 182, 183
Bradbury, Ray, 208
Brando, Marlon, 245
Brantley, Ben, 77
The Breakfast Club, 101, 104–106, 109
Breaking Bad, 143
Breen, Joseph, 47, 58, 236, 238
Bressart, Felix, 10
Breu, Christopher, 69, 77
Bride of Frankenstein, 110, 113
Bridge of Spies, 220n2
Brody, Richard, 36, 37, 132
Brooks, Peter, 258
Brown, Clarence, 22, 24–26
Brutus, Marcus Junius, 259, 263
Burns, Robert, 259
BuzzFeed, 105, 108
BuzzFeed Theory, 13, 104, 106–110, 115, 116, 205

C
Caesar, Julius, 263
Cagle, Jess, 203
Cahn, Billy, 73, 76

Cain, James M., 48, 55, 58, 236, 237, 238n2
Caine, Michael, 243
Caldwell-Gervais, Noah, 150, 151
Caleb Williams, 167, 171, 173
Calhoun, John C., 197
Call BuzzFeed Theory, 100
Camus, Albert, 253
Cancel, 102, 207
Cancel culture, 197, 198, 207, 209
Cancelation, 107, 200, 209
Canceled, 99
Canceling, 210
Canon(s), 5, 6, 197, 207, 209
Carné, Marcel, 57
Carnival, 7
Carrière, Jean-Claude, 231
Carter, Graydon, 198
Cartmell, Deborah, 15, 182
Caspary, Vera, 48, 55
CD Projekt Red (CDPR), 146, 150, 151
Cecilia después, o por qué la tierra, 82
Cecilia (1982), 82, 85, 86, 88, 89, 92
Cecilia Valdés, 13, 81–96
Censorship, 15, 195–210
 and adaptation, 204
 and curation, 208
Century Fox, 210
Chandler, Raymond, 16, 48, 55, 237
Chaplin, Charlie, 8
Chartier, Jean-Pierre, 57
Chatman, Seymour, 159, 173
Chauvin, Derek, 197
Chaviano, Daína, 82
Cheng, Susan, 105
Cherkaoui, Sidi Larbi, 34
Chernobyl (2019), 142
Chernyshevsky, Nikolay, 259
Chijona, Gerardo, 82
Children of Men, 141
A Christmas Carol, 95

274 INDEX

Chung, Hye Seung, 216
Church, Ricky, 132
Cien años de soledad (*One Hundred Years of Solitude*), 83
Cills, Hazel, 103
Cinema studies, 4, 7
Citizen Kane, 71
C.K., Louis, 197
Clery, E.J., 160, 168, 173
Clift, Montgomery, 71
Clinamen, 158, 165
Cockle, Doug, 147
Cohn, Jesse, 108, 115
Coleridge, Samuel Taylor, 16–17, 253–257, 260–266
Collaboration, 3
Collaborative, 234
Collaborative art, 230
Colman, George, 15, 159–168, 171
Colonialism, 84
Coloniality, 86
Coloniality of power, 84
Colonial power, 82
Columbia, 236
Columbus, Christopher, 197
Composite nonfiction, 189
Concepts, 164
  and percept, 164
Confidential, 63, 67
Congregation for the Doctrine of the Faith, 208
Connery, Sean, 243
Conservatism, 166
Conservative, 159, 166, 172, 173
Contagion, 213–227
Containment, 166, 168
Continuation, 54
Cooke, Paul, 221
Copyright, 3, 43, 231
Cotton, Tom (Senator), 198
Coulter, Ann, 197

COVID-19, 144, 145, 150, 208, 255, 264
COVID-19 pandemic, 139, 140, 143, 234, 253
Cowart, David, 159, 163, 166, 168
Crash Bandicoot (1996–2020), 141
Creative nonfiction, 178, 180, 188n4, 189, 190
Crowley, John, 14, 119, 127, 130, 131
Crowther, Bosley, 8, 57
Cryer, Thomas, 259
Cuba, 82, 84, 85, 88, 91
Cuban(s), 83, 86, 88, 89, 92, 94
Cukor, George, 25, 205
Cultural patrimony, 82
Culture industry, 172
Cumandá, 83
Curly Sue, 109
Curtis, Tony, 64, 65, 69, 70, 77
Cutchins, Dennis, 188, 190
Cyberpunk, 151
Cyberpunk 2020, 140, 146, 147, 149, 150
Cyberpunk 2077, 14, 139–153
Cyberpunk Red, 148
Cyrus, Miley, 101

D
Dafoe, Willem, 255
Dahl, Roald, 243
Dahl, Tessa, 243
Damnatio memoriae, 199, 204
Damon, Matt, 218
Daniels, William, 22
Dark Like the Night, 38
Dark Like the Night. Anna Karenina-2019, 38
Das Leben der Anderen (*The Lives of Others*), 16, 215

David Copperfield, 133
Davies, Andrew, 3
Davis, Gary, 230
Davis, Marvin, 202
Dawkins, Richard, 214, 215, 227
Deakins, Roger, 132
Decameron, 253, 257
Defoe, Daniel, 253
De la Fouchardière, Georges, 45, 46, 53, 57
Deleuze, Gilles, 83
Delgado, Martín Morúa, 82
DeMille, Cecil B., 75
Dennis the Menace, 109
Desjardin, Mary, 68
Deus Ex, 148
De Vries, A.B., 123
Dickens, Charles, 6, 95, 131, 133
Dickinson, Thorold, 205
Didion, Joan, 179
Die Hard, 103
Diffrient, David Scott, 216
Dirty adaptation, 12
Dirty texts, 63
Disney, 205
Dmytryk, Edward, 55
Dobkin, Lawrence, 68
Documentary(ies), 181
Dodd, Dawn, 202
Domestico, Anthony, 131, 134
Donnersmarck, Florian Henckel von, 16, 221, 222, 226
Doom Eternal, 139
Doré, Gustav, 256
Dostoevskii, Fedor, 20
Double Indemnity, 16, 46, 58, 70, 230, 235, 236, 236n1, 238–240
Dou, Gerrit, 120
Downey, Robert Jr., 110
Dramatic nonfiction, 189
Dreiser, Theodore, 15, 158, 162, 168, 169, 171, 173

Dr. Seuss, 6
Druckmann, Neil, 142, 145
The Duchess, 35
Dugan, Tom, 9
Du Maurier, Daphne, 6
Dungeons & Dragons, 140, 147
Durran, Jacqueline, 36
Duryea, Dan, 45, 49, 55, 56
Duvillars, Pierre, 60
Duvivier, Julien, 33n8
Dwyer, Kevin, 179n1, 182, 187

E
Ebert, Roger, 142
E.C. Comics, 110, 114
Edwards, J. Gordon, 27
Eisenstein, Sergei, 15, 161, 162, 169
Elastextity, 94, 95
Elder Scrolls IV: Oblivion, 147
Elfman, Danny, 109
Elgort, Ansel, 127
Elliott, Kamilla, 7, 107
Emma, 6
Endogamous operations, 88
Endogamous practice, 82
Endogamy, 96
Enquiry Concerning Political Justice, 171
Epifantsev, Vladimir, 30
Espinosa Mendoza, Norge, 82, 92, 94, 95
Estorino, Abelardo, 82, 93
Ethical boundaries, 181
Ethical documentary, 181
Ethical implications, 191
Ethical questions, 178
Ethical responsibility, 182
Ethical standard, 179
Ethics, 177–191
Evolution, 183, 214

Exemplary or monumental, antiquarian, and critical history, 264
Experiment Schrodinger's Cat, 190
Exploitation, 15, 177–191
Exploitative, 181, 182, 188
Explorers, 101
Eyman, Scott, 11

F
Fabritius, Carel, 119–124, 126–131, 133
A Face in the Crowd, 64
Fahrenheit 451, 208, 209
Faithfull, Marianne, 255
Fallaha, Simon, 36
Far Cry, 150
Farewell, My Lovely, 55
Fashion, 5
Faulkner, William, 47, 230
F.E.A.R., 149
Fegley, Oakes, 128
Ferris Bueller's Day Off, 101, 109
Fiction, 190
Fictionalized nonfiction, 189
Fiddler on the Roof, 253
Fidelity, 16, 84, 172, 182, 183, 183n2, 191, 235, 242
Figes, Orland, 33
Film, 34
Film noir, 55, 63, 73
Final Fantasy VII Remake, 139
Finkelstein, Norman, 199
Firastopher, 251
Flamant, Georges, 52
Floyd, George, 197
Flubber, 109
Foreman, John, 241
Foucauldian governmentality, 166
Foucault, Michel, 83
Fox, Michael J., 112, 237
Franken, Al (Senator), 197
Frankenstein, 13, 100, 110, 112, 113
Freeman, Hadley, 103, 105
Fruit Still-Life with Squirrel and Goldfinch, 120

G
Gable, Clark, 245
Gabler, Neal, 65–68, 72, 73, 78
Garas, Márton, 27
Garbo, Greta, 22, 24–26, 32, 35, 36
The Garden of Earthly Delights, 120
Gardin, Vladimir, 27
Gaslight, 205
Gay, Roxane, 208
Gedeck, Martina, 222, 223
Geisel, Audrey, 6
Genre, 177–179, 187, 188n4, 189
Gerard, Philip, 179
Gessner, David, 205
Ghostbusters, 103
Ghosts of Tsushima, 139
Gibson, William, 140, 148
Giddins, Gary, 69
Gilbert, John, 23–25
Gilmartin, Kevin, 166, 168, 171
A Girl in a Window with a Bunch of Grapes, 120
Glance, Jonathan C., 16, 229
Gleiberman, Owen, 132
Globalism, 84
Godwin, William, 14, 158, 160, 161, 166–168, 171
Going viral, 107
Goldberg, Jonah, 198
The Goldfinch, 14, 119–134
The Goldfinch (2013), 124–127
Golitsyn, Count Vladimir, 20
Gone with the Wind, 15, 107, 188n5, 201–206, 209, 210
Gordenker, Emilie, 122
Gordon, Neve, 199

INDEX

Goulding, Edmund, 22–24, 26
Granados, Daisy, 85–87
Grand Theft Auto, 148, 150
Grant, Cary, 245
The Graveyard of the Angels (1987), 89–92
The Great Dictator, 8
Grebenshchikov, Boris, 38
Greenblatt, Bob, 203
Greene, Marjorie Taylor, 196
Griffith, D.W., 204
Gross, Halley, 142
Grossman, Julie, 12, 13, 63, 94
Guattari, Félix, 83
Guiraud, Edmond, 27
Gutkind, Lee, 178, 179, 188n4, 189
Gye-nam Myeong, 220

H
Ha, Jung Woo, 216
Ha, Quan Manh, 185
Half-Life: Alyx, 139
Hall, Anthony Michael, 99, 111
Hall, Dan, 103
Hall, Mordaunt, 24
Halton, Charles, 10
Hamilton, Patrick, 205
Hamlet, 5
Hamlisch, Marvin, 77
Hammett, Dashiell, 48
Han, Suk-kyu, 216
The Handmaid's Tale, 253
The Hangover, 109
Hans, Simran, 132
Hanson, Curtis, 64
Harari, Yuval Noah, 267
Harrington, James, 253
Harrison, Susan, 73–75
Hatmaker, Elizabeth A., 69, 77
Hawley, Josh (Senator), 196
Hay, James, 111

Hays Office, 207, 208, 210, 238
Hayslip, Phung Thi Le Ly, 184–186
HBO Max, 15, 103, 201–204, 210
HBO series (1989–1996), 110
Hearst, William Randolph, 71, 104
Heaven and Earth, 184–186
Hecht, Harold, 71
Heller-Nicholas, Alexandra, 99, 114
Herrick Library, 234, 241
Herrick, Margaret, 236
Hicks, Russell, 48–49
Hill, Gladys, 241, 242, 245
Hill, James, 71
Hirsch, E.D., 5
Historical fiction, 188n4
Historical–poetic interpolation, 16, 252, 254, 258, 260, 262–264
History, 17, 204, 251–267
Hitchcock, Alfred, 3, 88, 188n5, 234
Hitler, Adolf, 10, 67, 76, 247, 257
Hoberman, J., 114
Hoffman, Irving, 66, 78
Hogg, Trevor, 127
Hollyfield, Jerod Ra'Del, 13, 99, 205
Home Alone, 109
Homeland, 220n2
Honest, 179, 179n1
Hopper, Grace Murray, 197
Horkheimer, Max, 170, 171
Horton, Andrew, 233
Hotter, Parry, 199
Howe, James Wong, 73
Hoxter, Julian, 233
Hughes, John, 13, 99–116
Hugo, Victor, 6
Hungerford, Amy, 266
Hunt, Tim (Sir), 197
Hush-Hush, 67
Huston, John, 3, 16, 230, 234, 235, 239, 241, 242, 244, 245, 247
Hutcheon, Linda, 89, 94, 165, 183
Hytner, Nicholas, 77

I

Iliad, 266
Imperialism, 106
In a Lonely Place, 72, 75
Incest, 13, 81–96
Incestuous, 92, 94
Index Librorum Prohibitorum, 208
Infection, 107
Infidelity, 21
Integrity, 5–7, 26, 181, 214
Intermedial studies, 4, 7
International Pictures, 47
Iron Chest, 159–162, 165–168, 170, 172, 173
It Can't Happen Here, 253

J

James, Brian D'Arcy, 77
Jameson, Fredric, 160
Jauss, Hans Robert, 260, 261
Jellenik, Glenn, 14, 157
Jenner, Kylie, 101
Johnny Mnemonic, 146, 149
Johnson, Ashley, 141
Johnson, Nunnally, 46
John Wick, 149
Joint Security Area, 220
Jones, Tommy Lee, 186
Jordan, Michael B., 209
Journal of the Plague Year, 253
Joy, Robert, 128
Julius Caesar, 263
Jun Ji-Hyun, 216

K

Kael, Pauline, 9
Kakutani, Michiko, 131
Kamilla Elliott, 109
Kashner, Sam, 72
Kast, Pierre, 57
Kelly, Megyn, 203
Kennedy, Burt, 230
Kennedy, Matthew, 23
Keogh, John, 220
Kermode, Frank, 263
Kierkegaard, Søren, 191
The Killers, 75
Kim Jong-il, 216
King, Stephen, 131
Kipling, Rudyard, 106, 236, 240–242, 244–246
  Kim (1901), 106
Kitson, Peter, 253–255
Kleeman, Alexandra, 157
Knightley, Keira, 19, 32, 35, 36
Koch, Sebastian, 222
Kracauer, Siegfried, 56
Krasner, Milton, 47
Krauthammer, Charles, 198
Krawitz, Jan, 181
Krugman, Paul, 198
Kubrick, Stanley, 5
Kurosawa, Akira, 140

L

La Chienne, 45–48, 51, 54, 55, 58
L.A. Confidential, 64
Lady and the Tramp, 205
The Lady of the Lake, 147
The Ladykillers, 71
Lahr-Vivaz, Elena, 13, 81
La isla de los amores infinitos, 82
La loma del Ángel (The Graveyard of the Angels), 82
Lancaster, Burt, 64, 69, 71–76
Lang, Fritz, 12, 43–60
The Last of Us, 140–142, 147
The Last of Us Part II, 14, 139–153
Laura, 55
Laurence, Aimée, 129
La Virgencita de Bronce (The Little Bronze Virgin), 82
Law, Jude, 36

LeBrock, Kelly, 99
Le Colonel Chabert, 258
Lee Kyung-young, 219
Legion, 45, 51
Legion of Decency, 12, 45
Le, Hiep Thi, 186
Lehman, Ernest, 64–67, 69–74, 76, 78
Lehmann, David, 8
Leigh, Vivien, 35
Leitch, Thomas, 1, 7, 26n3, 66, 106, 107, 112, 172, 195, 229, 252, 260, 263
Le Jour se lève, 57
Lemire, Christy, 36
Lengyel, Melchior, 7
Lenin, V.I., 17, 259, 260
Lev, Peter, 232
Lewis, Sinclair, 253
Licensing Act and the Production Code, 162
Licensing Act of 1737, 161, 165
Liedtke, Walter, 122, 123
Lincoln, Abraham, 263
Lindsay, James, 107, 115
Literary studies, 4, 7
Lithgow, John, 77
The Little Bronze Virgin (2004), 92–95
The Little Friend, 131
Little Women, 5
The Lives of Others, 221, 222, 224–226
Lloyd, Christopher, 112
Locke, John, 254
Loft, Arthur, 56
Lola rennt, 217
Lolita, 5
Lone Star, 84
Lord of the Rings, 6
Love, 22–24
Lowry, Rich, 198
Lubitsch, Ernst, 7, 8, 47, 48
The Lucky Strike Dance Hour, 65

Lumières, 20
Lynch, David, 63

M
MacDonald, Ian, 232
Mackendrick, Alexander, 63, 69, 71, 73, 74, 76
MacKenzie, Aeneas, 241, 244–247
MacLeish, Archibald, 45
MacMurray, Fred, 240
Madonna del cardellino, 120
Madsen, Axel, 241
Maher, Bill, 198
Mainstreaming, 159
Maître, Maurice-André, 27
Makoveeva, Irina, 12, 19
Maladaptation, 13
The Maltese Falcon, 75
The Man from U.N.C.L.E., 220n2
Man Hunt, 47
Manvell, Roger, 230
The Man Who Would Be King, 16, 230, 235, 236, 236n1, 240–247
Marèse, Janie, 52
Margaret Herrick Library, 233
Marginalization, 5
Marion, Frances, 23, 24
Márquez, Gabriel García, 83
Marric, Linda, 131
Marvel's Avengers, 139
Marx, Karl, 111
Masque of the Red Death, 253, 262, 263
Mass Effect, 150
Massell, Samantha, 253
Masterpiece Theatre, 142
Match(es), 77
The Matrix, 140, 146, 149
Matto de Turner, Clorinda, 83
Maurier, Daphne du, 188n5
Mauritius, Carel, 14

Maus, 266
Mavrov, 27
Ma, Wenlei, 132
Max Payn, 149
Mayer, Edwin Justus, 7
Mayer, Louis B., 236
Mazin, Craig, 142
McBride, Joseph, 235
McCarthyist media, 67
McCarthy, Joseph (Senator), 69, 72, 76
McClafferty, Monsignor, 45
McCrory, Helen, 22
McGann, Jerome, 255
McGilligan, Patrick, 52
McGuigan, John, 183, 184
McIntush, Holly G., 101
McMillan, Kyle, 26
Mecholsky, Kristopher, 16, 251
Media, 3
Medium specificity, 16
Meme pool, 215, 227
Memes, 214
Memoir, 177, 178, 184
Memorable history, 264
Mera, Juan León, 83
The Merchant of Venice, 10
Merry, Stephanie, 128
Metaphor, 213
Metelitsa, Katia, 21n2
Mexican Gothic, 83
MGM, 13, 58, 205, 236
Mignon, Abraham, 120
Miller, Renata, 26
Milling, 261
Milner, Martin, 68, 76
Milton, John, 253, 254, 259, 260, 264–266
Miracle on 34th Street, 109
Mitchell, Margaret, 107, 206
Mitchell-Smith, Ilan, 99, 111
Molotov, Vayacheslav, 28
Mond, F., 82

Monet, Claude, 128
Monstrosity, 96
Monstrous present, 84
Monstrous progeny, 84, 94
Mooney, William, 16, 213, 265
More, Hannah, 168
Moreno-García, Silvia, 83
Morskaia, Marina, 27
Moscow Art Theater, 28, 28n6
Motion Picture Production Code, 236
Motion Picture Production Code of 1930, 165, 244
Movie franchise (1995, 1996), 110
Mühe, Ulrich, 222
Mulholland Drive, 63
Murder, My Sweet, 55
Murray, Simone, 5, 104, 108, 163, 232
My Science Project, 101

N
Nabokov, Vladimir, 5
Nance, Kevin, 131
Naremore, James, 70, 71, 74
A Nation at Risk, 101, 111, 113, 114
Nature morte, 124–127
Naughty Dog, 140, 142–144, 150
Naughty Dog Studios, 141
Neal, Patricia, 243
Nelmes, Jill, 231, 235
Nelson, Cary, 199
Nemirovich-Danchenko, Vladimir, 28
Nepomnyashchy, Catherine, 34
Neumeier, John, 31, 32
Neuromancer, 140, 146, 148, 150, 151
Neverwinter Nights, 147
Newell, Kate, 1, 14, 119
Nichols, Barbara, 67
Nichols, Dudley, 45, 47, 48, 55
Nietzsche, Friedrich, 17, 263–265, 267

INDEX   281

Noiradaptation, 63–78
Noir(s), 57, 69, 70, 72, 76
  affect, 77
Nonfiction, 177–191, 187n3, 188n4
  fiction, 189
  literary, 183
  texts, 7
  truth, 180
North by Northwest, 66
Novel, 119
Novikova, Radda, 38, 39

O

Objective truth, 179
Octopussy, 220n2
Odets, Clifford, 65, 70, 72
Old Boy, 221
Olivares, Jorge, 91
Oliver Twist, 133
101 Dalmatians, 28, 205
1972 ballet *Anna Karenina*, 32
1930 Production Code, 25
The 1776 Report, 200
1619 Project, 200, 201
Originality, 11, 123
Orwell, George, 196, 201, 253, 260
Orwell, George, *1984*, 196, 201, 253, 260, 263
Osteen, Mark, 60
Ottavini, Cardinal Alfredo, 208

P

Pahle, Rebecca, 130
Paine, Thomas, 253
Painting, 120–125, 127, 128, 130, 131, 133
Palance, Jack, 75
Palmer, R. Barton, 1, 12, 43, 44, 64, 227
Pandemic, 152, 258

Paradise Lost, 265
Paramount, 161, 162, 169, 237
Paramount Pictures, 58
Parasite, 221
Parece blanca, 82, 93
Paretsky, Sara, 6
Paris, Barry, 23
Parker, James, 255
Pas de deux, 35
Pasmurov, N., 30n7
Pasolini, Pier Paolo, 231
Paternity, 84
Paulson, Sarah, 128
Paxton, Bill, 112, 115
Pelizzon, V. Penelope, 67–69
Pence, Mike, 195, 263
Percepts, 164
Peretz, Evgenia, 131
Performance studies, 7
Perry, Dennis, 1
Petit theories, 7
Petry, Michael, 124n3, 127–128
Peyton Place, 210
Pimienta, José Dolores, 93
Pirates of the Caribbean, 35
Pirogova, Anna, 21n1
Pius XI, Pope, 45
The Plague, 253
Planes, Trains, and Automobiles, 109
Plato, 5
Plisetskaia, Maia, 32
Pluckrose, Helen, 107, 115
Poe, Edgar Allan, 253, 262, 263
Political acts, 168
Political containment, 158
Political engagements, 161
Political issues, 165
Politics, 15, 159, 161, 164, 168
Polk, Oscar, 202
Pondsmith, Mike, 148
Poor Sap, 51
Pop, Iggy, 255

Portrait, 121
Portraiture, 120, 122, 126, 127
Possokhov, Yuri, 32
The Postman Always Rings Twice, 58
Potente, Franka, 217
Power, 84
Preminger, Otto, 55, 230
Pretty in Pink, 101, 104–105
Price, Steven, 231, 234
Pride and Prejudice, 35
Primary Colors, 8
Process of adaptation, 213, 247
Production Code Administration (PCA), 12, 45, 47, 48, 52, 58, 236
Production Code (PC), 22, 45, 51, 58, 162, 238
Progressive valences, 159
Public humanities, 4
Puppet(s), 93, 94
  play, 93
  theater, 94
Putin, Vladimir, 257, 259, 261, 267
Putter, Cornelis de, 123
Pynchon, Thomas, 6

Q
Quasi-nonfiction, 189
Quijano, Anibal, 84

R
Rabinowitz, Paula, 70
Racial control, 82
Randall, Alice, 206
Raphael, Sanzio, 120
Rassokhin, S.F., 27n4
Ratmanskii, Aleksei, 30
Raw, Laurence, 2, 252
Ray, Nicholas, 114
Ray, Robert, 168

Raymond Chandler, 238
Reagan, Ronald, 111, 112, 114
Real Genius, 101
Rebecca, 188n5
Rebel Without a Cause, 114
Red Dead Redemption II, 148
Reeves, Keanu, 146, 149
Rehabilitation, 199, 200
Rehabilitative, 204
Rehabilitative approach, 201
Reiff, Marija, 254
Renoir, Jean, 46, 50, 51, 53, 57
Rentschler, Eric, 221, 226
Resident Evil (1999–2012), 142
Resident Evil (1996–2021), 141
Resident Evil 3, 139
Responsible, 191
Reviewers, 6
Rey, Henri-François, 57, 58
Reyes, Amanda, 99, 110
Ricoeur, Paul, 17, 260, 261, 263, 264
Ridges, Stanley, 8
Ridley, John, 201, 203
Rights of Man, 253
Ringwald, Molly, 99, 101–105
Riverdale, 102
RKO, 47, 58
Roberts, Stephen, 47
Robespierre, Maximilien, 259
Robinson, Edward G., 45, 50, 55, 61
Roblin, Isabelle, 231, 233
Rodenas, Adriana Méndez, 83
Roese, Vivian, 108
Rogan, Joe, 208
Roig, Gonzalo, 82, 93, 94
Rojas, Bravo, 82
Roleplaying game (RPG), 146, 147, 150
Roman Ignat'ev, 30
Roorbach, Bill, 180
Roosevelt, Theodore, 205
Rothman, Joshua, 37

Rowling, J.K., 6, 198
Ruman, Sig, 10
Rushdie, Salman, 198
Rusler, Robert, 110
Ryoo, Seung-bum, 216
Ryoo Seung-wan, 16, 215–218, 220, 221, 226

S
Sabrina, 66
Sadoul, Georges, 57
Safran Foer, Jonathan, 266
Said, Edward, 106, 107
Sakhnovskii, Vasilii, 28
Salaita, Steven, 199
Salazar, Rubén Darío, 93
Salinger, J.D., 6
Salovey, Peter, 197
Saltykov-Shchedrin, Mikhail, 20
Sanctuary, 47, 52
Sanders, Julie, 3, 52, 110, 158
Sant-Andrews, James, 82
Sapkowski, Andrzej, 146–148
Sayles, John, 84
Scandal(s), 1, 2, 5–7, 11, 13, 19, 21, 22, 30, 32, 39, 43–60, 81–96, 100–109, 119–134, 140, 146, 152, 157, 160, 162–170, 177–181, 187–190, 203, 209, 214, 227, 230, 251–267
  of adaptation, 4
  excessive, 92
  nature of adaptation, 12
  offspring, 91
  readers, 181
  sheet, 76
  of translation, 4
A Scanner Darkly, 149
Scarlet Street, 12, 43–61
Schickel, Richard, 46, 205
Schindel, Dan, 132

Schnittke, Alfred, 31
Scott, A.O., 37, 132, 134
Scott, Ridley, 183
Scott, Sir Walter, 164
Screen adaptations, 32
Screenplays, 16, 229–248
Scripts, 66, 204
The Secret History, 131
Secret Reunion, 220
Selznick, David O., 15, 25, 161–164, 169, 171, 188n5, 206, 236
Sequel(s), 142, 143
Seven Arts, 241
Seventh Seal, 262, 263
Shakespeare, William, 254, 257, 259, 264, 266
Shakira Caine, 243
Shannon, Michael, 209
Shary, Timothy, 113
She's Having a Baby, 109
Sheedy, Ally, 105
Shelley, Mary, 13, 110, 259
Sherrill, Matthew, 133
Sherry, Jamie, 232, 244
Shiri, 220
Shishkin, Oleg, 30
Sidney, Algernon, 253
Silent Hill, 142
Silver, Joel, 109, 110
Simon, Michel, 52
Singleton, Daniel, 14, 139
Sixteen Candles, 101, 104, 109
Skal, David J., 113
Skyrim, 150
Smith, Christina, 53
Smollett, Tobias, 172
Snyder, Mary, 183n2
Snydor, Emily, 106
Socrates, 197
Sofía, 82
Solás, Humberto, 82, 85, 86, 88, 89, 92
Sommer, Doris, 83

The Sopranos, 143
The Sound and the Fury, 159
The Sound of Music, 66
South Atlantic Modern Language Association (SAMLA), 1, 229
Spacey, Kevin, 197
Specificity of media, 233
Spider-Man, 6
Spiegelman, Art, 266
Spielberg, Steven, 220n2
The Spy Who Came in from the Cold, 220
Stack, Robert, 8
Stalin, Joseph, 28, 259
Stam, Robert, 6, 160, 165, 188, 191
Stanwyck, Barbara, 240
Stasov, Vladimir, 20
Steel, Danielle, 37
Steel Rain, 220
Stephens, Rebecca, 185
Sternberg, Josef von, 159, 161, 162, 168, 173
Stevens, Cat (Yusuf Islam), 31
Stewart, Jacqueline, 203, 204
Stiles, Julia, 218
Still life, 120, 122, 123, 127, 134
Stone, Oliver, 184–186
Stone-Ferrier, Linda, 122, 122n2, 123
Stoppard, Tom, 32, 37
The Story of Temple Drake, 47
Strange Days, 146, 148
Straughan, Peter, 119, 130
Subjective, 179n1, 183
Subjective truth, 179, 180
Subjectivity, 181
Subversion(s), 158
Succès de scandale, 19–40
Suchsland, Rüdiger, 221
Suchtelen, Ariane van, 123
Sunset Blvd, 75
Supergenre, 190
Super Mario Brothers games (1985–2017), 141

Swan Lake, 34
Sweet Smell of Success, 12, 63–78
Swinton, Tilda, 255
Swofford, Anthony, 181
Symbiosis, 160, 163

T

Tales from the Crypt, 110
Tammy and the Bachelor, 69
Tarasova, Alla, 28, 29
Tarrio, Enrique, 259
Tartt, Donna, 14, 119, 123, 125–128, 130–134
Tayler, Christopher, 131
Taylor, Antony, 259
Taylor, Elizabeth, 71
Taylor-Johnson, Aaron, 35
Tchaikovskii, Piotr, 31, 34
Teen film(s), 99, 102, 103, 111
Teen movie, 101
Temple Drake, 48, 52
Text, 3
Theater, 34
Theatrical adaptations, 26
Thieme, Thomas, 222–224
Things as They Are, or The Adventures of Caleb Williams, 14, 158, 160
Thoré-Bürger, Théophile, 119
Tiffany, Kaitlyn, 261
To Be or Not to Be, 7, 8
Todd, Chuck, 198
Tolstoi, Lev, 12, 19–21, 21n1, 27n4, 34, 259
Tomb Raider (1996–2022), 141
Toobin, Jeffrey, 197
Torn Curtain, 220n2
Translation, 43, 44, 229
 studies, 2–4
 theory and practice, 4
Trompe l'oeil(s), 14, 120–126, 133, 134
True, 179n1, 190

Trump, Donald J., 65, 68, 69, 195–197, 200, 253, 259, 260
Trump, Donald (Jr.), 196, 260
Truth, 189
  in an objective sense, 190
  truthfulness, 182
Tryon, Chuck, 106
Tsypkin, Aleksandr, 38
Turgenev, Ivan, 20
Turner, Joseph Mallord William, 128
Tutan, Defne Ersin, 252, 263
12 Years a Slave, 201
28 Days Later, 141
21 Jump Street, 109
Twitter, 195, 251
2019 film, 119, 133

U

Uncharted (2007–2017), 141
Uncle Buck, 109
  into a CBS sitcom, 109
Under-reading, 157, 162–170
Universal, 45, 47
Universal Pictures, 45
Universal Studios, 12, 241
Un paraíso bajo las estrellas, 82

V

Veiller, Tony, 241, 242, 245, 247
Venuti, Lawrence, 2–4, 16, 37, 43, 96, 227, 229
Veracini, Lorenzo, 107
Verevis, Constantine, 215n1
Vermeer, Johannes, 119
Vertigo, 88
Video game(s), 139, 142, 153
Viertel, Peter, 241, 242, 245, 247
Vietnam War, 184, 186
Vigilanti Cura, 45
Villaverde, Cirilo, 13, 81, 84, 88, 90, 92–94, 96

Viral, 107
Viral elements, 214
Virgencita, 93
Virus, 108, 213
Volkov, Nikolai, 28

W

Waiting for Lefty, 72
Wald, Priscilla, 213
The Walking Dead, 140, 142
Wallace, Chris, 198
Walsh, Joseph, 132
Wanger, Walter, 45, 47, 48, 51, 53, 55, 56
War literature, 178
  and film, 177
Warner Brothers, 230, 236
Warner, Jack L., 230, 236
Warners, 58
Watts, Naomi, 63
Weinstein, Harvey, 197
Weird Science, 13, 99–116
Weird Science spawned a USA Network television series, 109
Weiser, Frans, 252
Welles, Orson, 71
Wells-Lassagne, Shannon, 231, 233
Westermann, Mariët, 123
West, Nancy, 67–69
West, Nathanael, 159
West Side Story, 66
Westworld (2016–), 142
Whale, James, 110, 113
When Heaven and Earth Changed Places, 15, 184
White, David, 67
White, Hayden, 263, 264
Who's Afraid of Virginia Woolf?, 66
Wilder, Billy, 16, 46, 55, 230, 234, 235, 237–239
Williams, Bronwyn, 180, 181
Williams, Caroline Randall, 200

Wilson, John K., 199
Wilson, Luke, 128
Winchell, Walda, 73
Winchell, Walter, 12, 63, 65–70, 72, 73, 78
The Wind Done Gone, 206
Window, 54–56
Wist, Hailey, 129
The Witcher, 147
The Witcher 2: Assassins of Kings, 147
The Witcher 3: Wild Hunt, 147, 148, 150
Witschief, Graham, 169, 170
The Wizard of Oz, 205
The Woman in the Window, 12, 46, 47, 54
Wood, James, 131

Wood, Oliver, 218
Woolf, Virginia, 159, 164
Wright, Geoffrey A., 15, 177, 266
Wright, Joe, 32–35, 37, 38
Writer's Guild of America, 231
Wurbain, M.L., 123

Y
Yong, Ed, 255, 257

Z
Zarkhi, Aleksander, 32
Zarzuela, 82, 93, 94
Zelensky, Volodymyr, 257, 259
Zemeckis, Robert, 112
Zhang, Alex, 199–201, 204, 205

Printed and bound by CPI Group (UK) Ltd, Croydon, CR0 4YY

14/11/2024

01788762-0001